P9-CNB-655

Deliciously Low

THE GOURMET GUIDE TO LOW-SODIUM, LOW-FAT, LOW-CHOLESTEROL, LOW-SUGAR COOKING

Deliciously Low

THE GOURMET GUIDE TO LOW-SODIUM, LOW-FAT, LOW-CHOLESTEROL, LOW-SUGAR COOKING

---

by

Harriet Roth

FOREWORD BY JOHN W. FARQUHAR, M.D.

NEW YORK AND SCARBOROUGH, ONTARIO

NOTE TO THE READER

The information contained in this book is not intended as a substitute for consulting with your physician. All matters regarding your health require medical supervision. Please note also that many of the products mentioned in this book are registered trademarks.

Published simultaneously in Canada by The New American Library of Canada Limited

NAL BOOKS TRADEMARK REG. U.S. PAT. OFF. AND FOREIGN COUNTRIES
REGISTERED TRADEMARK—MARCA REGISTRADA
HECHO EN HARRISONBURG, VA., U.S.A.

SIGNET, SIGNET CLASSIC, MENTOR, PLUME, MERIDIAN and NAL BOOKS are published *in the United States* by The New American Library, Inc., 1633 Broadway, New York, New York 10019, *in Canada* by The New American Library of Canada Limited, 81 Mack Avenue, Scarborough, Ontario M1L 1M8

LIBRARY OF CONGRESS CATALOGING IN PUBLICATION DATA

Roth, Harriet.
Deliciously low.

Bibliography: p.
Includes index.
1. Cookery. 2. Nutrition. 3. Health. I. Title.
TX715.R8418 1983 641.5′63 83–11402
ISBN 0–453–00447–4

First Printing, November, 1983

1 2 3 4 5 6 7 8 9

PRINTED IN THE UNITED STATES OF AMERICA

This book is dedicated to the health of my family

my daughter, Sally

my son, Larry

and my husband, Harold,
whose love and encouragement
provided the energy for
writing this book

Acknowledgments

No book just happens, and this one is no exception. There are years of learning, teaching, anticipation, and, finally, realization. I would like to say thank you to *everyone* who contributed to this process for their sound advice, ideas, recipe-testing, editing and proofreading, typing, and always enthusiastic encouragement.

I will not enumerate what each individual has contributed, merely list them alphabetically. They are: Sandy Ackerman, Molly Allen, Irene Baron, Sharon Berryhill, Barbara Curry, John Dodds, Annette Drandell, Helen Eisenbach, John W. Farquhar, M.D., Barbara Frances, Harriet Friedman, Kenny Gonzales, Susan Herner, Lee Hochman, Esther Holsenberg, Ronny Johnson, Barrett S. Litt, Jill Neimark, Maryann Palumbo, Marge Perlow, Irene Pink, Nathan Pritikin, Harriet Root, Richard Rossiter, Penny Saltsburg, Eva Silver, David S. Sobel, M.D., Edith Wahl, Barbara Wolf, and my many friends and participants from the Pritikin Longevity Center, and Computrition, Inc.

A special note of thanks to my editor, Carole Hall, Joe Kirschbaum, and George Epstein for their guidance.

Again, my heartfelt thanks to you all.

—H. R.

Foreword

This excellent book provides both the neophyte and the seasoned veteran of culinary battles with a fresh, new approach to nutrition. Harriet Roth leaps into the future instead of timidly creeping toward a prudent lifestyle.

Too many "health" cookbooks heretofore have not addressed the central issue of our nation's need to *dramatically* alter its eating habits in order to eat lower on the food chain. The economic reasons have been most cogently described by Frances Moore Lappe. The health reasons for changing our eating habits in this manner have been put forth by the Stanford Heart Disease Prevention Program and by many other national and international health groups. Most recently the World Health Organization added its vote to the urgency of adopting a lowered sodium, low fat, and high complex carbohydrate diet as a means of preventing coronary heart disease. Similarly, a recent committee of the National Academy of Sciences advocated this nutritional change as a means of preventing various cancers.

Given this consensus, many people rightfully want to know how to change their eating habits. Harriet Roth gives us recipes with nutrient contents that will allow us to practice the art of changing our diets in a palate-pleasing manner. How better to avoid the familiar trap and common fear that the path toward health will be painful? This book will be a most welcome resource for millions of American families.

—John W. Farquhar, M.D.
Director, Stanford Heart Disease
Prevention Program

Contents

Deliciously Low

THE GOURMET GUIDE
TO LOW-SODIUM, LOW-FAT,
LOW-CHOLESTEROL,
LOW-SUGAR COOKING

Introduction

In 1978, my husband, Dr. Harold V. Roth, developed a coronary problem. At the time, I was steeped in a background of *haute cuisine*, having studied with some of the finest cooks in the world—Simone Beck, Roger Verget, Camille Cadier. In fact, for thirteen years I had been conducting cooking classes in the preparation of French and Italian foods. Suddenly I had to face the fact that the traditional style of cooking I loved might be dangerous to my husband's health.

Fortunately, I discovered Nathan Pritikin's concepts of life-style and nutrition and began to prepare food at home in accord with his ideas; that is, making sure that my husband's diet was high in complex carbohydrates, low in sodium and fat, and low in protein (also making it low in cholesterol)—with no added sugar. I found it fairly easy to follow these recommendations by eliminating added salt and sugar, and using fresh fruits and vegetables, whole grains, legumes, and only minimal amounts of animal protein.

I had always delighted in preparing elegant meals for my family and friends, and while it was not difficult to minimize the sodium, fat, cholesterol, or sugar in my favorite recipes, it was an enormous challenge to limit all four of those menaces at the same time. Determined to continue to prepare a wide variety of delicious and attractive meals but keep them very low in potentially harmful elements, I developed and tested countless new recipes. My husband was responding beautifully to the Pritikin diet, and seeing his health improve was all the incentive I needed to persevere.

I also got tremendous encouragement from an unexpected source—my cooking students. I had begun to experiment with Pritikin principles in my cooking classes because I could no longer reconcile myself to teaching people how to prepare food that did not contribute to their optimum health.

To my constant delight, every new class presentation was a success. I found that most of my favorite recipes could be modified to conform to low-sodium, low-fat, low-cholesterol, low-sugar standards. The new ingredients and cooking techniques produced very attractive, delectable, uniquely healthful dishes which I proudly served in my home—to both family and guests.

In 1981 my teaching and experimentation led to my appointment as Director of the Pritikin Longevity Center Cooking School. Fueled by the enthusiasm and needs of the participants at the Longevity Center—as well as by my husband's return to vigorous, tennis-playing good health—my personal culinary exploration became even more intense as I instructed others to prepare and create along with me so that when they left the Longevity Center they could take the Pritikin diet into their own kitchens, stick with it, and still enjoy eating.

A Pritikin-Style Diet to Live With

Many of my students had a misconceived image of wholesome cooking. Some thought that if you eliminated sugar, salt, refined flour, and the like from your diet, all you'd have left to cook with would be seaweed and lecithin. To the contrary, eliminating dangerous foods from your cooking can open the door to discovering scores of familiar foods and food products that you may have just never taken the time or effort to imaginatively prepare or even try. You don't have to be nutritionally deprived in order to feel gastronomic satisfaction. You *can* have healthful food and eat well at the same time.

Let me give you an example. Recently, I had an occasion to prepare lunch for some dear friends I hadn't seen for years. My friends went wild for the pasta salad with shiitake mushrooms and couldn't believe that the salmon mousse was neither fattening nor illegal. We had wonderful whole wheat muffins with a delightful sugar-free apple and black currant spread I'd found at the supermarket. And I filled an enormous basket with vegetables fresh from the grocer—not only the usual carrots, broccoli, and cauliflower, but lovely, crisp, sugar snap peas, rutabaga, turnips, Japanese radishes, and fennel as well—to serve with a piquant spinach dip. For dessert, I served my Perfect Pears in a gorgeous crystal bowl, its beauty only surpassed by the wonderful, natural flavor of the fruit.

It is my hope that nutritious foods, exotically flavored and handsomely displayed, will inspire you to take positive steps toward a healthier life through better cooking. This book is not intended as a cure-all, but every recipe has been carefully, creatively designed to show that beautiful, richly satisfying meals can be prepared in accordance with modern theories of healthful eating. For years we have been hearing that health problems related to diet begin very early in life, and that how we eat can make all the difference between being sick and being well. If you are still regularly eating foods that are high in salt, fat, cholesterol, and sugar, though, you may be wondering just what those modern theories are. The United States Department of Health and Human Services sums them up in the following recommendations.

1. Avoid Too Much Sodium and Salt

The average person in the United States consumes 10 to 20 times more sodium than he needs. Limited amounts of sodium are necessary so the body can maintain a proper water balance, but in excessive amounts sodium causes the body to adjust to holding excessive fluids and contributes to high blood pressure, edema, and kidney disease.

There is enough sodium in the natural food and water we consume to answer our basic metabolic needs. Additional sodium is hidden in various products such as medications and dentifrices. The recipes in this book add no salt in food preparation, and will help you decrease your use of sodium-packed convenience and fast foods. Whenever my recipes call for prepared ingredients, I'll be recommending either low-sodium or no-sodium products or ways to dilute the sodium content of commercial products that are not low-sodium already.

2. Avoid Too Much Fat and Cholesterol

About 40 percent of the total calories the average American consumes are derived from fat. An ounce of fat contains over twice as many calories as either protein or complex carbohydrates, and high fat diets have been shown to contribute to heart disease, hypertension, coronary artery disease, cancer, and diabetes. My recipes are designed to help you lower your fat intake to a safer 15 to 20 percent of your total calories by avoiding vegetable oils, mayonnaise, prepared salad dressings, margarine, butter, lard, bacon, pork, lamb, chicken fat, ice cream, whole milk products and cheeses, and too much beef.

Cholesterol is a sterol, not a fat. It is naturally manufactured by the body and found in all foods derived from animal sources but not in foods from plant sources. For example, egg yolks, not whites, are high in cholesterol but relatively low in fat and calories, while chocolate is *high in fat* and *calories* but contains *no cholesterol.* Cholesterol is another part of our diet that bears watching. Because we all manufacture different amounts of cholesterol in our bodies, the American Heart Association recommends that we control the amount of cholesterol we include in our diets and hold the amount down to 100 to 300 milligrams per day, depending upon the state of your health. One egg yolk contains 285 milligrams. Other high-cholesterol foods to avoid are beef, veal, lamb, pork, some shellfish, organ meats, butter, ice cream, and whole milk dairy products, such as sour cream, cheeses, and yogurt—all examples of animal protein.

Nathan Pritikin recommends we reduce our fat intake to less than 10 percent of total calories and limit our cholesterol intake to 100 milligrams per day. Even with this cholesterol limitation you can still eat as much as a total of 24 ounces of fish, fowl, and/or meat in a week. On a daily basis, this is about 3 to 4 ounces; practically all my recipes, with the exception of those using ricotta and mozzarella cheeses, meet these limitations.

The recipes in this book use nonfat dairy products and will help you limit the amount of animal protein you consume. Judging by the diets of most Americans, the role of and need for protein are grossly misunderstood. For decades, Americans have been taught that a healthy diet should contain generous amounts of protein, the more the better. On the contrary, nutritionally, this is no advantage, but rather a disadvantage. Recent studies have found that excess protein prevents absorption of calcium in the body and may contribute to osteoporosis. Animal protein, in particular, poses the danger of excess fat and cholesterol. Not only do we need less protein—no more than 12 to 15 percent of our caloric intake, but less should come from animal sources and more from other sources such as vegetables, legumes, and whole grains.

3. Avoid Too Much Sugar and Eat a Diet High in Complex Carbohydrates and Fiber

We know that excessive sugar in our diet contributes to tooth decay and obesity but current research points to the fact that a high sugar intake also contributes to the development of heart disease. (Refined, simple sugars tend to increase triglyceride levels in the blood.) To maximize the nutritional benefits of the calories you consume it makes sense to limit your sugar intake. It's up to you to avoid sugar-laden soft drinks, cakes, cookies, and candy, but I've included recipes in this book to satisfy your desire for sweets while limiting all sugars, including molasses, honey, and syrups.

There is more to the low-sugar story. According to Dr. John W. Farquhar of Stanford University, "Complex carbohydrates found in grains and vegetables are a common casualty of a sugar-rich diet. Complex carbohydrates once constituted a major and valuable part of the American diet. Unfortunately, starch and carbohydrates have fallen into disrepute in recent years because of popular fads, including 'low-carbohydrate high-protein' diets. In fact, complex carbohydrates are potentially the slimmer's greatest ally. As a group they not only provide more complex nutrition than do refined carbohydrates, but are also lower in caloric density than are fatty or sugary foods; they tend to slow down the rapid intake of calories that often leads to weight gain." An additional benefit of a diet high in complex carbohydrates is that it will also be naturally high in fiber, a known protection against certain forms of cancer.

My recipes will help you restore complex carbohydrates to their proper place in your diet. You will be using more dried peas, beans, lentils, whole grain cereals, whole grain breads, whole grain pastas, whole raw vegetables, and whole raw fruits and enjoying them more. Why waste your calories?

4. Maintain Your Ideal Weight

If you've seen a table of desirable heights and weights before, it was probably based on the one developed by the Metropolitan Life Insurance Company. The latest table developed by Metropolitan (see page 328) allows you one to sixteen pounds more (depending on your height) than the older one did. But it is important to remember that these tables were never meant to be taken literally, and the new standard should not be used as an excuse to fatten up. These figures are simply a useful guide that points in the direction of a longer, healthier life. Cardiovascular disease, diabetes, gout, osteoarthritis, gallbladder disease, and high blood pressure have all been associated with obesity.

My recipes will help you keep your weight down because they will help you minimize the amount of fat, sugar, fluid-retaining salt, and high-calorie animal protein in your daily diet.

Compare the Difference

Every recipe in this book has been computer-analyzed for its per-serving calorie count and its content of eighteen essential nutrients plus fiber. The analysis is printed at the foot of each recipe based on data compiled by Computrition, Inc., Chatsworth, California. You can use this information if you are closely monitoring and controlling your diet (see page 329 for the daily dietary allowances recommended by the Food and Nutrition Board of the National Academy of Sciences).

If you're wondering how well my recipes stack up against conventional recipes, the computer analyses will convince you that there's a major improvement. I asked Computrition to analyze a few of my old recipes so I could compare them to the ones I've recently created, and even I was astonished by the degree of difference that my approach to cooking made in lowering the sodium, fat, cholesterol, and caloric content of conventional dishes.

Rumaki, for instance, is an appetizer high in popularity, but even higher in sodium, fat, cholesterol, and calories. Here are the ingredients for 12 servings from my old favorite rumaki recipe:

12 chicken livers, cut in half
12 slices bacon, cut in half
½ cup soy sauce
2 tablespoons sugar
2 tablespoons sherry or saki
2 tablespoons water
1 teaspoon garlic powder
1 teaspoon ground ginger
¼ cup catsup
2 tablespoons Dijon mustard

Computrition analyzed the key nutrients in that recipe as follows: 245 calories, 991 milligrams of sodium, 20.8 grams of fat, and 177 milligrams of cholesterol per serving.

The ingredients in my new recipe, which follows, produce a comparable taste sensation, but without the health risk.

Chicken Rumaki

Serves: 12

10 ounces slightly frozen skinned and boned chicken breasts
12 fresh or canned unsweetened pineapple chunks
12 whole canned water chestnuts, drained
3 tablespoons mild soy sauce
¼ cup water
2 tablespoons frozen unsweetened pineapple juice concentrate
2 tablespoons dry sherry or sake
1 teaspoon garlic powder
1 teaspoon ground ginger

Chicken Rumaki has only 48 calories, 163 milligrams of sodium, 0.33 gram of fat, and 14 milligrams of cholesterol per serving.

In case you think rumaki is just an especially dramatic example, I'd like to compare three more sets of recipes to demonstrate how contrary to good health traditional recipes can be and how my recipes can help you make a change for the better. The ingredients in Veal Tonnato, an Italian entrée, are a high-cholesterol case in point.

According to Computrition, they add up to 572 calories, 523 milligrams of sodium, 41.9 grams of fat, and 131 milligrams of cholesterol per serving.

In my recipe on page 172 I changed the veal to turkey, tuna in oil to tuna in salt-free water pack, and omitted the anchovies and mayonnaise. This vastly improves the nutritional quality without sacrificing flavor.

Each serving has only 200 calories, 96 milligrams of sodium, 3.7 grams of fat, and 85 milligrams of cholesterol. The nutritional advantage is impressive, and—served as I suggest, with a colorful garnish of cherry tomatoes and radish roses accompanied by a cold rice salad—so is the dish.

You will find my recipes provide new rewards for your palate that more than compensate for an inevitable loss of certain familiar flavors that come from the liberal use of salt, butter, egg yolks, cream, and the like. I'd be the last person to deny that the flavors in Pasta Florentine are wonderful. But think of the price you pay by overindulging in the ingredients: according to Computrition, many Pasta Florentines have 531 calories, 594 milligrams of sodium, 38.4 grams of fat, and 141 milligrams of cholesterol per serving. My adapted recipe is a spectacular alternative. By eliminating butter, cream, frozen spinach soufflé, and Gruyère cheese and substituting low-calorie cottage cheese, skimmed evaporated milk, frozen spinach, and my Bolognese sauce, I've brought my Pasta Florentine on page 250 down to only 266 calories, 106 milligrams of sodium, 5.4 grams of fat, and *no* cholesterol in each serving.

Sometimes even recipes with healthy-sounding names can be loaded with potentially harmful ingredients. A muffin recipe I used to enjoy is a perfect example. The difference in the calorie count between these muffins and my adaptation is only about 50 calories per muffin, but there is an enormous difference in the nutritional quality. One recipe I used to use contained 181 calories, 179 milligrams of sodium, 5.6 grams of fat, and 27.8 milligrams of cholesterol per serving.

My recipe for Geneva's Extra-Special Muffins on page 297 is high in fiber and has only 126 calories, 56 milligrams of sodium, 0.8 grams of fat, and no cholesterol per serving. To get these results I use unsweetened cereal, fruit instead of sugar, whole grain flour instead of bleached white flour, and eliminate oil and egg yolks.

Sometimes you can feel the placque in your arteries forming as you read traditional ingredient lists. Eggs Benedict is a good example: there are an incredible 1142 calories, 3912 milligrams of sodium, 81 grams of fat, and 1132 milligrams of cholesterol per serving.
substitute with only 148 calories, 185 milligrams of sodium, 1.47 grams of
My Tuna Benedictine on page 309 is an attractive, considerably lighter
fat, and 16 milligrams of cholesterol per serving.

Where There's a Will, There's a Way

In changing from *haute cuisine* to healthful cooking, I learned many new things. They include cooking methods, that now have become second nature to me. Once you learn them yourself, you can begin to improvise your own low-sodium, low-fat, low-cholesterol, low-sugar recipes. Here are some of the methods I've adopted.

Substitutions

Instead of	*Use*
canned fruit	fresh fruit
fruit juice	whole fruit
fat or oil	nonstick spray, nonstick pan, or broth for sautéeing
canned soup	homemade or acceptable commercial product (see Preferred Products list, page 323)
sugar, molasses, or syrup	unsweetened fruit juice or fruit concentrate or ripe banana
sour cream, cream cheese, or mayonnaise	nonfat yogurt
oil-packed tuna	water-packed tuna
whole milk	nonfat milk and milk products, dry skim milk plus water, or canned skim milk
whipped cream	whipped nonfat milk, whipped nonfat evaporated milk, or whipped dry skim milk
white breads or flours	use whole grain breads or flours
whole eggs	egg whites only
salt	low-sodium vegetable seasoning, herbs, and other piquant seasonings such as pepper

Better Recipes for the Basics

Instead of	*Use*
chicken stock	Basic Chicken Stock (see page 26)
bouillon cubes	Bouillon Cubes (see page 25) This low-sodium alternative is handy for stir-frying, sautéeing, or seasoning.
cream cheese or sour cream	Our Cream Cheese and Sour Cream (see page 27) The key to making these nonfat alternatives is to use only the freshest ingredients.
salt	Harriet's No-Salt Vegetable Seasoning (see page 28) or an acceptable low-Sodium Seasoning
packaged bread crumbs	Seasoned Bread Crumbs (see page 29)

How to Start Eating Better

It is my sincere hope that after you try some of my recipes, you will be motivated to change your cooking and eating habits. But the degree to which you follow my suggestions is up to you. Any positive changes that you make will be in your best interests, so don't be discouraged and feel that if you don't radically change all your food habits at once, you can't change at all.

You may start by omitting salt—omitting added salt in your cooking and removing the salt shaker from your table.

Using nonfat dairy products is most desirable, but you can *start* by changing to low-fat dairy products—that's a 50 percent reduction in your fat intake. Using oil-free salad dressing, light salad dressings, or yogurt instead of mayonnaise or sour cream and baking and broiling foods instead of frying will all help reduce your total fat intake.

You may have been having eggs or even bacon for breakfast every morning, and red meat four to five times a week. Limit your red meat to no more than a weekly serving of very lean beef such as flank steak, round steak, or rump, and increase the use of fish and poultry. Have an egg just once a week, if you must. This will enormously lower your intake of cholesterol.

Try satisfying your "sweet tooth" by choosing some of the wonderful, seasonally fresh or dried fruits available in the market today or preparing a sorbet or treat as listed in Sweets and Treats (pages 261–99). Fruit concentrates can take the place of refined sugars usually found in "traditional" recipes. Be creative and try adjusting some of your favorite recipes with the ingredients listed in the next section.

Helpful Hints

Preferred Products

Caveat emptor means "let the buyer beware." Indeed, as prudent consumers we must use judgment and take the *time to read labels*. (The federal government and private agencies are trying to make explicit labeling mandatory.) Be aware of the sodium, fat, sugar, and preservatives that are being added to the foods you buy. I have compiled a list of some of my favorite food products (see Appendix, page 323). Perhaps they are not available in the markets in your area, but they will give you an indication of what to look for and what to ask your local store managers for. Keep these general shopping guidelines in mind:

1. Avoid buying food with any of the following ingredients listed on the label, as they raise the *sodium content* of the product: salt (should be listed at least after the third ingredient), sodium chloride, sea salt, MSG (monosodium glutamate), sodium saccharin, sodium nitrite, sodium nitrate, sodium propionate, sodium benzoate, sodium bisulfite, or any ingredient with sodium in its name should be shunned.
2. Do not buy seasoning such as onion salt, garlic salt, celery salt, catsup, chili sauce, barbecue sauce, cooking wines (salt is added), miso, soy sauce or tamari (unless low-sodium), and prepared mustard (unless salt-free). Capers must be rinsed before using to remove some salt and then used only as a seasoning. Worcestershire sauce (French's) contains 150 milligrams of sodium per tablespoon; use it judiciously as a seasoning.
3. If you use salt-free tomato products instead of the usual canned tomato products you will substantially further lower the sodium content of our recipes. One cup canned Italian plum tomatoes contains 250 to 300 milligrams of sodium, whereas one cup salt-free or no-salt-added tomatoes contains 30 milligrams of sodium.
4. Sugar on labels appears under listings such as sucrose, glucose, dextrose, lactose, fructose, corn sugar, corn syrup or corn sweetener, cane sugar, raw sugar, sorghum, molasses, and honey. Avoid buying products with any of these ingredients.

5. Fat content in processed foods is listed as shortening, oil, mayonnaise, butter, margarine, monoglycerides, diglycerides or triglycerides, lard, tallow, suet, chicken fat, egg yolks, lipids, or lecithin. Avoid these if you can.

6. When buying cereals, choose whole grain cereals that have no salt or sugar added.

7. Whole grain flours are preferred. If you buy white flour, at least buy the unbleached variety.

8. If you use canned fruits purchase only those canned in natural, unsweetened fruit juices. Frozen fruits should be unsweetened.

9. Canned soups should have no fat, MSG, or sweetener added. If any salt is added, it should appear after the third ingredient listed. Try making your own soup. It will taste better and be cheaper and more nourishing.

10. Above all, be an alert and concerned consumer. Become a detective. The quality of the products that appear in our markets is improving daily. This is only because consumers like you and I have requested, in some cases demanded, nourishing food products not disturbed by unnecessary processing, additives, and preservatives.

A Note on Herbs and Spices

My recipes always use dried herbs unless fresh herbs are specified. Of course, if you have access to fresh herbs, use them. They will add a gentle seasoning you will enjoy. To convert from dried to fresh herbs, triple the amounts specified for dried.

Herbs and spices should be stored in a cool, dry, dark place (not over the kitchen stove). They have a shelf life of about six months, so the ones you do not use a great deal should be divided at time of purchase and placed in plastic bags in the freezer. I write the date on my herb jars when I fill them and empty those not used within six months. Stale herbs taste like sawdust, not a very delicate flavor to add to your foods, so do not buy in bulk and only buy herbs and spices in sealed containers.

Our Vinaigrette or Italian Dressings

Whenever the recipes call for our Italian or our Vinaigrette Dressing, you may use any commercial Italian or vinaigrette dressing that is low-sodium, and sugar-free. Any commercial product is acceptable if it meets those standards. If you buy a commercial dressing that is low-fat and sugar-free but not low-sodium, you can make it acceptable by making two bottles out of one. Here's how: mix your bottled dressing with an equal amount of a solution that is half water and half of a quality vinegar

Useful Ingredients

Applesauce

Perk up the flavor of canned applesauce by topping with lemon or orange zest, cinnamon, freshly ground nutmeg, or plumped raisins.

Baking Powder

In an emergency 1 teaspoon of a tartrate baking powder may be substituted for ¼ teaspoon of baking soda and ½ teaspoon of cream of tartar.

If not using a low-sodium baking powder such as Cellu or Featherweight, I recommend baking powder without aluminum or alum.

Bananas

A very ripe banana is a good sweetener. Bananas may be flash-frozen on a baking sheet and stored in tightly closed plastic bags. Defrost slightly before using, except in preparing sorbet.

Bouquet Garni

A bouquet garni is a combination of parsley, thyme, bay leaf, and crushed red pepper used in flavoring soups, stews, vegetables, and sauces. Combine the ingredients in cheesecloth tied with string or unwaxed dental floss or use a stainless steel tea caddy, which may be reused each time.

Buttermilk

When using buttermilk always strain fat globules, which have been added at the dairy, before using. If a recipe calls for buttermilk, you may substitute milk which has been soured in this fashion: Add 1 tablespoon of brown rice vinegar to 1 cup of nonfat milk. Let stand a few moments until it curdles.

Carob Powder

Carob powder is made from the dried pods of the carob tree. It is used as a substitute for chocolate or cocoa (which contains caffeine). There is a difference in flavor, but it is quite acceptable. A rule of thumb for substitution is 3 tablespoons of carob plus 2 tablespoons of liquid equals one square unsweetened chocolate. Sugar substitutions are made with fruit juice concentrate or ripe banana to suit your taste.

Chicken Stock (see recipe page 26)

Save skin, bones, giblets, and wing tips from poultry and freeze in plastic bags. Use as part of base when making chicken stock. (Chicken necks and backs are good and cheap to use in making stock.)

TO CLARIFY CHICKEN OR FISH STOCK

Add 1 egg white plus 2 teaspoons of water, and the eggshell to 1 quart boiling stock. Boil 2 minutes and strain.

TO ADD A RICH BROWN COLOR TO CHICKEN STOCK

Add 1 tablespoon tomato paste to 1 quart stock.

Duxelles

Minced mushrooms and shallots sautéed in our Bouillon Cubes (see page 25) as follows: Take ½ pound of mushrooms and mince in food processor. Squeeze dry in corner of a kitchen towel. (Save juice for soup or sauce.) Add to minced green onions or shallots and sauté in 2 Bouillon Cubes and 2 tablespoons of dry vermouth. Stir frequently until mushrooms are dry and begin to separate. Add 1 teaspoon of vegetable seasoning (see page 28) and sauté a few more minutes. Store in refrigerator for several weeks in airtight container or freeze. Used in sauces, stuffings, and vegetable purees, this will be a cherished ingredient.

Flours, Cereals

Flours and cereals should be stored in airtight jars. Because the germ is not removed in whole grain products, they are a bit more perishable. (The fat content of germ causes this.) I keep my whole wheat flour in the freezer. Odds and ends of dry cereal may be pulverized, appropriately seasoned, and used to bread fish or chicken or as a topping for vegetables.

Garlic

If you are a garlic lover as I am, try adding a bit of additional minced garlic to a dish ten minutes before the cooking time is over. It gives a fresh, delicious taste to the food.

To make garlic toast croutons, toast whole wheat bread and rub whole cloves of garlic on hot toast. It will melt into toast and make a flavorful garlic toast—without fat. If croutons are desired, cut into cubes and toast on baking sheet in 400° oven until crisp. (If your hands smell garlicky, rinse in cold water and rub in salt; we finally found something it is good for.)

Ginger Root

May be stored in a plastic bag or the freezer or in a bottle of dry sherry if you promise not to nip.

Green Onions or Scallions

The white portion may be used to substitute for shallots in cooking, and the green part for chives.

Leftovers

YESTERDAY'S VEGETABLES BECOME TODAY'S SALAD

Mix our Vinaigrette Dressing (see page 12) in a generous-sized jar. Each day, add any leftover bits of raw or cooked vegetables. (Exception is salad greens.) In a few days, lift marinated vegetable mixture with slotted spoon onto lettuce leaves and serve as a delicious salad. You will discover unusual and flavorful mixtures this way.

LEFTOVER COOKED MEATS

Use leftover cooked meats (chicken, turkey, or flank steak) in salads; puree and use as a seasoned sandwich spread or as a pâté appetizer.

LEFTOVER COOKED RICE OR SPAGHETTI

May be used in salads, soups, or as a crust. Season and blend with slightly beaten egg white and Weight Watcher's cottage cheese. Press over bottom and sides of pie plate, and fill with vegetable mixture and bake.

Lemons

Lemon juice is a marvelous flavor enhancer to be used on fish, chicken, game, and turkey. It develops a flavor without a lemony taste, if used judiciously. Add grated lemon zest to salads or vinaigrette dressings. Float lemon slices on black bean soup or serve with jellied consommés. Lemon wedges served with fresh melon add extra zip. Lemons may be stored at room temperature for about ten days and in the refrigerator in crisper or plastic bag for about six weeks. Lemons yield more juice when at room temperature. If chilled, place under hot water or in a microwave oven for about fifteen seconds. Roll on counter before squeezing to release more juice.

Mirepoix

A mirepoix is a mixture of 1 carrot, 1 small onion, and 1 stalk of celery (sometimes a shallot) that have been chopped and sautéed in chicken broth until transparent. It is used as a base in roasting or braising meat or chicken and sometimes with added liquid as a base for poaching fish.

Popcorn

May be seasoned with vegetable seasoning, curry powder, garlic powder, or onion powder as a snack substitute for "junk foods."

Sap Sago Cheese (nonfat herb cheese from Switzerland)

When using Sap Sago cheese as a seasoning or topping, grate it fine, then place it on a baking sheet in a 375° oven until golden brown. Stir from time to time while toasting. If it lumps, do not become alarmed, simply crush it between your fingers until it resembles the texture of Parmesan, for which it is frequently substituted. Sap Sago cheese may be frozen.

Soy Sauce

Use only mild soy sauce. If you cannot find mild salt-reduced soy sauce, you can dilute regular soy sauce (1 part water to 1 part soy sauce) before measuring and using.

Thickeners
For thickening a sauce, 1 tablespoon of cornstarch, arrowroot, or potato starch equals 2 tablespoons of flour. Use cornstarch, arrowroot, or potato starch when you want a translucent look. Mix thickener with cold water before adding to hot liquid.

Tofu (soy bean curd)
Tofu is a vegetable cheese made from soy milk. It has been used as a meat exchange in China and Japan for centuries as a major source of protein. Since it is not of animal origin, it contains no cholesterol. Because of its fat content, it must be used as an exchange for fish or poultry; however, it has fewer calories—about 72 calories in a 3½-ounce serving, whereas a skinned chicken breast has about 110 calories.

Tofu has a bland taste, but it absorbs the flavors of the food with which it is combined. Hence, it lends itself to marinades or stir-frying. When cubed, it is a good protein addition to soups. It may be blended in your food processor and used as a cheese in lasagna, as a substitute for mayonnaise, or seasoned and used instead of yogurt in a dip.

Tomato Products
Blend 1 can of salt-free tomato paste with 1 can of cold water to make a salt-free tomato puree, 2 cans of water with paste to make a sauce, and 3 cans of water plus 1 teaspoon of apple juice concentrate, lemon juice, and Tabasco to make a pleasant-tasting (and less expensive) tomato juice. It is important to blend juice well and chill before serving.

For catsup, combine a 6-ounce can of salt-free tomato paste, 2 cans of water, 2 tablespoons of apple cider, brown rice vinegar, or raspberry wine vinegar, and 1½ tablespoons of frozen unsweetened pineapple juice concentrate. Blend well and refrigerate. (If you like a spicier catsup, a few drops of Tabasco may be added.)

Truffles
Truffles are round, wrinkled, black or white aromatic fungi, which are dug up by pigs in certain regions of France and Italy. They are expensive, especially the fresh, which are seldom found in the United States. The flavor of canned truffles can be enhanced by sprinkling 1 tablespoon of Madeira over them a short time before serving. They lend exquisite flavor to sauces and salads; leftovers, if you can use such a plebian term in connection with truffles, may be frozen and are wonderful shredded and added to pasta.

Vinegar
There is a soggy mass that may develop in vinegar when it ages. This is called mother-of-vinegar. If it is present, you may make your own vinegar by adding leftover wine (white or red depending on the vinegar) to it

and letting the bottle stand in a cool, dark place for several weeks before using.

Herb vinegars are more expensive. You may make your own by adding a bunch of fresh basil, tarragon, dill, or 3 crushed garlic cloves to the plain vinegar of your choice. (It makes a lovely gift, also.)

Wine

Don't be concerned about adding wine to your cooking; 85 percent of the calories and all of the alcohol cook off at about 175°.

Yogurt

Contains the same nutrients as the milk from which it is made. Therefore, 8 ounces of nonfat yogurt contain about 90 calories. Compare this to 1 cup of sour cream with 485 calories, or worse yet, 1 cup of mayonnaise with 1400 calories. Yogurt is also a good source of protein, calcium, potassium, and other minerals. It is a perishable dairy product and must be refrigerated. The longer it is stored, the more tart it becomes. Yogurt made from a Bulgarian starter is innately more tart. Liquid naturally separates from the solid as it stands, so for a thicker yogurt, drain off the liquid before stirring it. Commercial yogurt has a date stamped on the bottom to indicate the last day it can be sold. Yogurt may be used in dips, as a base in desserts or fruited toppings, in baking, in soups, and in marinating or cooking poultry, fish, or meats. Naturally, it can be adapted and substituted whenever sour cream or mayonnaise is used.

Cooking Tips

To Beat Egg Whites

The bowl, beaters, and egg whites should be at room temperature to increase the volume of the beaten egg whites. Do not use a plastic bowl because it retains grease from previous cooking and inhibits egg whites from becoming stiff. If you add half of a very ripe banana, pureed, to softly beaten egg whites, you will further increase their volume.

To Whip Skimmed Evaporated Milk

Canned milk should be thoroughly chilled for about one hour or two in the freezer. The bowl and beater to be used should also be chilled in the freezer first. If all ingredients and utensils are thoroughly chilled, milk will triple in bulk when beaten.

To Whip Fresh Skimmed Milk

Follow the same procedure used to whip skimmed evaporated milk. A special hand-held mixer, such as the Bamix (made in Switzerland, but available in the United States), the Maxi-Mix, or the Minipimer, is required to whip fresh skimmed milk.

Steam, Broil, Use Pressure Cooker or Microwave Raw Vegetables to Preserve Vitamins

When possible, eat raw. Don't thaw frozen vegetables before cooking, and use as little water as possible to cook them. (It saves the nutrients.) Any leftover vegetable liquid should be saved for soups, sauces, or gravy.

To Remove Fat from Liquids

Let liquids chill so that the fat rises and hardens. Remove the fat several hours later or the next day. If you want to remove fat immediately, there is a wonderful piece of equipment called a gravy strain that removes all fat from liquids by just pouring. The spout is on the bottom so that defatted liquid can be removed quite simply.

To Prepare Dried Orange Peel

To prepare dried orange peel, remove zest of orange (not white part) with vegetable peeler and let it hang in your kitchen for several days to dry. When dried, store in airtight spice jar or in freezer for future use.

Taste Your Marinara Sauce

Dip a small piece of whole wheat or Italian bread into your marinara or tomato sauce while cooking to check the seasoning. It will give you a good idea of what the sauce tastes like served over pasta. (Besides, it also gives you an excuse to dunk while cooking.) If you are concerned about calories, try the following: blanch fresh bean sprouts in boiling water about one minute. Drain *quickly* and serve with marinara sauce. *Voilà*—almost-pasta with few calories.

Control Yogurt Curdling

Yogurt is very sensitive to heat. It curdles under high temperatures. When a recipe calls for you to heat yogurt, start with it at room temperature and add it to the other ingredients at the end of the cooking time. Continue cooking at a low temperature for a brief period of time. Cornstarch blended with yogurt—1 teaspoon of cornstarch to ½ cup of yogurt—also helps stabilize it.

To Process Garlic

Add garlic while the machine is in motion; otherwise, it may lodge under the blade of the processor and not be chopped.

To Clean Mushrooms

Wipe with damp paper towels or a mushroom brush. As a last resort, you may wash quickly under cold running water. *Never* soak mushrooms in water to clean. They absorb too much water and dilute flavor in cooking. If mushroom caps are not tightly closed and you can see the gills, the mushrooms are too old and you should not buy them. If, however, you have them at home, they can be used. Mushrooms can be sliced and placed in freezer bags for future use in cooking.

To Cook Whole Onions
Cut an X in the root end of an onion to prevent it from slipping apart in cooking.

To Plump Raisins
In order to enhance the flavor and texture of raisins they need to be plumped in a hot liquid of your choice such as fresh orange juice, water, sherry, or brandy. Simply cover raisins with hot liquid for fifteen minutes and drain well before using. They may also be heated in the microwave oven on high for three minutes.

To Peel Tomatoes
Immerse in boiling water for two minutes. Rinse in cold water, core and peel. They may also be placed on a fork over an open flame and turned until skin bursts, then peeled. To seed tomatoes, cut in half crosswise and gently squeeze to remove seeds.

Marvelous Menus

The recipes for all of the dishes in the following menus can be found in this book. I've included them as a spur to your own creativity as well as to give you some suggestions for memorable meals. When planning your own menus, start with your entrée as the focal point and build around it. Remember to allow yourself plenty of time to enjoy both the preparation and the meal. One way to do that in the midst of a busy life is to plan and cook ahead. All the dishes marked with an asterisk (*) below may be partially or totally prepared several hours before serving or the day before, or they may be frozen for future use.

AN EXCELLENT MOVABLE FEAST
*Quick, Cold Cucumber Soup with Homemade Crisp Chips
*Pan Bagna
*Green Bean Salad
Assorted fresh fruits and *Harriet's Pumpkin Bread

A COMPANY DINNER
*Broccoli Dip with Crudités
Hearts of Palm and Watercress Salad
*Bracciole
Barley Casserole
Sesame, Zucchini, and Tomatoes
*Raspberry Mousse

A FORMAL DINNER
*Tuna Pâté with Slim Rye
Orange-Glazed Cornish Hens
Cracked Wheat Pilaf
*Layered Vegetable Mold
Bibb lettuce salad with *Vinaigrette Dressing
*Floating Islands with Raspberry Sauce

LET'S EAT CHINESE
*Marinated Chicken Drummettes
*Chinese Hot and Sour Soup
Chinese Minced Chicken in Lettuce Leaves
Steamed Brown Rice
Nanette's Microwaved Oriental Vegetables
Chopped Broccoli, Chinese Style
Fresh pineapple wedges

AFTER THE GAME
*Queso con Salsa and/or *Spicy Pink Dip
with Crudités and Homemade Crisp Chips
*Venison Stew Mexicana—Chili Verde
Sliced fresh pineapple, papaya, melon, and strawberries

YOUR HOLIDAY DINNER
*Tomato Aspic Supreme with Cucumber Sauce
Roast turkey with gravy
Wild Rice, Brown Rice, and Mushrooms
*Cranberry, Pineapple, and Yogurt Freeze
*Spinach Ring with carrots *Sweet Potato Mélange
*Yogurt-Pumpkin Pie—or—*Festive Fruitcake with Low-Calorie
Whipped Topping

A SPECIAL SUMMER VEGETARIAN BUFFET OR BRUNCH
*Gazpacho
*Liptauer Cheese and Finn Crisp crackers
Salad Medley
*Confetti Rice Salad *Marinated Bean Salad
Sliced tomatoes and red onions with fresh basil
*Noodle Pudding I or II
*Boysenberry-Yogurt Sorbet

A PLEASANT DINNER
Bean Sprout, Spinach, and Mushroom Salad
*Anna's Tomato Chicken with pasta
*Your Perfect Pear

A MENU FOR EACH SEASON
Summer
*Chilled Puree of Cauliflower Soup
Eva's Easy-Does-It Poached Salmon
Steamed red potatoes Asparagus
*Cucumber, Green Onion, and Yogurt Salad
*Banana and Pineapple Sorbet

Winter
*Split Pea Soup
*Old-Fashioned Baked Meat Loaf
Mixed green salad with *My Favorite Russian Dressing
Plain baked potato with
*Our Sour Cream and chives
Steamed Summer Squash with Carrots
*Apple Crisp

Spring
*Chicken Paprika with Yogurt
Zucchini with Linguini
*Gingered Cucumbers
*Mrs. Latterman's Strawberry Chiffon Pie
—or—
*Strawberries with Strawberry Sauce

Fall
*Antipasto à la Roma
Bucatini Primavera
Whole Wheat Garlic Toast
*Citron Soufflé

Dining Out

Speak up for your diet preferences!

Appetizer: Have a fruit, juice, or raw vegetable salad with lemon or vinegar. A restaurant salad bar usually offers a good variety.

Soup: Ask if soups are canned—if so, avoid. Choose a vegetable soup—not a creamed soup. Taste—if too salty, pass.

Main Dish: Choose broiled, grilled, or roasted poultry or fish, prepared without fat, sauce or gravy. Again ask for lemon. Order steamed rice, boiled potato, or baked potato with chives.

Vegetable: Choose steamed vegetables without added butter or sauce.

Dessert: Fruit is a good choice. Order melon or berries in season, or a basket of fresh fruit *without the accompanying cheese.*

If fast food is your only choice, try a pizzeria where you can have pizza made with vegetables and marinara sauce only—*no cheese or oil*—or a restaurant with a good salad bar.

Six Easy Basics

Bouillon Cubes

2 cups our Basic Chicken Stock (see page 26)
½ cup dry white wine or vermouth
1 bay leaf
2 shallots, chopped

1. Combine above ingredients.
2. Simmer until reduced to 1 cup. (If by chance you have stored your chicken stock in the refrigerator for more than 3 days, bring the stock to a boil before using in order to destroy any harmful bacteria.)
3. Pour into ice cube tray and freeze.
4. Remove from tray and seal tightly in plastic bags. (Don't get cubes wet when removing from ice cube tray or they will stick together.) These are handy to use in stir-frying or sautéeing ingredients, instead of fat or oil. Also nice for seasoning steamed vegetables.

Per serving: 5 calories; 0.4 gm protein; 0 gm fat; 0.8 gm carbohydrate; 0 gm fiber; 0 mg cholesterol; 0 mg iron; 0.7 mg sodium; 0 IU Vitamin A; 0 mg thiamine; 0 mg riboflavin; 0 mg Vitamin C; 0 mg potassium; 0 mg zinc; 0 mg niacin; 0 mcg Vitamin B_6; 0 mcg Vitamin B_{12}; 0 mcg folic acid

Basic Chicken Stock

Yield: 2 quarts (1 cup = 1 serving)

The preparation of a delicious low-fat, low-sodium chicken stock is essential in our type of food preparation. It serves as the base of many other soups, is an essential cooking liquid in a large variety of dishes and sauces, and is required in making your own frozen bouillon cubes to use in stir-frying, sautéing, and seasoning. As of this writing there is no chicken stock available commercially that has no salt, MSG, sugar, or fat added. Besides, yours will taste much better. You can make it in bulk once a month to freeze for future use. If by chance you have stored your chicken stock in the refrigerator for more than 3 days, bring the stock to a boil before using in order to destroy harmful bacteria—Salmonella—that increase with lengthy storage.

4 quarts cold water
4 pounds chicken necks and backs (all visible fat removed)
2 whole chicken breasts, halved
3 carrots
3 stalks celery with leaves
1 parsnip
2 leeks, well washed
1 turnip
1 bouquet garni (4 sprigs Italian parsley, ½ teaspoon crushed red pepper, 2 bay leaves, 1 teaspoon thyme, 1 tablespoon Rokeach dried soup greens)
1 onion stuck with 4 whole cloves

1. Place chicken necks and backs in a 8- to 10-quart stainless steel stock pot.
2. Cover with *cold* water.
3. Bring to a boil; remove scum.
4. Add remaining ingredients, lower heat, and simmer for 2½ hours, partially covered. (Remove chicken breasts after 1 hour of cooking.*)
5. Strain through a stainless steel triple-mesh strainer, cool, and place in refrigerator overnight. Remove congealed fat before using or freezing. Keeps in refrigerator 3 days. For longer storage, freeze according to instructions on page 57.

To Use: Reheat and serve as broth or use as the base for a soup. (If you like, add fresh dill to the broth when reheating—it adds a surprisingly fresh flavor. Remember to remove the sprigs of dill before serving.) Use some to prepare our valuable Bouillon Cubes (see page 25).

* Reserve chicken breasts for use in salads or sandwiches, or serve as chicken in the pot with broth for dinner!

Helpful Hints: Always use cold water in starting a stock. It allows the flavor to flow into the stock instead of being sealed in the bones or meat.

There is a cup called a gravy strain that may be used to defat broth *before* chilling or freezing.

Per serving: 34 calories; 2.6 gm protein; 0 gm fat; 5.5 gm carbohydrate; 0 gm fiber; 0 mg cholesterol; 0 mg iron; 5 mg sodium; 0 mg calcium; 0 mg phosphorus; 0 IU Vitamin A; 0 mg thiamine; 0 mg riboflavin; 0 mg Vitamin C; 0 mg potassium; 0 mg zinc; 0 mg niacin; 0 mcg Vitamin B_6; 0 mcg Vitamin B_{12}; 0 mcg folic acid

Our Cream Cheese and Sour Cream

Yield: 2½ cups (1 tablespoon = 1 serving)

This is a nonfat substitute for cream cheese and sour cream that is not only easy to prepare but may be frozen for future use.

½ pound *fresh* hoop cheese or skim milk ricotta*
½ cup fresh nonfat yogurt, or more to reach desired consistency
½ cup buttermilk, strained to remove fat globules (for sour cream only)

1. Crumble *fresh* hoop cheese into a food processor or blender.
2. Process cheese until it forms a ball.
3. Add yogurt gradually while creaming. *This produces a cream cheese.*
4. *When a smooth, sour cream consistency is desired,* add ½ cup buttermilk and process until smooth.
5. Keep in refrigerator for 1 week; for longer storage, put in freezer.

To Use: May be served or used as a cooking ingredient whenever cream cheese or sour cream is indicated. Try the cream cheese on bagels for Sunday brunch, the sour cream as a topping for baked potatoes. If frozen, defrost and blend well before using.

Variation: If hoop cheese is not available, sour cream can be made by pureeing 1%- or 2%-fat cottage cheese in the food processor until smooth. Use as a sour cream topping.

Per serving: 9 calories; 1.8 gm protein; 0.09 gm fat; 0.63 gm carbohydrate; 0 gm fiber; 0.08 mg cholesterol; 0 mg iron; 22 mg sodium; 12 mg calcium; 8 mg phosphorus; 33 IU Vitamin A; 0 mg thiamine; 0.01 riboflavin; 0.04 mg Vitamin C; 13 mg potassium; 0.05 mg zinc; 0 mg niacin; 2.67 mcg Vitamin B_6; 0.03 mcg Vitamin B_{12}; 0.58 folic acid

* The freshness of the hoop cheese *(check the date on the label)* determines the quality of the cream cheese or sour cream.

Harriet's No-Salt Vegetable Seasoning

Yield: 7 tablespoons (½ teaspoon = 1 serving)

If a low-sodium vegetable seasoning is not available in your area, try making your own. It is quite simple, and you may even find that you prefer it to those commercially available.

¼ cup Rokeach dried soup greens
1 tablespoon dried shallots or dried mushrooms
¼ teaspoon ground bay leaf
⅛ teaspoon celery seed
2 teaspoons toasted onion flakes
1 teaspoon garlic powder
1 teaspoon herbes de Provence or thyme
1 teaspoon Hungarian paprika
¼ teaspoon crushed red pepper or chili powder
¼ teaspoon dry mustard

1. Blend all ingredients in blender until granulated and powdery. (If you do not have a blender, try a mortar and pestle.)
2. Store in a screw-top jar in a cool, dark, dry place.

To Use: This snappy seasoning is appropriate for salads, vegetables, fish, and poultry, and can be used in cooking wherever vegetable seasoning is indicated.

Variation: Add 1 teaspoon toasted sesame seeds, ground ginger, or dill weed to vary the flavor.

Per serving: 3 calories; 0.1 gm protein; 0 gm fat; 0.4 gm carbohydrate; 0.1 gm fiber; 0 mg cholesterol; 0.3 mg iron; 1 mg sodium; 6 mg calcium; 3 mg phosphorus; 171 IU Vitamin A; 0 mg thiamine; 0.01 riboflavin; 1 mg Vitamin C; 11 mg potassium; 0 mg zinc; 0 mg niacin; 2 mcg Vitamin B_6; 0 mcg Vitamin B_{12}; 1 mcg folic acid

Seasoned Bread Crumbs

Yield: approx. 1 cup (1 tablespoon = 1 serving)

Try making your own seasoned bread crumbs. Simply combine one tablespoon of your favorite unsalted herb seasoning with one cup of bread crumbs. Or for a more interesting and zesty flavor prepare the following recipe. Store it in the refrigerator to preserve its freshness. If you read the label on commercial bread crumbs carefully, you will note that in most circumstances they have fat, salt and sodium preservatives, and sugar added. With this in mind it behooves us to prepare our own—besides you can also economize by using up stale bread.

1 cup dried fine bread crumbs (preferably made from Pritikin whole wheat bread)
Freshly ground pepper
Few grains crushed red pepper
½ teaspoon Hungarian paprika
1 teaspoon low-sodium vegetable seasoning (see page 28)
¼ teaspoon dried savory, crushed
½ teaspoon dried basil, crushed
½ teaspoon dried thyme, crushed
2 tablespoons grated Sap Sago cheese, toasted (see page 15)

1. Combine all ingredients in a small bowl. Mix well.
2. Store in refrigerator in an airtight container or freeze for future use.

Per serving: 16 calories; 3.7 gm protein; 0.3 gm fat; 2.0 gm carbohydrate; 0.2 gm fiber; 0 mg cholesterol; 0.3 mg iron; 35 mg sodium; 24 mg calcium; 12 mg phosphorus; 147 IU Vitamin A; 0.03 mg thiamine; 0.02 mg riboflavin; 0 mg Vitamin C; 19 mg potassium; 0 mg zinc; 0.2 mg niacin; 1 mcg Vitamin B_6; 0 mcg Vitamin B_{12}; 0 mcg folic acid

Basic White Sauce

Yield: 2⅓ cups (3 tablespoons = 1 serving)

A sauce is meant to heighten the flavor of the food it covers. This basic white sauce or Béchamel, as it is sometimes called, is delicate in flavor, yet makes an interesting addition on occasion to already wonderful, crisp steamed vegetables.

3 our Bouillon Cubes (see page 25) or 3 tablespoons our Chicken or Vegetable Stock (see pages 25, 60)
4 tablespoons unbleached flour
1 slice onion or 1 teaspoon chopped shallots
2 cups nonfat milk
⅓ cup dry nonfat milk
1 bay leaf
½ teaspoon thyme, crushed
½ teaspoon white pepper
1 teaspoon vegetable seasoning
2 tablespoons dry sherry, sauterne, or vermouth (optional)

1. Melt bouillon cubes in a nonstick saucepan over moderate heat. Add flour and onion; blend with a wooden spoon or whisk.
2. Simmer over low heat for several minutes, *stirring constantly. Do not allow to brown.*
3. Remove from heat, add milks, bay leaf, thyme, white pepper, and vegetable seasoning. Return to heat, stirring constantly until mixture coats the spoon. If desired, add wine and simmer 5 minutes more to evaporate alcohol.
4. Remove onion and bay leaf.
5. Cover and store until used, or place in an airtight container and refrigerate for several days, or freeze for future use.

Serving Suggestions: This sauce may be used over 8 cups of steamed vegetables such as broccoli florets, diced potatoes, quartered mushrooms, peas, asparagus, or sliced carrots. To serve, place vegetables in a shallow, ovenproof serving dish. Drizzle sauce over vegetables, sprinkle with 2 tablespoons Parmesan or Sap Sago cheese or with Hungarian paprika, and place under broiler to brown lightly before serving.

Variations: Instead of sprinkling cheese on top of vegetables, you may add 2 tablespoons Parmesan cheese to the white sauce and heat for 5 minutes. This is called a Mornay sauce. You may also substitute ⅔ cup of vegetable stock for ⅔ cup of nonfat liquid milk. Proceed as in recipe.

Per serving: 34 calories; 2.7 gm protein; 0.1 gm fat; 5.5 gm carbohydrate; 0.1 gm fiber; 1 mg cholesterol; 0.3 mg iron; 36 mg sodium; 90 mg calcium; 71 mg phosphorus; 97 IU Vitamin A; 0.05 mg thiamine; 0.11 mg riboflavin; 1 mg Vitamin C; 126 mg potassium; 0.28 mg zinc; 0.2 mg niacin; 26 mcg Vitamin B_6; 0.27 mcg Vitamin B_{12}; 3 mcg folic acid

Appetizers and Hors d'Oeuvres

A GOOD FIRST ACT ISN'T HARD TO FOLLOW

Spicy Bean Dip
Broccoli Dip
Cottage Cheese Caper
Spicy Pink Dip
Tuna Dip Tapénade
Salsa Dip with Fresh Vegetables
Herbed Yogurt Dip
Queso con Salsa
Homemade Crisp Chips
Caponata
Texas Caviar
Marinated Chicken Drummettes
Chicken Rumaki
Liptauer Cheese
Marinated Mushrooms
Stuffed Mushrooms with Shallots
Petite Meatballs on Toast
Spinach-Stuffed Mushrooms
Marvelous Marinated Salmon
Salmon Steak Tartare
Seviche
Tomato Aspic Supreme with Cucumber Sauce
Salmon Pâté
Tuna Pâté

It has always been my contention that appetizers should be something special—a savory treat. As is so frequently the case, the French have a word for it—"*amuse gueule*": that which amuses the palate. It implies that appetizers are to be served to heighten the pleasure of eating. This may be accomplished by simply presenting fresh, unpeeled vegetables as crudités with a dipping sauce or by choosing a dramatic presentation, such as an antipasto or an attractively garnished seviche. Vegetables such as green and red peppers, eggplants, or cooked artichokes can be hollowed to form edible containers for cheese mixtures or dips. Our Cream Cheese (see page 27) may be flavored to be served with crackers and Iverson's Slim-Rye or molded into a log or ball and coated with freshly chopped parsley, herbs, chives, or Hungarian paprika.

Perhaps hot hors d'oeuvres, painstakingly prepared, are more to your liking. Whatever your choice may be, try to make it look and taste special—if not, forget it!

Spicy Bean Dip

Yield: 2½ cups (1 tablespoon = 1 serving)

1 15-ounce can chili beans
1 clove garlic
½ cup nonfat yogurt
½ cup tomato sauce
½ small red onion, quartered
3 tablespoons green chili salsa, or to taste
1 whole red or green pepper for serving
2 tablespoons chopped tomato for garnish
1 tablespoon chopped fresh cilantro for garnish

1. Place beans, garlic, yogurt, and tomato sauce in blender or food processor. Blend until smooth.
2. Add onion and blend until chopped.
3. Add salsa to taste and blend briefly.
4. Chill several hours before serving to let flavors blend.

To Serve: Place in hollowed red or green pepper garnished with chopped tomato and chopped cilantro and surround with our Homemade Crisp Chips (see page 39).

Per serving: 43 calories; 2.1 gm protein; 2 gm fat; 3.9 gm carbohydrate; 0.1 gm fiber; 0 mg cholesterol; 0.1 mg iron; 91 mg sodium; 10 mg calcium; 3 mg phosphorus; 96 IU Vitamin A; 0.01 mg thiamine; 0.02 mg riboflavin; 1 mg Vitamin C; 5 mg potassium; 0.01 mg zinc; 0.1 mg niacin; 3 mcg Vitamin B_6; 0 mcg Vitamin B_{12}; 1 mcg folic acid

Broccoli Dip

(Almost Mimosa)

Yield: 2½ cups (1 tablespoon = 1 serving)

1 10-ounce package frozen chopped broccoli, cooked, drained, and cooled
¼ cup hoop cheese or skim-milk ricotta cheese
¾ cup nonfat yogurt
½ teaspoon thyme
½ teaspoon marjoram
1 tablespoon toasted onion flakes
3 green onions
3 hard-cooked eggs, whites only (reserve 1 for garnish)
½ cup fresh parsley
1 teaspoon low-sodium vegetable seasoning (see page 28)
2 tablespoons fresh dill

1. Squeeze out excess moisture from broccoli and combine with cheese, yogurt, thyme, marjoram, onion flakes, green onions, 2 egg whites, parsley, vegetable seasoning, and dill in blender or food processor.

2. Blend until finely chopped.

3. Chill several hours before serving to let flavors blend.

To Serve: Place dip in bowl, garnish with grated egg white, and surround with your choice of assorted raw vegetables, such as radishes, cherry tomatoes, cauliflower, sugar snap peas, jicama, carrots, cucumber, zucchini, or mushrooms.

Per serving: 35 calories; 3.9 gm protein; 0.6 gm fat; 4.2 gm carbohydrate; 0.6 gm fiber; 2 mg cholesterol; 1.0 mg iron; 41 mg sodium; 81 mg calcium; 38 mg phosphorus; 1126 IU Vitamin A; 0.05 mg thiamine; 0.13 mg riboflavin; 26 mg Vitamin C; 149 mg potassium; 0.09 mg zinc; 0.5 mg niacin; 6 mcg Vitamin B_6; 0.03 mcg Vitamin B_{12}; 2 mcg folic acid

Cottage Cheese Caper

Yield: 1¼ cups (1 tablespoon = 1 serving)

This dip can also be used as a salad dressing.

1 cup Weight Watchers cottage cheese, rinsed and drained
¼ cup buttermilk, strained to remove fat globules
1 clove garlic
2 green onions, chopped
1 tablespoon capers, rinsed and drained
2 tablespoons lime juice
½ teaspoon low-sodium vegetable seasoning (see page 28)
Few grains cayenne pepper

Hungarian paprika for garnish

1. Whirl cottage cheese and buttermilk in blender or food processor until smooth.

2. Add garlic, green onions, capers, lime juice, vegetable seasoning, and cayenne. Blend until smooth.

3. Chill at least 1 hour to let flavors blend.

To Serve: If used as a dip, place in a bowl, sprinkle with Hungarian paprika, and serve with crackers or assorted raw vegetables.

Per serving: 29 calories; 3.9 gm protein; 0.3 gm fat; 2.4 gm carbohydrate; 0.2 gm fiber; 0 mg cholesterol; 0.3 mg iron; 75 mg sodium; 42 mg calcium; 12 mg phosphorus; 136 IU Vitamin A; 0.03 mg thiamine; 0.09 mg riboflavin; 2 mg Vitamin C; 55 mg potassium; 0.01 mg zinc; 0.2 mg niacin; 0 mcg Vitamin B_6; 0 mcg Vitamin B_{12}; 0 mcg folic acid

Spicy Pink Dip

Yield: about 3 cups (1 tablespoon = 1 serving)

1½ cups Weight Watchers cottage cheese, rinsed and drained
½ cup salt-free tomato sauce
1 small onion, quartered
2 tablespoons horseradish, or to taste
1 4-ounce can diced green chilies

1. Place the first 4 ingredients in food processor or blender. Process until smooth.
2. Pour into a bowl and fold in chilies.
3. Cover with plastic wrap and chill.

To Serve: Serve with our Homemade Crisp Chips (see page 39) or assorted crisp raw vegetables.

Per serving: 10 calories; 0.9 gm protein; 0.3 gm fat; 0.8 gm carbohydrate; 0.1 gm fiber; 0 mg cholesterol; 0.1 mg iron; 19 mg sodium; 8 mg calcium; 2 mg phosphorus; 38 IU Vitamin A; 0 mg thiamine; 0.02 mg riboflavin; 0 mg Vitamin C; 11 mg potassium; 0.01 mg zinc; 0.1 mg niacin; 3 mcg Vitamin B_6; 0 mcg Vitamin B_{12}; 1 mcg folic acid

Tuna Dip Tapénade

Yield: 2¼ cups (2 tablespoons = 1 serving)

½ cup Weight Watchers cottage cheese, rinsed and drained
½ cup nonfat yogurt
1 7½-ounce can salt-free tuna in water, well drained
2 tablespoons lemon juice
¼ small onion
½ teaspoon Hungarian paprika
½ teaspoon salt-free mustard
1 tablespoon capers, rinsed and drained

1 whole red or green pepper for serving
1 tablespoon chopped fresh parsley for garnish

1. Place the first 7 ingredients in blender or food processor. Blend until mixture is smooth.
2. Add capers and process slightly.
3. Taste, and adjust seasonings.

To Serve: Remove stem and seeds from nicely shaped red or green pepper. Place tapénade in hollowed pepper. Sprinkle with parsley and surround with assorted crisp, raw vegetables, crackers, or our Homemade Crisp Chips (see page 39).

Per serving: 38 calories; 6.7 gm protein; 0.3 gm fat; 1.8 gm carbohydrate; 0.2 gm fiber; 11 mg cholesterol; 0.4 mg iron; 36 mg sodium; 27 mg calcium; 37 mg phosphorus; 158 IU Vitamin A; 0.02 mg thiamine; 0.07 mg riboflavin; 13 mg Vitamin C; 86 mg potassium; 0.01 mg zinc; 2.6 mg niacin; 25 mcg Vitamin B_6; 0 mcg Vitamin B_{12}; 1 mcg folic acid

Salsa Dip with Fresh Vegetables

Yield: 4 cups (2 tablespoons = 1 serving)

1 28-ounce can plum tomatoes in puree
1 small onion, red or white
½ green pepper
1 3½-ounce can green chilies
1 clove garlic
1½ tablespoons red wine vinegar
1 teaspoon oregano
½ teaspoon cumin
½ teaspoon Italian herb seasoning
½ cup cilantro

1 whole green pepper for serving (optional)

1. Add all ingredients except whole green pepper to food processor or blender. Blend until well chopped. *Don't overchop.* (If salt-free tomatoes are used, the sodium content will be considerably lower.)

2. Store in covered container in refrigerator. May be stored several weeks.

To Serve: Place dip in bowl or hollowed green pepper and surround with cut-up raw vegetables, such as green or red pepper strips, cucumber strips, zucchini strips, cauliflowerets, broccoli florets, rutabaga slices, mushrooms, celery sticks, or pea pods.

Per serving: 13 calories; 0.6 gm protein; 0.1 gm fat; 2.9 gm carbohydrate; 0.2 gm fiber; 0 mg cholesterol; 0.6 mg iron; 104 mg sodium; 8 mg calcium; 11 mg phosphorus; 490 IU Vitamin A; 0.03 mg thiamine; 0.02 mg riboflavin; 12 mg Vitamin C; 125 mg potassium; 0.01 mg zinc; 0.4 mg niacin; 10 mcg Vitamin B_6; 0 mcg Vitamin B_{12}; 1 mcg folic acid

Herbed Yogurt Dip

Yield: 2¼ cups (1 tablespoon = 1 serving)

16 ounces nonfat yogurt
¼ cup chopped fresh dill
¼ teaspoon celery seed
¼ teaspoon caraway seed
1 tablespoon grated onion
1 steamed artichoke or 1 whole red or green pepper for serving
Chopped fresh dill for garnish

1. Combine yogurt with dill, celery and caraway seeds, and onion.
2. Chill several hours or overnight to develop flavors.

To Serve: For a particularly attractive presentation, instead of a bowl, place yogurt in center of a chilled steamed artichoke, choke removed, or a hollowed-out red or green pepper. (The artichoke is especially nice because its leaves may be used for dipping and the heart eaten when the dip is finished.) Sprinkle with dill. Place container with dip in center of large platter or basket and surround with crisp, raw vegetables, such as cauliflower, broccoli florets, snow peas, jicama, rutabaga, turnip, celery, cucumber, fresh fennel, cherry tomatoes, red radishes, green onions, and zucchini.

Per serving: 8 calories; 1 gm protein; 0 gm fat; 2 gm carbohydrate; 0 gm fiber; 0 mg cholesterol; 0.5 mg iron; 10 mg sodium; 35 mg calcium; 7 mg phosphorus; 47 IU Vitamin A; 0 mg thiamine; 0 mg riboflavin; 4 mg Vitamin C; 34 mg potassium; 0 mg zinc; 0 mg niacin; 9 mcg Vitamin B_6; 0 mcg Vitamin B_{12}; 0 mcg folic acid

Queso con Salsa

(Cheese with Chili Salsa)

Yield: 1¼ cups yogurt cheese (2 tablespoons = 1 serving)

Our Yogurt Cheese, from 1 pint nonfat yogurt (see page 305)
1¼ cups chili salsa

Unmold cheese onto a serving plate and spoon salsa over and around cheese.

To Serve: Surround with crackers and crisp toasted pita bread.

Per serving: 33 calories; 4.0 gm protein; 0.2 gm fat; 4 gm carbohydrate; 0.5 gm fiber; 0 mg cholesterol; 0.3 mg iron; 33 mg sodium; 86 mg calcium; 19 mg phosphorus; 380 IU Vitamin A; 0.10 mg thiamine; 0.19 mg riboflavin; 11 mg Vitamin C; 80 mg potassium; 0 mg zinc; 0.5 mg niacin; 0 mcg Vitamin B_6; 0 mcg Vitamin B_{12}; 0 mcg folic acid

Homemade Crisp Chips

Yield: 96 chips (4 chips = 1 serving)

It is difficult to find commercial chips that are not high in sodium because of added salt or preservatives, or high in fat because of deep-frying. The following recipe gives you a low-sodium, low-fat snack that can be prepared in large amounts and frozen for future use. Serve with dips, soups, or salads.

1 dozen salt-free corn tortillas (prepared from corn and lime water), or 1 package (6) whole wheat pita bread
2 tablespoons mild soy sauce
½ cup water, our Chicken Stock (see page 26), or our Vegetable Stock (see page 60)
Onion powder (optional seasoning)
Garlic powder (optional)
Herbal bouquet (optional)
Hungarian paprika (optional)
Low-sodium vegetable seasoning (see page 28), optional

1. Cut through entire stack of 12 tortillas at once, making 4 cuts through center to make 96 chips, or cut 6 whole wheat pita breads in 4 cuts and separate.
2. Lay wedges on nonstick baking sheets in single layers; avoid overlapping.
3. Combine soy sauce and water or stock in a plastic spray bottle and spray the wedges; this helps seasoning stick to chips.
4. Sprinkle with seasoning of your choice.
5. Bake in a preheated 400° oven until lightly browned and sufficiently crisp—approximately 8 minutes.
6. Cool. Store in airtight plastic bags or freeze for future use.

Variation: Chips may be sprinkled with grated Sap Sago cheese (see page 15)—or Parmesan if your diet permits—before baking.

Per serving: 25 calories; 0.8 gm protein; 0.3 gm fat; 6 gm carbohydrate; 0 gm fiber; 0 mg cholesterol; 0.3 mg iron; 20 mg sodium; 1 mg calcium; 14 mg phosphorus; 33 IU Vitamin A; 0.2 mg thiamine; 0.01 mg riboflavin; 0 mg Vitamin C; 3 mg potassium; 0.12 mg zinc; 0 mg niacin; 0 mcg Vitamin B_6; 0 mcg Vitamin B_{12}; 0 mcg folic acid

Caponata

(An Eggplant Appetizer)

Serves: 10–12 (⅓ cup = 1 serving)

1 1½-pound eggplant, halved
1 teaspoon low-sodium vegetable seasoning (see page 28)
4 tablespoons our Chicken Stock (see page 26)
1 stalk celery, chopped
1 medium onion, chopped
2 cloves garlic, minced
½ green pepper, chopped
6 fresh mushrooms, cleaned, stemmed, and quartered
1½ cups canned Italian plum tomatoes in sauce, drained (sauce reserved) and chopped, or 2 large ripe tomatoes, peeled, seeded, and chopped
⅓ cup red wine vinegar
1 tablespoon unsweetened apple juice concentrate
3 tablespoons chopped fresh Italian parsley
1 tablespoon capers, rinsed and drained
3 tablespoons salt-free tomato paste, mixed with ½ cup water
⅓ cup drained sauce from tomatoes, or canned tomato sauce if using fresh tomatoes
Freshly ground pepper
1 teaspoon Italian herb seasoning, crushed

1. Place halved eggplant on nonstick baking pan. Add ¼ inch water. Bake in a preheated 400° oven for 15 to 20 minutes.
2. Cool, peel, and cube eggplant. Season with vegetable seasoning and place in colander to drain.
3. Place stock in a nonstick skillet. Add chopped celery. Sauté 5 minutes. Add onion, garlic, and green pepper. Sauté 10 minutes more. Add mushrooms, sauté 5 minutes more.
4. Add drained eggplant cubes and sauté until lightly browned, stirring with a wooden spoon. (If the mixture starts to stick, add a bit of tomato sauce.)
5. Add tomatoes, vinegar, and apple juice concentrate. Cook 5 minutes.
6. Add parsley, capers, tomato paste mixed with water, tomato sauce, pepper, and Italian herb seasoning.
7. Cook, uncovered, about 20 minutes, or until thick. Stir from time to time.
8. Adjust seasoning, cool, and chill in refrigerator container several hours or overnight before serving.

To Serve: Bring to room temperature, place in a bowl, and surround with toasted pita bread.

Variation: My friend Gracie tops each helping of Caponata with a dab of Hummus (see page 311); a wonderful combination of flavors with the welcome addition of the protein from the garbanzo beans.

Per serving: 43 calories; 1.8 gm protein; 0.9 gm fat; 8.4 gm carbohydrate; 1.7 gm fiber; 0 mg cholesterol; 1.4 mg iron; 8 mg sodium; 31 mg calcium; 43 mg phosphorus; 657 IU Vitamin A; 0.08 mg thiamine; 0.09 mg riboflavin; 21 mg Vitamin C; 289 mg potassium; 0.09 mg zinc; 1.1 niacin; 110 mcg Vitamin B_6; 0 mcg Vitamin B_{12}; 13 mcg folic acid

Texas Caviar

Yield: 7½ cups (½ cup = 1 serving)

The price of this high-protein, low-fat-and-cholesterol appetizer is certainly better than the real thing, and so is the food value. By the way, did you know that it's good luck to eat black-eyed peas on New Year's Day?

1 pound black-eyed peas
1 cup our Italian Dressing (see page 12)
2 cups diced onion (red or white)
1 cup finely chopped green onion
¼ cup finely chopped jalapeno peppers
1 2-ounce jar diced pimiento, drained
1 cup finely chopped jicama
3 cloves garlic, minced
Hot pepper sauce to taste

1. Soak beans in hot water in a large saucepan for 1 hour. Drain.
2. Add water to cover, about 3 inches. Place over high heat, bring to a boil, turn down to a simmer, and cook until tender.
3. Drain. Add Italian dressing while beans are warm. Marinate 2 to 4 hours, then add remaining ingredients and marinate overnight.

To Serve: Serve on individual plates on lettuce leaves with tomato wedges as an appetizer or in a bowl accompanied by whole wheat crackers as hors d'oeuvres.

Per serving: 126 calories; 7.8 gm protein; 0.6 gm fat; 24 gm carbohydrate; 2.1 gm fiber; 0 mg cholesterol; 2.2 mg iron; 62 mg sodium; 36 mg calcium; 146 mg phosphorus; 275 IU Vitamin A; 0.39 mg thiamine; 0.09 mg riboflavin; 20 mg Vitamin C; 403 mg potassium; 0.09 mg zinc; 0.9 mg niacin; 25 mcg Vitamin B_6; 0 mcg Vitamin B_{12}; 7 mcg folic acid

Marinated Chicken Drummettes

Serves: 12 (2 drummettes = 1 serving)

1½ pounds chicken drummettes (these are the single-boned portion of the wing), skinned
⅔ cup our Italian Dressing (see page 12)
1½ teaspoons Italian herb seasoning, crushed
1½ teaspoons Hungarian paprika
1½ tablespoons green chili salsa
1 tablespoon raspberry wine vinegar

Shredded lettuce for serving
Chopped fresh Italian parsley for garnish

1. Place skinned chicken drummettes in saucepan with remaining ingredients. Stir to combine.
2. Bring to a boil over medium heat, lower to a simmer, and cook, covered, for about 20 to 30 minutes.
3. Taste, and adjust seasonings.
4. Place in refrigerator and chill 4 to 6 hours or overnight before serving.

To Serve: Arrange chicken drummettes on a bed of shredded lettuce in a spokelike design. Sprinkle with Italian parsley and serve.

Per serving: 41 calories; 6.7 gm protein; 1.1 gm fat; 0.7 gm carbohydrate; 0.1 gm fiber; 24 mg cholesterol; 0.7 mg iron; 54 mg sodium; 7 mg calcium; 58 mg phosphorus; 237 IU Vitamin A; 0.02 mg thiamine; 0.06 mg riboflavin; 2 mg Vitamin C; 94 mg potassium; 0 mg zinc; 2.5 mg niacin; 1 mcg Vitamin B_6; 0 mcg Vitamin B_{12}; 0 mcg folic acid

Chicken Rumaki

Serves: 12 (2 rumaki = 1 serving)

10 ounces slightly frozen skinned and boned chicken breasts, thinly sliced across grain into 24 slices
12 whole canned water chestnuts, drained
12 fresh or canned unsweetened pineapple chunks
3 tablespoons mild soy sauce
¼ cup water
2 tablespoons frozen unsweetened pineapple juice concentrate
2 tablespoons dry sherry or sake
1 teaspoon garlic powder
1 teaspoon ground ginger

2 tablespoons salt-free Chinese mustard or Dijon mustard for serving (optional)

1. Wrap each of the water chestnuts and each of the pineapple chunks with a slice of chicken. Secure with toothpick.

2. Combine soy sauce, water, pineapple juice, sherry, garlic powder, and ginger in a plastic bag.

3. Add wrapped chestnuts and pineapple to bag. Marinate in refrigerator several hours or overnight.

4. Drain, place on broiler pan, and broil on high about 2 minutes. Turn over, baste with sauce, and broil 2 minutes more. Baste again with sauce.

To Serve: Serve hot, with Chinese mustard or Dijon mustard on the side for dipping if you like.

Per serving: 48 calories; 5.98 gm protein; 0.33 gm fat; 4.4 gm carbohydrate; 0.14 gm fiber; 14 mg cholesterol; 0.29 mg iron; 163 mg sodium; 6 mg calcium; 53 mg phosphorus; 12 IU Vitamin A; 0.04 mg thiamine; 0.04 mg riboflavin; 3 mg Vitamin C; 122 mg potassium; 0.2 mg zinc; 2.76 mg niacin; 136 mcg Vitamin B_6; 0.09 mcg Vitamin B_{12}; 1.3 mcg folic acid

Liptauer Cheese

Yield: 1½ cups (2 tablespoons = 1 serving)

8 ounces skim-milk ricotta or hoop cheese
⅓ cup nonfat yogurt
1 clove garlic, minced
1 tablespoon capers, rinsed and drained
2 teaspoons Hungarian paprika
1½ teaspoons caraway seeds
½ teaspoon salt-free Dijon mustard
1 teaspoon low-sodium vegetable seasoning (see page 28)
Few grains crushed red pepper
1 teaspoon mild soy sauce
2 tablespoons chopped green onions

1. Blend ricotta or hoop cheese in blender or food processor until smooth.

2. Add yogurt and process until smooth.

3. Add minced garlic, capers, paprika, caraway seeds, mustard, vegetable seasoning, crushed red pepper, soy sauce, and green onions. Process until well blended.

4. Taste, and adjust seasonings.

5. Pack in 3 individual soufflé dishes or ramekins, cover with plastic wrap and foil, and store in refrigerator 24 hours before using so that flavors may develop. Unused portion keeps well for about 1 week.

To Serve: Serve with unsalted whole wheat or rye crackers.

Per serving: 33 calories; 2.7 gm protein; 1.6 gm fat; 2.2 gm carbohydrate; 0.2 gm fiber; 6 mg cholesterol; 0.4 mg iron; 41 mg sodium; 67 mg calcium; 40 mg phosphorus; 420 IU Vitamin A; 0.02 mg thiamine; 0.06 mg riboflavin; 1 mg Vitamin C; 48 mg potassium; 0.26 mg zinc; 0.2 mg niacin; 4 mcg Vitamin B_6; 0.05 mcg Vitamin B_{12}; 0 mcg folic acid

Marinated Mushrooms

Serves: 12 (4 mushrooms = 1 serving)

1 cup our Chicken Stock (see page 26)
¼ cup water
⅔ cup red wine vinegar
4 cloves garlic, minced
¼ cup chopped fresh parsley
2 teaspoons crushed herbes de Provence
2 teaspoons salt-free Dijon mustard
1 2-ounce jar chopped pimiento, drained
1 pound small fresh mushrooms, wiped clean and stems removed

Red lettuce leaves for serving
1 bunch green onions, finely chopped, or 1 red onion, finely chopped, for garnish

1. Place stock, water, vinegar, garlic, parsley, herbs, mustard, and pimiento in jar. Shake to blend well.
2. Place mushrooms in bowl, cover with marinade, cover bowl, and chill in refrigerator overnight.

To Serve: Arrange crisp lettuce leaves on a platter and cover with drained mushrooms. Sprinkle mushrooms with chopped green onions or chopped red onion. This can also be served on a cold buffet surrounded by beefsteak tomato slices and red onion slices.

Helpful Hint: Save mushroom stems for Mushroom Sauce from Cuisine Minceur (page 318), soups, or Duxelles (page 14).

Per serving: 28 calories; 1.8 gm protein; 0.3 gm fat; 5.5 gm carbohydrate; 1.5 gm fiber; 0 mg cholesterol; 1.2 mg iron; 10 mg sodium; 33 mg calcium; 58 mg phosphorus; 450 IU Vitamin A; 0.05 mg thiamine; 0.19 mg riboflavin; 11 mg Vitamin C; 257 mg potassium; 0.07 mg zinc; 1.7 mg niacin; 69 mcg Vitamin B_6; 0 mcg Vitamin B_{12}; 16 mcg folic acid

Stuffed Mushrooms with Shallots

Serves: 12 (1 mushroom = 1 serving)

12 medium-to-large fresh mushrooms, wiped clean
2 tablespoons lemon juice
4 shallots, chopped
2 tablespoons chopped fresh parsley
2 tablespoons our Chicken Stock (see page 26), or 2 our Bouillon Cubes, melted (see page 25)
¼ cup hoop cheese or skim-milk ricotta
1 carrot, shredded
½ teaspoon herbes de Provence
Hungarian paprika
¼ cup salt-free tomato sauce
1 teaspoon mild soy sauce (optional)
1 bunch watercress or parsley for garnish

1. Remove mushroom stems. Sprinkle caps with lemon juice and set aside.
2. Chop shallots, mushroom stems, and parsley in blender or food processor, or by hand.
3. Sauté shallots, mushroom stems, and parsley in stock for 2 minutes, stirring constantly.
4. Add hoop cheese, carrot, herbs, and soy sauce if desired. Blend well.
5. Fill each mushroom cap with cheese and shallot mixture and sprinkle with Hungarian paprika.
6. Spread tomato sauce in bottom of shallow baking dish. Arrange mushrooms on top of sauce.
7. Bake uncovered in a preheated 350° oven for 25 minutes.

To Serve: Serve hot on a platter with a bunch of either watercress or parsley for garnish.

Per serving: 23 calories; 1.2 gm protein; 0.9 gm fat; 3 gm carbohydrate; 0.7 gm fiber; 2 mg cholesterol; 0.5 mg iron; 12 mg sodium; 25 mg calcium; 33 mg phosphorus; 950 IU Vitamin A; 0.03 mg thiamine; 0.09 mg riboflavin; 3.5 mg Vitamin C; 114 mg potassium; 0.09 mg zinc; 0.7 mg niacin; 30 mcg Vitamin B_6; 0.01 mcg Vitamin B_{12}; 4.5 mcg folic acid

Petite Meatballs on Toast

Serves: 24 (2 meatballs = 1 serving)

It is always such a hassle to prepare hors d'oeuvres on the day of a party that I find these a joy to serve because they can be prepared at my convenience and frozen for future use.

Thinly sliced Pritikin whole wheat or rye bread, cut into 48 1½-inch circles
2 tablespoons nonfat yogurt
1 teaspoon salt-free Dijon mustard
1 slice Pritikin whole wheat bread, crust removed, pulled into crumbs
2 tablespoons nonfat milk
1 pound ground flank steak, extra-lean ground beef, or ground turkey
3 tablespoons chopped fresh parsley
3 tablespoons grated onion
1 clove garlic, minced
1 tablespoon salt-free tomato juice
1 teaspoon Worcestershire sauce
1 teaspoon low-sodium vegetable seasoning (see page 28)
Freshly ground pepper
¼ cup salt-free tomato sauce or tomato puree
1 tablespoon chopped fresh basil

1. Place bread circles on baking sheet and toast lightly on both sides under broiler.
2. Mix yogurt and mustard together. Spread lightly on 1 side of toasted circles.
3. Pour nonfat milk over whole wheat bread crumbs. Let stand until milk is completely absorbed.
4. Combine meat, parsley, onion, garlic, tomato juice, Worcestershire sauce, vegetable seasoning, ground pepper, and soaked bread mixture. Mix thoroughly with a fork.
5. Roll into 48 balls approximately 1 inch in diameter (wetting hands with cold water in between to prevent sticking).
*6. Place balls on toasted bread circles. Make an indentation, about ¼ inch deep, in the center of each ball with the tip of your little finger.
7. Broil about 3 to 4 minutes.
8. Fill center with a dab of tomato sauce and basil.

To Serve: Serve hot. For an elegant look, place a doily on a serving platter with either parsley, watercress, or a lovely flower from your garden in the center and surround with meatballs and a few cherry tomatoes.

***To Freeze for Future Use:** Prepare through step 6. Place finished meatballs unbroiled on a shallow baking sheet or foil pan and flash-freeze.

Cover with plastic wrap or foil; seal tightly. Can be stored 2 to 3 months (label package with the date of freezing). For serving, frozen meatballs should be at least partially defrosted before broiling. If not completely defrosted, broil 5 to 6 minutes.

Per serving: 60 calories; 6 gm protein; 2.4 gm fat; 3.6 gm carbohydrate; 0.2 gm fiber; 18 mg cholesterol; 1 mg iron; 44 mg sodium; 14 mg calcium; 48 mg phosphorus; 1.06 IU Vitamin A; 0.04 mg thiamine; 0.06 mg riboflavin; 2 mg Vitamin C; 134 mg potassium; 0 mg zinc; 1.4 mg niacin; 2 mcg Vitamin B_6; 0 mcg Vitamin B_{12}; 2 mcg folic acid

Spinach-Stuffed Mushrooms

Serves: 12 (2 mushrooms = 1 serving)

2 10-ounce packages frozen chopped spinach
¼ pound hoop cheese or low-fat ricotta cheese
1 clove garlic, minced
1 teaspoon mild soy sauce
2 egg whites
1 pound or 25 medium-to-large fresh mushrooms, wiped clean and stems removed
Low-sodium vegetable seasoning (see page 28)
½ cup salt-free tomato sauce
2 tablespoons grated Sap Sago cheese, toasted (see page 15)
Hungarian paprika

1. Thaw spinach and squeeze dry.
2. Mix spinach with a fork, adding hoop cheese or ricotta, minced garlic, soy sauce, crushed red pepper, and egg whites.
3. Sprinkle mushroom caps with vegetable seasoning and stuff with spinach mixture.
4. Place in baking pan spread with tomato sauce and bake uncovered in a preheated 350° oven for 20 to 25 minutes, or until firm to touch.
5. Sprinkle with cheese and paprika.

To Serve: Serve hot as an hors d'oeuvre, or as an accompaniment or garnish to an entrée.

Variation: Use frozen chopped broccoli instead of spinach.

Helpful Hint: Save mushroom stems for Mushroom Sauce from Cuisine Minceur (page 318), soups, or Duxelles (page 14).

Per serving: 46 calories; 4.6 gm protein; 0 gm fat; 4.6 gm carbohydrate; 1.4 gm fiber; 1 mg cholesterol; 1.4 mg iron; 68 mg sodium; 84 mg calcium; 84 mg phosphorus; 2708 IU Vitamin A; 0.08 mg thiamine; 0.28 mg riboflavin; 14 mg Vitamin C; 236 mg potassium; 1.2 mg zinc; 1.8 mg niacin; 48 mcg Vitamin B_6; 0.04 mcg Vitamin B_{12}; 8 mcg folic acid

Marvelous Marinated Salmon

Serves: 10 (as an appetizer; as an entrée, serves 6)

This marvelous marinated salmon recipe is my answer to high-sodium gravlax. Marinated salmon can be served either as an appetizer or a buffet entrée.

1½ pounds center-cut salmon fillets, cut in *very thin* diagonal slices
3 tablespoons frozen unsweetened apple juice concentrate
1 tablespoon low-sodium vegetable seasoning (see page 28)
Freshly ground pepper
1½ cups thinly sliced onion (Maui or Vidalia onions preferred)
4 carrots, peeled and thinly sliced
2 small zucchini, thinly sliced
2 lemons, thinly sliced
6 ounces brandied cherries, well drained (optional)
Juice of 2 lemons
¼ cup dry white wine or vermouth
½ cup red wine vinegar or raspberry wine vinegar
1 tablespoon Worcestershire sauce (optional)

1. Sprinkle salmon slices with apple juice concentrate, vegetable seasoning, and ground pepper.
2. Make a layer of onions, carrots, zucchini, lemon slices, and, if desired, brandied cherries in an 8 x 8-inch glass or earthenware dish.
3. Cover with a layer of salmon. (*Do not overlap fish slices.*)
4. Repeat layers until all ingredients are used.
5. Combine lemon juice, wine, and vinegar and pour *carefully* over salmon mixture. If all fish is not covered in liquid, add more lemon juice.
6. Cover with plastic wrap and refrigerate at least 2 days before using —will keep in refrigerator up to 2 weeks.

To Serve: For appetizer, serve on individual plates with slices of Iverson's Slim-Rye. *For buffet,* place drained salmon on a lettuce-lined platter and garnish with the marinated cherries, carrots, onions, zucchini, and lemon slices. Sprinkle lightly with chopped fresh dill or parsley.

Per serving: 133 calories; 15.1 gm protein; 2.8 gm fat; 12 gm carbohydrate; 2.3 gm fiber; 24 mg cholesterol; 1.6 mg iron; 63 mg sodium; 130 mg calcium; 201 mg phosphorus; 3616 IU Vitamin A; 0.18 mg thiamine; 0.08 mg riboflavin; 27 mg Vitamin C; 472 mg potassium; 0.2 mg zinc; 5.5 mg niacin; 557 mcg Vitamin B_6; 2.72 mcg Vitamin B_{12}; 9 mcg folic acid

Salmon Steak Tartare

Serves: 8 (2 ounces = 1 serving)

This variation of beef tartare is even more pleasing than the recipe from which it is derived, and, of course, better for your health.

1 pound *very fresh* salmon, chopped fine
4 tablespoons capers, rinsed, drained, and chopped
1 teaspoon lemon juice
2 tablespoons salt-free Dijon mustard with herbs
2 tablespoons chopped fresh parsley
Red lettuce leaves for serving
2 6-ounce new potatoes, boiled, cooled, peeled, and diced small, for garnish
3 small beets, baked or boiled, cooled, peeled, and diced small, for garnish
4 tablespoons finely chopped red onion for garnish

Mix salmon, capers, lemon juice, mustard, and parsley together and chill to allow flavors to blend.

To Serve: Arrange salmon mixture in a flat mound on a serving plate covered with red lettuce leaves. Score top of salmon with metal spatula into diamond-shaped pattern and garnish attractively with rows of potatoes, beets, and red onion. Serve with slices of Pritikin whole wheat bread cut into quarters.

Variation: If capers are omitted in this recipe, the sodium content will be reduced to 40 mg. per serving. Either 1 tablespoon Worcestershire sauce or 2 tablespoons cognac may be used instead.

Helpful Hint: Chop salmon with a sharp knife or the chopping blade of a food processor. If using a food processor, be careful to process only until chopped, not pureed.

Per serving: 165 calories; 12.1 gm protein; 4.2 gm fat; 8.3 gm carbohydrate; 1.5 gm fiber; 19 mg cholesterol; 0.9 mg iron; 229 mg sodium; 56 mg calcium; 198 mg phosphorus; 182 IU Vitamin A; 0.1 mg thiamine; 0.15 mg riboflavin; 9 mg Vitamin C; 401 mg potassium; 0.14 mg zinc; 4.5 mg niacin; 90 mcg Vitamin B_6; 0 mcg Vitamin B_{12}; 7 mcg folic acid

Seviche

Serves: 10 (1½ ounces = 1 serving); (as an entrée, serves 5)

Seviche is a cold, marinated fish dish that makes an elegant presentation served as an hors d'oeuvre in the living room, as a first course at the table, or as one of the entrées on a hot-weather buffet.

1 pound corbina or halibut, cut in 1-inch cubes
2 shallots, minced
½ cup dry white wine or vermouth
2 cloves garlic, minced
4 tablespoons raspberry wine vinegar
2 dashes Tabasco
1 tablespoon fresh orange juice or lime juice
Few grains crushed red pepper
1 tablespoon mild soy sauce
2 tablespoons capers, rinsed and drained
1 10-ounce can quartered artichoke hearts, rinsed and drained
1 red onion, sliced thin
1 green pepper, diced
1 red pepper, diced, or 1 2-ounce jar chopped pimiento, drained

2 ripe tomatoes, peeled, seeded, and diced, for garnish
3 tablespoons chopped fresh Italian parsley or cilantro for garnish

1. Bring minced shallots and wine to a boil; add fish and blanch 1 minute (until fish turns opaque). Drain, *saving liquid.**
2. Combine remaining ingredients except tomatoes and parsley in a glass or stainless steel bowl.
3. Add drained fish with 2 tablespoons blanching liquid and marinate at least 4 hours in refrigerator before serving.

To Serve: Place on individual plates or in a serving bowl and top with diced tomato and chopped parsley. When served on a buffet or as an entrée, slices of cold steamed corn on the cob or cooked sweet potato may be added to the garnish before serving.

Variation: If your diet allows, as a treat use half scallops, half fish. Remember, however, that the scallops will raise the cholesterol level in the recipe.

***Helpful Hint:** Blanching liquid may be refrigerated or frozen and used at another time as a poaching liquid for fish.

Per serving: 83 calories; 11.2 gm protein; 0.8 gm fat; 7.8 gm carbohydrate; 1.6 gm fiber; 23 mg cholesterol; 1.2 mg iron; 91 mg sodium; 34 mg calcium; 136 mg phosphorus; 815 IU Vitamin A; 0.09 mg thiamine; 0.08 mg riboflavin; 31 mg Vitamin C; 452 mg potassium; 0.10 mg zinc; 4.3 mg niacin; 77 mcg Vitamin B_6; 0 mcg Vitamin B_{12}; 7 mcg folic acid

Tomato Aspic Supreme with Cucumber Sauce

Yield: 12 servings (⅔ cup = 1 serving aspic; 1½ tablespoons = 1 serving sauce)

For a pleasant change in texture, I like to serve molded salads occasionally. I only use plain, unflavored gelatin, since all flavored gelatins have too much sugar or artificial sweetener added. This aspic may be served as a first course or as a buffet or luncheon dish.

Juice of 1 lemon or lime
4 cups salt-free tomato juice
Few drops Tabasco
2 envelopes plain, unflavored gelatin
⅔ cup diced celery
⅔ cup diced green pepper
½ cup chopped green onions
1 tablespoon horseradish (no preservatives, creaming agent, or oil added)
¾ pound poached halibut,* drained, flaked, and chilled

1 hothouse cucumber, chopped, shredded, and squeezed dry**
½ pint nonfat yogurt
1 teaspoon garlic powder
1 teaspoon unsweetened apple juice concentrate
1 tablespoon grated onion (optional)

2 ripe tomatoes, peeled, seeded, and diced, for garnish
4 tablespoons chopped fresh dill for garnish

1. Combine lemon or lime juice, tomato juice, and Tabasco in a small saucepan and bring to a boil.
2. Place gelatin in a large bowl. Add boiling juice and stir until gelatin is completely dissolved.
3. Chill mixture until it becomes the consistency of unbeaten egg whites.
4. Add celery, green pepper, green onions, horseradish, and chilled, flaked fish. Mix gently to combine.
5. Place in an attractive glass serving bowl and chill until firm, or overnight (I use an old, treasured cut-glass bowl).
6. *To make sauce:* Shred and squeeze cucumbers. Combine with yo-

* *To poach halibut,* bring 2 cups dry white wine, 1 sliced onion, 1 sliced carrot, 1 bay leaf, a few grains crushed red pepper, and 2 sprigs fresh dill or parsley to a boil. Add fish fillet and poach 10 minutes, or until fish flakes. Remove fish, drain, and cool.
** Hothouse cucumbers have a thin, delicate skin, are unwaxed, and do not have to be seeded. They are generally twice as long as traditional cucumbers, which in most instances are waxed in order to preserve them. If using traditional cucumbers, peel and seed before shredding.

gurt, garlic powder, apple juice concentrate, and, if desired, grated onion, just before serving.

To Serve: Sprinkle diced tomato over aspic. Garnish with dollops of cucumber sauce and sprinkle with freshly chopped dill. When served on a buffet or as a luncheon entrée, accompany with a green salad and crispy rye sourdough rolls.

Per serving: 77 calories; 9.6 gm protein; 0.6 gm fat; 9.3 gm carbohydrate; 1.2 gm fiber; 14 mg cholesterol; 1.7 mg iron; 49 mg sodium; 80 mg calcium; 96 mg phosphorus; 1173 IU Vitamin A; 0.11 mg thiamine; 0.14 mg riboflavin; 32 mg Vitamin C; 488 mg potassium; 0.06 mg zinc; 3.5 mg niacin; 47 mcg Vitamin B_6; 0 mcg Vitamin B_{12}; 3.4 mcg folic acid

Salmon Pâté

Serves: 20 (2 tablespoons = 1 serving)

This attractive pâté can be used in many interesting ways and freezes beautifully.

1 15½-ounce can red salmon, drained, skin and bones removed, or 1¼ pounds fresh salmon, poached in court bouillon,* drained, skinned, boned, and flaked
½ cup our Sour Cream (see page 27) or skim-milk ricotta
3 artichoke hearts, rinsed and drained
1 green onion
3 tablespoons chopped fresh dill
3 drops Tabasco
1 teaspoon salt-free Dijon mustard
1 tablespoon fresh lemon juice, or to taste
1 tablespoon chopped fresh tarragon
1 tablespoon chopped chives
3 tablespoons chopped fresh parsley
2 ounces pimiento, drained
1 tablespoon capers, rinsed and drained

1. Place salmon in a blender or food processor with our Sour Cream, artichokes, green onion, dill, Tabasco, mustard, and lemon juice. Blend well.
2. Add tarragon, chives, parsley, pimiento, and capers. Blend until specks of each still appear.
3. Chill in covered refrigerator container for several hours or overnight to permit flavors to blend.

* *To poach salmon:* Combine 1 cup dry white wine, 1 teaspoon thyme, 1 small sliced carrot, ¼ onion, 1 bay leaf, few grains crushed red pepper, and 1 cup water. Simmer 10 minutes. Add salmon and poach about 10 minutes, or until fish flakes. Cool in broth.

To Serve: Serve as an hors d'oeuvre or on a cold buffet. Mound pâté onto a coquille shell or flat serving dish and serve chilled with assorted crisp raw vegetables or crackers. For an elegant presentation, just before serving layer on thinly sliced cucumber to simulate scales of a fish and sprinkle with chopped fresh dill.

Variations: Pâté may be used to stuff eggs (see page 97), cherry tomatoes, or artichoke bottoms for a cold buffet or a salade composée.

To make a molded salmon mousse, soak ½ envelope of plain, unflavored gelatin in ¼ cup poaching liquid. Dissolve over low heat and stir into salmon mixture. Pour into a 3- to 4-cup fish mold sprayed with nonstick spray. Chill 4 to 6 hours or overnight. Unmold onto a bed of greens and garnish with cucumber as in pâté.

Helpful Hints: Drain liquid from canned salmon through cheesecloth or a triple-mesh strainer. Remember, if you use the drained canned salmon liquid in making the pâté, it will raise the sodium level considerably!

Reserve drained poaching liquid for use in making molded salmon mousse (see Variations).

Per serving: 47 calories; 5.4 gm protein; 2.2 gm fat; 1.4 gm carbohydrate; 0.2 gm fiber; 8 mg cholesterol; 0.8 mg iron; 76 mg sodium; 76 mg calcium; 84 mg phosphorus; 208 IU Vitamin A; 0.02 mg thiamine; 0.07 mg riboflavin; 4 mg Vitamin C; 127 mg potassium; 0 mg zinc; 1.7 mg niacin; 1 mcg Vitamin B_6; 0 mcg Vitamin B_{12}; 0.5 mcg folic acid

Tuna Pâté

Serves: 20 (2 tablespoons = 1 serving; as an entrée, serves 10)

1 13-ounce can salt-free tuna in water, drained and flaked
⅔ cup Weight Watchers cottage cheese, rinsed and drained
3 green onions
1 tablespoon lemon juice
1 tablespoon green chili salsa
2 tablespoons chopped green chilies
Freshly ground pepper
½ teaspoon herbes de Provence

1 2-ounce jar chopped pimiento, drained
2 tablespoons capers, rinsed and drained

2 tablespoons chopped fresh Italian parsley for garnish
1 small green pepper, seeded and cut into ½-inch strips, for garnish
4 cherry tomatoes, halved, for garnish

1. Place tuna, cottage cheese, green onions, lemon juice, salsa, chilies, pepper, and herbs in blender or food processor and process until smooth.
2. Add pimiento and capers; process until chopped (flecks of pimiento and capers remain).
3. Spoon mixture into a 3-cup terrine or loaf pan that has been sprayed with nonstick spray.
4. Cover with plastic wrap and chill in refrigerator 24 hours or overnight.

To Serve: Several hours before serving, run a knife around pâté and unmold onto a serving platter. At serving time, garnish pâté with chopped parsley, green pepper strips, and halved cherry tomatoes. As an hors d'oeuvre, surround with Finn Crisp crackers, Iverson's Slim-Rye, or small slices of rye bread. As an individual first course, place 1 slice of pâté on a Boston lettuce leaf with a dab of Dijon mustard, several cherry tomatoes, and strips of warm whole wheat toast (Pritikin). Tuna Pâté can also be served as a summer luncheon entrée.

Per serving: 35 calories; 6.3 gm protein; 0.3 gm fat; 1.3 gm carbohydrate; 0.2 gm fiber; 12 mg cholesterol; 0.6 mg iron; 41 mg sodium; 17 mg calcium; 39 mg phosphorus; 217 IU Vitamin A; 0.02 mg thiamine; 0.05 mg riboflavin; 12 mg Vitamin C; 96 mg potassium; 0.01 mg zinc; 2.6 mg niacin; 18 mcg Vitamin B_6; 0 mcg Vitamin B_{12}; 1 mcg folic acid

Soups

SOME LIKE IT HOT–
SOME LIKE IT COLD

Some Basic Stocks

Basic Turkey Stock
Basic Fish Stock
Basic Vegetable Stock

Hot Soups

Basic Broccoli Soup
Puree of Cauliflower Soup
Mushroom, Bean, and Barley Soup
Fresh Mushroom Soup
Old-Fashioned Black Bean Soup
Split Pea or Lentil Soup
Chinese Hot and Sour Soup
Mediterranean Fish Soup
One-Two-Three Minestrone
Spicy Pumpkin Soup
Election Night Borscht
French Country Winter Vegetable Soup
Turkey-Vegetable Soup
Quick Cream of Leftover Vegetable Soup

Cold Soups

Gazpacho
Jellied Fish Consommé
Quick Cold Cucumber Soup
Nearly Vichyssoise
Fresh Strawberry Soup

Whether you are huddled by a roaring fire on a cold winter's evening or pausing at the end of a hot summer's day, you will find that a good soup—a hearty country vegetable soup or a cup of chilled gazpacho—will have a comforting and soothing effect on the psyche as well as the appetite. Soups, served hot or cold, add variety to our meals.

General Information for Freezing Soups

1. Cool soup, uncovered, at room temperature.

2. Chill overnight in refrigerator and remove any visible congealed fat before freezing.

3. Freeze in suitable plastic freezer containers or jars, leaving 1 inch head space for expansion. (At this time you will want to remember to freeze in portion sizes that suit your family and life-style. I like to freeze single 1-cup portions—I may want split pea soup when my partner has been looking forward to mushroom-barley!)

4. Cover containers tightly. (If soup is not tightly sealed, it will lose much of its flavor.)

5. Label with content and date.

6. To serve frozen soup, thaw to room temperature and reheat or put container of frozen soup in the microwave oven for 12 to 15 minutes, depending upon the amount.

Helpful Hints: Always use cold water to start a soup. Hot water seals the flavor into the bones and meat instead of allowing it to flow into the soup.

Do not put hot soup in the refrigerator. It makes the motor work too hard to cool it down.

Some Basic Stocks

These basic stocks should be prepared when you have time. They may be frozen for future use. For Basic Chicken Stock, see Six Easy Basics, page 26.

Basic Turkey Stock

Yield: 2–2½ quarts (1 cup = 1 serving)

3 quarts cold water
Entire carcass of roast turkey with skin, meat scraps, and giblets (not liver)*
1 large onion stuck with 4 cloves
3 medium carrots, cut in chunks
2 stalks celery with leaves, cut in chunks
2 large leeks, split and well washed
1 parsnip, cut in chunks
1 tomato, coarsely chopped
1 bouquet garni (4 sprigs Italian parsley, ½ teaspoon crushed red pepper, 2 bay leaves, 1 teaspoon thyme, 1 tablespoon Rokeach dried soup greens)

1. Break up turkey carcass and place in a 6-quart stainless steel stock pot with bones, skin, and meat scraps. Cover with cold water.
2. Bring to a boil, remove scum, and add remaining ingredients.
3. Bring to a second boil and reduce heat to barely simmer.
4. Half cover the pot and simmer 3 hours.
5. Strain stock through triple-mesh stainless steel strainer. Let cool, then cover and refrigerate.

* Any chicken backs, necks, or skins you have on hand may also be added.

6. Remove hardened fat before using or freezing. Keeps in refrigerator 3 to 4 days. For longer storage, freeze according to instructions on page 57.

To Use: Reheat and serve as a broth, or use as a base in preparing Turkey-Vegetable Soup (page 73) or Mushroom, Bean, and Barley Soup (page 63).

Variation: Serve as a *turkey-vegetable bouillon* by adding 1 20-ounce package frozen mixed vegetables, 2 chopped Roma tomatoes, and 1 cup Steamed Brown Rice (see page 254). Bring to a boil, reduce to simmer, and cook 15 minutes before adding ¼ cup chopped fresh Italian parsley or fresh basil.

Per serving: 34 calories; 2.6 gm protein; 0 gm fat; 5.5 gm carbohydrate; 0 gm fiber; 0 mg cholesterol; 0 mg iron; 5 mg sodium; 0 mg calcium; 0 mg phosphorus; 0 IU Vitamin A; 0 mg thiamine; 0 mg riboflavin; 0 mg Vitamin C; 0 mg potassium; 0 mg zinc; 0 mg niacin; 0 mcg Vitamin B_6; 0 mcg Vitamin B_{12}; 0 mcg folic acid

Basic Fish Stock

Yield: approx. 2½ quarts (1 cup = 1 serving)

2–3 pounds fish bones with skin and head,* washed
2 cups dry white wine
3 quarts cold water
2 onions, coarsely chopped
2 stalks celery with leaves, chopped
2 large carrots, chopped
1 leek (white part only), split, well washed, and chopped
1 lemon, sliced
1 bouquet garni (4 sprigs parsley, 2 bay leaves, ½ teaspoon crushed red pepper, 1 teaspoon thyme, 1 tablespoon Rokeach dried soup greens)

1. Place bones in a 6-quart stainless steel stock pot. Add wine and simmer on high heat 5 minutes.

2. Add remaining ingredients and simmer 1 hour.

3. Strain, cool, and store in refrigerator or freezer (see instructions for freezing, page 57). Stock may be stored safely in refrigerator for 3 to 5 days.

To Use: Use as a poaching liquid for fish or as a base for fish soup or bouillabaisse.

Per serving: 29 calories; 0 gm protein; 0 gm fat; 1.5 gm carbohydrate; 0 gm fiber; 0 mg cholesterol; 0.1 mg iron; 2 mg sodium; 3 mg calcium; 4 mg phosphorus; 0 IU Vitamin A; 0 mg thiamine; 0 mg riboflavin; 0 mg Vitamin C; 33 mg potassium; 0 mg zinc; 0 mg niacin; 14 mcg Vitamin B_6; 0 mcg Vitamin B_{12}; 0 mcg folic acid

* Do not use scales or gills. Do not use salmon, mackerel, or bluefish bones; they are too oily.

Basic Vegetable Stock

Yield: 2½ quarts (1 cup = 1 serving)

½ cup dry white wine
2 onions, chopped
2 shallots, chopped
2 leeks, split, well washed, and chopped
4 carrots, chopped
1 turnip, chopped
1 rutabaga, chopped
1 kohlrabi, chopped
1 parsnip, chopped
3 Roma tomatoes, chopped
2 stalks celery with leaves, chopped
2 tablespoons Rokeach dried soup greens
3 quarts cold water
1 bouquet garni (6 sprigs Italian parsley, ½ teaspoon crushed red pepper, 2 bay leaves, 2 teaspoons herbes de Provence, and 1 teaspoon thyme)
1 teaspoon low-sodium vegetable seasoning (see page 28)
Any leftover cooked or raw vegetables or vegetable liquid

1. Add wine to a 5-quart stainless steel stock pot. Heat to boiling and add onions, shallots, leeks, carrots, turnips, rutabaga, kohlrabi, parsnip, Roma tomatoes, and celery.
2. Simmer vegetables about 10 minutes, stirring from time to time.
3. Add dried soup greens, cold water, bouquet garni, vegetable seasoning, and leftover vegetables or liquids.
4. Bring to a boil, lower to simmer, and simmer gently 2½ to 3 hours.
5. Strain through a stainless steel triple-mesh strainer. (Press vegetables to release their juices.)
6. Cool and freeze according to instructions on page 57.

To Use: Use in preparing any of our soups or sauces or as a hot beverage.

Per serving: 37 calories; 2 gm protein; 0 gm fat; 5.1 gm carbohydrate; 0 gm fiber; 0 mg cholesterol; 0.05 mg iron; 4 mg sodium; 1 mg calcium; 1 mg phosphorus; 0 IU Vitamin A; 0 mg thiamine; 0 mg riboflavin; 0 mg Vitamin C; 11 mg potassium; 0 mg zinc; 0 mg niacin; 4 mcg Vitamin B_6; 0 mcg Vitamin B_{12}; 0 mcg folic acid

Hot Soups

Basic Broccoli Soup

Serves: 6 (¾ cup = 1 serving)

2 cups our Chicken Stock (see page 26)
2 cups fresh broccoli,* cut in 1-inch pieces
1 slice onion
½ teaspoon herbal bouquet
½ cup instant nonfat dry milk (optional)

1. Place chicken stock, broccoli, onion, and herbs in a saucepan.
2. Bring to a boil and simmer until broccoli is tender.
3. Remove from heat, cool, and puree in food processor or blender.
4. At this point, add milk for a creamed soup if you like. Soup may be frozen for future use according to instructions on page 57.

To Serve: Reheat before serving. Soup also may be served chilled.

Variations: Instead of broccoli, you may use other fresh or leftover cooked vegetables such as carrots, zucchini, or peas.

Add ½ teaspoon curry powder, or to taste. This version is particularly good chilled.

Per serving: 29 calories; 2.6 gm protein; 0.2 gm fat; 5.2 gm carbohydrate; 2.2 gm fiber; 0 mg cholesterol; 0.9 mg iron; 10 mg sodium; 46 mg calcium; 33 mg phosphorus; 1411 IU Vitamin A; 0.04 mg thiamine; 0.06 mg riboflavin; 30 mg Vitamin C; 136 mg potassium; 0.01 mg zinc; 0.3 mg niacin; 93 mcg Vitamin B_6; 0 mcg Vitamin B_{12}; 29 mcg folic acid

* Broccoli stalks alone may be used, saving the florets for use as a vegetable dish at another time. You could use a few small florets for garnishing the soup at time of serving.

Puree of Cauliflower Soup

Serves: 8 (¾ cup = 1 serving)

4 cups nonfat milk
1 slice onion
1 bay leaf
1 medium head cauliflower*
(about 1 pound), cored and broken into florets
1 teaspoon low-sodium vegetable seasoning (see page 28)
1 teaspoon powdered horseradish (optional)

Chopped chives, watercress, or Hungarian paprika for garnish

1. In a large saucepan, bring milk to a boil with onion and bay leaf. Add cauliflowerets and cook, partially covered, until tender when pierced with a fork.

2. Remove bay leaf and place drained cauliflower and onion slice into blender or food processor. Puree until smooth.

3. Return puree to milk in saucepan; whisk thoroughly until smooth. Add vegetable seasoning to taste. If you prefer a zippier flavor, add horseradish. Soup may be frozen according to instructions on page 57.

To Serve: Serve in mugs or soup bowls garnished with chopped chives, watercress, or Hungarian paprika. Soup may also be served chilled.

Per serving: 57 calories; 5.6 gm protein; 0.3 gm fat; 8.7 gm carbohydrate; 1 gm fiber; 2 mg cholesterol; 0.6 mg iron; 69 mg sodium; 165 mg calcium; 140 mg phosphorus; 57 IU Vitamin A; 0.11 mg thiamine; 0.26 mg riboflavin; 28 mg Vitamin C; 285 mg potassium; 0.5 mg zinc; 0.5 mg niacin; 53 mcg Vitamin B_6; 0.49 mcg Vitamin B_{12}; 2 mcg folic acid

* Leftover cooked cauliflower (about 3 cups) may be used instead.

Mushroom, Bean, and Barley Soup

Yield: 12 servings to eat; 12 for the freezer (1 cup = 1 serving)

I came from a large family—the youngest of nine children—and cooking could be a daily chore, not an adventure. Good hearty soups, served hot, were a veritable staple. Here is one of my favorites. For best results, preparation must be started a day in advance. Of course, if you have stock on hand, you may start with step 6 and make the soup in one day.

2 pounds beef soup bones
4 pounds chicken necks and backs
1 5-pound stewing hen or roaster, quartered, all visible fat removed
8 quarts cold water
2 large onions
2 leeks, split and well washed
4 carrots
6 stalks celery with leaves
1 bouquet garni (3 bay leaves, 4 sprigs parsley, a few grains crushed red pepper, 1 teaspoon thyme, and 3 whole cloves)

1½ cups barley
1 cup dried lima beans

4 carrots, diced
4 stalks celery, diced
2 cups fresh mushrooms, sliced
1 ounce dried mushrooms, soaked in 1 cup hot water for 30 minutes, then rinsed several times, squeezed dry, and sliced
1 cup chopped fresh parsley

1. Place bones, chicken backs, stewing hen, and *cold* water in a 12-quart stainless steel stock pot.
2. Bring to a boil and *simmer* 30 minutes, removing scum as it comes to top with a stainless steel triple-mesh strainer.
3. Add onions, leeks, carrots, celery, and bouquet garni. Continue to simmer stock 2½ to 3 hours.
4. Remove vegetables, soup bones, and chicken,* and strain the stock.
5. Cool, uncovered, and chill in refrigerator overnight. Remove congealed fat.
6. Add barley and beans to soup and simmer 2 hours.
7. Add carrots, celery, fresh mushrooms, and dried mushrooms and continue to simmer 30 minutes.
8. Stir in chopped parsley before serving. If you like, you may freeze half of the soup according to instructions on page 57.

Variation: For a heartier soup, part of the meat from the hen may be diced and added 30 minutes before serving.

Per serving: 138 calories; 7.3 gm protein; 0.4 gm fat; 26.9 gm carbohydrate; 2.7 gm fiber; 0 mg cholesterol; 1.6 mg iron; 37 mg sodium; 36 mg calcium; 97 mg phosphorus; 3121 IU Vitamin A; 0.1 mg thiamine; 0.1 mg riboflavin; 12 mg Vitamin C; 373 mg potassium; 0.36 mg zinc; 1.3 mg niacin; 121 mcg Vitamin B_6; 0 mcg Vitamin B_{12}; 18 mcg folic acid

* Remove the meat from the chicken and freeze for use later in salad, pâté, or other recipes calling for cooked chicken.

Fresh Mushroom Soup

Serves: 8 (¾ cup = 1 serving)

1¼ pounds fresh mushrooms, wiped clean
2 bunches green onions with tops
3 our Bouillon Cubes, melted (see page 25), or 3 tablespoons our Chicken Stock (see page 26)
Freshly ground pepper
½ teaspoon thyme
½ teaspoon herbes de Provence
Few grains freshly ground nutmeg
1 quart our Chicken Stock
1 cup nonfat evaporated milk (optional)

1. Mince mushrooms in food processor or blender.
2. Mince green onions in food processor or blender.
3. Place melted bouillon cubes or stock in a 2-quart saucepan. Add mushrooms and green onions and sauté 10 minutes.
4. Add freshly ground pepper, thyme, herbs, and nutmeg.
5. Add the 1 quart stock, bring to a boil, and simmer 30 minutes.
6. If desired, add evaporated milk and heat 5 minutes before serving. This soup may also be frozen (see instructions page 57).

Variation: Add 1 tablespoon Rokeach dried soup greens or 1 tablespoon dry sherry to the mushrooms and green onions while they are sautéing.

Per serving: 42 calories; 3.5 gm protein; 0.3 gm fat; 7 gm carbohydrate; 2.1 gm fiber; 0 mg cholesterol; 1.1 mg iron; 14 mg sodium; 19 mg calcium; 87 mg phosphorus; 164 IU Vitamin A; 0.08 mg thiamine; 0.33 mg riboflavin; 4 mg Vitamin C; 321 mg potassium; 0.02 mg zinc; 3 mg niacin; 89 mcg Vitamin B_6; 0 mcg Vitamin B_{12}; 18 mcg folic acid

Old-Fashioned Black Bean Soup

Serves: 20 (1 cup = 1 serving)

2 cups dried black beans, washed and soaked in water to cover overnight
2 pounds beef bones, fat removed
4 large our Bouillon Cubes (see page 25), or ¼ cup our Chicken Stock (see page 26)
2 large onions, chopped
2 carrots, chopped
2 cloves garlic, chopped
2 leeks (white part only) split, well washed, and chopped
2 ripe tomatoes, peeled, seeded, and chopped
1 stalk celery with leaves, chopped
5 quarts cold water
1 tablespoon Rokeach dried soup greens
1 bouquet garni (2 bay leaves, 4 sprigs parsley, 1 teaspoon thyme, ½ teaspoon crushed red pepper, and 2 whole cloves)
Freshly ground pepper
1 teaspoon low-sodium vegetable seasoning (see page 28)
⅓ cup Madeira

Lemon slices for garnish

1. Place beef bones on a shallow baking sheet and brown in a preheated 450° oven for about 20 minutes.
2. Melt bouillon cubes in a 4-quart stock pot. Add onions, carrots, garlic, leeks, tomatoes, and celery. Sauté over low heat for about 10 minutes. Stir occasionally.
3. Add browned beef bones, cold water, soup greens, and bouquet garni. Bring water to a boil, remove scum, reduce heat, and simmer 2 hours.
4. Drain beans, add to stock pot, and simmer 2½ hours more. *Stir occasionally.* (Add more liquid if necessary.)
5. Remove beef bones and puree beans and vegetables in blender or food processor.
6. Return to stock pot. Add freshly ground pepper, vegetable seasoning, and Madeira. Bring soup to a boil; taste, and adjust seasonings. If soup is too thick, thin with our Chicken Stock.
7. Soup may be prepared the day before and reheated for serving, or frozen for future use (see page 57).

To Serve: Serve in warm soup bowls garnished with a slice of lemon and accompanied by Corn Sticks or Corn Bread (page 296). This soup even tastes good when taken in a thermos for lunch.

Variation: To prepare as a vegetarian soup, omit beef bones.

Per serving: 87 calories; 5.2 gm protein; 0.4 gm fat; 15.8 gm carbohydrate; 5.9 gm fiber; 0 mg cholesterol; 2 mg iron; 13 mg sodium; 45 mg calcium; 101 mg phosphorus; 1176 IU Vitamin A; 0.14 mg thiamine; 0.06 mg riboflavin; 9 mg Vitamin C; 322 mg potassium; 0.1 mg zinc; 0.7 mg niacin; 43 mcg Vitamin B_6; 0 mcg Vitamin B_{12}; 5 mcg folic acid

Split Pea or Lentil Soup

Serves: 14 (1 cup = 1 serving)

12 cups our Chicken Stock (see page 26) or water
1 pound beef soup bones (optional)
1 pound green or yellow split peas or lentils or a combination of the three
1 bouquet garni (2 bay leaves, ½ teaspoon thyme, a few parsley sprigs and celery leaves, and a few grains red pepper)
1 clove garlic, chopped
6 small carrots, chopped
3 stalks celery with leaves, chopped
1 onion, chopped
1 leek, split, well-washed, and chopped
1 turnip, chopped
1 teaspoon thyme

Whole wheat croutons or chopped fresh Italian parsley for garnish

1. Combine the stock, soup bones (if desired), peas, bouquet garni, and garlic and cook in a 6-quart stock pot for 30 minutes.
2. Add the carrots, celery, onion, leek, turnip, and thyme and cook an additional hour.
3. Remove the bouquet garni and bones.
4. Puree all vegetables in food processor or blender and return to stock.
5. Reheat thoroughly before serving. May be frozen for future use (see instructions page 57).

To Serve: Place in warm soup bowls and garnish with whole wheat croutons or chopped Italian parsley.

Variations: Add 1 cup nonfat evaporated milk after soup has been pureed to make a cream soup.

For a heartier soup, add 1 cup Steamed Brown Rice (see page 254) after pureeing.

Diced cooked carrots and celery may be added to soup after soup has been pureed.

Per serving: 158 calories; 10.6 gm protein; 0.4 gm fat; 28.7 gm carbohydrate; 5 gm fiber; 0 mg cholesterol; 2.1 mg iron; 36 mg sodium; 28 mg calcium; 102 mg phosphorus; 2418 IU Vitamin A; 0.26 mg thiamine; 0.11 mg riboflavin; 4 mg Vitamin C; 411 mg potassium; 1.15 mg zinc; 1.2 mg niacin; 89 mcg Vitamin B_6; 0 mcg Vitamin B_{12}; 21 mcg folic acid

Chinese Hot and Sour Soup

Serves: 8 (1 cup = 1 serving)

8 cups our Chicken Stock (see page 26)
1 8-ounce chicken breast, skinned, boned, and sliced thin
10 dried mushrooms (preferably Chinese), soaked in 1 cup hot water 30 minutes, rinsed well, squeezed dry, and sliced thin*
1 7½-ounce can bamboo shoots, sliced thin
6 tablespoons white wine vinegar or brown rice vinegar
2 tablespoons mild soy sauce
Freshly ground pepper
1 tablespoon cornstarch
½ cup water
Dash Tabasco
2 egg whites, lightly beaten
3 green onions, minced
½ cup fresh pea pods

1. Bring stock to a boil in a 3-quart saucepan; add chicken and mushrooms. Bring to a boil again and simmer 10 minutes.
2. Add bamboo shoots and simmer 10 minutes.
3. Add vinegar, soy sauce, and pepper.
4. Mix cornstarch with water and add to soup. Return to a boil.
5. Add Tabasco and slightly beaten egg white to soup and stir.
6. Add green onions and pea pods. Soup may be refrigerated and reheated and served several days later.

Variations: If your diet allows, add 1 tablespoon sesame oil in step 6.

Add 2 ounces finely cubed tofu (Chinese bean curd) in step 6 for additional protein.

***Helpful Hint:** Strain and save mushroom liquid to add to soup.

Per serving: 105 calories; 12.1 gm protein; 1.1 gm fat; 11.8 gm carbohydrate; 0.8 gm fiber; 19 mg cholesterol; 0.9 mg iron; 159 mg sodium; 14 mg calcium; 107 mg phosphorus; 167 IU Vitamin A; 0.11 mg thiamine; 0.14 mg riboflavin; 5 mg Vitamin C; 347 mg potassium; 0.01 mg zinc; 4 mg niacin; 16 mcg Vitamin B_6; 0.01 mcg Vitamin B_{12}; 4 mcg folic acid

Mediterranean Fish Soup

Serves: 12 (1 cup = 1 serving)

Mediterranean Fish Soup is found on the menu frequently in both Italy and France. Each soup is slightly different, reflecting the taste and the supplies of the cook preparing it. Try it my way first—then vary it to suit your palate.

¼ cup our Fish Stock (see page 59) or dry white wine
1 cup finely chopped onion
1 cup finely chopped carrots
1 bulb fennel, finely chopped, or 1 teaspoon fennel seed, crushed
1 cup well-washed and finely chopped leek (white part only)
4 cloves garlic, minced
4 large ripe tomatoes, peeled, seeded, and chopped, or 6 canned plum tomatoes, chopped
1 slice dried orange peel
1 bay leaf
1 teaspoon thyme or savory, crushed
1 teaspoon dried basil, crushed
Few grains crushed red pepper
½ teaspoon powdered saffron, or 2 pinches saffron threads
¼ cup Pernod or dry white wine
1 cup salt-free tomato sauce
2½ quarts our Fish Stock
1 pound fresh cod, halibut, haddock, snapper, sole, or sea bass (if possible, use at least 2 different fishes for better flavor), cut into ½-inch cubes

1. Place the ¼ cup fish stock in a 5-quart saucepan. Add onion, carrots, fennel, leek, and garlic. Sauté 5 minutes or until soft, stirring constantly.

2. Add tomatoes, orange peel, bay leaf, thyme, basil, crushed red pepper, and saffron. Cook 5 minutes more.

*3. Add Pernod or wine, tomato sauce, and fish stock. Simmer uncovered, for 1 hour.

4. Add cubed fish and cook 15 minutes before serving.

To Serve: Serve from a heated tureen at the table or in individual warmed bowls from the kitchen. Top each serving with a slice of French baguette dried in the oven and rubbed with a clove of garlic, or place a slice of garlic-flavored dried bread in each bowl first and ladle soup over it. This may be followed by a crisp green salad and fresh fruit.

Variation: For a heartier soup, add 2 cups Steamed Brown Rice (see page 254) to soup before serving, or serve over a spoonful of rice.

* Soup may be frozen for future use after step 3.

Helpful Hints: If you have no fish stock in your freezer, use 2½ quarts water and 2 pounds fresh fish trimmings. (Do not use scales or gills. Do not use any trimmings from salmon, mackerel, or bluefish; they are too oily.) Be sure to remove trimmings by straining stock before the final 15 minutes of cooking with the added fish. Return strained vegetables to stock.

Per serving: 114 calories; 10.5 gm protein; 2 gm fat; 13.1 gm carbohydrate; 1.7 gm fiber; 19 mg cholesterol; 1.2 mg iron; 39 mg sodium; 36 mg calcium; 111 mg phosphorus; 1849 IU Vitamin A; 0.09 mg thiamine; 0.07 mg riboflavin; 19 mg Vitamin C; 391 mg potassium; 0.19 mg zinc; 1.5 mg niacin; 88 mcg Vitamin B_6; 0 mcg Vitamin B_{12}; 9 mcg folic acid

One-Two-Three Minestrone

Serves: 12–14 (1 cup = 1 serving)

Isn't it nice that a few convenience foods that have no added salt, preservatives, or MSG are starting to be available to us?

8 cups cold water
2 packages Hain's hearty vegetable soup or minestrone mix, *no salt added*
2 8-ounce cans salt-free tomato sauce
1 bunch green onions, thinly sliced
1 teaspoon dried oregano*
1 teaspoon dried basil,* crushed, or 1 tablespoon fresh basil
1 10-ounce package frozen chopped spinach, cut in 4 chunks
½ cup chopped fresh Italian parsley
½ cup uncooked small whole wheat shells or macaroni

1. Place water in a 4-quart Dutch oven, add soup mix, tomato sauce, green onions, oregano, basil, and frozen spinach.
2. Bring to a boil and simmer 30 minutes. Stir occasionally.
3. Add parsley and macaroni and simmer 30 additional minutes, or until pasta is tender.
4. The soup is enhanced if it is made several hours ahead of time so that the flavors can blend, then reheated.

To Serve: Serve piping hot with crisp sourdough rolls or crusty whole wheat bread.

Per serving: 130 calories; 4.6 gm protein; 1.3 gm fat; 20.2 gm carbohydrate; 0.9 gm fiber; 0 mg cholesterol; 1.6 mg iron; 15 mg sodium; 48 mg calcium; 51 mg phosphorus; 2629 IU Vitamin A; 0.19 mg thiamine; 0.12 mg riboflavin; 17 mg Vitamin C; 157 mg potassium; 0.28 mg zinc; 1.5 mg niacin; 17 mcg Vitamin B_6; 0 mcg Vitamin B_{12}; 2 mcg folic acid

* 1 tablespoon Italian herb seasoning may be used instead of the oregano and basil.

Spicy Pumpkin Soup

Serves: 10 (1 cup = 1 serving)

The innately autumnal flavor of pumpkin makes a perfect soup to start a fall meal.

1 large onion, finely minced
2 small carrots, finely minced
2 our Bouillon Cubes, melted (see page 25), or 2 tablespoons our Chicken Stock (see page 26)
3 cups pumpkin puree or canned pumpkin
¼ teaspoon freshly grated nutmeg
Few grains crushed red pepper
6 cups our Chicken Stock or our Vegetable Stock (see page 60)
1 cup nonfat evaporated milk
½ teaspoon curry powder (optional)

Chopped cilantro for garnish

1. Sauté minced onion and carrots in the bouillon cubes or the 2 tablespoons stock until transparent. *Do not brown.*
2. Add pumpkin puree, nutmeg, and crushed red pepper.
3. Simmer slowly while adding the 6 cups stock and stir until mixture is smooth.
4. Add evaporated milk and stir to blend.
5. Taste to correct seasonings (curry may be added at this point if desired), and simmer 5 minutes until piping hot. This soup may be frozen for future use (see page 57).

To Serve: A hollowed-out pumpkin makes a dramatic soup tureen for this soup. Heat the bowls before serving, and sprinkle each serving with chopped cilantro. You may enjoy this as a fall or winter entrée, served with hearty whole wheat bread, a crisp green salad, and fresh fruit.

Per serving: 76 calories; 4.5 gm protein; 0.4 gm fat; 14.5 gm carbohydrate; 1.7 gm fiber; 0 mg cholesterol; 0.5 mg iron; 39 mg sodium; 100 mg calcium; 79 mg phosphorus; 5951 IU Vitamin A; 0.04 mg thiamine; 0.13 mg riboflavin; 6 mg Vitamin C; 331 mg potassium; 0.29 mg zinc; 0.6 mg niacin; 90 mcg Vitamin B_6; 0.06 mcg Vitamin B_{12}; 13 mcg folic acid

Election Night Borscht

Serves: 12 (1 cup = 1 serving)

I like to have my guests serve themselves this soup right from the stove so that an air of informality prevails while watching the election returns. I arrange all the bowls, sour cream, dill, and bread conveniently.

1 small head green cabbage, finely shredded
2 onions, thinly sliced
1 stalk celery, thinly sliced
3 shallots, finely minced
6 large, fresh beets, peeled and shredded
3 ripe tomatoes, peeled, seeded, and chopped, or 4 drained Italian plum tomatoes, chopped
2 quarts our Chicken Stock (see page 26)
1 bouquet garni (4 sprigs parsley, 2 bay leaves, 1 teaspoon thyme, several celery leaves, few grains crushed red pepper)
1 tablespoon frozen unsweetened apple juice concentrate
Juice of ½ lemon
½ cup vermouth or dry white wine
Freshly ground pepper
1 teaspoon low-sodium vegetable seasoning (see page 28)
3 tablespoons chopped fresh dill, or 1 teaspoon dry dill weed

Our Sour Cream (see page 27) or nonfat yogurt and freshly chopped fresh dill for garnish

1. In a 6-quart kettle, combine green cabbage, onions, beets, celery, shallots, tomatoes, stock, and bouquet garni. Bring to a boil, cover, and simmer 1 hour or until cabbage is tender.

2. Add apple juice concentrate, lemon juice, vermouth, freshly ground pepper, vegetable seasoning, and dill. Cover and simmer 40 minutes.

3. Taste, and adjust seasonings.

4. Soup tastes even better served the next day and reheated. May also be frozen for future use (see page 57); it keeps well for 3 to 4 months in the freezer.

To Serve: Serve piping hot with dollops of our Sour Cream and chopped dill for a garnish. Heavy whole wheat or seven-grain bread makes a wonderful accompaniment.

Per serving: 76 calories; 4.2 gm protein; 0.3 gm fat; 13.8 gm carbohydrate; 3.3 gm fiber; 0 mg cholesterol; 0.9 mg iron; 42 mg sodium; 49 mg calcium; 42 mg phosphorus; 358 IU Vitamin A; 0.07 mg thiamine; 0.07 mg riboflavin; 34 mg Vitamin C; 335 mg potassium; 0.32 mg zinc; 0.6 mg niacin; 133 mcg Vitamin B_6; 0 mcg Vitamin B_{12}; 23 mcg folic acid

French Country Winter Vegetable Soup

Serves: 12 (1 cup = 1 serving)

3 our Bouillon Cubes, melted (see page 25)
1 red onion, minced
3 cloves garlic, minced
1 tablespoon minced shallot
1 leek, split, well washed, and minced
1 carrot, minced
1 large potato, minced
2 celery stalks, minced
¼ small head green cabbage, minced
4 fresh mushrooms, minced
3 fresh ripe tomatoes, peeled, seeded, and minced
1 parsnip, minced (if available)
1 kohlrabi, minced (if available)
1 turnip, minced (if available)
1 rutabaga, minced (if available)
1 small celeriac, minced (if available)
½ fresh fennel bulb, minced (if available)
½ cup fresh sorrel or fresh basil
3 bay leaves
2 teaspoons herbes de Provence
Any minced leftover cooked vegetables, stock, or defatted gravy
4 cups our Chicken Stock (see page 26)
4 cups water

1. Place bouillon cubes in an 8-quart stock pot or Dutch oven. Add minced onion, garlic, shallot, and leek and sauté until transparent.

2. Add remaining vegetables, sorrel or basil, bay leaves, herbs, and any leftover cooked vegetables, stock, or defatted gravy to stock pot. Cook 5 minutes, stirring constantly.

3. Add chicken stock and water and cook until vegetables are tender —about 30 minutes.

4. If a finer texture is desired, puree entire mixture in food processor or blender in batches.

5. Taste and season with additional herbs such as thyme, basil, or low-sodium vegetable seasoning (see page 28) if desired. This soup may also be frozen for future use (see page 57).

Variations: Use 8 cups water instead of half water, half stock.

For a creamier consistency, add 1 cup skimmed evaporated milk after step 4. Heat 10 minutes before serving.

For a spicy tomato-vegetable soup, add 1 4-ounce can salt-free tomato paste and 1 teaspoon of your favorite curry powder after step 4. Heat 10 minutes before serving, and garnish with chopped fresh Italian parsley or cilantro.

Per serving: 63 calories; 3.0 gm protein; 0.4 gm fat; 13.5 gm carbohydrate; 3.2 gm fiber; 0 mg cholesterol; 2.5 mg iron; 21 mg sodium; 111 mg calcium; 61 mg phosphorus; 1428 IU Vitamin A; 0.08 mg thiamine; 0.07 mg riboflavin; 28 mg Vitamin C; 438 mg potassium; 0.18 mg zinc; 1.1 mg niacin; 83 mcg Vitamin B_6; 0 mcg Vitamin B_{12}; 11 mcg folic acid

Turkey-Vegetable Soup

Serves: 20 (1 cup = 1 serving)

1 turkey carcass with any skin or bits of turkey
4 quarts cold water
1 onion stuck with 3 whole cloves
1 whole leek, split and thoroughly washed
1 cup barley, rinsed
2 packages Manischewitz mushroom soup mix, *seasoning packets removed*
1 bouquet garni (2 bay leaves, 4 sprigs parsley, 4 celery leaves, ½ teaspoon crushed red pepper, 1 teaspoon thyme)
6 carrots, thinly sliced
4 stalks celery, thinly sliced
1 ounce dried mushrooms, soaked 30 minutes in hot water, rinsed, squeezed dry, and cut into slivers
1 20-ounce package frozen mixed vegetables, or any leftover cooked vegetables
¼ cup chopped fresh Italian parsley

1. Place turkey carcass in an 8-quart stainless steel stock pot. Add cold water, onion, and leek.

2. Bring to a boil and simmer 30 minutes.

3. Add barley, soup mix, and bouquet garni. Simmer 2 hours.

4. Remove turkey carcass and skin and the onion and leek. Scrape off any bits of turkey meat from carcass and return to pot.

5. Add carrots, celery, and mushrooms. Simmer 20 minutes, then add frozen vegetables and parsley and cook 15 minutes.

6. This soup, as is so often the case, tastes even better the next day. Or, it may be frozen for future use (see page 57).

To Serve: Serve hot. Add crusty sourdough or whole wheat bread, a green salad, and fresh fruit, and your supper is complete. If, when serving this soup the next day, it seems a bit thick, you may want to add some of our Turkey, Chicken, or Vegetable Stock (see pages 58, 26, and 60).

Per serving: 106 calories; 1.5 gm protein; 0.6 gm fat; 17 gm carbohydrate; 2.3 gm fiber; 0 mg cholesterol; 0.7 mg iron; 35 mg sodium; 22 mg calcium; 35 mg phosphorus; 4012 IU Vitamin A; 0.06 mg thiamine; 0.05 mg riboflavin; 7 mg Vitamin C; 178 mg potassium; 0.09 mg zinc; 0.7 mg niacin; 42 mcg Vitamin B_6; 0 mcg Vitamin B_{12}; 3 mcg folic acid

Quick Cream of Leftover Vegetable Soup

Serves: 10 (¾ cup = 1 serving)

1 medium onion, minced
1 stalk celery with leaves, minced
2 green onions, minced
½ cup our Chicken Stock (see page 26) or Vegetable Stock (see page 60)
1 leftover baked potato, or 1 cup mashed or steamed potatoes
2 cups our Chicken Stock or leftover vegetable soup liquid
½ teaspoon low-sodium vegetable seasoning (see page 28)
1 bay leaf
2 cups leftover cooked vegetables (broccoli, carrots, peas, beans, corn, cauliflower, ratatouille, or whatever you have)
2 cups nonfat milk
¼ cup nonfat dry milk
½ cup tomato puree (optional)
1 teaspoon curry powder (optional)

¼ cup minced fresh Italian parsley for garnish

1. Sauté onion, celery, and green onion in the ½ cup stock in saucepan. Stir until transparent.
2. Add potato, the 2 cups stock, vegetable seasoning, bay leaf, and all leftover vegetables.
3. Bring to a boil and simmer 2 minutes.
4. Remove all vegetable solids with a slotted spoon or strainer and puree.
5. Return puree to liquids in saucepan. Stir in nonfat milk and nonfat dry milk until well blended.
6. Simmer 5 minutes. If tomato puree and/or curry are desired, add them here. Taste, and adjust seasonings.

To Serve: Serve hot with chopped parsley garnish.

Per serving: 76 calories; 4.3 gm protein; 0.2 gm fat; 15.1 gm carbohydrate; 1.5 gm fiber; 1 mg cholesterol; 1.2 mg iron; 57 mg sodium; 83 mg calcium; 96 mg phosphorus; 2522 IU Vitamin A; 0.11 mg thiamine; 0.13 mg riboflavin; 15 mg Vitamin C; 321 mg potassium; 0.3 mg zinc; 1 mg niacin; 79 mcg Vitamin B_6; 0.16 mcg Vitamin B_{12}; 9 mcg folic acid

Cold Soups

Gazpacho

Serves: 10 (1 cup = 1 serving)

This cold soup is an important part of the hot-weather cuisine in the south of Spain. The proportions may be varied to suit your taste.

5 large, ripe tomatoes, peeled and seeded
1 large cucumber, peeled and seeded, or ½ Belgian or European cucumber, no peeling or seeding required
1 green or red pepper
½ red or white onion
2 shallots
1 large clove garlic
3 slices fresh Pritikin whole wheat bread, crusts removed, cut into eighths
1 cup our Chicken Stock (see page 26) or water
2 10-ounce cans salt-free tomato juice
Few grains cayenne pepper
⅓–½ cup red wine vinegar
1 teaspoon Hungarian paprika
1 teaspoon dried oregano, or 1 tablespoon fresh oregano

1. Puree tomatoes, cucumber, pepper, onion, shallots, and garlic in food processor or blender.
2. Add bread to the vegetable sauce and process.
3. Place pureed vegetables in a large bowl and add chicken stock, tomato juice, cayenne, vinegar, paprika, and oregano.
4. Blend thoroughly. Chill several hours; adjust seasonings before serving. (Note that chilled soups need heavy seasoning.) Soup may be frozen for future use (see page 57).

To Serve: Serve as is, or garnish with the following diced vegetables: green pepper, red pepper, cucumber, green onion, peeled seeded tomato, and our bite-sized garlic croutons, toasted (see page 14). May also be served with a dollop of our Sour Cream (see page 27) or nonfat yogurt and freshly chopped dill. Gazpacho makes a different and delicious first course at a luncheon or a barbecue.

Per serving: 58 calories; 2.5 gm protein; 0.5 gm fat; 12.5 gm carbohydrate; 2 gm fiber; 0 mg cholesterol; 1.4 mg iron; 28 mg sodium; 25 mg calcium; 44 mg phosphorus; 1460 IU Vitamin A; 0.11 mg thiamine; 0.08 mg riboflavin; 44 mg Vitamin C; 420 mg potassium; 0.19 mg zinc; 1.3 mg niacin; 119 mcg Vitamin B_6; 0 mcg Vitamin B_{12}; 9 mcg folic acid

Jellied Fish Consommé

Serves: 8 (½ cup = 1 serving)

Don't save the bones for Henry Jones, freeze them and prepare this elegant first course. *Jellied Fish Consommé must be prepared the day before serving.*

3½ pounds fish bones and heads (choose from flounder, sole, bass, halibut, haddock, turbot, whiting, or any local *fresh, nonoily* white fish—see note page 59)
1 large onion, peeled and chopped
1 leek (white part only), well washed and chopped
4 fresh mushrooms, chopped
1 carrot, chopped
1 shallot, chopped
1 celery stalk, chopped
2 Roma tomatoes, chopped
½ small stalk fennel, chopped
½ cup dry white wine or vermouth
8 cups *cold* water
1 bouquet garni (4 sprigs parsley, 1 strip orange zest, ½ teaspoon crushed red pepper, ½ teaspoon thyme, and 1 bay leaf)

Our Sour Cream (see page 27) and chopped chives for garnish

1. Wash fish trimmings in cold water, drain, and place in a stainless steel stock pot.

2. Add chopped vegetables to trimmings. Add white wine and boil 15 minutes.

3. Add cold water and bouquet garni, and bring to a boil. Reduce heat and simmer slowly for 30 minutes. Skim off scum periodically as it rises to the surface.

4. Continue to simmer over low heat for about 3 to 3½ hours, or until reduced by half. Skim during this time as often as necessary.

*5. Line a stainless steel triple-mesh strainer with cheesecloth and strain consommé into a container for storage. (Press down lightly to remove juices from vegetables and bones.)

6. Cool, cover, and refrigerate for use the next day. It will become jellied as it chills. Remove any fat that may surface and harden before serving.

To Serve: Spoon jellied consommé into chilled glass serving bowls, garnish with a dollop of our Sour Cream, and sprinkle with chives. This makes an elegant first course at a formal dinner party.

Per serving: 46 calories; 2.7 gm protein; 0 gm fat; 6.1 gm carbohydrate; 0 gm fiber; 0 mg cholesterol; 0.1 mg iron; 6 mg sodium; 1 mg calcium; 1 mg phosphorus; 0 IU Vitamin A; 0 mg thiamine; 0 mg riboflavin; 0 mg Vitamin C; 14 mg potassium; 0 mg zinc; 0 mg niacin; 6 mcg Vitamin B_6; 0 mcg Vitamin B_{12}; 0 mcg folic acid

* If you wish to clarify the consommé at this point so that it has a clear, jewel-like appearance, see instructions on page 13.

Quick Cold Cucumber Soup

Serves: 10 (¾ cup = 1 serving)

2 large hothouse cucumbers (see note page 51), or 4 regular cucumbers, peeled and seeded
4 green onions
½ cup fresh parsley
1 clove garlic
3 tablespoons chopped fresh dill, or 1 tablespoon dill weed
1 cup nonfat yogurt
1 cup our Chicken Stock (see page 26)
2 cups buttermilk, strained
2 drops Tabasco
Juice of ½ lemon (optional)

½ green pepper, ½ red pepper, ½ cucumber, and 2 Roma tomatoes, all diced for garnish
Nonfat yogurt and chopped fresh dill for garnish

1. Cut up cucumber lengthwise and in eighths crosswise.
2. Place cucumber, green onion, and parsley in food processor or blender.
3. While pureeing mixture, add garlic, dill, and yogurt. Blend well.
4. Place mixture in a bowl, add chicken stock, buttermilk, and Tabasco. Add lemon juice, if desired.
5. Chill 4 to 6 hours or overnight before serving.

To Serve: Serve from chilled tureen and garnish with diced vegetables and, if desired, a dollop of yogurt. Sprinkle with freshly chopped fresh dill.

Variation: Sometimes I just combine all the diced garnish vegetables with the pureed cucumber soup and serve in chilled bowls with a bit of yogurt on top.

Per serving: 51 calories; 4 gm protein; 0.2 gm fat; 9 gm carbohydrate; 1.5 gm fiber; 1 mg cholesterol; 0.8 mg iron; 85 mg sodium; 120 mg calcium; 71 mg phosphorus; 990 IU Vitamin A; 0.08 mg thiamine; 0.2 mg riboflavin; 39 mg Vitamin C; 283 mg potassium; 0.06 mg zinc; 0.7 mg niacin; 45 mcg Vitamin B_6; 0 mcg Vitamin B_{12}; 5 mcg folic acid

Nearly Vichyssoise

Serves: 12 (1 cup = 1 serving)

Vichyssoise is a favorite hot-weather cold soup. We have varied the recipe and made a cold soup higher in protein by using white beans instead of potatoes.

3 cups well washed and sliced leeks (white part only), or 1½ cups onions, sliced
1 clove garlic, minced
4 tablespoons our Chicken Stock (see page 26), or 4 of our Bouillon Cubes, melted (see page 25)
1 cup dry white northern beans, rinsed, sorted, and soaked according to direction on package
5 cups water
2 cups nonfat milk
½ cup nonfat dry milk
½ teaspoon crushed red pepper

Nonfat yogurt, cumin-garlic croutons,* and 2 tablespoons minced chives or green part of scallion for garnish

1. Cook leeks and garlic in stock until tender.
2. Add white beans and water and cook until beans are tender.
3. Puree bean mixture in batches; add milk and mix until smooth.
4. Add crushed red pepper.
5. Chill soup in refrigerator for 4 hours or overnight. This soup may be frozen for future use (see page 57).

To Serve: Serve in chilled bowls or from a chilled tureen, and garnish with a dollop of nonfat yogurt, cumin-garlic croutons, and chopped chives.

Variations: For a change in flavor, add 1 cup nonfat yogurt to the chilled soup, blend well, and serve.

3 cups sliced russet potatoes may be substituted for the beans.

Soup may be heated *slowly over low heat* and served hot with croutons and chopped chives.

Per serving: 108 calories; 7.2 gm protein; 0.6 gm fat; 19.1 gm carbohydrate; 4.3 gm fiber; 0 mg cholesterol; 1.6 mg iron; 67 mg sodium; 123 mg calcium; 147 mg phosphorus; 201 IU Vitamin A; 0.15 mg thiamine; 0.19 mg riboflavin; 3 mg Vitamin C; 344 mg potassium; 0.8 mg zinc; 0.6 mg niacin; 137 mcg Vitamin B_6; 0.27 mcg Vitamin B_{12}; 25 mcg folic acid

* *To make cumin-garlic croutons:* Shake 1 cup bread cubes made from Pritikin bread in a plastic bag with ½ teaspoon each cumin and garlic powder. Bake on nonstick baking sheet in a 375° oven for *5 minutes* only, until lightly toasted.

Fresh Strawberry Soup

Serves: 6 (¾ cup = 1 serving)

Cold fruit soups are more popular in Europe than in the United States. This one, with its beautiful deep pink color, is lovely to serve as a first course at a bridal shower or luncheon.

2 pints fresh sweet, ripe strawberries, washed, then hulled and cut in halves
1 tablespoon cornstarch
1 cup fresh orange juice
1 cup red wine
¼ cup frozen unsweetened apple juice concentrate, or to taste
1 cup nonfat yogurt

Fresh mint leaves for garnish

1. Puree half of the strawberries in a blender or food processor. Add remaining berries and puree.
2. Blend cornstarch with ¼ cup of the orange juice in a 2-quart saucepan. Add remaining orange juice, the red wine, apple juice concentrate, and pureed strawberries.
3. *Heat just to boiling* over medium heat, *stirring frequently;* remove from heat. Cool.
4. Stir in nonfat yogurt with a whisk.
5. Cover and refrigerate 2 to 4 hours before serving. This soup may be frozen (see page 57).

To Serve: This beautiful deep pink soup makes a dramatic presentation. Serve in chilled glass or elegant white china bowls garnished with whole or chopped fresh mint leaves and a stemmed whole strawberry.

Per serving: 107 calories; 2.6 gm protein; 0.5 gm fat; 17.1 gm carbohydrate; 1.5 gm fiber; 0 mg cholesterol; 1 mg iron; 25 mg sodium; 76 mg calcium; 26 mg phosphorus; 213 IU Vitamin A; 0.08 mg thiamine; 0.15 mg riboflavin; 60 mg Vitamin C; 225 mg potassium; 0.01 mg zinc; 1 mg niacin; 69 mcg Vitamin B_6; 0 mcg Vitamin B_{12}; 7 mcg folic acid

Salads

CRISP, COLD, AND COLORFUL

Antipasto à la Roma
Marinated Bean Salad
Bean Sprout, Spinach, and Mushroom Salad
Spicy Broccoli Salad
Green Bean Salad
Cabbage, Apple, and Raisin Slaw
Chinese Cabbage Salad
Chef's Salad
Chinese Minced Chicken in Lettuce Leaves
Calico Corn Salad
Tabouli
Gingered Cucumbers
Cucumber, Green Onion, and Yogurt Salad
Heavenly Stuffed Eggs
Hearts of Palm and Watercress Salad
A Lobster and Truffle Salad to Be Remembered
Roasted Pepper and Mushroom Vinaigrette
Crunchy Pea Salad
Potato Salad with Yogurt Dressing
Orange and Onion Salad
Confetti Rice Salad
Special Salmon Mousse
Two-Way Tomatoes
Tuna Vinaigrette
Turkey and Orange Salad
Zucchini "Coleslaw"

A Few Salad Dressings

Buttermilk Dressing
Herb Dressing
Cucumber Yogurt Dressing
Zesty Buttermilk Dressing
My Favorite Russian Dressing

Somehow, when we think of salads we think of all the wonderful fresh vegetables that spring and summer bring. However, there are many salads equally tasty that can be prepared year-round, even when the selection of fresh produce is limited, using dried peas and beans, cucumbers, onions, green onions, green peppers, carrots, cabbages, potatoes, and selected salt-free frozen vegetables.

The French have traditionally served their salads *after* the main course. Many years ago, Californians started serving their salads as a separate course before the entrée instead of with or after the main course. This custom has become widely accepted in the United States. It is advantageous to serve a salad as a first course, because this is when we are most hungry and larger amounts of food are eaten. A salad will therefore help satisfy this hunger while supplying us with vitamins, minerals, and fiber. The need for larger portions of an entrée is decreased and the result is a diet lower in calories yet nourishing and satisfying.

Antipasto à la Roma

Serves: 10–12

Antipastos lead the procession in all fine Italian meals. You could serve a salmon pâté with crackers alone, or a more elaborate platter of assorted vegetables and mixtures. Here we have a simple assortment—try it once, then add your own individual interpretation.

1 16-ounce package frozen ready-to-eat bean salad mix, or 1 15-ounce can garbanzo beans, drained
1 7½-ounce can salt-free tuna in water, drained and flaked
½ cup our Italian Dressing (see page 12)
1 10-ounce can quartered artichoke hearts, rinsed and well drained
1 2-ounce jar chopped pimiento, drained
½ cup our Italian Dressing
¼ pound whole small fresh mushrooms, cleaned and stems removed
1 8-ounce can salt-free tomato sauce
1 teaspoon Italian herb seasoning, crushed
¼ cup chopped fresh Italian parsley
1 head butter lettuce, washed and dried
1 green pepper, sliced in rings
1 red pepper, sliced in rings
2 heads Belgian endive, sliced lengthwise
2 tablespoons capers, rinsed and drained
3 tablespoons chopped fresh parsley

1. Prepare beans according to package directions. Drain. Add tuna and the first ½ cup Italian dressing and marinate in refrigerator for 4 hours.
2. Combine artichokes with pimiento and the second ½ cup Italian dressing and marinate for 4 hours.
3. Combine mushrooms, tomato sauce, herb seasoning, and parsley and marinate for 4 hours.
4. Arrange dry lettuce leaves in bottom of a shallow salad bowl, platter, or lazy Susan. Arrange drained bean mixture, drained artichoke hearts, and mushrooms in groups on lettuce. Intersperse pepper rings and endive slices attractively on platter. Sprinkle with capers and chopped parsley.
5. Platter may be prepared several hours in advance and covered with plastic wrap.

To Serve: This appetizer is suitable to be served to guests in the living room before an Italian-style dinner. To complete the menu, serve Buccatini Primavera (page 242) or Ragù alla Bolognese (page 240), hot crusty Italian bread, and Strawberry Chiffon Pie (page 281) or cheesecake for dessert. Antipasto also could be served as a luncheon entrée. Salt-free breadsticks or crusty sourdough rolls are a good complement.

Variation: Omit tuna and add turkey slices rolled and placed intermittently on platter.

Per serving: 209 calories; 15.7 gm protein; 4.2 gm fat; 30.5 gm carbohydrate; 6.7 gm fiber; 13 mg cholesterol; 4.7 mg iron; 95 mg sodium; 114 mg calcium; 223 mg phosphorus; 2357 IU Vitamin A; 0.21 mg thiamine; 0.28 mg riboflavin; 52 mg Vitamin C; 708 mg potassium; 0 mg zinc; 4.8 mg niacin; 50 mcg Vitamin B_6; 0 mcg Vitamin B_{12}; 22 mcg folic acid

Marinated Bean Salad

Serves: 12 (1 cup = 1 serving)

1½ cups cooked red kidney beans
1½ cups cooked garbanzo beans
1½ cups cooked pinto beans
1½ cups cooked white northern beans
1½ cups cooked cut green beans
1 cup sliced, cooked carrots
1 cup sliced water chestnuts
1 medium red onion, thinly sliced, or 6 green onions, thinly sliced
1 green pepper, diced
4 ounces diced pimiento
½ cup chopped fresh parsley
1 large clove garlic, minced
1 teaspon dried basil, crushed, or 1 tablespoon chopped fresh basil
⅔ cup our Italian Dressing (see page 12)

Tomato wedges and chopped fresh parsley for garnish

1. Combine cooked beans, carrots, water chestnuts, onion, green pepper, pimiento, and parsley with garlic, basil, and dressing.

2. Marinate 4 to 6 hours or overnight before serving. Salad may be stored in refrigerator for 7 to 10 days.

To Serve: Place in a large glass bowl and garnish with tomato wedges and chopped parsley. May also be used in a pita bread sandwich for lunch or as an accompanying salad with a turkey sandwich for dinner.

Variation: Add 4 quartered artichoke hearts, 4 sliced hearts of palm, or 1 cup sliced button radishes.

Per serving: 167 calories; 9.4 gm protein; 1.3 gm fat; 31.3 gm carbohydrate; 5.7 gm fiber; 0 mg cholesterol; 3.5 mg iron; 46 mg sodium; 76 mg calcium; 175 mg phosphorus; 1996 IU Vitamin A; 0.18 mg thiamine; 0.15 mg riboflavin; 30 mg Vitamin C; 588 mg potassium; 0.23 mg zinc; 1.2 mg niacin; 41 mcg Vitamin B_6; 0 mcg Vitamin B_{12}; 5 mcg folic acid

Bean Sprout, Spinach, and Mushroom Salad

Serves: 8

1 pound fresh bean sprouts, rinsed and drained
1 bunch fresh spinach (1 pound), washed and drained, stems removed
⅓ pound fresh mushrooms,* cleaned and sliced
1 2-ounce jar chopped pimiento, drained
1 shallot, finely minced
2 tablespoons red wine or brown rice vinegar
Juice of 1 lemon
1 tablespoon mild soy sauce
1 teaspoon salt-free Dijon mustard
1 teaspoon Hungarian paprika
½ cup our Chicken Stock (see page 26)
Freshly ground pepper
1 small red onion, thinly sliced (optional)

1. In a large salad bowl, combine bean sprouts, spinach, mushrooms, and pimiento. Cover with plastic wrap and refrigerate.

2. *To make salad dressing,* combine shallot, vinegar, lemon juice, soy sauce, mustard, paprika, chicken stock, and pepper in a screw-top jar. Shake well.

3. At serving time, add well-blended salad dressing to chilled vegetables. If desired, add red onion at this time. Mix well but gently with 2 forks.

Per serving: 40 calories; 3.6 gm protein; 0.3 gm fat; 6.7 gm carbohydrate; 13.6 gm fiber; 0 mg cholesterol; 1.6 mg iron; 79 mg sodium; 27 mg calcium; 69 mg phosphorus; 1482 IU Vitamin A; 0.11 mg thiamine; 0.2 mg riboflavin; 26 mg Vitamin C; 303 mg potassium; 0.11 mg zinc; 1.4 mg niacin; 66 mcg Vitamin B_6; 0 mcg Vitamin B_{12}; 16 mcg folic acid

* 1 package Enoki mushrooms (fresh Japanese mushrooms) may be substituted.

Spicy Broccoli Salad

Serves: 6–8 (½ cup = 1 serving)

This tasty salad has one exceptional ingredient—a small amount of sliced almonds. I made this exception because I felt it added so much to the flavor and texture of the recipe. You may omit it, of course, but check the nutritional analysis first.

3–4 cups broccoli florets, steamed until crisp
½ cup nonfat yogurt
⅛ teaspoon garlic powder
1 teaspoon low-sodium vegetable seasoning (see page 28)
1 tablespoon onion, grated
3 tablespoons tomato sauce
4–6 drops Tabasco
1½ ounces sliced almonds, toasted in 350° oven until lightly browned

1. Cut steamed broccoli into 1-inch pieces and place in a bowl.
2. Blend yogurt with garlic powder, vegetable seasoning, grated onion, tomato sauce, and Tabasco.
3. Combine yogurt sauce with broccoli and half of the toasted almonds. Blend ingredients gently with a fork.
4. Place in a 1-quart glass or stainless steel mixing bowl, cover with plastic wrap, and chill several hours.

To Serve: Run a spatula around the broccoli mixture in bowl, and unmold onto a serving platter. Sprinkle with remaining toasted almonds and surround with cherry tomatoes or sliced beefsteak tomatoes topped with fresh chopped basil.

Variation: ¼ cup light-style salad dressing may be substituted for the yogurt. It has about 40 calories in each tablespoon, while regular mayonnaise has 100 calories.

Per serving: 65 calories; 3.7 gm protein; 4.2 gm fat; 6.8 gm carbohydrate; 3.2 gm fiber; 0.29 mg cholesterol; 10.6 mg iron; 27 mg sodium; 118 mg calcium; 107 mg phosphorus; 2043 IU Vitamin A; 0.01 mg thiamine; 0.25 mg riboflavin; 71 mg Vitamin C; 303 mg potassium; 0.16 mg zinc; 0.9 mg niacin; 16.3 mcg Vitamin B_6; 0.1 mcg Vitamin B_{12}; 5 mcg folic acid

Green Bean Salad

Serves: 8 (¾ cup = 1 serving)

½ hothouse cucumber (see note page 51), thinly sliced, or 1 regular cucumber, peeled, cut in half lengthwise, seeded, and thinly sliced
1 20-ounce package frozen salt-free French-cut green beans, thawed, cooked 2 minutes, and drained
1 15-ounce can garbanzo beans, rinsed and drained
½ bell pepper, seeded and finely chopped
½ small red onion, finely chopped
1 2-ounce jar pimientos, drained
1 clove garlic, pressed
⅔ cup our Italian Dressing (see page 12)
½ cup chopped fresh Italian parsley*
1 teaspoon dried basil,* crushed

Red lettuce leaves for serving
Peeled, seeded tomato wedges and chopped fresh parsley for garnish

1. Combine all ingredients except lettuce and tomato wedges in salad bowl and mix thoroughly.
2. Allow to marinate in refrigerator several hours before serving.

To Serve: Line a serving platter with red lettuce leaves. Mound vegetable mixture lightly on platter. Garnish with peeled, seeded tomato wedges dipped in chopped fresh parsley.

Per serving: 134 calories; 7.7 gm protein; 1.5 gm fat; 24.5 gm carbohydrate; 5.6 gm fiber; 0 mg cholesterol; 3.2 mg iron; 52 mg sodium; 89 mg calcium; 129 mg phosphorus; 1016 IU Vitamin A; 0.16 mg thiamine; 0.14 mg riboflavin; 33 mg Vitamin C; 445 mg potassium; 0.02 mg zinc; 1.0 mg niacin; 33 mcg Vitamin B_6; 0 mcg Vitamin B_{12}; 4 mcg folic acid

* ½ cup chopped fresh basil may be substituted for the parsley and dried basil.

Cabbage, Apple, and Raisin Slaw

Serves: 8 (¾ cup = 1 serving)

This salad is high in Vitamins A and C and potassium. When buying cabbage, choose firm, crisp green heads.

1 small head green cabbage (approx. 1½ pounds), finely shredded
3 carrots, coarsely shredded
2 stalks celery, thinly sliced
1 teaspoon low-sodium vegetable seasoning (see page 28)
Freshly ground white pepper
⅓ cup seeded muscat raisins
2 crisp green apples (Pippin, Granny Smith, or Gravenstein), peeled, cored, and sliced
1½–2 tablespoons white wine or raspberry vinegar
2–3 tablespoons unsweetened apple juice concentrate
½–⅔ cup nonfat yogurt

1 sprig fresh parsley and thinly sliced red apple, such as Delicious, for garnish

1. Cut cabbage in quarters, remove core, and shred.
2. Add shredded carrots and sliced celery.
3. Season with vegetable seasoning and ground pepper.
4. Add raisins and apples.
5. Combine vinegar, apple juice concentrate, and yogurt. Add to cabbage mixture. Mix with a fork until salad is well blended. Taste, and adjust seasonings.
6. Place in a serving bowl and garnish with a sprig of fresh parsley in center of salad and thin apple slices (with red skin up) in spokelike fashion around the parsley. Cover with plastic wrap and chill several hours before serving to blend flavors.

To Serve: This is a wonderful salad to serve with broiled fish, steamed peas, and new potatoes.

Variation: Substitute 1 cup drained, crushed unsweetened pineapple or fresh chopped pineapple for the apples and 3 tablespoons frozen unsweetened pineapple juice concentrate for the apple juice concentrate.

Per serving: 82 calories; 2.2 gm protein; 0.3 gm fat; 19.7 gm carbohydrate; 4.6 gm fiber; 0 mg cholesterol; 1 mg iron; 46 mg sodium; 77 mg calcium; 44 mg phosphorus; 3265 IU Vitamin A; 0.09 mg thiamine; 0.1 mg riboflavin; 36 mg Vitamin C; 368 mg Potassium; 0.38 mg zinc; 0.7 mg niacin; 168 mcg Vitamin B_6; 0 mcg Vitamin B_{12}; 25 mcg folic acid

Chinese Cabbage Salad

Serves: 6

Chinese cabbage (Napa or celery cabbage) is a mild-tasting vegetable that is delicious served raw or braised in chicken broth until crisp. When shopping for this salad, make certain that your Chinese cabbage is long, straight, slightly green, and crisp—if not, choose another salad.

3 cups shredded Chinese cabbage
1 cup diced hothouse cucumber (see note page 51)
1 red pepper, thinly sliced
⅔ cup our Vegetable Stock (see page 60) or Chicken Stock (see page 26)
2 tablespoons red wine vinegar
2 tablespoons brown rice vinegar
½ teaspoon salt-free Dijon mustard
Freshly ground pepper
½ small red onion, finely chopped

1. Place shredded cabbage, cucumber, and red pepper slices in a bowl.

2. *To make vinaigrette dressing,* combine stock, vinegar, mustard, pepper, and chopped red onion in a jar. Shake thoroughly.

3. Add dressing to vegetables in bowl, toss thoroughly, and serve.

To Serve: This is a crisp salad, the flavor of which complements Marinated Broiled Flank Steak (page 176).

Per serving: 23 calories; 1.3 gm protein; 0.2 gm fat; 5.1 gm carbohydrate; 1 gm fiber; 0 mg cholesterol; 0.5 mg iron; 14 mg sodium; 25 mg calcium; 28 mg phosphorus; 802 IU Vitamin A; 0.04 mg thiamine; 0.04 mg riboflavin; 46 mg Vitamin C; 188 mg potassium; 0.03 mg zinc; 0.4 mg niacin; 11 mcg Vitamin B_6; 0 mcg Vitamin B_{12}; 2 mcg folic acid

Chef's Salad

Serves: 6 (1½ cups = 1 serving)

A hot-weather meal-in-one, and a delightful way to use leftover turkey.

1 16-ounce package frozen carrots, cauliflower, and French-cut green beans, cooked and cooled
1 10-ounce package frozen artichoke hearts, cooked and cooled
4 fresh mushrooms, cleaned and sliced
2 green onions, thinly sliced
⅔ cup our Vinaigrette or Italian Dressing (see page 12)
½ head romaine lettuce, washed, dried, and shredded
12 ounces roast turkey breast, shredded
1 cup defrosted frozen peas

1 tomato, seeded and cut into wedges, for garnish

1. Combine cooked and cooled vegetables and artichoke hearts with mushrooms and green onions.

2. Add vinaigrette dressing and marinate 1 hour in refrigerator.

3. Combine romaine, turkey, and peas in a salad bowl. Add marinated vegetables with dressing and toss lightly.

To Serve: Serve immediately, garnished with tomato wedges and accompanied by crisp sourdough rolls or Italian bread.

Per serving: 165 calories; 23 gm protein; 2.7 gm fat; 9.8 gm carbohydrate; 2.3 gm fiber; 44 mg cholesterol; 2.1 mg iron; 167 mg sodium; 55 mg calcium; 219 mg phosphorus; 1216 IU Vitamin A; 0.17 mg thiamine; 0.25 mg riboflavin; 18 mg Vitamin C; 698 mg potassium; 1.38 mg zinc; 7.7 mg niacin; 76 mcg Vitamin B_6; 0 mcg Vitamin B_{12}; 30 mcg folic acid

Chinese Minced Chicken in Lettuce Leaves

Serves: 8 (¾ cup = 1 serving)

4 cups cooked chicken,* shredded or chopped in food processor
4 dried black mushrooms, soaked in 1 cup hot water for 30 minutes, rinsed well, squeezed dry, and chopped
1 cup dry sherry
¼ cup our Chicken Stock (see page 26)
1 tablespoon mild soy sauce
1 teaspoon juice from grated ginger
1 tablespoon unsweetened pineapple juice concentrate
1 teaspoon Chinese Five Spices
1 tablespoon white sesame seeds
1 7-ounce can water chestnuts, rinsed, drained, and chopped
6 green onions, sliced
Freshly ground pepper

8 cold, crisp lettuce leaves

1. Marinate chopped chicken and mushrooms in sherry for about 1 hour.
2. Blend chicken stock, soy sauce, ginger juice, pineapple juice, and Five Spices with sherry drained from chicken. Mix well.
3. Heat dry pan and toast sesame seeds quickly and lightly.
4. Combine drained chicken and mushrooms and chopped chestnuts with soy sauce mixture. Heat about 5 minutes, or until heated through.
5. Add sliced green onions and pepper.

To Serve: Mound mixture on a heated platter surrounded by cold, crisp lettuce leaves, and sprinkle with toasted sesame seeds. Each person may spoon some of the mixture into a lettuce leaf, roll it up, and savor the flavor.

Variation: If your diet allows, 1 teaspoon sesame oil may be added to the soy sauce mixture in step 2.

Per serving: 176 calories; 17.7 gm protein; 4 gm fat; 8.9 gm carbohydrate; 0.8 gm fiber; 61 mg cholesterol; 1.7 mg iron; 116 mg sodium; 21 mg calcium; 172 mg phosphorus; 280 IU Vitamin A; 0.09 mg thiamine; 0.21 mg riboflavin; 5 mg Vitamin C; 404 mg potassium; 0.1 mg zinc; 6.6 mg niacin; 11 mcg Vitamin B_6; 0 mcg Vitamin B_{12}; 5 mcg folic acid

* Any cooked chicken can be used, but leftover roast or broiled chicken is best.

Calico Corn Salad

Serves: 10 (⅔ cup = 1 serving)

1 16-ounce package salt-free frozen kernel corn, cooked and cooled in cooking liquid
1 4-ounce jar pimiento, sliced
½ cup chopped fresh Italian parsley
1 bunch green onions, chopped
1 green pepper, chopped
1 red pepper, chopped
1 7½-ounce can hearts of palm, rinsed, drained, and cut in ¼-inch circles
20 cherry tomatoes, halved
4 tablespoons white wine vinegar
1 teaspoon dried tarragon, crushed, or 1 tablespoon chopped fresh tarragon
1 teaspoon dry mustard
Freshly ground white pepper

1. Drain corn and save cooking liquid.
2. Combine corn, pimiento, parsley, green onions, green and red pepper, hearts of palm, and halved tomatoes.
3. *To make salad dressing,* combine remaining ingredients and 1 cup liquid from cooked corn. Blend well.
4. Mix salad dressing with corn mixture and marinate 2 to 4 hours before serving.

To Serve: Serve in a large glass bowl or on bed of green, leafy lettuce.

Variation: If your diet allows, 1 tablespoon safflower oil may be added to the salad dressing.

Per serving: 75 calories; 2.3 gm protein; 0.5 gm fat; 12.9 gm carbohydrate; 1.2 gm fiber; 0 mg cholesterol; 1.2 mg iron; 9 mg sodium; 24 mg calcium; 91 mg phosphorus; 1577 IU Vitamin A; 0.08 mg thiamine; 0.08 mg riboflavin; 60 mg Vitamin C; 614 mg potassium; 0.06 mg zinc; 1.1 mg niacin; 53 mcg Vitamin B_6; 0 mcg Vitamin B_{12}; 5 mcg folic acid

Tabouli

(Cracked Wheat Salad)

Serves: 8 (1 cup = 1 serving)

Bulgur, or cracked wheat, is a grain commonly used in the Middle East. Tabouli is a Lebanese dish. If you like, you may substitute buckwheat groats, commonly called kasha, for the bulgur wheat.

1½ cups cracked wheat
6 cups boiling water
½ cup fresh lemon juice
⅓ cup our Chicken Stock (see page 26)
1 tablespoon mild soy sauce
1 teaspoon low-sodium vegetable seasoning (see page 28)
Freshly ground crushed red pepper
½ cup chopped fresh mint
1 cup chopped red onion, or 1 bunch green onions, chopped
1 cup minced fresh Italian parsley
½ eggplant, peeled, diced, and steamed
1 cup sliced radishes
½ hothouse cucumber (see note page 51), diced, or 1 regular cucumber, peeled, seeded, and diced
2 ripe tomatoes, peeled, seeded, and diced

1 head Boston lettuce, washed and crisped, for serving
1 small green pepper, cut into rings, for garnish
1 10-ounce can artichoke quarters, rinsed and drained, for garnish

1. Combine cracked wheat with boiling water and let stand 45 minutes, or until firm but not crunchy and the liquid is absorbed.
2. Combine lemon juice, chicken stock, soy sauce, vegetable seasoning, crushed red pepper, and mint. Mix.
3. Add drained cracked wheat, onions, parsley and eggplant to lemon mixture. Mix thoroughly, cover and chill several hours.
4. When ready to serve, add radishes, cucumber, and tomatoes. Mix gently with a fork.

To Serve: Mound salad mixture on a serving platter surrounded with lettuce leaves. Place a row of green pepper rings down center of salad and garnish with artichokes. Additional chopped parsley may be sprinkled on top.

Per serving: 139 calories; 5 gm protein; 0.7 gm fat; 30.2 gm carbohydrate; 2.6 gm fiber; 0 mg cholesterol; 3.4 mg iron; 75 mg sodium; 70 mg calcium; 129 mg phosphorus; 2417 IU Vitamin A; 0.17 mg thiamine; 0.12 mg riboflavin; 56 mg Vitamin C; 452 mg potassium; 0.13 mg zinc; 2 mg niacin; 86 mcg Vitamin B_6; 0 mcg Vitamin B_{12}; 13 mcg folic acid

Gingered Cucumbers

Serves: 8 ($\frac{1}{2}$ cup = 1 serving)

½ cup white wine vinegar or brown rice vinegar
¼ cup water
1 tablespoon mild soy sauce
1½ teaspoons grated fresh ginger
2 tablespoons frozen unsweetened apple juice concentrate
1 hothouse cucumber (see note page 51), thinly sliced, or 2 regular cucumbers, peeled, seeded, and thinly sliced
1 large carrot, shredded
3 green onions, sliced
2 tablespoons chopped fresh Italian parsley

1. Combine vinegar, water, soy sauce, ginger, and apple juice concentrate. Blend well.
2. Add cucumber, carrot, green onions, and parsley. Toss and cover.
3. Refrigerate 1 to 2 hours. Toss again before serving.

To Serve: This salad is particularly tasty served with broiled or barbecued chicken.

Per serving: 36 calories; 0.8 gm protein; 0.1 gm fat; 7.1 gm carbohydrate; 1.5 gm fiber; 0 mg cholesterol; 0.3 mg iron; 71 mg sodium; 22 mg calcium; 11 mg phosphorus; 1524 IU Vitamin A; 0.01 mg thiamine; 0.02 mg riboflavin; 11 mg Vitamin C; 185 mg potassium; 0.06 mg zinc; 0.3 mg niacin; 20 mcg Vitamin B_6; 0 mcg Vitamin B_{12}; 2 mcg folic acid

Cucumber, Green Onion, and Yogurt Salad

Serves: 8 (½ cup = 1 serving)

1 hothouse cucumber (see note page 51), halved lengthwise and thinly sliced, or 2 regular cucumbers, peeled, seeded, and thinly sliced
½ green pepper, diced
6 green onions, chopped
4 tablespoons chopped fresh dill
Freshly ground pepper
1 cup nonfat yogurt
3 tablespoons frozen unsweetened apple juice concentrate

1 ripe tomato, seeded and chopped, for garnish
Chopped fresh parsley or dill for garnish

1. Squeeze cucumber dry to remove excess liquid, and place in a bowl with green pepper, green onions, fresh dill, and ground pepper. Mix with a fork.
2. Cover with plastic wrap and chill until 1 hour before serving.
3. Add yogurt and frozen apple juice concentrate to cucumber mixture. Mix thoroughly with a fork and place in a serving bowl and chill. (This hour of marinating gives flavors a chance to blend—but is not so long that mixture will become watery.)
4. Garnish with chopped tomato and chopped parsley or dill before serving.

Per serving: 48 calories; 2 gm protein; 0.1 gm fat; 7.7 gm carbohydrate; 1.4 gm fiber; 0 mg cholesterol; 0.4 mg iron; 20 mg sodium; 62 mg calcium; 20 mg phosphorus; 270 IU Vitamin A; 0.03 mg thiamine; 0.09 mg riboflavin; 26 mg Vitamin C; 164 mg potassium; 0.02 mg zinc; 0.4 mg niacin; 33 mcg Vitamin B_6; 0 mcg Vitamin B_{12}; 2 mcg folic acid

Heavenly Stuffed Eggs

Serves: 12 (2 egg halves and approx. 2 teaspoons pâté = 1 serving)

12 extra-large eggs
½ recipe Salmon Pâté (see page 52) for stuffing
Coarsely chopped fresh dill, or 2 tablespoons chopped fresh parsley mixed with 1 teaspoon dill weed

2–3 bunches watercress

Cherry tomatoes and carrot sticks for garnish

1. Hard-cook the eggs in simmering water for 20 minutes.

2. Cool eggs quickly in cold water, *crack* shells, and let cool in cold water.*

3. Peel eggs, cut in half lengthwise or crosswise, and remove the yolks. (Your dog will love them.)

4. Stuff whites with pâté and sprinkle with freshly chopped dill.

To Serve: To serve as a salad, for each serving place 2 stuffed egg whites on a bed of watercress and garnish with cherry tomatoes with stems and carrot sticks. The eggs may also be placed on a platter and served as hors d'oeuvres or part of a buffet.

***Helpful Hint:** Adding ice cubes to the water hastens chilling of eggs and allows eggs to be peeled more readily. It also *prevents* the formation of a dark ring around the yolk formed by iron in the white and sulfur in the yolk.

Per serving: 76 calories; 10.4 gm protein; 2.5 gm fat; 4 gm carbohydrate; 0.7 gm fiber; 7 mg cholesterol; 1.2 mg iron; 123 mg sodium; 57 mg calcium; 92 mg phosphorus; 2067 IU Vitamin A; 0.03 mg thiamine; 0.17 mg riboflavin; 18 mg Vitamin C; 280 mg potassium; 0.07 mg zinc; 2.5 mg niacin; 26 mcg Vitamin B_6; 0.05 mcg Vitamin B_{12}; 2 mcg folic acid

Hearts of Palm and Watercress Salad

Serves: 12 (¼ cup = 1 serving)

1½ tablespoons minced shallots
1 clove garlic, minced
1 teaspoon mild soy sauce
2 teaspoons salt-free Dijon mustard
Freshly ground pepper
Juice of ½ lemon
4 tablespoons red wine vinegar or raspberry wine vinegar
⅓ cup our Chicken Stock (see page 26)
½ tablespoon chopped fresh parsley
1 tablespoon chopped chives
3 tablespoons finely diced green pepper
½ teaspoon low-sodium vegetable seasoning (see page 28)
2 14-ounce cans hearts of palm, rinsed and drained
1 2-ounce jar chopped pimiento, drained
2 heads Boston lettuce, leaves separated, washed, and well drained
1 bunch watercress, washed, tough stems removed

Cherry tomatoes for garnish (optional)

1. *To make vinaigrette dressing,* combine first 12 ingredients in a screw-top jar and shake vigorously. Chill 1 hour.

2. Cut hearts of palm into ¼-inch circles or into strips and place in a bowl. Add pimiento and vinaigrette dressing. Mix lightly and marinate in refrigerator for 1 hour.

To Serve: Arrange lettuce leaves on a large serving platter. Place hearts of palm and pimiento mixture on lettuce and top with watercress. Garnish with cherry tomatoes.

Per serving: 31 calories; 2.5 gm protein; 0.4 gm fat; 5.9 gm carbohydrate; 0.8 gm fiber; 0 mg cholesterol; 1.3 mg iron; 26 mg sodium; 36 mg calcium; 56 mg phosphorus; 877 IU Vitamin A; 0.14 mg thiamine; 0.08 mg riboflavin; 21 mg Vitamin C; 491 mg potassium; 0 mg zinc; 0.6 mg niacin; 7 mcg Vitamin B_6; 0 mcg Vitamin B_{12}; 8 mcg folic acid

A Lobster and Truffle Salad to Be Remembered

Serves: 6

Lobster has the same amount of cholesterol as flank steak. So try this as an occasional treat—if you can float the loan—it is a salad to be remembered.

½ cup Weight Watchers cottage cheese, rinsed and drained
¼ cup very fresh nonfat yogurt
1 tablespoon unsweetened apple juice concentrate
½ teaspoon low-sodium vegetable seasoning (see page 28)
2 cups washed, crisped, and shredded romaine lettuce
2 cups washed, crisped, and shredded red lettuce
16 ounces or 2 cups cooked lobster, cut into small chunks
1 cup diced cooked artichoke bottoms, or 1 10-ounce package frozen artichoke hearts, cooked, drained, and halved
1 cup diced peeled and seeded cucumber
4 tablespoons chopped fresh dill
12 cherry tomatoes
6 thin slices black truffle, shredded

1. *To make salad dressing,* combine first 4 ingredients in blender or food processor and process until smooth. Refrigerate at least 2 hours.

2. Place shredded greens, lobster, artichokes, and cucumber in a salad bowl. Cover with plastic wrap and chill until serving time.

3. Combine salad dressing with salad mixture, using 2 forks to toss gently. Add chopped dill and tomatoes and toss lightly. Sprinkle with shredded black truffles.

To Serve: If salad is served in individual plates, top each salad with shredded black truffles. This can be served as a main dish for a special luncheon or as an elegant appetizer. For luncheon, serve with crisp sourdough rolls, broccoli vinaigrette, and fresh pineapple with Strawberry Sauce (see page 272).

Per serving: 119 calories; 17.7 gm protein; 2 gm fat; 8.7 gm carbohydrate; 1.3 gm fiber 113 mg cholesterol; 1.7 mg iron; 236 mg sodium; 95 mg calcium; 186 mg phosphorus; 825 IU Vitamin A; 0.39 mg thiamine; 0.23 mg riboflavin; 15 mg Vitamin C; 462 mg potassium; 0.11 mg zinc; 2.1 mg niacin; 35 mcg Vitamin B_6; 0 mcg Vitamin B_{12}; 13 mcg folic acid

Roasted Pepper and Mushroom Vinaigrette

Serves: 8 (1 cup = 1 serving)

A bright red pepper is a fully matured, ripe green bell pepper. It is sweeter and has about fourteen times as much Vitamin A as a green pepper. Unfortunately, it is not always available, is quite perishable, and because of its late harvest, is more expensive. Try using it raw in salads or stuffed, and for a delicious change, roast it before using (see steps 2, 3, and 4 below).

2 tablespoons lemon juice
2 tablespoons red wine vinegar
2 tablespoons white wine vinegar or brown rice vinegar
2 cloves garlic, minced
Freshly ground pepper
1 tablespoon chopped fresh basil, or 1 teaspoon dried basil, crushed
⅔ cup our Chicken Stock (see page 26) or Vegetable Stock (see page 60)
3 red peppers
3 green peppers
1 pound fresh mushrooms, cleaned, stemmed, and sliced
1 red onion, thinly sliced

Butter lettuce leaves for serving
Chopped fresh Italian parsley or chopped fresh basil for garnish

1. *To make vinaigrette dressing,* combine the first 7 ingredients in a screw-top jar and shake thoroughly. Adjust flavors to your taste.
2. *To roast peppers,* lay them on broiling pan close to broiler and scorch skin on all sides. Watch closely so peppers do not get too burned.
3. Remove roasted peppers to brown paper bag or wrap in kitchen towel and "sweat" for 10 or 15 minutes.
4. Scrape off charred skins and remove stems and seeds.
5. Cut into strips.
6. Combine sliced peppers with vinaigrette dressing and chill several hours.
7. An hour before serving, add mushrooms and red onion. Mix lightly and refrigerate.
8. Drain salad before serving.

To Serve: Line a large platter or individual salad plates with butter lettuce and mound with salad mixture. Sprinkle with chopped Italian parsley.

Other Uses for Roasted Red or Green Peppers: Plain sliced roasted peppers are a wonderful ingredient in preparing a pipérade (a mixture of tomatoes, onions, and peppers used with fish or chicken). Marinated sliced roasted peppers are delicious as an addition to a green salad, as a low-calorie snack, or as part of a relish tray or antipasto. *To marinate the roasted pepper slices*, sprinkle them with 1 tablespoon olive oil, 2 tablespoons red wine vinegar, and 1 minced clove garlic, and store, covered, in refrigerator. They'll keep this way for 1 week. (Plain roasted pepper slices should be used the same day.)

Per serving: 45 calories; 3 gm protein; 0.4 gm fat; 9.1 gm carbohydrate; 2.8 gm fiber; 0 mg cholesterol; 1.5 mg iron; 19 mg sodium; 27 mg calcium; 94 mg phosphorus; 1443 IU Vitamin A; 0.12 mg thiamine; 0.32 mg riboflavin; 90 mg Vitamin C; 447 mg potassium; 0.06 mg zinc; 2.8 mg niacin; 157 mcg Vitamin B_6; 0 mcg Vitamin B_{12}; 25 mcg folic acid

Crunchy Pea Salad

Serves: 8 (⅔ cup = 1 serving)

10 ounces frozen petits pois, defrosted in strainer under spray of cold water, or 2 cups fresh peas, steamed and chilled
1 7-ounce can water chestnuts, drained and sliced
3 stalks celery,* thinly sliced
1 cup shredded carrots
4 green onions, thinly sliced
2 tablespoons salt-free tomato juice
2 tablespoons red wine vinegar
1 tablespoon mild soy sauce
1 teaspoon salt-free Dijon mustard
1 clove garlic, minced
1 teaspoon Hungarian paprika
1 teaspoon frozen unsweetened apple juice concentrate

1. Combine peas, water chestnuts, celery, carrots, and green onions.
2. *To make the marinade,* mix the remaining ingredients and beat well.
3. Pour over salad; blend well.
4. Cover and chill for about 1 hour.
5. Drain excess marinade before serving.

To Serve: May be served as is or with the addition of 1 teaspoon nonfat yogurt per serving as a garnish. A sliced tomato wedge and chopped parsley may also be added to each serving. Delightful with cold broiled chicken for a summer picnic.

Variation: Add 2 cups fresh bean sprouts.

Per serving: 60 calories; 2.8 gm protein; 0.3 gm fat; 12.4 gm carbohydrate; 1.7 gm fiber; 0 mg cholesterol; 1.1 mg iron; 131 mg sodium; 19 mg calcium; 60 mg phosphorus; 1958 IU Vitamin A; 0.17 mg thiamine; 0.1 mg riboflavin; 11 mg Vitamin C; 284 mg potassium; 0.07 mg zinc; 1.1 mg niacin; 78 mcg Vitamin B_6; 0 mcg Vitamin B_{12}; 12 mcg folic acid

* Celery can be omitted to lower the sodium content.

Potato Salad with Yogurt Dressing

Serves: 10 (1 cup = 1 serving)

3 pounds potatoes, steamed, cooled, skinned, and diced
½ cucumber, peeled, seeded, and diced
3 hard-cooked egg whites, coarsely grated
1 cup diced celery
½ cup diced green pepper
½ cup chopped green onions
¼ cup minced fresh parsley
½ teaspoon Italian seasoning
1 teaspoon low-sodium vegetable seasoning (see page 28)
Freshly ground white pepper
⅔ cup nonfat yogurt
1–2 tablespoons tarragon vinegar
1 tablespoon frozen unsweetened apple juice concentrate
2 teaspoons salt-free Dijon mustard
½ teaspoon celery seed, crushed

1. Toss diced potatoes with cucumber, grated egg whites, celery, green pepper, green onions, parsley, Italian seasoning, vegetable seasoning, and white pepper.
2. Combine remaining ingredients and pour over vegetables. Toss to mix.
3. Chill for several hours before serving to allow flavors to blend.

To Serve: Serve with cold chicken, cold sliced turkey, or leftover chilled Meat Loaf (page 178).

Variation: Cold steamed cauliflower may be substituted for the potatoes for fewer calories.

Per serving: 114 calories; 5 gm protein; 0.3 gm fat; 23.8 gm carbohydrate; 3.5 gm fiber; 0 mg cholesterol; 1.4 mg iron; 46 mg sodium; 56 mg calcium; 72 mg phosphorus; 442 IU Vitamin A; 0.16 mg thiamine; 0.13 mg riboflavin; 39 mg Vitamin C; 514 mg potassium; 0.43 mg zinc; 2 mg niacin; 267 mcg Vitamin B_6; 0.01 mcg Vitamin B_{12}; 12 mcg folic acid

Orange and Onion Salad

Serves: 6 (1 cup = 1 serving)

1 head romaine lettuce
6 navel oranges
1 large red or white onion (Maui, Walla Walla, or Vidalia onions are superdelicious)
4 tablespoons our Chicken Stock (see page 26) or water
2 tablespoons raspberry wine vinegar or red wine vinegar
1 clove garlic, minced
1 teaspoon low-sodium vegetable seasoning (see page 28)
½ teaspoon dry mustard
1 tablespoon frozen unsweetened apple juice concentrate
Few grains crushed red pepper

1. Wash and dry romaine leaves. Arrange in a salad bowl or on a platter.
2. Using a sharp, serrated knife, peel the oranges (removing all white portion of skin). Slice thinly.
3. Peel onion and slice into thin rings, or chop.
4. Arrange orange slices and onion in salad bowl.

*5. *To make salad dressing,* combine the remaining ingredients in a screw-top jar. Shake thoroughly.

6. Just before serving, pour dressing over salad.

To Serve: This salad makes a colorful and flavorful accompaniment for a stuffed cabbage or a meat loaf.

Variation: In the fall, red pomegranate seeds make an attractive and tasty garnish. Spinach leaves may be substituted for romaine.

***Helpful Hint:** Salad and dressing may be prepared separately, covered, and refrigerated early in the day. Combine just before serving.

Per serving: 85 calories; 2.4 gm protein; 0.5 gm fat; 20.3 gm carbohydrate; 3.3 gm fiber; 0 mg cholesterol; 1.4 mg iron; 8 mg sodium; 86 mg calcium; 49 mg phosphorus; 935 IU Vitamin A; 0.17 mg thiamine; 0.09 mg riboflavin; 69 mg Vitamin C; 389 mg potassium; 0.45 mg zinc; 0.8 mg niacin; 128 mcg Vitamin B_6; 0 mcg Vitamin B_{12}; 25 mcg folic acid

Confetti Rice Salad

Serves: 8 (⅔ cup = 1 serving)

2 cups Steamed Brown Rice (see page 254), cooled
1 cup frozen or cooked fresh green peas
½ green pepper, finely diced
½ red pepper, finely diced, or 1 4-ounce can chopped pimiento, drained
½ cup finely chopped green onions
½ cup finely chopped fresh Italian parsley

½ cup our Vinaigrette Dressing (see page 12)
2 tablespoons nonfat yogurt
½ teaspoon salt-free Dijon mustard

Lettuce leaves for serving
1 10-ounce can artichoke hearts, rinsed, drained, and rolled in chopped fresh parsley, for garnish

1. Combine cooled rice with peas, green pepper, red pepper, green onions, and parsley.
2. Mix vinaigrette dressing with yogurt and Dijon mustard. Add to rice mixture and combine gently with a fork.
3. Chill 2 to 3 hours or overnight until ready to serve.

To Serve: Place chilled rice mixture in a lettuce-lined bowl and garnish with parsleyed artichoke hearts. This is lovely served as an accompaniment for luncheon or dinner with Turkey Tonnato (page 172) or cold broiled chicken.

Variations: This rice salad may be used for stuffing 8 small tomatoes.
To serve as a main-dish salad, add 2 cups diced leftover roast chicken.

Per serving: 89 calories; 3.1 gm protein; 0.5 gm fat; 18.4 gm carbohydrate; 2.3 gm fiber; 0 mg cholesterol; 1.2 mg iron; 30 mg sodium; 36 mg calcium; 66 mg phosphorus; 1123 IU Vitamin A; 0.13 mg thiamine; 0.07 mg riboflavin; 38 mg Vitamin C; 167 mg potassium; 0.04 mg zinc; 1.3 mg niacin; 49 mcg Vitamin B_6; 0 mcg Vitamin B_{12}; 9 mcg folic acid

Special Salmon Mousse

Serves: 12 (⅔ cup = 1 serving)

1 16-ounce can red salmon, drained, skinned, and bones removed
½ cup nonfat yogurt
¼ cup Weight Watchers cottage cheese, rinsed and drained
1 tablespoon lemon juice
½ teaspoon dry horseradish
1 teaspoon dry mustard or salt-free Dijon mustard with herbs
Few grains cayenne pepper
2 packages plain, unflavored gelatin
1½ cups our Chicken Stock (see page 26)
1 cup skimmed evaporated milk, *well chilled*
3 cups finely shredded romaine

Red lettuce leaves for serving
6 limes or lemons for garnish
1 4-ounce jar chopped pimiento, drained and chopped, for garnish

1. Combine salmon, yogurt, cottage cheese, lemon juice, horseradish, mustard, and cayenne in blender or food processor. Blend until smooth. (*Do not overmix.*)
2. Soften gelatin in ½ cup of the cool chicken stock. Liquefy over hot water or heat and add to salmon with the remaining cup of chicken stock.
3. Whip thoroughly chilled milk in chilled bowl until stiff. Fold salmon mixture and romaine into whipped milk.
4. Spray a 6-cup fish mold with nonstick spray and turn salmon mixture into mold. Cover with plastic wrap.
5. Chill overnight or until firm.

To Unmold and Serve: Unmold onto a platter lined with red lettuce leaves. (To facilitate unmolding, loosen around edges with a metal spatula, invert mold over platter, and shake gently until unmolded.) Cut limes in half with saw-tooth edges and top with chopped pimiento. If necessary, slice off ends of limes so that they stand straight. Surround mold with lime cups. Complete luncheon menu with Cucumber, Green Onion, and Yogurt Salad (page 96), Pickled Beets (page 312), crisp sourdough rolls, and pineapple or melon in Strawberry Sauce (page 272) for dessert.

Per serving: 120 calories; 14.9 gm protein; 5.4 gm fat; 6.4 gm carbohydrate; 0.1 gm fiber; 20 mg cholesterol; 1 mg iron; 159 mg sodium; 176 mg calcium; 181 mg phosphorus; 569 IU Vitamin A; 0.05 mg thiamine; 0.18 mg riboflavin; 21 mg Vitamin C; 291 mg potassium; 0.16 mg zinc; 3 mg niacin; 21 mcg Vitamin B_6; 0.03 mcg Vitamin B_{12}; 4 mcg folic acid

Two-Way Tomatoes

Serves: 4 (1 cup = 1 serving)

The same ingredients give you two different recipes—a cold soup and a salad—either of which is lovely served with broiled fish.

4 large ripe tomatoes, peeled, seeded, and cut into wedges
1½ cups nonfat yogurt
1 large clove garlic, minced
Dash Tabasco
15 fresh mint leaves, chopped
Red lettuce leaves (for serving salad)
2 tablespoons chopped fresh dill for garnish

To Make Salad:

1. Put sliced tomatoes in a bowl.
2. Combine yogurt, garlic, Tabasco, and chopped mint, pour over tomatoes, and toss gently with a fork.
3. Chill several hours.

To Serve: Place on small platter lined with red lettuce leaves and sprinkle with chopped dill.

To Make Soup:

1. Combine all ingredients except red lettuce (use the dill) and process in blender or food processor.
2. Chill and serve as soup the next day. If mixture is too thick, add a bit more yogurt or tomato juice.

To Serve: Serve in chilled bowls.

Per serving: 78 calories; 5.8 gm protein; 0.4 gm fat; 14.5 gm carbohydrate; 2.7 gm fiber; 0 mg cholesterol; 1.3 mg iron; 57 mg sodium; 160 mg calcium; 52 mg phosphorus; 2051 IU Vitamin A; 0.16 mg thiamine; 0.28 mg riboflavin; 47 mg Vitamin C; 463 mg potassium; 0.34 mg zinc; 2.1 mg niacin; 176 mcg Vitamin B_6; 0 mcg Vitamin B_{12}; 15 mcg folic acid

Tuna Vinaigrette

Serves: 6 (1 cup = 1 serving)

1/3 cup raspberry wine vinegar
2/3 cup our Chicken Stock (see page 26)
1/2 teaspoon low-sodium vegetable seasoning (see page 28)
Freshly ground pepper
1/2 teaspoon oregano, crushed
1/2 teaspoon chervil, crushed
1 tablespoon chopped fresh parsley
2 tablespoons chopped pimiento
1 clove garlic, minced
1 13-ounce can salt-free tuna in water, rinsed, drained, and flaked
2 1-pound cans quartered artichoke hearts, rinsed and drained
8 fresh mushrooms, cleaned and sliced
1 cup frozen petits pois, defrosted, or fresh peas, steamed and chilled
3 hard-cooked egg whites, coarsely chopped
1/2 green pepper, diced
1/2 cucumber, peeled, seeded, and diced

2 tablespoons toasted sesame seeds for garnish
12 cherry tomatoes for garnish
1 bunch watercress, washed and tough stems removed, for garnish

1. *To make vinaigrette dressing,* combine the first 9 ingredients in a screw-top jar. Shake well to blend.

*2. Place tuna, artichokes, mushrooms, peas, egg whites, green pepper, and cucumber in a salad bowl.

3. Add salad dressing to salad ingredients; toss with 2 forks.

To Serve: Sprinkle with toasted sesame seeds and arrange cherry tomatoes and sprigs of watercress on top.

***Helpful Hint:** The salad may be prepared through step 2 early in the day and combined with salad dressing later on for serving.

Per serving: 185 calories; 26.7 gm protein; 2.8 gm fat; 18.5 gm carbohydrate; 3.1 gm fiber; 39 mg cholesterol; 3.1 mg iron; 173 mg sodium; 88 mg calcium; 278 mg phosphorus; 1672 IU Vitamin A; 0.26 mg thiamine; 0.49 mg riboflavin; 51 mg Vitamin C; 863 mg potassium; 0.04 mg zinc; 11.2 mg niacin; 91 mcg Vitamin B_6; 0.02 mcg Vitamin B_{12}; 12 mcg folic acid

Turkey and Orange Salad

Serves: 6 (1 cup = 1 serving)

2 cups cubed cooked turkey
½ cup sliced celery
½ cup sliced water chestnuts
½ cup our Vinaigrette Dressing (see page 12)
¼ teaspoon curry powder (optional)
2 cups orange segments
1 small red onion, thinly sliced

Red lettuce leaves for serving
Chopped fresh parsley for garnish

1. Marinate turkey, celery, and water chestnuts in vinaigrette dressing (add curry to dressing if desired).

2. Add 1 cup of the orange segments and the red onion just before serving.

To Serve: Arrange on red lettuce leaves; garnish with parsley and the remaining 1 cup orange segments.

Variation: Mix with 4 cups shredded romaine before serving.

Per serving: 133 calories; 16.3 gm protein; 3.1 gm fat; 10.4 gm carbohydrate; 1.9 gm fiber; 42 mg cholesterol; 1.7 mg iron; 86 mg sodium; 69 mg calcium; 151 mg phosphorus; 1160 IU Vitamin A; 0.1 mg thiamine; 0.15 mg riboflavin; 47 mg Vitamin C; 418 mg potassium; 1.15 mg zinc; 4.1 mg niacin; 61 mcg Vitamin B_6; 0 mcg Vitamin B_{12}; 12 mcg folic acid

Zucchini "Coleslaw"

Serves: 6 (½ cup = 1 serving)

The term "coleslaw" means a cabbage salad; however, there are many other vegetable combinations that can be used for a similar effect. If you have access to home-grown zucchini, it's especially delicious, but fresh zucchini from the market in season also makes a wonderful "slaw."

6 small zucchini, scrubbed, trimmed, and coarsely shredded
1 clove garlic, minced
1 tablespoon grated onion
3 small carrots, shredded
Freshly ground pepper
½ cup our Chicken Stock (see page 26)
3 tablespoons white wine vinegar
1 shallot, finely minced
½ teaspoon thyme, crushed
½ teaspoon chervil, crushed
½ teaspoon basil, crushed
½ teaspoon salt-free Dijon mustard

1. Place shredded zucchini on paper towels. Pat gently to remove moisture.
2. Turn zucchini into salad bowl with minced garlic, onion, carrots, and ground pepper. Toss to blend.
3. *To make vinaigrette dressing,* place stock, vinegar, shallot, thyme, chervil, basil, and mustard in screw-top jar. Shake vigorously.
4. Add dressing to zucchini mixture and blend well.
5. Cover and chill in refrigerator for several hours until icy cold.

To Serve: Place in a chilled bowl or on a bed of greens with a garnish of crisp red button radishes or cherry tomatoes.

Per serving: 33 calories; 1.7 gm protein; 0.2 gm fat; 7.2 gm carbohydrate; 3.5 gm fiber; 0 mg cholesterol; 0.9 mg iron; 14 mg sodium; 44 mg calcium; 38 mg phosphorus; 3043 IU Vitamin A; 0.06 mg thiamine; 0.09 mg riboflavin; 19 mg Vitamin C; 283 mg potassium; 0.11 mg zinc; 1 mg niacin; 40 mcg Vitamin B_6; 0 mcg Vitamin B_{12}; 2 mcg folic acid

A Few Salad Dressings

Buttermilk Dressing

Yield: 3½ cups (1 tablespoon = 1 serving)

1 cup unsalted tomato juice or tomato sauce
½ cup red wine vinegar
1 teaspoon chervil
1 teaspoon basil
2 cloves garlic, minced
2 cups buttermilk, strained to remove fat globules

Put all ingredients in a bowl, blend well with whisk, and store in screw-top container. Keeps well in refrigerator.

Per serving: 4 calories; 0.3 gm protein; 0 gm fat; 0.7 gm carbohydrate; 0 gm fiber; 0 mg cholesterol; 0.1 mg iron; 9 mg sodium; 9 mg calcium; 8 mg phosphorus; 29 IU Vitamin A; 0 mg thiamine; 0.01 mg riboflavin; 1 mg Vitamin C; 23 mg potassium; 0 mg zinc; 0 mg niacin; 0 mcg Vitamin B_6; 0 mcg Vitamin B_{12}; 0 mcg folic acid

Herb Dressing

Yield: 3¼ cups (1 tablespoon = 1 serving)

1 cup raspberry wine vinegar
½ tablespoon basil
1 tablespoon rosemary
1 tablespoon thyme
1 bay leaf
1 clove garlic, mashed
2 cups our Chicken Stock (see page 26), chilled
½ red onion, minced

Put all ingredients in a bowl, blend well with whisk, and store in screw-top container. Keeps well in refrigerator.

Per serving: 3 calories; 0.1 gm protein; 0 gm fat; 0.7 gm carbohydrate; 0.1 gm fiber; 0 mg cholesterol; 0.2 mg iron; 0 mg sodium; 4 mg calcium; 1 mg phosphorus; 10 IU Vitamin A; 0 mg thiamine; 0 mg riboflavin; 0 mg Vitamin C; 9 mg potassium; 0 mg zinc; 0 mg niacin; 1 mcg Vitamin B_6; 0 mcg Vitamin B_{12}; 0 mcg folic acid

Cucumber Yogurt Dressing

Yield: 2 cups (1 tablespoon = 1 serving)

1 cup nonfat yogurt
1 teaspoon lemon juice
1 clove garlic, minced
1 tablespoon minced fresh parsley
1 tablespoon chopped chives
Few grains red pepper
1 teaspoon salt-free Dijon mustard
1 cup cucumber, peeled, seeded, and shredded

Put all ingredients in a bowl, blend well with whisk, and store in screw-top container. Keeps well in refrigerator.

Per serving: 6 calories; 0.6 gm protein; 0 gm fat; 1 gm carbohydrate; 0 gm fiber; 0 mg cholesterol; 0 mg iron; 7 mg sodium; 19 mg calcium; 2 mg phosphorus; 82 IU Vitamin A; 0.01 mg thiamine; 0.03 mg riboflavin; 1 mg Vitamin C; 13 mg potassium; 0 mg zinc; 0.1 mg niacin; 0 mcg Vitamin B_6; 0 mcg Vitamin B_{12}; 0 mcg folic acid

Zesty Buttermilk Dressing

Yield: 2¾ cups (1 tablespoon = 1 serving)

1 cup nonfat yogurt
1 cup buttermilk, strained to remove fat globules
¼ cup fresh parsley, chopped
1 tablespoon instant toasted onion flakes
1 large clove garlic, crushed
¼ teaspoon dried basil, or 1 tablespoon fresh basil
¼ teaspoon dried oregano, or 1 tablespoon fresh oregano
¼ teaspoon dried rosemary, or 1 tablespoon fresh rosemary
½ cup watercress leaves, chopped
½ teaspoon low-sodium vegetable seasoning (see page 28)

1. Blend yogurt and buttermilk in blender or food processor.
2. Add remaining ingredients and blend well.
3. Refrigerate for at least 1 hour before using so that flavors may develop.

Per serving: 7 calories; 0.6 gm protein; 0 gm fat; 1 gm carbohydrate; 0 gm fiber; 0 mg cholesterol; 0.1 mg iron; 12 mg sodium; 20 mg calcium; 8 mg phosphorus; 141 IU Vitamin A; 0.01 mg thiamine; 0.03 mg riboflavin; 2 mg Vitamin C; 20 mg potassium; 0 mg zinc; 0.1 mg niacin; 1 mcg Vitamin B_6; 0 mcg Vitamin B_{12}; 0 mcg folic acid

My Favorite Russian Dressing

Yield: 1½ cups (1 tablespoon = 1 serving)

1 cup nonfat yogurt
¼ cup salt-free tomato sauce
2 hard-cooked egg whites, chopped
¼ cup diced green pepper
½ teaspoon onion powder
¼ teaspoon garlic powder
¼ teaspoon low-sodium vegetable seasoning (see page 28)
Dash Tabasco

Place all ingredients into a bowl and blend well with whisk.

To Use: Especially good served over hearts of romaine salad, garnished with chopped pimiento and freshly chopped parsley.

Per serving: 7 calories; 0.6 gm protein; 0.2 gm fat; 0.8 gm carbohydrate; 0 gm fiber; 0 mg cholesterol; 0 mg iron; 8 mg sodium; 11 mg calcium; 1 mg phosphorus; 50 IU Vitamin A; 0.01 mg thiamine; 0.03 mg riboflavin; 2 mg Vitamin C; 7 mg potassium; 0 mg zinc; 0.1 mg niacin; 3 mcg Vitamin B_6; 0 mcg Vitamin B_{12}; 0 mcg folic acid

Traditional Entrées

LIMITED PORTIONS–HEIGHTENED APPEAL

At the risk of not "beefing up" your diet, let us turn our attention to the preparation of entrées. Entrées are commonly regarded as our principal source of protein, and traditionally they have included either fish, poultry, game, or red meat. This chapter contains a wide variety of delectable recipes using those ingredients. In order to minimize the intake of cholesterol and fat, I limit the use of red meat to flank steak or lean ground round. Fatty fishes are used only occasionally. All shellfish except lobster are off limits. Poultry is used with skin and all visible fat removed. And the amount of meat in each serving is limited to 4 ounces.

Other entrées using little or no meat or fish can be found in the chapters on Casseroles, Pastas and Grains, Soups, and Salads.

Fish

Catch of the Day

Bouillabaisse
My Favorite Flounder Fillets
Filets de Poisson aux Tomates
Simply Baked Salmon Fillets
Shirley's Barbecued Teriyaki Salmon
Five-Minute Fillet of Sole
Hap's Vegetable-Stuffed Fillet of Sole
Fillet of Sole in Tomato-Orange Sauce
Eva's Easy-Does-It Poached Salmon
Easy Summer Fish Casserole
Poached Halibut, English Style
Herbed Baked Halibut
Sea Bass with Julienne Vegetables
Baked Salmon Loaf
Halibut Creole for a Crowd
Broiled Swordfish Steaks
Jellied Fish
Sweet and Pungent Fish
Red Snapper à la Mexicaine

Not too many years ago fish was considered an inexpensive meal. With the new national awareness of the importance of proper nutrition, fish—with its low-fat, low-cholesterol, high-protein content—has proven to be a high-quality entrée. The increased demand for and limited supply of fish has unfortunately also increased its cost.

Fish contains adequate amounts of Vitamin B and D and large amounts of phosphorus, potassium, iron, and other trace minerals such as iodine and fluorine. A 4-ounce serving of fish will supply approximately half of the total protein required by the body each day. The high-quality protein of fish is complemented by its low calories. Fish has fewer calories than beef, and is lower in cholesterol and fat. The fat content of fish does vary, however, from under 1 percent to over 15 percent. The following fishes are listed in order of their approximate fat content—starting with those with a minimal fat content and progressing to those with a high fat content. If you are counting calories, you should of course choose from among those fishes considered lean or containing less than 3 percent fat. My overall suggestion is that you choose fish as an entrée several times a week.

The following are considered lean fish:

.3% fat—Cod or Scrod
Haddock
Hake
Pollack
Flat Fish, such as Sole, Flounder, Turbot, and Halibut
Red Snapper
Sea Bass
Sturgeon
Brook Trout
Tile Fish, such as Yellow Pike and Yellow Snapper

The following are considered moderately fat fish:

Bluefish
Striped Bass
Catfish
Carp
Shark
Swordfish
Tuna
Whiting or Silver Hake

The following are considered fat fish:

Butterfish
Lake Trout
Mullet
Mackerel
Lake Whitefish
Pompano
15% fat—Salmon

There is a rule of thumb to be followed when cooking fish. Measure the fish at its thickest point and cook it 10 minutes for each measured inch. This rule of thumb applies to all cooking methods, whether it be baking, broiling, or poaching. Frozen fish (not thawed) takes twice the cooking time but ends up being overcooked on the outside while still cold on the inside. Frozen fish should therefore be thawed at room temperature and cooked immediately for best results; however, I recommend the use of frozen fish only as a last resort. When you think the fish has finished cooking, take a fork and gently flake it; if it passes the test, it's yours to serve and enjoy.

Fresh fish, properly prepared, will be a memorable main dish.

Bouillabaisse

(Fish Chowder)

Serves: 8 (1½ cups = 1 serving)

This easily prepared bouillabaisse, made with low-calorie whitefish, can be made a day ahead or frozen for future use. Company loves it and it's a natural for large, informal groups.

1 onion, minced
2 whole leeks, minced
1 carrot, minced
1 stalk celery, minced
3 cloves garlic, minced
1 cup our Fish Stock (see page 59) or water
2 bay leaves
2 teaspoons thyme, crushed
½ teaspoon basil, crushed
½ cup minced fresh fennel, or ½ tablespoon dried fennel seed
⅔ cup dry white wine
3 potatoes cut into ½-inch cubes
1 28-ounce can Italian peeled plum tomatoes, pureed
2 fresh tomatoes, peeled, seeded, and diced
1 16-ounce can salt-free tomato sauce or tomato bits
1 3-inch strip fresh orange zest
1 quart water
Juice of 1 lemon
1½–2 pounds rockfish (a firm whitefish such as flounder, sole, halibut, turbot, loup, cod), cut into 1-inch cubes
½ cup chopped fresh parsley
Few grains crushed red pepper
2 frozen 8-ounce lobster tails, defrosted, cut into serving pieces with shell (optional)

1. Simmer minced ingredients in fish stock or the 1 cup water for 10 minutes.

*2. Add bay leaves, thyme, basil, fennel, wine, potatoes, tomatoes, tomato sauce, orange zest and the 1 quart water. Simmer for 30 minutes, or until potatoes are tender.

3. While ingredients are simmering, squeeze lemon over fish cubes and let marinate for 30 minutes.

4. After chowder has simmered about 30 minutes, add fish, parsley, and crushed red pepper. Continue to simmer 20 minutes more. (If you are adding the lobster, do so 5 minutes before serving.)

To Serve: This dish may be served in individual ramekins or soup plates with rounds of toasted sourdough baguette rubbed with fresh garlic. A roasted red pepper and mushroom salad is a delicious beginning, and Grapefruit Baked Alaska (page 273) a satisfying end.

Per serving: 262 calories; 23.2 gm protein; 6.3 gm fat; 25.5 gm carbohydrate; 3.5 gm fiber; 57 mg cholesterol; 3.6 mg iron; 234 mg sodium; 75 mg calcium; 312 mg phosphorus; 3446 IU Vitamin A; 0.22 mg thiamine; 0.17 mg riboflavin; 54 mg Vitamin C; 1053 mg potassium; 1.16 mg zinc; 4.3 mg niacin; 370 mcg Vitamin B_6; 1.36 mcg Vitamin B_{12}; 14 mcg folic acid

* May be prepared a day ahead or frozen after step 2. See instructions for freezing soups, page 57.

My Favorite Flounder Fillets

Serves: 4 (4 ounces cooked fish = 1 serving)

On the day your local fishmonger has really fresh flounder or heavy sole, buy it and try this recipe. Its success depends solely (no pun intended) on the freshness of the fish.

4 thick flounder or sole fillets*
(1¼ pounds fish)
Juice of ½ lemon
1 tablespoon mild soy sauce
1 teaspoon onion powder
1 teaspoon low-sodium vegetable seasoning (see page 28)
Hungarian paprika

2 tablespoons chopped fresh parsley for garnish
4 lemon wedges for garnish

1. Wash fish in acidulated water (1 pint cold water with 1 tablespoon lemon juice added) and pat dry with paper towels.
2. Line broiler pan with foil. Lay fillets on foil.
3. Sprinkle with lemon juice, soy sauce, onion powder, and vegetable seasoning. Marinate at room temperature for 30 minutes.
4. Sprinkle with paprika and place in preheated broiler, 6 inches from flame.
5. Broil 10 minutes, or until fish flakes.

To Serve: Garnish with chopped parsley and lemon wedges. Serve with steamed potatoes and broccoli spears.

Variation: I like to double my recipe so that I can prepare cold fish salad for the next day. After broiling, wrap the remaining fish in plastic wrap and refrigerate overnight. Serve cold the next day with our Herb Dressing (page 110) on a bed of greens. Garnish with a marinated cucumber salad, sliced beefsteak tomatoes, and red onions sprinkled with chopped fresh basil.

Per serving: 130 calories; 24.6 gm protein; 1.3 gm fat; 4.3 gm carbohydrate; 0.3 gm fiber; 65 mg cholesterol; 1.9 mg iron; 235 mg sodium; 41 mg calcium; 291 mg phosphorus; 370 IU Vitamin A; 0.12 mg thiamine; 0.09 mg riboflavin; 21 mg Vitamin C; 573 mg potassium; 0.99 mg zinc; 2.6 mg niacin; 248 mcg Vitamin B_6; 1.7 mcg Vitamin B_{12}; 1 mcg folic acid

* Whitefish may be substituted, but remember, it is higher in fat.

Filets de Poisson aux Tomates

(Fish Fillets with Tomato Puree)

Serves: 6 (4 ounces cooked fish = 1 serving; ½ cup sauce = 1 serving)

½ cup dry white wine
1 pound fish bones*
1 pint water
Few slices leek (white part only)
1 bouquet garni (3 sprigs parsley, 1 teaspoon thyme, 1 bay leaf)
1 small onion stuck with 2 whole cloves
½ lemon, sliced
1 teaspoon crushed red pepper
1 large shallot, finely chopped
1 large onion, finely chopped
1 leek, chopped (green part only)
2 pounds ripe tomatoes, peeled, seeded, and chopped, or 1 28-ounce can of Italian peeled plum tomatoes, drained and chopped
1 teaspoon thyme
1 bay leaf
1 slice ginger root
Few grains crushed red pepper
2 pounds fish fillets (such as flounder, sea bass, cod, trout, or striped bass)
Chopped fresh parsley and lemon wedges or slices for garnish

1. *To make court bouillon:*** Combine wine, fish bones, water, leek, bouquet garni, onion, lemon, and crushed red pepper in nonaluminum saucepan.
2. Bring to a boil and simmer 30 minutes.
3. Strain and use for steaming the fish in step 6.
4. *To make sauce:* Combine shallot, onion, leek, and tomatoes in a saucepan.
5. Add thyme, bay leaf, ginger root, and pepper and cook slowly 30 minutes. Remove bay leaf and ginger root and puree.
6. *To steam fish:* Place fish fillets on rack in skillet or fish poacher and add about 2 inches of steaming court bouillon.
7. Cover and let steam 5 minutes, or until fish flakes. (It takes about 10 minutes for each inch of thickness of fish.) Serve at once.

To Serve: Place several spoonfuls of puree on a hot plate and top with a fish fillet. Sprinkle fish with chopped parsley and top with a lemon wedge or slice. The meal is completed with a baked potato and chives and steamed julienne green beans.

Per serving: 182 calories; 28.6 gm protein; 1.6 gm fat; 12.7 gm carbohydrate; 3 gm fiber; 76 mg cholesterol; 2.4 mg iron; 128 mg sodium; 52 mg calcium; 349 mg phosphorus; 1459 IU Vitamin A; 0.18 mg thiamine; 0.15 mg riboflavin; 38 mg Vitamin C; 951 mg potassium; 1.45 mg zinc; 3.7 mg niacin; 440 mcg Vitamin B_6; 1.82 mcg Vitamin B_{12}; 19 mcg folic acid

* Do not use salmon, mackerel, or bluefish bones; they are too oily.
** This court bouillon may also be used as a poaching or steaming liquid for other fish. After cooking, it may be frozen for future use; see instructions for freezing soups on page 57.

Simply Baked Salmon Fillets

Serves: 4 (4 ounces cooked fish = 1 serving)

4 5-ounce salmon fillets, at room temperature
3 tablespoons lemon juice
1 tablespoon dry vermouth or white wine
1 teaspoon onion powder
½ teaspoon oregano, crushed
Freshly ground pepper
Hungarian paprika

1. Rinse fish in acidulated water (see page 119) and pat dry with paper towels.

2. Arrange fillets close together in a shallow baking dish sprayed with nonstick spray.

3. Stir together lemon juice, vermouth, onion powder, and crushed oregano. Pour evenly over fish.

4. Sprinkle with freshly ground pepper and Hungarian paprika.

5. Bake in a preheated 350° oven about 10 to 15 minutes (depending upon the thickness of the fish), or until the fish flakes with a fork.

To Serve: Spoon the juices over the fish, garnish with chopped parsley and lemon wedges, and serve with steamed red new potatoes, peas, and a cucumber-yogurt salad.

Per serving: 304 calories; 29 gm protein; 11 gm fat; 1.9 gm carbohydrate; 0.2 gm fiber; 53 mg cholesterol; 1.6 mg iron; 144 mg sodium; 9 mg calcium; 446 mg phosphorus; 342 IU Vitamin A; 0.18 mg thiamine; 0.07 mg riboflavin; 5 mg Vitamin C; 509 mg potassium; 0 mg zinc; 10.5 mg niacin; 7 mcg Vitamin B_6; 0 mcg Vitamin B_{12}; 0 mcg folic acid

Shirley's Barbecued Teriyaki Salmon

Serves: 6 (4 ounces cooked fish = 1 serving)

2 tablespoons mild soy sauce
2 tablespoons dry sherry or sake
3 tablespoons frozen unsweetened pineapple juice
½ teaspoon garlic powder
1 teaspoon low-sodium vegetable seasoning (see page 28)
6 5-ounce fresh salmon fillets (2 pounds fish)
3 cups shredded romaine for serving
12 cherry tomatoes for garnish
2 lemons, cut in 6 wedges, rolled in 2 tablespoons chopped fresh parsley, for garnish

1. Combine soy sauce, sherry, pineapple juice, garlic powder, and vegetable seasoning in a plastic bag.

2. Add salmon fillets to bag and marinate in refrigerator 1 to 2 hours.

3. Spray a metal fish basket with nonstick spray. Place drained salmon in basket and secure tightly.

4. Barbecue on preheated charbroiler about 4 to 5 minutes on each side.

To Serve: Place salmon fillets on a platter, sprinkle with shredded romaine, and garnish with cherry tomatoes and parsley-dipped lemon wedges. Serve with our Tabouli Salad (page 94), crisp sourdough rolls, and, for dessert, a light fresh fruit compote.

Per serving: 308 calories; 29 gm protein; 11 gm fat; 4.7 gm carbohydrate; 0.08 gm fiber; 53 mg cholesterol; 1.38 mg iron; 260 mg sodium; 12 mg calcium; 489 mg phosphorus; 533 IU Vitamin A; 0.22 mg thiamine; 0.08 mg riboflavin; 10.5 mg Vitamin C; 472.5 mg potassium; 0.01 mg zinc; 9.65 mg niacin; 934 mcg Vitamin B_6; 5.29 mcg Vitamin B_{12}; 1 mcg folic acid

Five-Minute Fillet of Sole

Serves: 6 (4 ounces cooked fish = 1 serving)

6 fillets of sole (2 pounds fish)
1½ teaspoons low-sodium vegetable seasoning (see page 28)
⅓ cup nonfat yogurt
1½ tablespoons fresh lemon juice
1 tablespoon salt-free Dijon mustard
1 tablespoon beet horseradish

Chopped fresh parsley for garnish

1. Wash fish in acidulated cold water (see page 119). Pat fish dry with paper towel and sprinkle with vegetable seasoning.
2. Combine yogurt, lemon juice, mustard, and horseradish.
3. Place fish in broiling pan and spread some of yogurt mixture over each fillet.
4. Broil 5 minutes, or until fish flakes. Serve immediately.

To Serve: Garnished with chopped parsley, this fish, served with Zucchini with Linguini (page 249), presents a colorful yet quick dinner plate.

Per serving: 134 calories; 26.1 gm protein; 1.6 gm fat; 1.8 gm carbohydrate; 0.1 gm fiber; 76 mg cholesterol; 1.6 mg iron; 133 mg sodium; 48 mg calcium; 302 mg phosphorus; 80 IU Vitamin A; 0.12 mg thiamine; 0.11 mg riboflavin; 2 mg Vitamin C; 542 mg potassium; 1.06 mg zinc; 2.8 mg niacin; 260 mcg Vitamin B_6; 1.82 mcg Vitamin B_{12}; 0 mcg folic acid

Hap's Vegetable-Stuffed Fillet of Sole

Serves: 6 (4 ounces cooked fish = 1 serving)

24 slim, fresh asparagus spears, tough ends removed
24 green beans, ends removed
6 small carrots, quartered lengthwise
6 fillets of sole (2 pounds fish)
Juice of 1 lemon
8 crushed fennel seeds
1 teaspoon celery seed, crushed
1 teaspoon low-sodium vegetable seasoning (see page 28)
Freshly ground pepper
3 shallots, minced, or 3 green onions, chopped
1 cup dry white wine or vermouth

1. Steam vegetables until barely tender. Set aside.
2. Sprinkle both sides of fish fillets with lemon juice, crushed fennel, celery seed, vegetable seasoning, and ground pepper.
3. Sprinkle bottom of a 13 x 9 x 2-inch baking dish with chopped shallots or green onion.
4. Divide vegetables into 6 portions* and place 1 portion across dark side of each fillet; roll up.
5. Place seam-side-down on shallots in baking dish and pour wine over fish.
6. Place in a preheated 350° oven and bake for 20 minutes, or until fish flakes with a fork. *Serve immediately.*

To Serve: Since you already have your lovely vegetables included in the recipe, complete your meal with a baked potato, baked beet salad (see page 213) on crisp lettuce, and Yogurt Dessert Mold (page 283), for dessert.

Helpful Hint: Asparagus should be lightly peeled with a vegetable peeler to take off the tough outer coating.

Per serving: 205 calories; 28.1 gm protein; 1.7 gm fat; 12.6 gm carbohydrate; 3.6 gm fiber; 76 mg cholesterol; 3.1 mg iron; 148 mg sodium; 89 mg calcium; 374 mg phosphorus; 6191 IU Vitamin A; 0.26 mg thiamine; 0.25 mg riboflavin; 31 mg Vitamin C; 982 mg potassium; 1.26 mg zinc; 4.1 mg niacin; 352 mcg Vitamin B_6; 1.82 mcg Vitamin B_{12}; 4 mcg folic acid

* 1 portion of vegetables equals 4 asparagus spears, 4 green beans, and 4 carrot strips.

Fillet of Sole in Tomato-Orange Sauce

Serves: 8 (3 ounces cooked fish = 1 serving)

We seldom think of oranges and tomatoes as the right combination of sweet and savory flavors, but here they are—elegant but easy.

8 Petrale sole fillets (2 pounds fish)
Juice of ½ lemon
1 teaspoon low-sodium vegetable seasoning (see page 28)
¼ cup dry vermouth or white wine
1 large onion, chopped
2 shallots chopped
4 ripe, large tomatoes, peeled, seeded, and chopped, or 6 canned Italian plum tomatoes, drained
1 cup fresh orange juice
2 tablespoons frozen unsweetened orange juice concentrate
2 tablespoons frozen unsweetened apple juice concentrate
Few grains crushed red pepper
½ teaspoon herbes de Provence for fish

Fresh parsley sprigs and orange slices for garnish

1. Season sole fillets with lemon juice and vegetable seasoning. Roll fillets, skin-side-inside, and place in a shallow baking dish sprayed with a nonstick spray.
2. *To make sauce:* Place vermouth in small saucepan and bring to a boil. Add onion and shallots and sauté until transparent.
3. Add tomatoes and simmer 10 minutes.
4. Add orange juice, apple juice and orange juice concentrates, red pepper, and herbs and simmer 5 minutes.
5. Pour sauce over fish fillets in baking dish and bake in a preheated 350° oven for 25 to 30 minutes, or until fish flakes with a fork.

To Serve: Garnish fish with parsley sprigs and orange slices; to complete meal, serve steamed peas and pea pods with toasted sesame seeds and parsleyed brown rice.

Per serving: 151 calories; 20.7 gm protein; 1.3 gm fat; 12.7 gm carbohydrate; 1.7 gm fiber; 57 mg cholesterol; 2 mg iron; 95 mg sodium; 48 mg calcium; 262 mg phosphorus; 845 IU Vitamin A; 0.16 mg thiamine; 0.11 mg riboflavin; 42 mg Vitamin C; 714 mg potassium; 1.01 mg zinc; 2.7 mg niacin; 304 mcg Vitamin B_6; 1.36 mcg Vitamin B_{12}; 12 mcg folic acid

Eva's Easy-Does-It Poached Salmon

Serves: 2 (4 ounces cooked fish = 1 serving)

1 cup water
1 cup dry white wine or vermouth
1 bay leaf
⅛ teaspoon freshly ground crushed red pepper
1 10-ounce salmon steak or fillet
1 stalk celery, cut in 1-inch pieces
2 small carrots, cut in 1-inch pieces
4 slices onion
1 small green pepper, seeded and cut in 1-inch pieces
4 sprigs fresh parsley or fresh dill
3 lemon slices

1. Place water, wine, bay leaf, and crushed red pepper in a small skillet. Bring to a boil.
2. Add salmon, celery, carrots, onions, green pepper, and parsley.
3. Lay lemon slices on top of salmon.
4. Bring to a second boil, lower heat, cover skillet, and simmer 10 to 15 minutes, or until fish flakes with a fork. (Remember the rule of thumb is 10 minutes of cooking time for each inch of thickness.)
5. Cool in cooking liquid.

To Serve: Serve with the vegetables (they will be crisp) and lemon wedges. To complete your meal, add a sliced tomato salad with mustard-yogurt dressing and Pritikin whole wheat bread, and finish with a serving of fresh fruit.

Helpful Hint: Save strained fish stock; store in refrigerator for up to 3 days, or freeze to use for poaching liquid for salmon at some future date.

Per serving: 319 calories; 33.1 gm protein; 11 gm fat; 7.7 gm carbohydrate; 1.6 gm fiber; 53 mg cholesterol; 2.3 mg iron; 144 mg sodium; 36 mg calcium; 292 mg phosphorus; 2759 IU Vitamin A; 0.29 mg thiamine; 1.16 mg riboflavin; 40 mg Vitamin C; 809 mg potassium; 0.15 mg zinc; 10.6 mg niacin; 87 mcg Vitamin B_6; 0 mcg Vitamin B_{12}; 11 mcg folic acid

Easy Summer Fish Casserole

Serves: 6 (3 ounces cooked fish = 1 serving)

2 medium russet potatoes, washed and thinly sliced
1 teaspoon low-sodium vegetable seasoning (see page 28)
½ small onion, thinly sliced
½ pound fresh mushrooms, cleaned and sliced
1 pound small zucchini, thinly sliced
4 ripe tomatoes, peeled, seeded, and chopped, or 6 canned Italian plum tomatoes, drained and chopped
6 4-ounce fillets of flounder, sole, scrod, or snapper (1½ pounds fish)
Juice of ½ lemon
1 teaspoon low-sodium vegetable seasoning (see page 28)
1 teaspoon thyme or herbes de Provence
1 tablespoon fresh basil, chopped, or 1 teaspoon dry basil, crushed
Hungarian paprika
3 green onions, thinly sliced
2 tablespoons dry vermouth or white wine

6 thin lemon slices for garnish
3 tablespoons chopped fresh Italian parsley for garnish

1. Spray a 2-quart shallow baking dish with nonstick spray.

2. Layer sliced potatoes in baking dish and season with the first teaspoon vegetable seasoning. Arrange sliced onion over potatoes and cover with foil. Bake in a preheated 350° oven for 15 minutes.

*3. Place mushrooms, zucchini, and tomatoes over partially cooked potato mixture. Arrange fish over vegetables. Sprinkle with lemon juice, the second teaspoon vegetable seasoning, thyme, basil, and Hungarian paprika. Cut diagonal slices in fish and top with sliced green onions and dry vermouth.

4. Bake 20 to 25 minutes more, *uncovered*, or until fish flakes with fork. If not sufficiently browned, place under broiler for a minute or two before serving.

To Serve: Garnish with lemon slices and chopped parsley. Complete the meal with a pickled beet and endive salad.

Per serving: 189 calories; 23.6 gm protein; 1.5 gm fat; 20.5 gm carbohydrate; 6.7 gm fiber; 57 mg cholesterol; 3.5 mg iron; 102 mg sodium; 93 mg calcium; 358 mg phosphorus; 1438 IU Vitamin A; 0.29 mg thiamine; 0.37 mg riboflavin; 53 mg Vitamin C; 1223 mg potassium; 1.03 mg zinc; 6 mg niacin; 349 mcg Vitamin B_6; 1.36 mcg Vitamin B_{12}; 20 mcg folic acid

* The dish may be prepared through step 3, then covered with foil and placed in the refrigerator until you are ready to finish the cooking sometime later in the day or even the next day. Hence, you could prepare it in the morning and then do the final baking in the evening just before serving dinner.

Poached Halibut, English Style

Serves: 6 (3 ounces cooked fish = 1 serving)

Adding milk to your poaching liquid gives the fish a sweeter and milder taste.

6 1-inch-thick halibut fillets (1½ pounds fish), skinned
3 cups fish stock*
1 cup nonfat milk
1 bay leaf

Lemon wedges and watercress for garnish

1. Place fish in skillet.
2. Heat stock with milk. Pour hot mixture over fish; add bay leaf.
3. Cover and *simmer gently* for about 10 minutes, or until fish flakes.

To Serve: Remove fish from skillet carefully with broad spatula, place on a warm platter, and surround with boiled potatoes, lemon wedges, and watercress.

Variation: *To make Halibut with Red Pepper Sauce:* Roast 1½ pounds red peppers as described on page 100. In blender or food processor with steel blade, puree peppers. Add cayenne and freshly ground pepper to taste. Blend until smooth. Before removing fish from poaching liquid, place a layer of red pepper sauce on a platter; then top with fish and surround with boiled potatoes, steamed carrots, lemon wedges, and watercress.

Per serving: 134 calories; 25.4 gm protein; 1.4 gm fat; 3.3 gm carbohydrate; 0 gm fiber; 57 mg cholesterol; 0.9 mg iron; 68 mg sodium; 26 mg calcium; 280 mg phosphorus; 510 IU Vitamin A; 0.08 mg thiamine; 0.1 mg riboflavin; 0 mg Vitamin C; 523 gm potassium; 0.03 mg zinc; 9.4 mg niacin; 4 mcg Vitamin B_6; 0.03 mcg Vitamin B_{12}; 0 mcg folic acid

* If you have no fish stock, use all milk with 1 slice of onion and a bouquet garni (4 sprigs parsley, 1 bay leaf, 1 teaspoon thyme, ½ teaspoon crushed red pepper).

Herbed Baked Halibut

Serves: 4 (4 ounces cooked fish = 1 serving)

4 5-ounce fresh halibut or scrod fillets
Juice of ½ lemon or lime
1 teaspoon crushed Italian herb seasoning
Freshly ground pepper
1 8-ounce can salt-free tomato sauce
1 small onion, chopped
½ cup chopped celery
1 green pepper, chopped
2 ripe plum tomatoes, chopped
6 fresh mushrooms, sliced

1. Sprinkle halibut with lemon juice, herb seasoning, and pepper. Marinate 10 to 20 minutes.
2. Pour a bit of tomato sauce in the bottom of a small, shallow baking dish.
3. Lay fish on top of sauce and bake in upper third of a preheated 375° oven for 10 minutes.
4. Layer top of fish with onion, celery, green pepper, tomatoes, and mushrooms.
5. Pour remaining tomato sauce over vegetables and bake at 375° for 20 to 25 minutes, or until fish flakes.

To Serve: Serve with Steamed Brown Rice (page 254) with peas and baked beet salad (page 213). If you like, the fish may be prepared and served directly in individual baking dishes.

Per serving: 252 calories; 32.8 gm protein; 2.2 gm fat; 14.7 gm carbohydrate; 3 gm fiber; 71 mg cholesterol; 3.1 mg iron; 107 mg sodium; 77 mg calcium; 372 mg phosphorus; 2266 IU Vitamin A; 0.21 mg thiamine; 0.25 mg riboflavin; 60 mg Vitamin C; 1053 mg potassium; 0.23 mg zinc; 13.6 mg niacin; 198 mcg Vitamin B_6; 0 mcg Vitamin B_{12}; 19 mcg folic acid

Sea Bass with Julienne Vegetables

Serves: 6 (4 ounces cooked fish = 1 serving)

If all the vegetables are cut ahead of time, this dish will only take about 20 to 25 minutes to prepare.

2 pounds sea bass or heavy sole fillets
2 shallots, minced
Dry white wine
1 teaspoon low-sodium vegetable seasoning (see page 28)
2 turnips, peeled and cut julienne
4 carrots, peeled, and cut julienne
8 green beans, cut julienne
6 fresh mushrooms, cleaned and cut julienne
1 teaspoon herbes de Provence
⅓ cup nonfat evaporated milk, or ⅓ cup nonfat yogurt mixed with 1 teaspoon cornstarch
Few grains cayenne pepper
Lemon juice

Chopped fresh parsley for garnish

1. Cut fish into 6 portions.
2. Sprinkle shallots on bottom of shallow casserole dish and lay fish in dish on top of shallots. Add white wine to barely cover fish. Sprinkle with vegetable seasoning.
3. Bake fish in a preheated 350° oven for 10 to 15 minutes, or until fish flakes.*
4. Sauté vegetables in ¼ cup liquid from fish; add herbs.
5. Pour off remaining liquid from fish; reduce by half.
6. Add nonfat evaporated milk or yogurt mixed with cornstarch. Simmer slowly, stir, add cayenne pepper, sautéed vegetables, and lemon juice to taste.

To Serve: This is an elegant meal-in-one, best served on individual plates. Place fish on a bed of *al dente* linguini, top with vegetables and sauce, and garnish with chopped parsley.

Per serving: 187 calories; 34.2 gm protein; 1 gm fat; 8.5 gm carbohydrate; 2.6 gm fiber; 83 mg cholesterol; 2.4 mg iron; 150 mg sodium; 132 mg calcium; 258 mg phosphorus; 5677 IU Vitamin A; 0.23 mg thiamine; 0.42 mg riboflavin; 10 mg Vitamin C; 840 mg potassium; 0.2 mg zinc; 5.6 mg niacin; 89 mcg Vitamin B_6; 0 mcg Vitamin B_{12}; 6 mcg folic acid

* Keep fish warm during remainder of preparation by covering with foil.

Baked Salmon Loaf

Serves: 6

1 small zucchini
1 small carrot
½ onion
1 6-ounce russet potato, peeled, diced, and cooked
2 egg whites
1 teaspoon Worcestershire sauce
Dash cayenne pepper
1 tablespoon lemon juice
1 1-pound can red salmon, drained, bones and skin removed
1 cup fresh whole wheat bread crumbs, made from Pritikin bread
⅔ cup nonfat milk
1 teaspoon low-sodium baking powder
1 10-ounce package frozen mixed vegetables

Watercress for garnish

1. Place zucchini, carrot, and onion in food processor. Process until minced.
2. Add potato, egg whites, Worcestershire sauce, cayenne, and lemon juice. Blend well.
3. Add flaked salmon, bread crumbs, and milk; process until just combined.
4. Add baking powder and blend briefly.
5. Spray a 9 x 5-inch loaf pan with nonstick spray.
6. Place half of salmon mixture in pan, layer with frozen mixed vegetables, and top with remainder of salmon mixture.
7. Bake in a preheated 375° oven for 45 minutes, or until loaf is firm and lightly browned.

To Serve: Unmold onto a heated platter, slice, and garnish with watercress. To complete the meal, serve steamed asparagus, baked potatoes, and Cabbage, Apple, and Raisin Slaw (see page 89).

Per serving: 257 calories; 21.8 gm protein; 8.9 gm fat; 22.5 gm carbohydrate; 2.4 gm fiber; 27 mg cholesterol; 2.3 mg iron; 172 mg sodium; 183 mg calcium; 302 mg phosphorus; 3532 IU Vitamin A; 0.24 mg thiamine; 0.22 mg riboflavin; 16 mg Vitamin C; 677 mg potassium; 0.27 mg zinc; 6.9 mg niacin; 88 mcg Vitamin B_6; 0.12 mcg Vitamin B_{12}; 6 mcg folic acid

Halibut Creole for a Crowd

Serves: 18 (1 cup = 1 serving)

Entertaining a large number of people can be a chore, but this adaptation of my sister Edie's high-cholesterol shrimp creole makes informal entertaining a pleasure for both host and guests.

½ cup dry white wine or vermouth
3 cups diced green pepper
5 cups diced onion
2 cups diced celery with leaves
½ cup chopped fresh Italian parsley
2 28-ounce cans Italian plum tomatoes, crushed, in sauce
1 8-ounce can salt-free tomato sauce
1 teaspoon low-sodium vegetable seasoning (see page 28)
2 bay leaves
1 teaspoon curry powder, or to taste
Dash cayenne pepper
4 pounds fresh halibut or haddock fillets, cut in 1-inch dice

1. Place wine in Dutch oven, bring to a boil, and add green pepper, onion, and celery. Sauté until transparent, about 10 minutes.

*2. Add parsley, tomatoes, tomato sauce, vegetable seasoning, bay leaves, curry, and cayenne pepper. Simmer 45 minutes to 1 hour. Stir from time to time to prevent sticking.

3. Add diced fish to simmering Creole sauce. Simmer 15 to 20 minutes before serving.

To Serve: Place Creole mixture in a large, heated tureen or chafing dish and serve with a casserole of Steamed Brown Rice (page 254). Complete the meal with a crisp green salad with our Vinaigrette Dressing (page 12), a platter of steamed vegetables, hot sourdough baguettes, and Citron Soufflé (page 292) for dessert.

Per serving: 175 calories; 23.3 gm protein; 1.5 gm fat; 11.1 gm carbohydrate; 1.9 gm fiber; 50 mg cholesterol; 1.9 mg iron; 183 mg sodium; 44 mg calcium; 259 mg phosphorus; 1553 IU Vitamin A; 0.16 mg thiamine; 0.15 mg riboflavin; 56 mg Vitamin C; 809 mg potassium; 0.32 mg zinc; 9.4 mg niacin; 204 mcg Vitamin B_6; 0 mcg Vitamin B_{12}; 18 mcg folic acid

* May be prepared the day before through step 2.

Broiled Swordfish Steaks

Serves: 4 (4 ounces cooked fish = 1 serving)

1 tablespoon mild soy sauce
1 teaspoon garlic powder
Juice of ½ lemon
4 5-ounce swordfish (or halibut) steaks
Hungarian paprika

Lemon wedges and chopped fresh parsley for garnish

1. Combine soy sauce, garlic powder, and lemon juice.
2. Pour over fish in plastic bag and let marinate at least 30 minutes or several hours.
3. Drain fish (reserving marinade)* and place on broiling pan, sprinkle with paprika, and broil 10 minutes, or until fish flakes. If fish seems to dry excessively while broiling, baste with reserved marinade. Serve immediately.

To Serve: Garnish with chopped parsley and lemon wedges. To round out the meal, serve steamed, frozen salt-free French-cut green beans and corn, crisp French bread or sourdough rolls, and a lightly seasoned green salad. Top with a slightly chilled 4-ounce glass of California chardonnay.

***Helpful Hint:** The marinade may be refrigerated for about 10 days and used for basting other broiled fish dishes.

Per serving: 186 calories; 27.7 gm protein; 5.7 gm fat; 1.3 gm carbohydrate; 0.1 gm fiber; 62 mg cholesterol; 1.4 mg iron; 183 mg sodium; 28 mg calcium; 225 mg phosphorus; 1946 IU Vitamin A; 0.08 mg thiamine; 0.08 mg riboflavin; 3 mg Vitamin C; 657 mg potassium; 0 mg zinc; 9.1 mg niacin; 3 mcg Vitamin B_6; 0 mcg Vitamin B_{12}; 0 mcg folic acid

Jellied Fish

Serves: 8 (3 ounces cooked fish = 1 serving)

3 pounds striped bass or pike
2 teaspoons low-sodium vegetable seasoning (see page 28)
1 cup apple cider vinegar, brown rice vinegar, or white wine vinegar
1 cup cold water
3 bay leaves
1 teaspoon pickling spice
Few sprigs fresh Italian parsley
2½ large onions, sliced
1½ tablespoons unsweetened apple juice concentrate
½ lemon, sliced
2 carrots, sliced ¼ inch thick

1. Cut fish in 1-inch slices. Wash well in acidulated water (1 pint cold water with 1 tablespoon of lemon juice added), season with vegetable seasoning, and refrigerate several hours.

2. Combine the vinegar, water, bay leaves, pickling spice, parsley, 1 slice of onion, and apple juice concentrate and simmer partially covered for 25 minutes.

3. Add lemon slices, cook 5 minutes, and remove lemon slices (reserve).

4. Add fish and carrots and simmer gently about 15 to 20 minutes, or until the fish flakes.

5. Place fish in casserole, alternating in layers with remaining sliced raw onions and cooked carrots.

6. Pour strained hot cooking liquid over fish. Top with cooked lemon slices, cover, and chill overnight before serving. May be prepared ahead and stored in the refrigerator several weeks.

To Serve: Serve Jellied Fish on lettuce leaves with a horseradish sauce, boiled potatoes, and hearty whole wheat bread for a nice summertime supper.

Per serving: 221 calories; 26 gm protein; 4.8 gm fat; 10.4 gm carbohydrate; 2 gm fiber; 94 mg cholesterol; 2.9 mg iron; 132 mg sodium; 72 mg calcium; 396 mg phosphorus; 2223 IU Vitamin A; 0.23 mg thiamine; 0.09 mg riboflavin; 10 mg Vitamin C; 641 mg potassium; 0.24 mg zinc; 0.4 mg niacin; 90 mcg Vitamin B_6; 0 mcg Vitamin B_{12}; 15 mcg folic acid

Sweet and Pungent Fish

Serves: 6 (4 ounces cooked fish = 1 serving)

6 5-ounce fillets of sole, halibut, haddock, or red snapper (2 pounds fish)
Juice of ½ lemon
1 teaspoon low-sodium vegetable seasoning (see page 28)
⅓ cup brown rice vinegar
2 tablespoons cornstarch
3 tablespoons frozen unsweetened apple juice concentrate
1 tablespoon mild soy sauce
½ tablespoon ground ginger
1 20-ounce can unsweetened pineapple chunks with juice
1 green pepper, seeded and cut in strips
1 red pepper, seeded and cut in strips
1 medium onion, chopped
2 tablespoons dry sherry

1. Arrange fish fillets in a shallow glass or ceramic baking dish sprayed with nonstick spray and sprinkle with lemon juice and vegetable seasoning.

2. *To make sauce:* Combine vinegar, cornstarch, apple juice concentrate, soy sauce, and ginger in a saucepan.

3. Cook over moderate heat, stirring constantly, until thickened. *Do not overcook.*

4. Add pineapple chunks and juice, green and red pepper strips, onion, and sherry. Blend.

5. Pour sauce over fish and bake in a preheated 350° oven for 30 minutes.

To Serve: Serve with Steamed Brown Rice (see page 254) and peas.

Variation: This pungent sauce is also delicious served over a whole steamed red snapper, as you frequently find it served in Chinese restaurants.

Per serving: 189 calories; 23.5 gm protein; 1.3 gm fat; 19.9 gm carbohydrate; 1.3 gm fiber; 66 mg cholesterol; 2 mg iron; 208 mg sodium; 45 mg calcium; 285 mg phosphorus; 884 IU Vitamin A; 0.20 mg thiamine; 0.13 mg riboflavin; 70 mg Vitamin C; 729 mg potassium; 1 mg zinc; 2.8 mg niacin; 361 mcg Vitamin B_6; 1.59 mcg Vitamin B_{12}; 6.8 mcg folic acid

Red Snapper à la Mexicaine

Serves: 4 (4 ounces cooked fish = 1 serving)

4 5-ounce red snapper fillets
1 tablespoon lime juice
2 shallots, minced
1 large clove garlic, minced
¼ cup dry white wine or vermouth
4 ripe tomatoes, peeled, seeded, and chopped, or 5 canned Italian plum tomatoes, drained
Dash Tabasco
3 tablespoons chopped fresh cilantro or fresh parsley
1 tablespoon chopped mixed fresh oregano, thyme, and chervil, or 1½ teaspoons dried herb mixture

Lime slices and fresh cilantro or parsley sprigs for garnish

1. Spray a shallow flameproof baking dish with nonstick spray, arrange fillets close together in dish, and sprinkle with lime juice.
2. Sauté minced shallots and garlic in white wine or vermouth until wilted.
3. Add chopped tomatoes and Tabasco, and cook about 2 minutes.
4. Add cilantro and herbs.
5. Pour tomato mixture over fish and cover with waxed paper.
6. Place in a preheated 350° oven and bake 25 to 30 minutes, or until fish flakes.
7. Lift fish to platter carefully. Place baking dish over flame and reduce liquid a bit.

To Serve: Pour sauce over fish and garnish with thin lime slices and cilantro or parsley sprigs. Warm corn tortillas and a papaya and butter lettuce salad make wonderful accompaniments.

Per serving: 183 calories; 30 gm protein; 1.6 gm fat; 9 gm carbohydrate; 2.3 gm fiber; 78 mg cholesterol; 2.6 mg iron; 103 mg sodium; 62 mg calcium; 351 mg phosphorus; 1536 IU Vitamin A; 0.34 mg thiamine; 0.1 mg riboflavin; 39 mg Vitamin C; 873 mg potassium; 0.28 mg zinc; 6.1 mg niacin; 153 mcg Vitamin B_6; 0 mcg Vitamin B_{12}; 12 mcg folic acid

Game
Better Than Fair Game

Life-style is important in animals as well as humans. Both game hens and game animals are lower in fat than the domestic ones because of the type of food they eat and the increased exercise they get while searching for it. Since cornish game hens have little fat under the skin, we do not suggest removing the skin before cooking since the meat would become excessively dry. It may, of course, be removed before eating, if you choose.

Venison Stew Mexicana
(Chili Verde)

Serves: 6 (1 cup = 1 serving)

Venison is a pleasant change for a stew. The long, slow cooking of this recipe helps tenderize the meat, and the Mexican-style seasonings complement its flavor.

2 pounds venison, cut in ¾-inch cubes
Juice of 1½ limes
1 teaspoon low-sodium vegetable seasoning (see page 28)
3 cups peeled, seeded, and coarsely chopped ripe tomatoes, or 1 28-ounce can Italian plum tomatoes, drained and chopped
1 large onion, chopped
2 cloves garlic, minced
1 4-ounce can green chilies, chopped (for a spicier flavor, use 2 cans chilies)
1 teaspoon oregano, crushed
½ teaspoon ground cumin
Freshly ground pepper

1. Place venison in a single layer in an ovenproof casserole and season with lime juice and vegetable seasoning.
2. Brown venison under broiler until golden brown on all sides.

*3. After meat is browned, add remaining ingredients, stir to pick up drippings, and cover.

4. Simmer in a preheated 325° oven until meat is tender, approximately 2 hours. (The cooking time, of course, depends upon the tenderness of the meat used.)

5. Taste, and adjust seasonings before serving.

To Serve: This recipe makes a lovely entrée for a Mexican-style dinner served with hot tortillas, refried beans,** and Steamed Brown Rice (see page 254). My family loves to spoon the meat mixture into corn tortillas, roll it up, and eat it à la chili verde.

Variation: 3 cups diced cooked turkey may be used instead of venison, in which case simmer for 1 hour only.

Per serving: 224 calories; 33.3 gm protein; 5.4 gm fat; 6.9 gm carbohydrate; 2.1 gm fiber; 98 mg cholesterol; 3.8 mg iron; 103 mg sodium; 53 mg calcium; 415 mg phosphorus; 1814 IU Vitamin A; 0.44 mg thiamine; 0.79 mg riboflavin; 0.33 mg Vitamin C; 750 mg potassium; 0.23 mg zinc; 10.3 mg niacin; 71 mcg Vitamin B_6; 0 mcg Vitamin B_{12}; 10 mcg folic acid

* May be prepared through step 3 and reheated for use the next day. I happen to prefer making the stew a day or two before, since, of course, as with all stews, the flavor improves as it stands. This stew also freezes beautifully for future use.

** Do not use regular canned refried beans; they are too high in fat and sodium. Puree a can of chili beans with an onion. It works quite well. Or look for vegetarian refried beans.

Orange-Glazed Cornish Hens

Serves: 8 (½ Cornish game hen = 1 serving)

⅓ cup finely chopped onion
1 shallot, finely chopped
1 large clove garlic, minced
3 tablespoons minced fresh Italian parsley
2 cups fresh orange juice
Grated zest of 1 orange
1 teaspoon mild soy sauce
4 Cornish game hens, halved, wing tips and all visible fat removed
Juice of 1 lemon
1 teaspoon low-sodium vegetable seasoning (see page 28)
Freshly ground pepper
½ cup seeded muscat raisins
½ cup chopped chestnuts
2 tablespoons cornstarch
3 tablespoons cold water

3 cups Steamed Brown Rice (see page 254) or wild rice for serving
Watercress for garnish
3 navel oranges, peeled with sharp knife, all white removed, cut into ¼-inch slices, for garnish

1. Combine onion, shallot, garlic, parsley, orange juice, zest, and soy sauce in a large bowl.

2. Add hens, mix, and marinate several hours at room temperature.

3. Remove hens from marinade and place skin-side-up in a shallow casserole. Season with lemon juice, vegetable seasoning, and pepper.

4. Place in upper third of a preheated 400° oven. Bake uncovered for 30 minutes.

5. Heat remaining marinade until boiling and pour over hens. Sprinkle with raisins and chestnuts.

6. Cover and bake 30 additional minutes. Remove hens from casserole and keep warm.

7. Blend cornstarch with the 3 tablespoons cold water. Blend into sauce in baking dish. Cook over medium heat until thickened.

To Serve: Place rice on a large, warm serving platter, arrange hens on rice, and spoon sauce with raisins and chestnuts over hens. Surround with watercress and orange slices and serve immediately.

Per serving: 512 calories; 55.1 gm protein; 12.9 gm fat; 41.4 gm carbohydrate; 3.4 gm fiber; 100 mg cholesterol; 4.1 mg iron; 125 mg sodium; 58 mg calcium; 348 mg phosphorus; 613 IU Vitamin A; 0.25 mg thiamine; 0.31 mg riboflavin; 38 mg Vitamin C; 797 mg potassium; 3.18 mg zinc; 18 mg niacin; 921 mcg Vitamin B_6; 0.72 mcg Vitamin B_{12}; 10 mcg folic acid

Irene's Cornish Game Hens Supreme

Serves: 8 (½ Cornish game hen = 1 serving)

An evening of good food and good conversation shared with good friends is a memory to be cherished. My dear friend Irene served this delicious dish on one such occasion.

1 medium onion, chopped
1 shallot, chopped
1 carrot, chopped
4 our Bouillon Cubes, melted (see page 25), or ¼ cup our Chicken Stock (see page 26)
2 small heads green cabbage (3 pounds), shredded
1 teaspoon thyme or herbes de Provence
½ cup dry white wine or vermouth
½ cup seeded muscat raisins
4 Cornish game hens, halved, wing tips and all visible fat removed
Juice of ½ lemon
2 teaspoons low-sodium vegetable seasoning (see page 28)
Hungarian paprika
¼ cup dry white wine

Chopped fresh parsley for garnish

1. Sauté onion, shallot, and carrot in a sauté pan with bouillon cubes until they are transparent. Stir constantly.
2. Add shredded cabbage, thyme, the ½ cup white wine, and raisins. Cover and cook until wilted (about 20 minutes).
3. Season halved game hens with lemon juice, vegetable seasoning, and paprika. Place in roaster. Brown under broiler about 7 minutes on each side.
4. Add cabbage mixture to roaster, lay browned game hens on top, and sprinkle with the ¼ cup dry white wine.
5. Cover and bake in a preheated 450° oven for 10 minutes.
6. Remove cover and continue baking at 350° until tender, about 20 to 30 minutes.

To Serve: Serve hens and cabbage on an attractive serving platter, surrounded with broiled tomatoes and garnished with chopped parsley. Cooked pasta shells with peas make a nice accompaniment.

Per serving: 430 calories; 54 gm protein; 8.5 gm fat; 22.8 gm carbohydrate; 7.4 gm fiber; 107 mg cholesterol; 4.1 mg iron; 122 mg sodium; 136 mg calcium; 348 mg phosphorus; 1727 IU Vitamin A; 0.25 mg thiamine; 0.31 mg riboflavin; 85 mg Vitamin C; 1042 mg potassium; 3.92 mg zinc; 18 mg niacin; 1197 mcg Vitamin B_6; 0.72 mcg Vitamin B_{12}; 66 mcg folic acid

Rock Hens Rôti

Serves: 8 (½ Cornish game hen with stuffing = 1 serving)

4 1-pound Cornish game hens, halved, wing tips and all visible fat removed
1 cup cold water
1 carrot, sliced
1 slice onion
1 bay leaf
1 teaspoon thyme
½ small onion, minced
1 clove garlic, minced
1 shallot, minced
1 our Bouillon Cube, melted (see page 25)
½ 10-ounce package frozen spinach, defrosted and squeezed dry
½ teaspoon herbes de Provence or basil, crushed
3 tablespoons chopped fresh parsley
Few grains crushed red pepper
1½ cups our Yogurt Cheese (see page 305) or skim milk ricotta
1 tablespoon grated Sap Sago cheese, toasted (see page 15)
2 egg whites
1 tablespoon low-sodium vegetable seasoning (see page 28)
2 teaspoons grated lemon zest or orange zest
½ cup fresh orange juice
3 tablespoons salt-free Dijon mustard with herbs
1 teaspoon Worcestershire sauce
½ cup white wine

Watercress for serving

1. While preparing hens, cook Cornish hen stock for sauce. In a saucepan combine water, hen giblets and wing tips, carrot, onion, bay leaf, and thyme. Simmer 30 minutes.
2. *To make stuffing:* Sauté onion, garlic, and shallot in the bouillon cube. When transparent, add spinach, sauté 2 minutes, and add herbs, parsley, and pepper.
3. Cool slightly and add cheeses and egg whites. Blend entire mixture thoroughly.
4. Using kitchen shears and your fingers, loosen hen skin, forming pockets to hold the stuffing.
5. Season hens with vegetable seasoning, especially under loosened skin.
6. Stuff under loosened skin with 2–3 tablespoons cheese mixture. Secure skin with toothpicks.
7. Place hens in roasting pan breasts up, sprinkle with lemon zest, and bake in a preheated 350° oven for 45 minutes.

8. While hens are roasting make sauce. Strain Cornish hen stock. Combine 1 cup stock with orange juice, mustard, and Worcestershire sauce. Bring to a boil.

9. After hens have roasted 45 minutes, reduce oven to 325°, pour sauce over hens, and bake 30 to 50 additional minutes, basting hens with sauce every 15 to 20 minutes.

10. Transfer hens to a warm serving platter. Degrease sauce, add ½ cup dry white wine, cook 2 minutes, strain sauce, and reduce for 5 minutes.

11. Taste sauce, adjust seasoning, and pour into a warmed gravy boat to serve with hens at table.

To Serve: Place roasted hens on a bed of watercress and surround with cherry tomatoes and steamed broccoli.

Per serving: 423 calories; 59 gm protein; 16 gm fat; 6.8 gm carbohydrate; 1 gm fiber; 113 mg cholesterol; 4.1 mg iron; 240 mg sodium; 178 mg calcium; 357 mg phosphorus; 2234 IU Vitamin A; 0.16 mg thiamine; 0.4 mg riboflavin; 22 mg Vitamin C; 697 mg potassium; 3.89 mg zinc; 16.9 mg niacin; 933 mcg Vitamin B_6; 0.85 mcg Vitamin B_{12}; 22 mcg folic acid

Poultry

It's Easy to Wing It with These Recipes

In these times of rising food costs, the popularity of poultry is at an all-time high. This is not only because of its low cost per serving and low cholesterol content, but also because of the many different and delectable ways it can be prepared. Always remove all visible fat and skin and the wing tips (*including the double-bone portion* of the wings, because it is extremely difficult to skin; the first portion can remain) from poultry *before* preparing. Discard the fat, but the scraps of skin, the giblets, and the wing tips should be stored in a container in your freezer to use in preparing stock.

Chicken à l'Orange with Sunchokes

Serves: 12 (4 ounces cooked chicken = 1 serving)

Sunchokes, sometimes called Jerusalem artichokes, are tuberous starchy vegetables that look something like ginger root. If they are not available in your market, substitute slices of russet potatoes.

½ onion, chopped
1 carrot, chopped
1 shallot, chopped
1 stalk celery, chopped
1 teaspoon Worcestershire sauce
3 our Bouillon Cubes, melted (see page 25)
6 whole chicken breasts (6 pounds chicken), split, skinned, all visible fat removed
Juice of 1 lemon
2 teaspoons Hungarian paprika
1 teaspoon garlic powder
1 teaspoon low-sodium vegetable seasoning (see page 28)
3–4 sunchokes, cut in ½-inch slices
12 ounces pearl onions, fresh or frozen
1 10-ounce package frozen artichoke hearts, or 6 canned artichoke bottoms, rinsed and drained
2 cups fresh orange juice
½ cup dry vermouth or dry white wine
2 tablespoons cornstarch (optional)

1. Sauté onion, carrot, shallot, celery, and soy sauce in bouillon cubes until transparent. Transfer mixture to an ovenproof casserole.
2. Season chicken breasts with lemon juice, paprika, garlic powder, and vegetable seasoning and place on sautéed vegetables.
3. Add sunchokes, peeled pearl onions, and artichokes.
4. Pour orange juice and vermouth over chicken and vegetables.
5. Bake uncovered in a preheated 375° oven for 50 to 60 minutes, or until lightly browned.
6. Remove chicken to a warmed serving platter. If you wish, thicken remaining juice and vegetables with cornstarch before spooning over chicken.

To Serve: Serve with Wild Rice, Brown Rice, and Mushrooms (page 257) and steamed vegetables.

Per serving: 211 calories; 29.1 gm protein; 4.6 gm fat; 12.7 gm carbohydrate; 0.8 gm fiber; 99 mg cholesterol; 3 mg iron; 104 mg sodium; 34 mg calcium; 270 mg phosphorus; 982 IU Vitamin A; 0.16 mg thiamine; 0.29 mg riboflavin; 27 mg Vitamin C; 534 mg potassium; 0.05 mg zinc; 10.8 mg niacin; 39 mcg Vitamin B_6; 0 mcg Vitamin B_{12}; 3 mcg folic acid

Baked Chicken Breasts Supreme

Serves: 12 (4 ounces cooked chicken = 1 serving)

This recipe uses seasoned yogurt as a marinade for chicken breasts, adding a piquant and interesting taste.

6 whole chicken breasts (about 6 pounds chicken), skinned, boned, halved, and flattened*
2 tablespoons lemon juice
3 cloves garlic, minced
1½ tablespoons mild soy sauce, or 1 tablespoon Worcestershire sauce (it has ⅓ the sodium)
1 teaspoon Hungarian paprika
2 teaspoons celery seed
1 tablespoon salt-free mustard
Few grains crushed red pepper
1 cup nonfat yogurt
1 cup dry whole wheat bread crumbs
Hungarian paprika

3 tablespoons chopped fresh parsley for garnish
Watercress for garnish
18 cherry tomatoes for garnish

1. Combine lemon juice, garlic, soy sauce, paprika, celery seed, mustard, crushed red pepper, and yogurt in a bowl. Mix well.
2. Add chicken breasts to yogurt mixture and marinate overnight (24 to 48 hours).
3. Remove chicken breasts from yogurt mixture and arrange in rows in a shallow 3-quart baking dish sprayed with nonstick spray.
4. Sprinkle with whole wheat bread crumbs and paprika and bake in a preheated 350° oven for 45 to 55 minutes.

To Serve: Sprinkle with chopped parsley, arrange watercress and tomatoes attractively around chicken, and serve.

Variation: For variety in flavor, a bed of Duxelles (see page 14) may be placed in the bottom of the baking dish before the yogurt-marinated chicken is added.

***Helpful Hints:** Many times, I skin chicken breasts but leave the bone. Meat cooked on the bone has an added flavor. The skin may be frozen and used in a future chicken stock preparation.

To flatten chicken breasts, place half breast between two pieces of waxed paper or plastic wrap and pound until it is ¼ inch thick.

Per serving: 190 calories; 24.2 gm protein; 3.6 gm fat; 7.8 gm carbohydrate; 0.7 gm fiber; 92 mg cholesterol; 2.1 mg iron; 118 mg sodium; 59 mg calcium; 245 mg phosphorus; 774 IU Vitamin A; 0.11 mg thiamine; 0.36 mg riboflavin; 12 mg Vitamin C; 429 mg potassium; 0.06 mg zinc; 7.9 mg niacin; 33 mcg Vitamin B_6; 0 mcg Vitamin B_{12}; 3 mcg folic acid

Chicken Breasts Supreme with Poached Cucumbers

Serves: 4 (4 ounces cooked chicken = 1 serving)

This recipe requires about 15 minutes of last-minute preparation. I suggest that you serve your salad at the end of the meal so that its vinegary flavor does not mask the delicate flavor of the sauce.

2 whole chicken breasts, skinned, boned, halved, and flattened (see page 145)
1 teaspoon low-sodium vegetable seasoning (see page 28)
3 our Bouillon Cubes (see page 25)
2 cloves garlic, finely minced
¼ cup shallots, finely minced
8 whole fennel seeds, crushed
1 cup dry white wine or vermouth
2 large cucumbers, peeled, cut in half, seeded, and cut into ¼-inch crescents
⅔ cup nonfat yogurt
2 teaspoons cornstarch
1 teaspoon salt-free Dijon mustard with herbs
4 Roma tomatoes, diced, or 4 canned Italian plum tomatoes, diced

2 tablespoons chopped fresh Italian parsley for garnish

1. Season chicken with vegetable seasoning several hours before serving.
2. In a large sauté pan, melt 3 bouillon cubes. Add garlic, shallots, and fennel seeds. Sauté 2 minutes over medium heat.
3. Add wine and bring to a boil.
4. Add chicken breasts, cover, and poach 3 to 4 minutes per side.
5. Remove chicken to a heated platter and keep covered and warm.
6. Reduce pan liquid to about two thirds. Add cucumber crescents and poach, covered, about 5 minutes, until translucent but crisp. Arrange on heated platter around chicken.
7. Place yogurt in a small bowl and whisk in 2 teaspoons cornstarch. *Slowly* whisk hot pan juices into yogurt until well blended. Add mustard. Return sauce to sauté pan and stir 2 minutes over *low heat* until thickened. Taste, and adjust seasonings.
8. Add tomatoes and heat until warmed through.

To Serve: Pour sauce over chicken and cucumbers and sprinkle with chopped parsley. May be served with bulgur wheat or brown rice cooked in our Chicken Stock (see page 26).

Per serving: 227 calories; 25 gm protein; 3.4 gm fat; 13.1 gm carbohydrate; 1.6 gm fiber; 92 mg cholesterol; 2.7 mg iron; 98 mg sodium; 111 mg calcium; 273 mg phosphorus; 665 IU Vitamin A; 0.17 mg thiamine; 0.42 mg riboflavin; 18 mg Vitamin C; 624 mg potassium; 0.06 mg zinc; 8.2 mg niacin; 58 mcg Vitamin B_6; 0 mcg Vitamin B_{12}; 3 mcg folic acid

Chicken Breasts Italiano

Serves: 6 (4 ounces cooked chicken = 1 serving)

The sauce in this recipe should be prepared several days before serving.

¼ cup our Chicken Stock (see page 26)
1 large red onion, minced
3 cups plum tomatoes, drained
¼ cup dry Marsala wine
2 cloves garlic, minced
1 teaspoon basil, crushed
½ teaspoon oregano, crushed
1 teaspoon Italian seasoning, crushed
1 bay leaf
¼ teaspoon coriander seed
¼ teaspoon fennel seed, crushed
1 3-inch piece orange zest
½ cup minced fresh Italian parsley
3 whole chicken breasts (3 pounds chicken), skinned, boned, halved, and flattened (see page 145)
Juice of ½ lemon
1 teaspoon low-sodium vegetable seasoning (see page 28)
½ teaspoon garlic powder
Hungarian paprika
3 tablespoons grated Sap Sago cheese, toasted (see page 15)

1. *To make sauce:* Heat stock in a skillet; add minced onion and sauté until lightly browned.
2. Stir in the next 10 ingredients; cover and simmer 1 hour.
3. Remove sauce from heat, adjust seasonings, and add parsley.
4. Refrigerate or freeze sauce until needed. When ready to use, reheat.
5. Season flattened chicken breasts on both sides with lemon juice, vegetable seasoning, garlic powder, and paprika.
6. Heat a nonstick skillet or an iron skillet sprayed with nonstick spray and sear breasts for 3 to 5 minutes on each side (or broil on each side).
7. Remove breasts to a heated ovenproof platter; cover with heated sauce and sprinkle with toasted Sap Sago cheese.
8. Heat under broiler until sauce bubbles, and serve immediately.

To Serve: Complete the meal with parsleyed spaghettini with peas and carrots, and an Italian salad of crisp greens and marinated garbanzo beans. Lila's Frozen Dessert (page 291) would end the meal on a light note.

Variation: If your diet permits, you may use grated Parmesan cheese instead of Sap Sago.

Per serving: 191 calories; 25.7 gm protein; 4.6 gm fat; 12 gm carbohydrate; 1.6 gm fiber; 92 mg cholesterol; 3.8 mg iron; 255 mg sodium; 118 mg calcium; 307 mg phosphorus; 1894 IU Vitamin A; 0.18 mg thiamine; 0.38 mg riboflavin; 39 mg Vitamin C; 748 mg potassium; 0.33 mg zinc; 8.5 mg niacin; 153 mcg Vitamin B_6; 0 mcg Vitamin B_{12}; 14 mcg folic acid

Company's-Coming Chicken, with Brown and Wild Rice

Serves: 8 (4 ounces cooked chicken = 1 serving)

1 cup corn flakes (no salt or sugar added), crushed
1 teaspoon curry powder*
4 whole chicken breasts, skinned, boned, halved
1 cup buttermilk, strained to remove fat globules
½ cup seeded muscat or manouka raisins
¼ cup dry sherry, or ½ cup pineapple juice (drained from canned, crushed pineapple below)
½ cup wild rice
½ cup brown rice
2¼ cups our Vegetable Stock (see page 60), our Chicken Stock (see page 26), or water
½ cup crushed, unsweetened, canned pineapple, drained

Watercress for garnish

1. Crush corn flakes; add curry powder.
2. Dip chicken breasts in buttermilk, coating both sides; then roll breasts in seasoned corn flakes, coating evenly.
3. Place on a shallow nonstick baking pan and bake in a preheated 375° oven 45 to 60 minutes, or until tender. Prepare rice as follows while chicken is baking.
4. Plump raisins in warmed sherry or pineapple juice. Drain, reserving liquid.
5. Combine drained juice and stock in a large saucepan and bring to a boil. Add rice, bring to a second boil; *don't stir.*
6. Cover and simmer about 45 minutes, or until all liquid is absorbed. Keep covered, remove from heat, and allow to steam for about another 10 to 15 minutes.
7. Stir raisins and pineapple into rice with a fork before serving.

To Serve: Place a bed of rice on a large warmed serving platter; top with baked chicken breasts and garnish with watercress. Hollowed summer squash filled with shredded carrots and steamed makes a lovely accompaniment to this elegant and delicious presentation.

Per serving: 271 calories; 25.9 gm protein; 3.6 gm fat; 31.6 gm carbohydrate; 2 gm fiber; 93 mg cholesterol; 2.7 mg iron; 134 mg sodium; 68 mg calcium; 339 mg phosphorus; 268 IU Vitamin A; 0.22 mg thiamine; 0.46 mg riboflavin; 3 mg Vitamin C; 519 mg potassium; 0.46 mg zinc; 9 mg niacin; 98 mcg Vitamin B_6; 0 mcg Vitamin B_{12}; 10 mcg folic acid

* 1 teaspoon low-sodium vegetable seasoning (see page 28) and ½ teaspoon garlic powder can be substituted for the curry.

Tandoori Chicken

Serves: 8 (4 ounces cooked chicken = 1 serving)

Tandoori chicken is delicious either hot or cold.

2 2-pound broiling chickens, quartered and skinned, with wing tips removed, or 4 whole chicken breasts, skinned and halved
2 cups nonfat yogurt
3 cloves garlic, minced
1 tablespoon grated fresh ginger
¼ cup lime or lemon juice
½ teaspoon ground coriander
½ teaspoon cumin
¼ cup frozen unsweetened apple juice concentrate
Few drops Tabasco
1 bunch scallions (white part only), chopped, or ¼ cup grated onion
2 tablespoons mild soy sauce or 1 tablespoon Worcestershire sauce

1. Cut small slits in each piece of chicken with the point of a sharp knife.
2. Combine remaining ingredients in a bowl and stir to blend.
3. Marinate quartered chicken in yogurt mixture 24 to 48 hours.
4. Remove chicken from marinade and broil or barbecue on grill until golden brown on both sides—about 15 to 20 minutes on each side.

To Serve: Serve on a bed of watercress, garnished with cherry tomatoes, with Raita (page 316) as a condiment. Spinach, Cheese, and Mushroom Squares (page 222), steamed carrots, toasted whole wheat pita bread, and the always enjoyed fresh fruit platter complete a delicious meal.

Helpful Hint: Remaining marinade may be stored in refrigerator and used to prepare additional chicken up to 10 to 12 days later.

Per serving: 160 calories; 23.7 gm protein; 3.2 gm fat; 8 gm carbohydrate; 0.2 gm fiber; 92 mg cholesterol; 1.8 mg iron; 145 mg sodium; 63 mg calcium; 240 mg phosphorus; 180 IU Vitamin A; 0.11 mg thiamine; 0.36 mg riboflavin; 8 mg Vitamin C; 407 mg potassium; 0.02 mg zinc; 7.7 mg niacin; 9 mcg Vitamin B_6; 0 mcg Vitamin B_{12}; 1 mcg folic acid

Anna's Tomato Chicken

Serves: 6 (4 ounces cooked chicken = 1 serving)

3 whole chicken breasts, skinned, halved, and all visible fat removed
½ teaspoon onion powder
½ teaspoon garlic powder
2 teaspoons low-sodium vegetable seasoning (see page 28)
2 teaspoons Hungarian paprika
3 cloves garlic, minced
1 medium onion, sliced
1 green pepper, cut in 1-inch cubes
1 sweet potato, cut in 1-inch cubes
1 rutabaga, cut in 1-inch cubes
4 carrots, cut in 1-inch cubes
1 stalk celery, sliced diagonally
1 bouquet garni (3 sprigs parsley, 1 teaspoon thyme, ½ teaspoon crushed red pepper, 1 bay leaf)
1 28-ounce can Italian plum tomatoes in puree, coarsely chopped
1 8-ounce can salt-free tomato sauce
⅓ pound fresh mushrooms, wiped clean and quartered
1 teaspoon Italian seasoning or oregano, crushed
8 ounces fusilli (spiral spaghetti)
10 ounces frozen petits pois

3 tablespoons grated Sap Sago cheese, toasted (see page 15) optional garnish
3 tablespoons chopped fresh Italian parsley for garnish

1. Season skinned chicken breasts with onion and garlic powders, vegetable seasoning, and paprika.
2. Place minced garlic and sliced onions in bottom of baking pan or casserole. Lay seasoned chicken breasts over onions. Cover chicken and roast in a preheated 375° oven for 20 minutes.
3. Add green pepper, sweet potato, rutabaga, carrots, celery, and bouquet garni and cover with chopped tomatoes and tomato sauce. Cover mixture, return to oven, and cook 1 hour. Uncover and baste mixture with tomato sauce every 30 minutes.
4. After 1 hour of baking, add quartered mushrooms and sprinkle with crushed Italian seasoning or oregano.
5. Return to oven and bake 30 minutes, or until tender.
6. Cook pasta in 2 quarts briskly boiling water, stirring with a wooden spoon. When pasta is *al dente,* drain well, return to saucepan, and add 2 cups of the tomato sauce from the chicken and the frozen petits pois. Keep covered until ready to serve. Pasta may be prepared 30 minutes before serving.

To Serve: Arrange chicken breasts and vegetables on a warmed serving platter. Place spoonfuls of fusilli and peas around platter. Cover entire platter with generous amounts of tomato sauce. If desired, sprinkle with

3 tablespoons toasted Sap Sago cheese. Garnish with chopped Italian parsley.

Variation: If your diet permits, you may use Parmesan cheese instead of Sap Sago.

Per serving: 447 calories; 33.6 gm protein; 4.5 gm fat; 61.4 gm carbohydrate; 7.2 gm fiber; 92 mg cholesterol; 6.6 mg iron; 331 mg sodium; 127 mg calcium; 454 mg phosphorus; 10,427 IU Vitamin A; 0.77 mg thiamine; 0.72 mg riboflavin; 78 mg Vitamin C; 1275 mg potassium; 0.54 mg zinc; 13.7 mg niacin; 374 mcg Vitamin B_6; 0 mcg Vitamin B_{12}; 33 mcg folic acid

Barbecue-Style Broiled Chicken

Serves: 4 (4 ounces cooked chicken = 1 serving)

1 2-pound broiling chicken, sectioned, skinned, and wing tips and all visible fat removed
1 teaspoon onion powder
Juice of 1 lemon
1 12-ounce can salt-free tomato juice
Few drops Tabasco
Juice of ½ lemon
1 cup fresh whole wheat bread crumbs
¼ cup whole wheat flour
1 teaspoon Hungarian paprika
1 teaspoon garlic powder
½ teaspoon chili powder
½ teaspoon thyme
½ teaspoon oregano
½ teaspoon sage (optional)

1. Sprinkle skinned chicken pieces with onion powder and half the lemon juice.
2. Combine tomato juice, Tabasco, and remaining lemon juice.
3. Combine bread crumbs, flour, paprika, garlic powder, chili powder, thyme, and oregano. Add sage if desired.
4. Dip chicken pieces in tomato juice mixture, then in seasoned bread crumb mixture.
5. Place on nonstick shallow baking pan and bake in upper third of a preheated 350° oven—it browns more readily in this section—for 45 to 60 minutes.

To Serve: For indoor or outdoor entertaining, this is lovely served with baked beans and a salad bar of raw vegetables for making your own salad. To complete the meal, serve a large platter of sliced fresh fruits.

Per serving: 270 calories; 31.9 gm protein; 4.8 gm fat; 23.9 gm carbohydrate; 0.8 gm fiber; 116 mg cholesterol; 4.1 mg iron; 165 mg sodium; 43 mg calcium; 325 mg phosphorus; 1272 IU Vitamin A; 0.21 mg thiamine; 0.45 mg riboflavin; 20 mg Vitamin C; 670 mg potassium; 0.05 mg zinc; 10.6 mg niacin; 10 mcg Vitamin B_6; 0 mcg Vitamin B_{12}; 1 mcg folic acid

Chicken and Vegetable Mousse

Serves: 12 (1 slice = 1 serving)

A little extra preparation the day before will produce a light and eye-appealing entrée—or, if you choose, an elegant appetizer.

1–2 bunches fresh spinach or Boston lettuce, well washed
2 green onions, chopped
1½ pounds ground chicken*
1 teaspoon low-sodium vegetable seasoning (see page 28)
Few grains crushed red pepper
4 egg whites
2 small zucchini, cut in 4 strips lengthwise**
1 10-ounce package frozen broccoli spears or florets, or 1 pound fresh broccoli
3 small carrots, cut in 4 strips lengthwise
4 canned artichoke bottoms, cut in 4 strips
2 cups Fresh Tomato Sauce with Fresh Basil (see page 241)

1. Remove stems from the spinach. Drop spinach or lettuce leaves into boiling water and blanch 30 seconds. Remove and pat dry with paper towels. (Handle leaves carefully.)
2. Spray a 9 x 5 x 4-inch loaf pan with nonstick spray. Overlap spinach or lettuce leaves on bottom and sides of pan.
3. Place green onion in blender or food processor and chop. Add chicken, vegetable seasoning, and crushed red pepper, and blend thoroughly. Add egg whites and blend until mixture is a fine paste.
4. Spread one-third of this mixture over spinach leaves. Pack down with a metal spatula, reaching into the corners of the pan.
5. Arrange half of the zucchini, broccoli, carrots, and artichokes on top of the chicken puree, *placing vegetables lengthwise.*
6. Repeat, adding a layer of one-third of the chicken, then the remaining vegetables, and ending with chicken puree.
7. Press the mixture lightly with your hand to remove any air pockets.
8. Cover pan with foil and place in a baking pan with 1 inch hot water.
9. Bake in preheated 350° oven 1 hour, or until a knife comes out clean.
10. Remove loaf pan from hot water and cool. At this point, if there is any excess liquid, pour it off, and then place covered loaf pan in refrigerator overnight to set.

To Unmold and Serve: Place a bed of tomato sauce on a serving platter and unmold the mousse on top of the sauce. To facilitate unmolding, loosen around edges with spatula, invert mold over platter, and shake

* Preground chicken is very fatty. It is better to make your own with a grinder or food processor, or have it done to order for you with the fat and skin removed.
** Fresh asparagus spears or whole green beans may be substituted for the zucchini.

gently until unmolded. This mousse makes a delicious luncheon entrée served with a green salad and crisp rolls. Spoon some tomato sauce on top of each serving.

Per serving: 140 calories; 15 gm protein; 3.3 gm fat; 9.1 gm carbohydrate; 2.4 gm fiber; 46 mg cholesterol; 2.3 mg iron; 82 mg sodium; 65 mg calcium; 170 mg phosphorus; 5340 IU Vitamin A; 0.12 mg thiamine; 0.3 mg riboflavin; 38 mg Vitamin C; 475 mg potassium; 0.27 mg zinc; 4.6 mg niacin; 95 mcg Vitamin B_6; 0.01 mcg Vitamin B_{12}; 20 mcg folic acid

Onion Lover's Chicken with Onions

Serves: 4 (4 ounces cooked chicken = 1 serving)

1 2-pound broiling chicken, skinned, defatted, with wing tips removed, and cut into 4 portions
Juice of ½ lemon
Freshly ground pepper
½ teaspoon garlic powder
Hungarian paprika
1 teaspoon herbal bouquet
2½ pounds onions, sliced
3 cloves garlic
1 cup dry white wine
1 tablespoon red wine vingear
1 bay leaf
1 teaspoon thyme, crushed, or 4 sprigs fresh thyme

¼ cup chopped fresh Italian parsley for garnish

1. Season chicken with lemon juice, freshly ground pepper, garlic powder, paprika, and herbal bouquet.
2. In a heavy, nonstick skillet, or one sprayed with nonstick spray, sear the chicken parts. (If they stick, add a touch of dry white wine.)
3. When chicken is browned, add onions, garlic, white wine, vinegar, bay leaf, and thyme.*
4. Cover and simmer 30 to 40 minutes, until chicken juices run clear, stirring occasionally.
5. Taste, and adjust seasonings before serving.

To Serve: Remove chicken and onions to a warm platter, surround with steamed potatoes and carrots, and sprinkle with chopped parsley.

Variation: Add 3 cups cooked pasta shells 15 minutes before chicken is finished cooking and omit the potatoes.

Per serving: 237 calories; 25.2 gm protein; 3.4 gm fat; 20.4 gm carbohydrate; 4.3 gm fiber; 92 mg cholesterol; 3.7 mg iron; 89 mg sodium; 97 mg calcium; 313 mg phosphorus; 573 IU Vitamin A; 0.14 mg thiamine; 0.38 mg riboflavin; 26 mg Vitamin C; 720 mg potassium; 0.59 mg zinc; 7.8 mg niacin; 230 mcg Vitamin B_6; 0 mcg Vitamin B_{12}; 48 mcg folic acid

* Can also be transferred to a casserole dish and baked in a preheated 375° oven for 30 to 40 minutes.

Terrine of Chicken

Serves: 6 (1 slice = 1 serving)

Served hot, this dish is plain country cooking; and served cold, elegant haute cuisine.

¼ onion, minced
¼ green pepper, minced
¼ cup chopped fresh parsley
1 clove garlic, minced
1 pound ground chicken
1 2-ounce jar chopped pimiento, drained
1 extra-large egg white
1 teaspoon salt-free Dijon mustard
2 teaspoons mild soy sauce
1 teaspoon low-sodium vegetable seasoning (see page 28)
1 teaspoon herbes de Provence, crushed
Freshly ground pepper
½ cup oatmeal
3 tablespoons oat bran
3 tablespoons salt-free tomato paste
1 8-ounce can salt-free tomato sauce

1. Place onion, green pepper, and parsley in a blender or food processor; mince. Add garlic while machine is in motion.
2. Add ground chicken, pimiento, egg white, mustard, soy sauce, vegetable seasoning, herbs, pepper, oatmeal, bran, tomato paste, and 2 tablespoons of the tomato sauce.
3. Process briefly until well combined.
4. Place in 3-cup earthenware terrine or loaf pan. Pat down firmly.
5. Cover with remaining tomato sauce and bake in a preheated 325° oven for 50 to 60 minutes.

To Serve: This may be served hot, sliced as a meat loaf on a platter, sprinkled with chopped parsley, and surrounded by an assortment of steamed vegetables such as whole new potatoes, carrots, summer squash, and broccoli. Many times, however, I cool and chill the terrine overnight in the refrigerator and serve it cold. *To serve cold,* thinly slice terrine (as a pâté) and place on a large, lettuce-lined platter with mounds of chopped onion, tomato, green pepper, and salt-free Dijon mustard. Accompany with thin slices of rye bread. If there is any left over, it makes a delicious appetizer or office lunch.

Per serving: 182 calories; 18.3 gm protein; 2.6 gm fat; 14.4 gm carbohydrate; 0.9 gm fiber; 61 mg cholesterol; 3.1 mg iron; 115 mg sodium; 50 mg calcium; 248 mg phosphorus; 928 IU Vitamin A; 0.15 mg thiamine; 0.25 mg riboflavin; 20 mg Vitamin C; 368 mg potassium; 0.59 mg zinc; 6.1 mg niacin; 59 mcg Vitamin B_6; 0.01 mcg Vitamin B_{12}; 13 mcg folic acid

Addie's Broiled Chicken

Serves: 8 (4 ounces cooked chicken = 1 serving)

1 cup white wine
1 clove garlic, minced
1 tablespoon mild soy sauce
1 teaspoon salt-free mustard
1 teaspoon low-sodium vegetable seasoning (see page 28)
1 teaspoon rosemary, crushed
Juice of ½ lemon
4 whole chicken breasts (4 pounds chicken; leave bone in for flavor), skinned, halved, and all visible fat removed
Hungarian paprika

1. Combine the first 7 ingredients in a bowl for marinade. Add chicken breasts to marinate.
2. Cover and refrigerate 4 to 6 hours or overnight.
3. Place chicken on broiling rack and sprinkle with paprika. Broil 4 inches from heat, about 20 minutes on each side, basting with remaining marinade from time to time.

To Serve: Serve from broiler to table in order to savor the flavorful and juicy quality of the chicken. Can be accompanied by Spanish Rice (page 203) and Chopped Broccoli Chinese Style (page 214).

Helpful Hint: Leftover marinade can be refrigerated and used to marinate chicken for another meal.

Per serving: 152 calories; 22.2 gm protein; 3.2 gm fat; 2.2 gm carbohydrate; 0.1 gm fiber; 92 mg cholesterol; 1.9 mg iron; 129 mg sodium; 24 mg calcium; 238 mg phosphorus; 203 IU Vitamin A; 0.09 mg thiamine; 0.29 mg riboflavin; 2 mg Vitamin C; 369 mg potassium; 0 mg zinc; 7.4 mg niacin; 13 mcg Vitamin B_6; 0 mcg Vitamin B_{12}; 0 mcg folic acid

Chicken and Pears au Vinaigre

Serves: 8 (4 ounces cooked chicken = 1 serving)

This delectable company dish will establish you as a gourmet cook.

4 whole chicken breasts, halved, skin and all visible fat removed, or 3-pound frying chicken, cut in eighths, wing tips and all visible skin and fat removed
Freshly ground pepper
Juice of ½ lemon
1 teaspoon low-sodium vegetable seasoning (see page 28)
2 onions, chopped
3 our Bouillon Cubes, melted (see page 25), or ¼ cup our Chicken Stock (see page 26)
8 cloves garlic, crushed
4 tomatoes, seeded and diced
2 bay leaves
2 cups red wine vinegar
2 cups red wine

1 bouquet garni (4 celery leaves, 1 teaspoon thyme, 4 sprigs parsley, 2 bay leaves, ½ teaspoon crushed red pepper)
3 cups red wine
½ cup water
½ cup frozen unsweetened pear-grape concentrate
4 whole cloves
Zest of ½ orange and ½ lemon
2 tablespoons lemon juice
1 stick of cinnamon, or 2 teaspoons vanilla
6 pears, peeled, cored, and quartered

Watercress for garnish

1. Season chicken breasts generously with freshly ground pepper, lemon juice, and vegetable seasoning. Broil until golden brown on both sides.
2. Sauté chopped onions in bouillon cubes until lightly browned. Stir constantly.
3. Add crushed garlic, diced tomatoes, and bay leaves.
4. Place vegetables in a roasting pan and lay chicken breasts on top of vegetables.
5. Deglaze broiling pan with vinegar and wine. Bring to a boil, and reduce to about 1 cup.
6. Pour over chicken breasts; add bouquet garni, cover, and simmer over medium heat 25 minutes or until tender. While chicken is cooking, poach pears.
7. Combine red wine, water, pear-grape concentrate, cloves, zest, lemon juice, and cinnamon in a saucepan and bring to a boil. Boil 10 minutes.
8. Add pears to simmering poaching liquid and simmer 10 minutes.

*9. Cool pears 20 minutes in syrup.

10. Remove chicken when tender. Reduce liquid with vegetables by half (simmer about 10 minutes).

11. Place vegetables and liquid in a blender or food processor and puree. Strain vegetable mixture.

12. Add strained vegetable sauce to chicken.

**13. Line roasting pan with drained poached pear slices; place chicken in sauce on top of pears.

14. Cover with foil and reheat in a preheated 350° oven for 30 minutes.

To Serve: Serve in the baking pan if attractive, or on a warm platter topped with strained sauce. Arrange pear slices around chicken and garnish with watercress. Serve with Wild Rice, Brown Rice, and Mushrooms (page 257) and Spinach Ring with carrots and pea pods (page 223), crispy rolls, and a salad of butter lettuce and hearts of palm. For an elegant finish, try a Citron Soufflé (page 292) with a fresh stemmed-strawberry garnish.

Per serving: 261 calories; 24 gm protein; 3.6 gm fat; 25.1 gm carbohydrate; 3.5 gm fiber; 92 mg cholesterol; 3.1 mg iron; 78 mg sodium; 55 mg calcium; 286 mg phosphorus; 621 IU Vitamin A; 0.15 mg thiamine; 0.36 mg riboflavin; 21 mg Vitamin C; 748 mg potassium; 0.21 mg zinc; 7.9 mg niacin; 128 mcg Vitamin B_6; 0 mcg Vitamin B_{12}; 14 mcg folic acid

* Pears prepared in this manner may also be chilled and served as a dessert. Syrup may be reserved for poaching pears again at another time.

** Recipe may be prepared several hours ahead of time through step 13.

Chicken Breasts with Artichokes

Serves: 8 (4 ounces cooked chicken = 1 serving)

4 whole chicken breasts, skinned, halved, and all visible fat removed
Juice of ½ lemon
1 teaspoon low-sodium vegetable seasoning (see page 28)
1 teaspoon herbes de Provence, crushed
½ teaspoon crushed red pepper
Hungarian paprika
4 our Bouillon Cubes (see page 25)
½ pound fresh mushrooms, thinly sliced
3 green onions, chopped
3 tablespoons unbleached flour
⅔ cup our Chicken Stock (see page 26)
3 tablespoons dry sherry
2 10-ounce packages frozen artichoke hearts, or 2 10-ounce cans artichoke hearts, rinsed and drained

¼ cup minced fresh Italian parsley for garnish

1. Place chicken breasts in a roaster or ovenproof casserole.
2. Sprinkle both sides with lemon juice, vegetable seasoning, herbs, crushed red pepper, and paprika.
3. Broil chicken quickly, 5 minutes on each side.
4. Melt bouillon cubes in a sauté pan, add sliced mushrooms and green onions, and sauté 3 minutes over medium high heat.
5. Sprinkle flour on top, stirring constantly to blend in flour.
6. Slowly add chicken stock and sherry. Stir constantly.
7. Simmer uncovered for 5 minutes, or until sauce thickens, stirring occasionally.
8. Add artichoke hearts to sauce. Stir well.
*9. Pour sauce over browned chicken and cover pan.
10. Bake in a preheated 350° oven for 40 to 45 minutes.

To Serve: Sprinkle with chopped parsley and serve with Steamed Brown Rice (see page 254) and steamed broccoli florets.

Per serving: 167 calories; 24.7 gm protein; 3.5 gm fat; 8.3 gm carbohydrate; 1.5 gm fiber; 92 mg cholesterol; 2.8 mg iron; 90 mg sodium; 54 mg calcium; 302 mg phosphorus; 666 IU Vitamin A; 0.16 mg thiamine; 0.49 mg riboflavin; 11 mg Vitamin C; 607 mg potassium; 0.08 mg zinc; 9.1 mg niacin; 50 mcg Vitamin B_6; 0 mcg Vitamin B_{12}; 9 mcg folic acid

* May be prepared through step 9 in the morning and baked just before serving dinner.

Harold's Favorite Chicken with Cabbage

Serves: 4 (4 ounces cooked chicken = 1 serving)

My husband, Harold, is a cabbage lover, and this quick recipe satisfies both his palate and my busy time schedule.

1 tablespoon mild soy sauce
3 tablespoons lemon juice
2 cloves garlic, minced
1 teaspoon grated fresh ginger root
2 whole chicken breasts (2 pounds chicken), skinned, halved, and all visible fat removed
1 onion, sliced
1 teaspoon low-sodium vegetable seasoning (see page 28)
Hungarian paprika
½ head cabbage shredded

1. Combine soy sauce, lemon juice, garlic, and ginger root.
2. Place in a plastic bag with the chicken breasts and marinate overnight or all day.
3. Place onion slices in a roaster. Lay chicken breasts on onions, pour marinade over chicken, and sprinkle with vegetable seasoning and paprika. Cover and roast 50 minutes in a preheated 350° oven.
4. Remove cover and broil chicken until lightly browned, about 5 minutes on each side.
5. Add shredded cabbage, cover, and roast at 350° for 30 additional minutes.

To Serve: Serve with Cracked Wheat Pilaf (see page 256) and parslied carrots.

Variation: Omit the Cracked Wheat Pilaf. Add 3 cups pasta shells after completing step 5. Cover and bake 15 additional minutes before serving.

Per serving: 166 calories; 24.1 gm protein; 3.4 gm fat; 9.9 gm carbohydrate; 3.4 gm fiber; 92 mg cholesterol; 2.5 mg iron; 207 mg sodium; 71 mg calcium; 277 mg phosphorus; 405 IU Vitamin A; 0.16 mg thiamine; 0.34 mg riboflavin; 43 mg Vitamin C; 608 mg potassium; 0.39 mg zinc; 7.8 mg niacin; 158 mcg Vitamin B_6; 0 mcg Vitamin B_{12}; 32 mcg folic acid

Roast Chicken on a Bed of Vermicelli

Serves: 4 (4 ounces cooked chicken = 1 serving)

1 2-pound broiling chicken, quartered, skinned, and wing tips and all visible fat removed
Juice of ½ lemon
1 teaspoon low-sodium vegetable seasoning (see page 28)
½ teaspoon garlic powder
½ teaspoon onion powder
Hungarian paprika
1 onion, thinly sliced
2 carrots, thinly sliced
1 clove garlic, minced
½ cup our Chicken Stock (see page 26)
½ pound vermicelli or whole wheat spaghettini
1 tablespoon dry sherry
1 tablespoon mild soy sauce or Worcestershire sauce
4 green onions, sliced

2 tablespoons chopped fresh Italian parsley for garnish

1. Season chicken pieces on both sides with lemon juice, vegetable seasoning, garlic powder, onion powder, and paprika.
2. Place onion slices, carrot slices, and garlic on bottom of small, covered roaster. Lay seasoned chicken on top of onion mixture; add chicken stock.
3. Cover roaster and place in a preheated 350° oven for 45 minutes. While chicken is roasting, prepare pasta.
4. Cook vermicelli in boiling water according to package directions.
5. Drain pasta; return to pot, and add sherry, soy sauce, and green onions.
6. When chicken is done, remove cover and brown chicken under broiler for 5 minutes.

To Serve: Arrange pasta mixture on a large warmed platter or on individual plates. Cover pasta with vegetables and pan juices from roaster. Lay chicken pieces on top, sprinkle with chopped parsley, and serve immediately.

Per serving: 380 calories; 36.8 gm protein; 5.2 gm fat; 45.8 gm carbohydrate; 2.1 gm fiber; 92 mg cholesterol; 3.4 mg iron; 228 mg sodium; 53 mg calcium; 267 mg phosphorus; 4433 IU Vitamin A; 0.37 mg thiamine; 0.43 mg riboflavin; 13 mg Vitamin C; 556 mg potassium; 0.26 mg zinc; 9.2 mg niacin; 101 mcg Vitamin B_6; 0 mcg Vitamin B_{12}; 13 mcg folic acid

Chicken Paprika with Yogurt

Serves: 8 (4 ounces cooked chicken = 1 serving)

2 large onions, minced
1 large clove garlic, minced
3 our Bouillon Cubes, melted (see page 25), or ¼ cup our Chicken Stock (see page 26)
1 3-pound frying chicken, skinned, wing tips and all visible fat removed, and cut into 8 serving pieces
1 teaspoon low-sodium vegetable seasoning (see page 28)
1 large ripe tomato, peeled, seeded, and chopped
1½–2 tablespoons Hungarian paprika
1 cup our Chicken Stock
1 green pepper, seeded and sliced
1 bay leaf
2 tablespoons cornstarch or unbleached flour
4 tablespoons nonfat yogurt (optional)

1. In a 4- to 5-quart heavy casserole or Dutch oven, sauté onions and garlic in melted bouillon cubes or stock.
2. Cook over medium heat until wilted but not browned.
3. Add chicken, sprinkled with vegetable seasoning.
4. Cover and cook over low heat for 10 minutes.
5. Add diced tomato and coat pieces of chicken with paprika. Cover and cook 10 minutes over low heat.

*6. Add chicken broth, green pepper, and bay leaf and cook over *very low heat* for about 25 minutes, or until the chicken is tender.

7. Remove chicken and peppers.
8. Combine cornstarch or unbleached flour with 3 tablespoons cold water and add to onion mixture. Stir, bring to a boil, and cook mixture until thickened, stirring constantly.
9. Add yogurt,** and stir over *low heat* until well blended.
10. Return chicken and peppers to sauce and warm thoroughly. Adjust seasonings. Cover until ready to serve.

To serve: Place on a warm serving platter and garnish with dollops of yogurt, if desired. The pungent sauce is delicious served over plain Steamed Brown Rice (see page 254). Cabbage, Apple, and Raisin Slaw (page 89) is a wonderful accompaniment.

Per serving: 177 calories; 24.8 gm protein; 3.7 gm fat; 11.2 gm carbohydrate; 3 gm fiber; 92 mg cholesterol; 3.8 mg iron; 79 mg sodium; 75 mg calcium; 277 mg phosphorus; 4166 IU Vitamin A; 0.18 mg thiamine; 0.43 mg riboflavin; 59 mg Vitamin C; 628 mg potassium; 0.23 mg zinc; 8.4 mg niacin; 72 mcg Vitamin B_6; 0 mcg Vitamin B_{12}; 11 mcg folic acid

* May be prepared several hours ahead of time through step 6.
** You may omit yogurt entirely and serve chicken after sauce has been thickened with cornstarch or flour.

Chicken with Lobster Sauce

Serves: 8 (3 ounces cooked chicken and 1½ ounces cooked lobster = 1 serving)

Lovely to look at, delightful to serve, and heaven to eat.

4 whole chicken breasts (3 pounds chicken), halved, skinned, boned, and flattened (see page 145)
1 tablespoon low-sodium vegetable seasoning (see page 28)
1 teaspoon white pepper
2 tablespoons dry vermouth
2–2½ cups our Chicken Stock (see page 26), as needed
1 pint skim milk
½ cup flour
1½ tablespoons mild soy sauce, or 1 tablespoon Worcestershire sauce
1 1-pound lobster tail, cut into 1-inch pieces with the shell
1 cup sliced scallions

Chopped fresh parsley for garnish

1. Sprinkle chicken on all sides with vegetable seasoning and white pepper.
2. Place pieces side by side in a single layer in a shallow pan. Add vermouth and as much chicken stock as is needed to cover chicken.
3. Cover with foil and bake in a preheated 375° oven for 30 minutes, or until tender. Let chicken remain warm in broth while making sauce.
4. Mix skim milk with flour. Add 2 cups of poaching broth to milk mixture. Stir sauce over heat until it bubbles and thickens.
5. Add soy sauce to taste. Stir in lobster and scallions. Reheat for 5 minutes.

To Serve: Drain chicken breasts and serve topped with lobster sauce and sprinkled with chopped parsley. Complete this spectacular meal with steamed asparagus spears, Steamed Brown Rice (page 254), and Lila's Frozen Dessert (page 291) served in lemon cups.

Helpful Hint: I sometimes prevail upon my fishmonger to give me a few empty cooked lobster shells to use as a smashing garnish!

Per serving: 225 calories; 35.6 gm protein; 4.3 gm fat; 12.1 gm carbohydrate; 0.5 gm fiber; 150 mg cholesterol; 2.3 mg iron; 274 mg sodium; 117 mg calcium; 406 mg phosphorus; 373 IU Vitamin A; 0.37 mg thiamine; 0.45 mg riboflavin; 5 mg Vitamin C; 561 mg potassium; 0.33 mg zinc; 8.5 mg niacin; 30 mcg Vitamin B_6; 0.24 mcg Vitamin B_{12}; 3 mcg folic acid

Chicken and Vegetables Poached in White Wine

Serves: 4 (¼ chicken = 1 serving)

This chicken dish is an old favorite of the French in Provence—simple country cooking for a cold winter evening.

3 our Bouillon Cubes (see page 25), or 3 tablespoons white wine
2 carrots, chopped
1 medium onion, chopped
1 small turnip, chopped
1 leek (white part only), chopped
1 2-pound broiling chicken, sectioned, skinned, and wing tips and all visible fat removed
1 teaspoon low-sodium vegetable seasoning (see page 28)
Freshly ground white or green peppercorns
1–1½ cups dry white wine or dry vermouth
2 cups our Chicken Stock (see page 26)
1 bouquet garni (½ teaspoon thyme, 1 bay leaf, 4 sprigs Italian parsley, 4 celery leaves, 1 mashed clove garlic, ½ teaspoon tarragon, few grains crushed red pepper)

1. Melt bouillon cubes in ovenproof casserole. Add cut vegetables. Cook slowly in covered casserole for about 10 minutes, stirring frequently. *Do not allow to brown.*

2. Season chicken sections with vegetable seasoning and freshly ground pepper.

3. Spread chicken over and around cooked vegetables. (Arrange white meat on top, as it cooks more rapidly.)

4. Add wine and chicken stock to barely cover.

5. Bury bouquet garni in vegetables; bring to a simmer. Taste, and adjust seasonings.

6. Cover casserole and simmer slowly in a preheated 325° oven about 25 to 35 minutes. When done, meat should feel tender when pressed with a fork and juices should run clear yellow, not pink. *Do not overcook.*

7. Remove bouquet garni. Taste, and adjust seasonings again with herbs or vegetable seasoning.

To Serve: Take casserole to table (or transfer chicken to a heated tureen). Serve a scoop of Steamed Brown Rice (see page 254) in individual shallow soup dishes with chicken, vegetables, and broth. To complete the meal, serve crusty whole wheat bread or crisp sourdough rolls, Spicy Broccoli Salad (page 87), and a hot fruit compote (page 267 or 268).

Per serving: 234 calories; 24.5 gm protein; 3.3 gm fat; 13.7 gm carbohydrate; 2.3 gm fiber; 92 mg cholesterol; 2.6 mg iron; 97 mg sodium; 57 mg calcium; 272 mg phosphorus; 4387 IU Vitamin A; 0.14 mg thiamine; 0.33 mg riboflavin; 10 mg Vitamin C; 614 mg potassium; 0.26 mg zinc; 7.8 mg niacin; 124 mcg Vitamin B_6; 0 mcg Vitamin B_{12}; 12 mcg folic acid

Stuffed Roast Chicken

(Its Beauty Is Not Only Skin Deep)

Serves: 4 (¼ chicken with stuffing = 1 serving)

This is the only chicken recipe in this book in which the skin is not removed. I use a broiler instead of a roaster (because it's leaner), with all visible fat removed, and stuff the chicken under the skin. The skin keeps the stuffing and the chicken moist and may be removed before serving or eating.

1 2-pound broiling chicken, split; wing tips, excess skin, and all visible fat removed
Juice of ½ lemon
1 teaspoon herbes de Provence
1 small onion, minced
1 clove garlic, minced, or ½ teaspoon garlic powder
1 large shallot, minced, or 2 green onions, minced
2 our Bouillon Cubes, melted (see page 25)
1 pound zucchini, shredded and squeezed dry, or 1 10-ounce package chopped spinach, defrosted and squeezed dry
4 ounces skim-milk ricotta or hoop cheese
1 extra-large egg white
1 teaspoon low-sodium vegetable seasoning (see page 28)
Few grains crushed red pepper
Freshly ground nutmeg
2 tablespoons grated Sap Sago cheese, toasted (see page 15)
Hungarian paprika

Watercress and cherry tomatoes for garnish

1. Using kitchen shears and your fingers, loosen chicken skin, forming pockets to hold the stuffing.

2. Sprinkle chicken under skin with lemon juice and herbs. Marinate in refrigerator several hours or overnight.

3. *To make stuffing:* Sauté onion, garlic, and shallot in bouillon cubes until transparent. Add zucchini and sauté 5 minutes more. Cool slightly.

4. Blend cheese in blender or food processor. Add egg white, vegetable seasoning, crushed red pepper, nutmeg, and Sap Sago cheese and blend. Stir in zucchini mixture and blend well.

*5. Stuff pockets formed between skin and body of chicken with zucchini-cheese mixture and secure with toothpicks.

* May be prepared several hours ahead through step 5.

6. Place chicken in an attractive shallow roasting pan, skin-side-up. Sprinkle with Hungarian paprika.

7. Roast in a preheated 450° oven for 10 minutes; lower oven to 375° and continue to roast for 45 to 60 minutes, or until done.

8. Cut broiler into quarters. (Remove skin if desired and sprinkle stuffing with Hungarian paprika.)

To Serve: Garnish with watercress and fresh cherry tomatoes, and serve immediately.

Variations: Sometimes I just use small chicken breasts for stuffing, particularly if I'm serving 8 or more guests. I also vary the stuffing occasionally, sometimes using a favorite bread stuffing.

Per serving: 324 calories; 48.3 gm protein; 6.5 gm fat; 11 gm carbohydrate; 4.4 gm fiber; 113 mg cholesterol; 4.8 mg iron; 146 mg sodium; 174 mg calcium; 453 mg phosphorus; 916 IU Vitamin A; 0.19 mg thiamine; 0.53 mg riboflavin; 29 mg Vitamin C; 861 mg potassium; 0.47 mg zinc; 16.5 mg niacin; 40 mcg Vitamin B_6; 0.09 mcg Vitamin B_{12}; 7 mcg folic acid

Quick and Colorful Microwaved Chicken Orientale

Serves: 6 (4 ounces cooked chicken = 1 serving)

This dish has appeal because of its relatively short preparation time and low caloric content—to say nothing of its colorful appearance.

1 cup canned unsweetened pineapple chunks or crushed pineapple, drained (reserve juice)
¼ cup drained pineapple juice
2 tablespoons mild soy sauce
2 tablespoons dry sherry
2 tablespoons brown rice vinegar
2–3 tablespoons salt-free Dijon mustard with herbs
1 teaspoon ground ginger
1 clove garlic, minced
1 3-pound frying chicken, skinned, defatted, wing tips removed, and cut in serving pieces, or 3 skinned, defatted, and halved chicken breasts

2 cups washed and sliced fresh mushrooms
1 green pepper, seeded, cut in 1-inch cubes
1 red pepper, seeded, cut in 1-inch cubes
1 7½-ounce can bamboo shoots, drained
1 10-ounce package frozen broccoli florets, defrosted

1 cup green onions, diagonally sliced

1. Combine drained pineapple, pineapple juice, soy sauce, sherry, vinegar, mustard, ginger, and garlic in a large glass measuring cup or a 1-quart glass bowl. Cook in microwave oven on high until mixture boils. Taste, and adjust seasonings.

2. Arrange chicken in a shallow oval or rectangular glass or ceramic baking dish. (Place thick side of breast toward edge of dish.)

*3. Pour sauce over chicken, coating all sides.

4. Cover with waxed paper and cook in microwave on high for 10 minutes.

5. Turn chicken over. Add mushrooms and green and red pepper cubes, and cook on high 10 additional minutes. Baste chicken with sauce.

6. Add bamboo shoots and defrosted broccoli florets. Cook 3 additional minutes on high.

To Serve: Sprinkle with sliced green onions and serve with Steamed Brown Rice (page 254).

* May be prepared several hours ahead of time through step 3.

Variations: Boneless chicken breasts cut in 2-inch strips may be substituted for whole breasts. In this case, reduce cooking time in step 4 to 5 minutes.

If desired, you may thicken sauce by mixing 2 tablespoons cornstarch with ½ cup drained pineapple juice and add to mixture in step 6.

Per serving: 206 calories; 30.3 gm protein; 2.23 gm fat; 14.87 gm carbohydrate; 2.5 gm fiber; 66 mg cholesterol; 2.1 mg iron; 287 mg sodium; 64 mg calcium; 311 mg phosphorus; 2429 IU Vitamin A; 0.25 mg thiamine; 0.34 mg riboflavin; 100 mg Vitamin C; 811 mg potassium; 0.97 mg zinc; 14.5 mg niacin; 734 mcg Vitamin B_6; 0.43 mcg Vitamin B_{12}; 14 mcg folic acid

Turkey Piccata

Serves: 6 (3 ounces cooked turkey = 1 serving)

Turkey is no longer just associated with Thanksgiving dinner; it is a popular meat used in a variety of ways. Turkey breast slices nicely into scallops that have a relatively short cooking time. Be careful not to overcook them, they'll become dry and tough.

¼ cup unbleached flour
1 cup our Seasoned Bread Crumbs (see page 29)
Freshly ground pepper
½ teaspoon Hungarian paprika
6 thin turkey fillets (1½ pounds turkey breast), flattened (see page 145)
1 cup buttermilk, strained of fat
6 thin lemon slices
1 tablespoon capers, rinsed and drained
½ cup lemon juice

Watercress or parsley sprigs for garnish

1. Combine flour, bread crumbs, pepper, and paprika.
2. Dip turkey fillets in buttermilk, then bread crumb mixture.
3. Arrange on nonstick baking pan and bake in a preheated 375° oven for 30 minutes.
4. Place lemon slices and capers in the lemon juice and bring to a boil.

To Serve: Remove browned turkey to a heated platter; place a lemon slice on each fillet; drizzle with lemon juice and capers. Garnish with sprigs of watercress or parsley and serve immediately. To complete the meal, serve with penne (a tubular macaroni) with Fresh Tomato Sauce with Fresh Basil (page 241) and steamed asparagus. Banana and Pineapple Sorbet (page 289) would be a refreshing finish.

Variation: These same flattened turkey fillets can be seasoned with lemon juice and low-sodium vegetable seasoning, grilled on a nonstick griddle, and served as a turkey burger on a whole wheat bun.

Per serving: 293 calories; 39.6 gm protein; 7.5 gm fat; 15.4 gm carbohydrate; 0.4 gm fiber; 102 mg cholesterol; 2.7 mg iron; 246 mg sodium; 68 mg calcium; 346 mg phosphorus; 278 IU Vitamin A; 0.13 mg thiamine; 0.31 mg riboflavin; 14 mg Vitamin C; 540 mg potassium; 2.50 mg zinc; 9.3 mg niacin; 16 mcg Vitamin B_6; 0 mcg Vitamin B_{12}; 11 mcg folic acid

Turkey Curry
(When You're in a Hurry)

Serves: 12 (1¼ cups = 1 serving)

2 large onions, finely chopped
2 celery stalks, thinly sliced
¼ cup dry white wine
2 pounds fresh mushrooms, quartered or sliced
Juice ½ lemon
2 cloves garlic, minced
2 apples, peeled, cored, and diced
4 tablespoons flour
1 tablespoon curry powder, or to taste
3 cups our Chicken Stock (see page 26) or Turkey Stock (see page 58), or leftover turkey gravy
6 cups diced cooled turkey breast
3 tablespoons parsley

1. Sauté onions and celery in white wine until transparent and tender.
2. Add mushrooms, lemon juice, and garlic. Cook a few minutes, then add apples, flour, and curry; stir to combine. Add stock and continue to cook, stirring constantly, until sauce coats the spoon (15 to 20 minutes).
3. Add diced turkey and parsley. Simmer until heated through. Taste, and adjust seasonings.
4. May be frozen; if so, omit apples. May also be prepared a day ahead and reheated.

To Serve: Serve curried turkey in a ring of Steamed Brown Rice (page 254), with Raita (page 316) and several of the following condiments: chopped green onion, chopped green pepper, toasted horseradish,* plumped raisins or currants (or add directly to the curry), chutney, chopped egg whites, and sliced bananas in orange juice.

***Helpful Hint:** *To make toasted horseradish,* shred raw horseradish root and place on a baking sheet in a 375° oven until golden brown. You will be pleasantly surprised at the transformation in its taste—from sharp to scrumptious. The street vendors in Vienna, Austria, use this as a topping for (you should excuse the expression) knockwurst.

Per serving: 204 calories; 25.7 gm protein; 4.7 gm fat; 13.9 gm carbohydrate; 3.2 gm fiber; 62 mg cholesterol; 2.4 mg iron; 113 mg sodium; 27 mg calcium; 284 mg phosphorus; 220 IU Vitamin A; 0.14 mg thiamine; 0.5 mg riboflavin; 12 mg Vitamin C; 691 mg potassium; 1.57 mg zinc; 8.8 mg niacin; 138 mcg Vitamin B_6; 0 mcg Vitamin B_{12}; 32 mcg folic acid

Turkey Kabobs

Serves: 12 (3 ounces cooked turkey = 1 serving)

The turkey chunks for these kabobs should be marinated overnight before they are used so that they absorb the flavor of the marinade. This dish looks beautiful—without a lot of fuss and work.

1 onion, cut in 1-inch cubes
1 stalk celery with leaves, chopped
1 carrot, chopped
5 cloves garlic, minced
3 bay leaves, crumbled
2 teaspoons mixed thyme, marjoram, fennel, and savory
¾ cup dry red wine
Juice and zest of 1 lemon
¾ cup our Turkey Stock (see page 58) or Chicken Stock (see page 26)

1 4- to 5-pound turkey breast, boned and cut in chunks
3 red peppers, seeded and cut in eighths
3 green peppers, seeded and cut in eighths
1 pound fresh mushrooms, wiped clean and stemmed

12 bamboo skewers

1. Combine all ingredients except peppers and mushrooms. Pour over turkey and marinate overnight in refrigerator.

2. Drain turkey chunks, reserving marinade, and thread onto skewers alternating with peppers and mushrooms.

3. Brush kabobs with marinade and broil until crispy on all sides, about 10 minutes.

To Serve: Serve on a bed of Steamed Brown Rice (page 254) with steamed green beans and a wedge of fresh pineapple.

Per serving: 265 calories; 37.5 gm protein; 4.1 gm fat; 8.5 gm carbohydrate; 2.4 gm fiber; 100 mg cholesterol; 2.7 mg iron; 127 mg sodium; 39 mg calcium; 415 mg phosphorus; 2062 IU Vitamin A; 0.16 mg thiamine; 0.41 mg riboflavin; 89 mg Vitamin C; 878 mg potassium; 2.8 mg zinc; 16.4 mg niacin; 144 mcg Vitamin B_6; 0 mcg Vitamin B_{12}; 25 mcg folic acid

Sunday-Supper Ground Turkey Rolls

Serves: 16 (½ roll and ½ cup filling = 1 serving)

1 14-ounce package long sourdough or French rolls (without added fat), 8 per package
⅔ cup our Turkey Stock (see page 58) or Chicken Stock (see page 26)
½ cup minced fresh parsley
¼ cup salt-free Dijon mustard
3 egg whites, lightly beaten
1 teaspoon herbes de Provence, crushed
Few grains crushed red pepper
1 teaspoon low-sodium vegetable seasoning (see page 28)
1 large onion, chopped
½ green pepper, chopped
1 clove garlic, minced
1 shallot, chopped
2 tablespoons our Chicken Stock or Turkey Stock
2 pounds ground raw or leftover cooked turkey
⅔ cup salt-free tomato sauce, with ½ teaspoon crushed oregano

1. Halve the rolls lengthwise. Carefully remove the soft center with your fingers or a grapefruit spoon, leaving a ¼-inch shell.
2. Toast the rolls lightly under broiler.
3. Crumble the soft centers of the rolls in a blender or food processor. Transfer to a bowl and add the ⅔ cup stock, parsley, mustard, egg whites, herbs, crushed red pepper, and vegetable seasoning.
4. Sauté onion, pepper, garlic, and shallot in the 2 tablespoons stock until tender.
5. Add ground turkey and cook over medium heat until turkey is cooked through.
*6. Drain turkey mixture, combine with crumb mixture, and blend thoroughly. Taste, and adjust seasonings.
7. Divide mixture equally among rolls, mounding slightly.
8. Place on ungreased baking dish and drizzle with tomato sauce.
9. Bake in a preheated 400° oven 10 to 15 minutes, or until hot and lightly browned.

To Serve: Serve immediately. To complete the meal, add a green bean salad and fresh pineapple in Strawberry Sauce (page 272) for dessert.

Per serving: 183 calories; 20.9 gm protein; 3.6 gm fat; 13 gm carbohydrate; 0.5 gm fiber; 51 mg cholesterol; 2 mg iron; 190 mg sodium; 28 mg calcium; 169 mg phosphorus; 520 IU Vitamin A; 0.1 mg thiamine; 0.17 mg riboflavin; 10 mg Vitamin C; 288 mg potassium; 1.23 mg zinc; 5 mg niacin; 24 mcg Vitamin B_6; 0.01 mcg Vitamin B_{12}; 8 mcg folic acid

* May be prepared ahead through step 6 and refrigerated for use later on in the day or the next day.

Turkey Tonnato
(Roast Turkey with Tuna Sauce)

Serves: 8 (3 ounces cooked turkey = 1 serving)

Turkey tonnato is a low-cholesterol adaptation of the traditional Italian vitello tonnato (veal with tuna sauce). It may be served as a beautiful entrée on a cold buffet or as an elegant appetizer. The meat must be roasted a day ahead.

1 7-ounce can salt-free light-meat tuna in water, well drained
⅔ cup nonfat yogurt
2 tablespoons fresh lemon juice
1 teaspoon capers, drained and rinsed
½ cup watercress leaves, washed
1 2½–3½-pound turkey breast, roasted to 160°, and chilled overnight
1 bunch watercress, washed and tough stems removed, for serving and garnish
1 tablespoon capers, rinsed and drained, for garnish
Cherry tomatoes for garnish
Radish roses for garnish

1. *To make sauce:* Puree drained tuna in a blender or food processor.
2. Add yogurt gradually while machine is in motion. Scrape down bowl and blend thoroughly.
3. Add lemon juice, capers, and watercress. Process until flecks of green appear.
4. Chill sauce until serving time. Sauce may be prepared a day ahead.
5. Just before serving time, skin chilled turkey breast and slice into ¼-inch slices.

To Serve: Arrange overlapping turkey slices on a bed of watercress. Spoon sauce over turkey slices, sprinkle with capers, and garnish with cherry tomatoes and radish roses. When served as an entrée, a cold rice salad makes a lovely accompaniment.

Per serving: 200 calories; 37.5 gm protein; 3.7 gm fat; 1.6 gm carbohydrate; 0 gm fiber; 85 mg cholesterol; 1.5 mg iron; 96 mg sodium; 45 mg calcium; 288 mg phosphorus; 289 IU Vitamin A; 0.07 mg thiamine; 0.2 mg riboflavin; 4 mg Vitamin C; 454 mg potassium; 1.9 mg zinc; 13.5 mg niacin; 2 mcg Vitamin B_6; 0 mcg Vitamin B_{12}; 7 mcg folic acid

Red Meat
Served Rarely

Bracciole
Marinated Flank Steak
Marinated Beef and Vegetable Salad
Old-Fashioned Baked Meat Loaf
Stuffed Rutabaga Cups
Stuffed Cabbage Loaf
Hearty Steak with Peppers
Pan Bagna

Hamburgers are an American fast-food favorite. Yet few people realize that over 50 percent of the calories in the average hamburger are derived from fat.

Limit your red meat to a 4-ounce serving *no more than once a week.* Pork and lamb are to be limited also because of their high fat and cholesterol contents. Veal, comparable to beef in cholesterol because it is milk-fed, but half as high in fat because it is not old enough to be marbled, should also be eaten sparingly. Ham should also be avoided, not only because of its fat and cholesterol content, but because of its high sodium content resulting from processing. Beef, of course, is high in both cholesterol and fat.

In order to minimize your intake of fat and cholesterol when preparing red meat, use the leaner cuts of beef such as flank steak and top round. I particularly recommend flank steak because of its lack of marbling and the ease with which you can remove its visible fat.

Bracciole

(Stuffed Flank Steak)

Serves: 8 (3 ounces cooked beef = 1 serving)

Bracciole was first served to my husband and me when we were at an inn in the wine country of Torgiano, Italy. Here is my low-fat, low-cholesterol, low-sodium version.

1 2-pound flank steak, all visible fat removed
1 teaspoon low-sodium vegetable seasoning (see page 28)
1 teaspoon garlic powder
1 teaspoon onion powder
1 medium carrot, shredded
2 medium zucchini, shredded
½ small onion, minced
2 cloves garlic, minced
½ teaspoon rosemary or herbes de Provence
1 cup soft whole wheat bread crumbs, made from Pritikin bread
1 egg white
1 tablespoon grated Sap Sago cheese, toasted (see page 15)
3 tablespoons chopped fresh parsley
½ teaspoon crushed pepper
1 tablespoon Hungarian paprika
2½ cups our Vegetable Stock (see page 60) or Chicken Stock (see page 26)
1 small onion, diced
1 carrot, diced
1 stalk celery, diced
3 tablespoons flour
1 tablespoon tomato paste
3 tablespoons dry white wine

1. Season both sides of the flank steak with vegetable seasoning, garlic powder, and onion powder.
2. *To make stuffing,* combine the next 10 ingredients.
3. Spread on steak, leaving a 1-inch border all around.
4. Roll as a jelly roll and tie 3 times with either kitchen string or unwaxed dental floss. Sprinkle meat with Hungarian paprika and moisten with 1 tablespoon of the stock.
5. Place meat on broiler rack and brown slowly under broiler, basting with 1 tablespoon stock every 5 minutes for about 20 minutes, or until lightly browned.
6. Brown onion, carrot, and celery in 3 tablespoons stock in an ovenproof casserole. When vegetables are lightly browned, add 3 tablespoons flour. Continue to cook flour slowly to an even brown color, stirring constantly.

*7. Add 2 cups stock slowly, blend until smooth, bring to a simmer, add tomato paste and dry white wine, blend, and add browned meat.

8. Cover casserole, place in lower middle level of a preheated 350° oven, and cook about 2 hours or until a fork pierces the meat quite easily. Check meat and turn and baste every half hour.

9. When meat is done, remove from casserole; puree vegetables, return to liquid in casserole, and heat sauce to a simmer.

10. While sauce is simmering, slice meat into 1-inch diagonal slices.

To Serve: Arrange meat on a platter, glaze with a small portion of sauce (serve the remainder in a sauce boat), and serve with the steamed fresh vegetables of your choice (carrots, zucchini, broccoli, summer squash, crookneck squash, or steamed small red potatoes). Add a lovely mixed green salad with our Vinaigrette Dressing (see page 12), crisp sourdough rolls, and seasonal fresh fruit for dessert—and you're ready for all the guests.

Variations: If your diet permits, Parmesan cheese may be substituted for the Sap Sago.

Instead of rolling the meat, you can slit a pocket in one side of the flank steak, fill it with the stuffing, and skewer the pocket closed. The stuffing can be varied to suit your taste and creativity.

Per serving: 248 calories; 28 gm protein; 6.6 gm fat; 13.7 gm carbohydrate; 2.3 gm fiber; 73 mg cholesterol; 4.3 mg iron; 144 mg sodium; 51 mg calcium; 228 mg phosphorus; 2301 IU Vitamin A; 0.11 mg thiamine; 0.21 mg riboflavin; 12 mg Vitamin C; 611 mg potassium; 0.15 mg zinc; 6.5 mg niacin; 59 mcg Vitamin B_6; 0 mcg Vitamin B_{12}; 8 mcg folic acid

* May be prepared the day before through step 7.

Marinated Flank Steak

Serves: 6 (3 ounces cooked beef = 1 serving)

2 tablespoons mild soy sauce
1 teaspoon powdered ginger or grated fresh ginger root
2 tablespoons frozen unsweetened pineapple juice concentrate
4 green onions, diced
1 teaspoon garlic powder, or 2 cloves garlic, minced

1½ pounds flank steak (all visible fat removed), scored lightly

Watercress or parsley sprigs and 1 cup fresh pineapple chunks for garnish

1. Combine the first 5 ingredients, place in a plastic bag, add flank steak, and marinate 4 to 6 hours. Turn meat in marinade from time to time.

2. Remove meat from marinade and broil 5 minutes on each side, or as necessary for desired degree of doneness.

3. Cut *diagonally* into ½-inch slices for serving.

To Serve: Place flank steak slices on a warm platter, garnish with watercress or chopped parsley, and sprinkle pineapple chunks over meat. Accompany with Larry's Crispy Potatoes (page 220) and Zucchini Tian (page 231).

Per serving: 172 calories; 25 gm protein; 6.5 gm fat; 1.1 gm carbohydrate; 0.2 gm fiber; 70 mg cholesterol; 3.7 mg iron; 243 mg sodium; 16 mg calcium; 281 mg phosphorus; 13 IU Vitamin A; 0.1 mg thiamine; 0.35 mg riboflavin; 0 mg Vitamin C; 403 mg potassium; 0 mg zinc; 6.1 mg niacin; 0 mcg Vitamin B_6; 0 mcg Vitamin B_{12}; 0 mcg folic acid

Marinated Beef and Vegetable Salad

Serves: 12 (1 cup = 1 serving)

1 20-ounce package frozen salt-free French-cut green beans
1 10-ounce package frozen artichoke hearts, or 1 8½-ounce can quartered artichoke hearts
1–1½ pounds flank steak* (all visible fat removed), prepared and cooked as in Marinated Flank Steak (see page 176) and cooled
1 7½-ounce can hearts of palm, cut in 4-inch circles
1½ pounds fresh mushrooms, stemmed and sliced
4 green onions, chopped
1½ tablespoons red wine vinegar
6 tablespoons our Chicken Stock (see page 26)
2 tablespoons lemon juice
4 tablespoons nonfat yogurt
2 tablespoons salt-free Dijon mustard
Freshly ground pepper

1 head butter lettuce, rinsed and dried, for serving
1 cup cherry tomatoes, or 2 ripe tomatoes, peeled, seeded, and sliced, for garnish
4 tablespoons finely chopped fresh Italian parsley for garnish

1. Cook beans as directed on package, drain, and chill.
2. Cook artichoke hearts as directed on package, drain, and chill.
3. Slice cooked flank steak across the grain into ¼-inch slices.
4. Combine meat with beans, artichoke hearts, hearts of palm, mushrooms, and green onions in a salad bowl.

**5. *To make salad dressing:* Shake the next 6 ingredients in a screw-top jar until thoroughly blended.

6. Pour just enough salad dressing on salad to coat ingredients. Toss lightly and marinate 1 hour.

To Serve: Pile on a lettuce-lined platter or bowl. Arrange tomatoes around mixture and sprinkle with chopped parsley.

Variation: Leftover roast chicken may be substituted for flank steak.

For a delicious cold pasta salad, add 4 ounces of chilled cooked fusilli.

Per serving: 118 calories; 14.9 gm protein; 3.1 gm fat; 8.8 gm carbohydrate; 2.5 gm fiber; 35 mg cholesterol; 2.5 mg iron; 46 mg sodium; 42 mg calcium; 156 mg phosphorus; 518 IU Vitamin A; 0.14 mg thiamine; 0.45 mg riboflavin; 14 mg Vitamin C; 559 mg potassium; 0.04 mg zinc; 4.7 mg niacin; 89 mcg Vitamin B_6; 0 mcg Vitamin B_{12}; 15 mcg folic acid

* May also be prepared from leftover flank steak that has been frozen.
** May be prepared through step 5 the day before.

Old-Fashioned Baked Meat Loaf

Serves: 6 (2 slices = 1 serving)

1 carrot, cut in 4 pieces
1 onion, cut in 4 pieces
1 stalk celery, cut in 4 pieces
¼ cup fresh Italian parsley
1 large clove garlic
2 slices Pritikin whole wheat or rye bread, quartered
2 egg whites
½ cup nonfat milk
1 pound ground flank steak or very lean ground beef
Freshly ground pepper

1. Place carrot, onion, celery, and parsley in food processor or blender. Process until chopped.
2. While food processor is in motion, add garlic clove to vegetable mixture. Continue to process until finely chopped. Scrape down sides of bowl from time to time.
3. Add bread and process until crumbled.
4. Add egg whites and milk and process.
5. Place ground meat in a mixing bowl and add vegetable mixture. Sprinkle with ground pepper.
6. Blend gently with a fork until mixture is well blended. (Do not overmix; it will make the meat loaf tough.)
7. Shape into a loaf in an 8-inch-square glass baking dish and bake in a preheated 350° oven for 50 to 60 minutes.

To Serve: Serve with baked potatoes and broiled tomato halves.

Per serving: 150 calories; 18.6 gm protein; 4 gm fat; 8.8 gm carbohydrate; 1.1 gm fiber; 47 mg cholesterol; 2.8 mg iron; 96 mg sodium; 54 mg calcium; 113 mg phosphorus; 1686 IU Vitamin A; 0.7 mg thiamine; 0.33 mg riboflavin; 9 mg Vitamin C; 353 mg potassium; 0.2 mg zinc; 2.6 mg niacin; 66 mcg Vitamin B_6; 0.8 mcg Vitamin B_{12}; 9 mcg folic acid

Stuffed Rutabaga Cups

Serves: 8 (½ stuffed rutabaga = 1 serving)

1½ pounds ground flank steak or very lean ground beef
2 cloves garlic, minced
1 green pepper, chopped
1 large onion, chopped
½ cup salt-free tomato sauce
1½ cups our Vegetable Stock (see page 60)
¼ cup flour
8 ounces nonfat yogurt
4 large rutabagas, halved, peeled, and hollowed out into cups

Chopped fresh dill and chopped ripe tomato for garnish

1. Brown meat with garlic, green pepper, and onion until crumbly and no longer pink.
2. Add tomato sauce, and stir.
3. Mix stock and flour together and stir into beef.
4. Stir in yogurt. *Do not boil.*
5. Cook rutabagas in boiling water until tender but still firm.*
6. Drain well and fill with beef mixture.

To Serve: Serve garnished with chopped dill and chopped ripe tomato. Steamed broccoli spears and sliced baked beets (page 213) complete a colorful plate.

Per serving: 253 calories; 21.7 gm protein; 7.5 gm fat; 22.2 gm carbohydrate; 3.4 gm fiber; 60 mg cholesterol; 3.1 mg iron; 57 mg sodium; 132 mg calcium; 210 mg phosphorus; 1002 IU Vitamin A; 0.19 mg thiamine; 0.33 mg riboflavin; 68 mg Vitamin C; 695 mg potassium; 0.09 mg zinc; 5.7 mg niacin; 58 mcg Vitamin B_6; 0 mcg Vitamin B_{12}; 6 mcg folic acid

* May also be steamed or cooked in microwave. Rutabaga is also delicious baked as you would a potato.

Stuffed Cabbage Loaf

Serves: 8 (2 slices = 1 serving)

For those of you who find making traditional stuffed cabbage a chore, here is an easy version that is superdelicious. It may be made ahead of time and frozen before or after baking. In choosing your cabbage, look for firm, green, crisp heads.

1 medium head green cabbage, quartered and cored
1 medium onion, minced
1 clove garlic, minced
1 *thin slice* peeled ginger root, minced
¼ cup minced fresh Italian parsley
1 teaspoon low-sodium vegetable seasoning (see page 28)
Freshly ground pepper
2 egg whites
3 slices Pritikin whole wheat bread, pulled into fine crumbs
⅔ cup nonfat milk
1¼ pounds ground flank steak or very lean ground beef*
1 cup Steamed Brown Rice (see page 254)
1 16-ounce can salt-free tomato sauce
1 medium onion, chopped
¼ cup defrosted frozen unsweetened apple juice concentrate

Chopped fresh parsley for garnish

1. Cover cabbage with boiling water and cook 10 minutes. *Drain well.*
2. Combine onion, garlic, ginger root, parsley, vegetable seasoning, pepper, and egg whites in a large bowl. Mix well.
3. Soak bread crumbs in milk until milk is absorbed. Combine with onion mixture.
4. Add ground meat and brown rice to onion mixture. Stir lightly with a fork (or washed hands) until blended. *Do not overmix.*
5. Combine tomato sauce with chopped onion and apple juice concentrate.
6. Lightly spray a glass 9 x 5-inch loaf pan with nonstick spray. Fill loaf pan with alternate layers of meat mixture, cabbage leaves, and 3 tablespoons of tomato sauce mixture. Begin and end with meat.
7. Pour remaining tomato sauce over top of meat.
8. Bake in a preheated 375° oven for about 1 hour.

To Serve: Unmold meat loaf on a heated platter, sprinkle with additional chopped parsley, and surround with steamed new potatoes and

* You may substitute ground turkey for the ground flank steak or lean beef.

frozen petits pois, or, if you're watching calories, substitute carrots or asparagus for the potatoes. To complete the meal, serve with a crisp mixed green salad, applesauce, and Boysenberry-Yogurt Sorbet (page 290) for dessert.

Per serving: 250 calories; 20 gm protein; 4.7 gm fat; 27.1 gm carbohydrate; 3.9 gm fiber; 44 mg cholesterol; 3.3 mg iron; 96 mg sodium; 96 mg calcium; 160 mg phosphorus; 1106 IU Vitamin A; 0.15 mg thiamine; 0.25 mg riboflavin; 44 mg Vitamin C; 476 mg potassium; 0.46 mg zinc; 3.5 mg niacin; 160 mcg Vitamin B_6; 0.09 mcg Vitamin B_{12}; 32 mcg folic acid

Hearty Steak with Peppers

Serves: 8 (1 cup = 1 serving)

3 tablespoons burgundy wine
1 1½-pound flank steak (all visible fat removed), cut in 1-inch cubes
1 tablespoon unbleached flour
2 celery stalks with leaves, sliced
1 onion, peeled and sliced
2 cloves garlic, minced
½ cup our Vegetable Stock (see page 60) or water
1 teaspoon low-sodium vegetable seasoning (see page 28)
Few grains crushed red pepper
1 green pepper, seeded and cut in 1-inch cubes
1 red pepper, seeded and cut in 1-inch cubes

1. Heat burgundy in a sauté pan; when boiling, add flank steak and sauté until brown.

2. Add flour to steak mixture and stir.

3. Add celery, onion, garlic, and stock or water; stir and simmer 15 minutes covered.

4. Add vegetable seasoning, crushed red pepper, and green and red pepper cubes. Cover and cook 15 additional minutes, or until meat is tender.

To Serve: Serve over Steamed Brown Rice (page 254).

Per serving: 135 calories; 18.1 gm protein; 4.3 gm fat; 4.8 gm carbohydrate; 1 gm fiber; 53 mg cholesterol; 2.7 mg iron; 47 mg sodium; 24 mg calcium; 108 mg phosphorus; 709 IU Vitamin A; 0.08 mg thiamine; 0.16 mg riboflavin; 44 mg Vitamin C; 333 mg potassium; 0.08 mg zinc; 2.9 mg niacin; 62 mcg Vitamin B_6; 0 mcg Vitamin B_{12}; 6 mcg folic acid

Pan Bagna

(A Meal in a Sandwich)

Serves: 12 (1 slice = 1 serving)

A treat for *al fresco* dining, whether on your patio or at the park.

1 long loaf sourdough French bread
3 tablespoons salt-free Dijon mustard with herbs
2 large ripe tomatoes, sliced ½-inch thick
1 large red onion, sliced ¼-inch thick
1 roasted pepper (see page 100), sliced (optional)
1 pound ground flank steak or very lean ground beef
1 pound ground turkey or chicken
3 green onions, chopped
1 medium onion, chopped
1 large clove garlic, minced
1 carrot, chopped
½ green pepper, chopped
½ cup whole wheat bread crumbs made from Pritikin bread,* soaked in ½ cup nonfat milk
3 egg whites
1 teaspoon low-sodium vegetable seasoning (see page 28)
½ teaspoon herbal bouquet
Few grains crushed red pepper
1 tablespoon mild soy sauce
1 teaspoon salt-free Dijon mustard

1. Halve the loaf of bread lengthwise and remove the soft center, leaving a ½-inch shell all the way around.
2. Spread surface of bread with mustard and arrange tomato and onion slices, and pepper slices if you like, on top of bread. Wrap in plastic wrap until meat loaf filling is baked.
3. Combine ground beef, turkey, green onions, onion, garlic, carrot, green pepper, bread crumbs, egg whites, vegetable seasoning, herbal bouquet, crushed red pepper, soy sauce, and mustard in a mixing bowl. Mix lightly with a fork until blended.
4. Spray a small, shallow roasting pan with nonstick spray. Shape meat loaf to the approximate size of the hollowed-out loaf of bread.
5. Bake in a preheated 375° oven for about 1 hour.
6. When meat is cooked, place hot meat loaf inside loaf of bread on top of tomatoes and onions.
7. Tie loaf together with kitchen cord—as tightly as possible—in several places.
8. Weight tied loaf down with heavy cans so that juices and flavors

* You may use crumbs made from the inside of the loaf of bread instead of Pritikin whole wheat bread if you wish.

will blend and soak into bread. Let it stand 2 to 3 hours before cutting into 1½-inch slices for serving.

To Serve: Complete your picnic with a green salad, a basket of fresh fruit, and a glass of dry white wine.

Per serving: 212 calories; 21.1 gm protein; 4.3 gm fat; 20.7 gm carbohydrate; 1.5 gm fiber; 49 mg cholesterol; 2.8 mg iron; 180 mg sodium; 35 mg calcium; 153 mg phosphorus; 1134 IU Vitamin A; 0.15 mg thiamine; 0.21 mg riboflavin; 16 mg Vitamin C; 386 mg potassium; 0.77 mg zinc; 4.4 mg niacin; 77 mcg Vitamin B_6; 0.01 mcg Vitamin B_{12}; 12 mcg folic acid

Casseroles

THE EASY WAY OUT– THAT'S IN

Hungarian Stuffed Cabbage
Cabbage Soufflé Pudding
Chicken and Green Chili Casserole
Buenos Enchiladas Suiza
Fava Bean Peasant Casserole
Judith's Fish Goulash
Flageolets au Gratin
Those Mushrooms
Noodle Lasagna
Sally's Vegetarian Lasagna
Creole Tuna Pie
Christmas Eve Turkey Casserole
Red and Green Peppers Stuffed with Vegetables
Baked Potatoes Provençale
Spanish Rice
Scalloped Sweet Potatoes and Apples

Casseroles are especially desirable because we can minimize the animal protein content of the meal with the addition of vegetables, rice, pasta, and the like. We use the animal protein as a seasoning in the casserole, or in some cases we eliminate it completely.

Two questions that were frequently asked in my classes were: Can I make it ahead of time? Can I freeze it? Many of the casserole dishes that follow answer these needs. On that rainy day or on one when you have much energy that needs to be directed, try a few and put them away in the freezer for those unexpected but welcome guests that frequent every happy home.

If frozen, the casserole should be removed from the freezer and placed in the refrigerator the night before, defrosted at room temperature for 4 to 6 hours (depending on the casserole), and then baked at the oven temperature and baking time in the recipe. (If you don't have time to bring it to room temperature, place in a *cold* oven and double the baking time.)

Hungarian Stuffed Cabbage

Serves: 6 (2 cabbage rolls = 1 serving)

1 large green cabbage
1 small onion, grated
1 shallot, minced
2 egg whites
1 clove garlic, minced
1 carrot, shredded
½ cup parsley
½ cup brown rice, partially cooked in 1 cup our Chicken Stock (see page 26) for 25 minutes
½ pound ground flank steak or extra lean beef
¼ cup bread crumbs
1 teaspoon low-sodium vegetable seasoning (see page 28)
¼ cup salt-free tomato juice (optional)
⅔ cup frozen peas
1 16-ounce can tomato sauce, or 1 can Italian plum tomatoes in puree, pureed
3 ounces frozen unsweetened apple or pineapple juice concentrate
½ teaspoon Hungarian paprika

Chopped fresh parsley for garnish

1. Core the cabbage and cook it in boiling water until barely tender. Drain and separate 12 large leaves and trim ribs.
2. Combine onion, shallot, egg whites, garlic, carrot, and parsley until thoroughly blended.
3. Combine onion mixture with rice, ground beef, bread crumbs, vegetable seasoning, and tomato juice, using a fork to mix. Add frozen peas.
4. Place ⅓ cup of the mixture in each cabbage leaf and roll up, tucking in sides. Make 12 rolls.
5. Shred remaining cabbage; sprinkle in bottom of 2-quart casserole.
6. Place cabbage rolls in casserole seam-side down, packing tightly.
7. Combine tomato sauce, or pureed tomatoes, juice concentrate, and paprika.
8. Pour sauce over cabbage rolls. Cook, covered, in a preheated 325° oven for 2 hours.*
9. This recipe may be prepared a day before serving and reheated, or it may be frozen for future use. Double the recipe, use one casserole, freeze the other. *To Reheat:* Leave at room temperature for several hours and cook, covered, in 325° oven for 1 hour or until thoroughly heated.

To Serve: Garnish with chopped parsley and serve with noodle pudding and steamed carrots.

***Helpful Hint:** Place casserole on a baking sheet to collect the drips!

Per serving: 300 calories; 18.8 gm protein; 3.5 gm fat; 43.3 gm carbohydrate; 5.5 gm fiber; 36 mg cholesterol; 3.6 mg iron; 105 mg sodium; 91 mg calcium; 167 mg phosphorus; 3302 IU Vitamin A; 0.22 mg thiamine; 0.25 mg riboflavin; 65 mg Vitamin C; 552 mg potassium; 0.47 mg zinc; 3.9 mg niacin; 215 mcg Vitamin B_6; 0.01 Vitamin B_{12}; 41 mcg folic acid

Cabbage Soufflé Pudding
(Tastes Like Noodle Pudding)

Serves: 8 (1 cup = 1 serving)

Noodle puddings are perennial favorites. This marvelous adaptation of a recipe sent to me by Sylvia Hankins, a participant at the Pritikin Longevity Center, is low in cholesterol, fat, sodium, and sugar—and contains no noodles!

3 pounds green cabbage
1 tablespoon mild soy sauce
3 apples, peeled, cored, and coarsely chopped
1 cup seeded muscat raisins
⅔ cup hot fresh orange juice
1 tablespoon lemon juice
¼ cup frozen unsweetened apple juice concentrate
⅓ cup our Chicken Stock (see page 26)
½ cup matzo meal
1 teaspoon cinnamon
8 egg whites
⅛ teaspoon cream of tartar
Cinnamon
Freshly ground nutmeg

1. Rinse cabbage, core, and shred coarsely (like wide noodles).
2. Cover with boiling water, add soy sauce, and bring to a boil. Simmer until tender, about 20 to 25 minutes.
3. Drain well and spread out to cool quickly on a baking sheet.
4. Squeeze dry, by handfuls, and place in a large mixing bowl.
5. Add apples, raisins, orange juice, lemon juice, apple juice concentrate, and chicken stock to cabbage and mix gently.
6. Sprinkle matzo meal and cinnamon over mixture and combine.
7. Beat egg whites with cream of tartar until stiff (holds a peak; does not slide in bowl).
8. Fold egg whites into cabbage mixture and turn into a 2-quart rectangular casserole that has been treated with nonstick spray.
9. Sprinkle lightly with cinnamon and freshly ground nutmeg and bake 1 hour in a preheated 350° oven.

To Serve: Serve with roast chicken and steamed fresh peas. Baked Fruit Compote (page 267) makes an excellent dessert.

Per serving: 204 calories; 8 gm protein; 0.7 gm fat; 45.7 gm carbohydrate; 8.3 gm fiber; 0 mg cholesterol; 1.7 mg iron; 150 mg sodium; 106 mg calcium; 82 mg phosphorus; 288 IU Vitamin A; 0.14 mg thiamine; 0.21 mg riboflavin; 92 mg Vitamin C; 679 mg potassium; 0.69 mg zinc; 0.8 mg niacin; 326 mcg Vitamin B_6; 0.03 mcg Vitamin B_{12}; 57 mcg folic acid

Chicken and Green Chili Casserole

Serves: 12 (1 cup = 1 serving)

1 onion, minced
2 shallots, minced
4 tablespoons our Chicken Stock (see page 26)
1 green pepper, chopped
4 cans mushroom soup (a brand that has no salt, MSG, preservatives, or sugar)
2 4-ounce cans diced green chilies
4 cooked chicken breasts, skinned, boned, and diced
1 package corn tortillas (12)
2 corn tortillas, toasted and crumbled
4 tablespoons grated Sap Sago cheese, toasted (see page 15)

1. Sauté minced onion and shallots in chicken stock until transparent.
2. Add chopped green pepper and sauté 2 minutes more.
3. Add canned mushroom soup and chilies. Stir until blended.
4. Add diced chicken and blend.
5. Spray a large 3-quart earthenware or glass shallow casserole with nonstick spray. Place 3 corn tortillas on bottom of casserole. Spoon one-third of chicken mixture over tortillas.
6. Repeat layers twice, ending with chicken mixture on top.

*7. Sprinkle with 3 crumbled, toasted tortillas and cheese.

8. Bake in a preheated 375° oven for 45 minutes, or until golden brown on top and heated through.

To Serve: Serve with a crisp green salad and additional warmed tortillas.

Variations: If your diet permits, use Parmesan cheese instead of Sap Sago. Instead of serving a salad, top the casserole with shredded lettuce, chopped tomato, chopped green pepper, and chopped green onions.

Per serving: 272 calories; 22.9 gm protein; 8 gm fat; 35.7 gm carbohydrate; 0.4 gm fiber; 43 mg cholesterol; 2.1 mg iron; 91 mg sodium; 60 mg calcium; 246 mg phosphorus; 105 IU Vitamin A; 1.02 mg thiamine; 0.2 mg riboflavin; 1 mg Vitamin C; 246 mg potassium; 1.04 mg zinc; 6.9 mg niacin; 374 mcg Vitamin B_6; 0.24 mcg Vitamin B_{12}; 5 mcg folic acid

* May be prepared the day before through step 7, or wrapped carefully at that point and frozen for future use.

Buenos Enchiladas Suiza

Serves: 6 (2 enchiladas = 1 serving)

⅓ cup Weight Watchers cottage cheese, rinsed and drained
3 tablespoons nonfat yogurt
1 teaspoon low-sodium vegetable seasoning (see page 28)
1 pound leftover cooked turkey breast or chicken, chopped
3 tablespoons green onion, chopped
2 tablespoons green chilies, chopped
1 15-ounce can chili beans
½ red or white onion, cut in quarters
¼ cup mild chili salsa (optional)
12 corn tortillas
1 10-ounce can enchilada sauce

Shredded lettuce, our Sour Cream (see page 27), and chopped green onions for garnish

1. Puree cottage cheese in blender or food processor; add yogurt and vegetable seasoning and blend.
2. In a bowl, combine cheese mixture with turkey, green onion, and chilies.
3. Puree chili beans in food processor.
4. Add onion to beans and chop. If a thinner texture is desired, add chili salsa.
5. Warm tortillas for 10 seconds in microwave oven or steamer to soften, or sprinkle with 2 tablespoons of water, wrap lightly in foil, and heat in a preheated 375° oven for 5 minutes.
6. Lay a tortilla flat and place ¼ cup bean mixture along center. Place ¼ cup chicken mixture over beans.
7. Fold over ends to cover mixture and place seam-side-down in a 2-quart 13 x 9 x 2-inch glass casserole.

*8. When all tortillas have been filled and placed in the casserole, cover with enchilada sauce.

9. Bake 20 to 30 minutes in a preheated 350° oven.

To Serve: Pass shredded lettuce, our Sour Cream, and chopped green onions, for a garnish.

Per serving: 333 calories; 37.7 gm protein; 6 gm fat; 63.1 gm carbohydrate; 1.3 gm fiber; 60 mg cholesterol; 5.2 mg iron; 172 mg sodium; 76 mg calcium; 410 mg phosphorus; 925 IU Vitamin A; 1.77 mg thiamine; 0.25 mg riboflavin; 12 mg Vitamin C; 712 mg potassium; 2.54 mg zinc; 9.7 mg niacin; 15 mcg Vitamin B_6; 0 mcg Vitamin B_{12}; 10 mcg folic acid

* May be frozen after step 8 is completed.

Fava Bean Peasant Casserole

Serves: 8–10 (1 cup = 1 serving)

Most people are either not familiar with fava beans or do not know how to prepare them. They come inside a giant pod and look somewhat like plump lima beans.

3 our Bouillon Cubes (see page 25)
2 large onions, thinly sliced
3 cloves garlic, minced
6 ripe tomatoes, peeled, seeded, and chopped, or 1 28-ounce can Italian plum tomatoes in puree
½ cup tomato puree (if using fresh tomatoes)
Freshly ground white pepper
1 teaspoon Italian herb seasoning
2 teaspoons dried savory, crushed, or 2 tablespoons fresh savory, chopped
1 bay leaf
3 pounds fava beans, shelled
1 teaspoon crushed red pepper
1 pound beef knuckle bones, fat removed
½ cup our Chicken Stock (see page 26) optional

1. Melt bouillon cubes in a large nonstick skillet. Add onions and garlic, and cook, covered, over low heat about 15 minutes, or until transparent and lightly browned. Stir from time to time.

2. Add chopped tomatoes, puree, pepper, herb seasoning, savory, and bay leaf. Simmer a few minutes.

3. Put tomato mixture in a 2-quart covered casserole. Add beans, crushed red pepper, and bones.

*4. Blend mixture and cover tightly.

5. Place in a preheated 350° oven and bake 45 to 60 minutes, or until beans are tender. If the mixture seems too dry, add chicken stock.

6. Remove bones before serving.

To Serve: This casserole may be served as a main dish with steamed vegetables and brown rice or as an accompaniment to a hot or cold chicken entrée.

Per serving: 136 calories; 9.5 gm protein; 0.9 gm fat; 25.2 gm carbohydrate; 5.1 gm fiber; 0 mg cholesterol; 4.2 mg iron; 66 mg sodium; 83 mg calcium; 189 mg phosphorus; 3240 IU Vitamin A; 0.35 mg thiamine; 0.24 mg riboflavin; 77 mg Vitamin C; 845 mg potassium; 0.34 mg zinc; 2.6 mg niacin; 106 mcg Vitamin B_6; 0 mcg Vitamin B_{12}; 14 mcg folic acid

* May be prepared the day before through step 4.

Fish Goulash

Serves: 4 (1¼ cups = 1 serving)

2 tablespoons red or white wine
1 medium onion, chopped
1 clove garlic, minced
3 ripe tomatoes, peeled, seeded, and quartered
3 small zucchini, sliced
1 pound cod, cut into 1-inch cubes
2 cups Steamed Brown Rice (see page 254)
1 teaspoon low-sodium vegetable seasoning (see page 28)
Freshly ground pepper
Hungarian paprika
⅓ cup water
3 tablespoons chopped fresh Italian parsley

1. Heat the wine in a saucepan. Add chopped onion and garlic to the wine and sauté until transparent and wilted. Add tomatoes and blend.
2. Add, in alternate layers, tomatoes, zucchini, fish, and rice. Sprinkle each layer with vegetable seasoning, pepper, and paprika.
3. Add water and cover firmly with lid.
4. Allow to cook over medium heat for about 25 to 30 minutes.

To Serve: Sprinkle with freshly chopped parsley and serve.

Variation: The same dish may be prepared using 2 diced potatoes instead of rice and 2 leeks and 3 carrots instead of squash and tomatoes.

Per serving: 375 calories; 37.8 gm protein; 7.1 gm fat; 38.1 gm carbohydrate; 7 gm fiber; 57 mg cholesterol; 3.3 mg iron; 135 mg sodium; 107 mg calcium; 457 mg phosphorus; 1808 IU Vitamin A; 0.33 mg thiamine; 0.27 mg riboflavin; 46 mg Vitamin C; 1034 mg potassium; 0.32 mg zinc; 6.5 mg niacin; 153 mcg Vitamin B_6; 0 mcg Vitamin B_{12}; 18 mcg folic acid

Flageolets au Gratin

Serves: 8 (⅔ cup = 1 serving)

Flageolets are very small beans commonly used in France and Italy. They are usually available in Italian delicatessens or gourmet shops, but small white northern beans can be substituted.

2 cups dried flageolets or white northern beans
1 onion stuck with 3 whole cloves
1 bouquet garni (6 sprigs parsley, 1 bay leaf, few grains crushed red pepper, and 1 teaspoon thyme)
1 tablespoon mild soy sauce
1 onion, minced
1 large clove garlic, minced
2 our Bouillon Cubes (see page 25)
3 ripe tomatoes, peeled, seeded, and cut into ½-inch strips
2 cups our Chicken Stock (see page 26)
1 cup nonfat evaporated milk
Freshly ground pepper
1 teaspoon low-sodium vegetable seasoning (see page 28)
1 cup our Seasoned Bread Crumbs (see page 29)

½ cup chopped fresh Italian parsley for garnish

1. Soak beans overnight in water to cover.
2. Drain beans. Place in a heavy casserole with onion, bouquet garni, and soy sauce. Add water to cover by 2 inches.
3. Bring to a boil, skim off froth, lower heat, and simmer 1½ hours, or until tender.
4. Drain beans, and discard onion and bouquet garni.
5. Sauté onion and garlic in bouillon cubes.
6. Add tomatoes and simmer 5 minutes.
7. Add chicken stock and nonfat milk; bring to a simmer and add drained flageolets.
8. Mix and season with freshly ground pepper and vegetable seasoning.
9. Transfer to a gratin dish and sprinkle with seasoned bread crumbs.
10. Bake in a preheated 375° oven for 30 minutes. If beans seem too dry, add a bit more chicken stock during cooking.

To Serve: Sprinkle with chopped parsley before serving.

Variation: If your diet allows, 1 tablespoon Parmesan cheese may be sprinkled over bread crumbs.

Per serving: 229 calories; 14.1 gm protein; 1.2 gm fat; 42.2 gm carbohydrate; 12.8 gm fiber; 0 mg cholesterol; 4.8 mg iron; 128 mg sodium; 143 mg calcium; 255 mg phosphorus; 998 IU Vitamin A; 0.38 mg thiamine; 0.21 mg riboflavin; 25 mg Vitamin C; 826 mg potassium; 1.59 mg zinc; 1.9 mg niacin; 362 mcg Vitamin B_6; 0.04 mcg Vitamin B_{12}; 73 mcg folic acid

Those Mushrooms

Serves: 10 (1 cup = 1 serving)

This luscious dish is based on a recipe of my sister Edie's. What may appear to be a complicated preparation is simplified by being partially done the day before.

3 our Bouillon Cubes (see page 25)
2 tablespoons dry vermouth or dry white wine
1¼ pounds mushrooms, thickly sliced
2 shallots, finely minced
4 green onions, finely minced
½ cup finely chopped celery
½ green pepper, finely chopped
3 tablespoons chopped fresh parsley
2 tablespoons nonfat yogurt
1 teaspoon low-sodium vegetable seasoning (see page 28)
Freshly ground pepper
½ cup Weight Watchers cottage cheese, rinsed, drained, and pureed in blender or food processor
6 slices Pritikin whole wheat bread, crusts removed
2 cloves garlic
4 egg whites
1½ cups nonfat milk
1 10½-ounce or 15-ounce can salt-free, undiluted cream of mushroom soup
¼ cup our Seasoned Bread Crumbs (see page 29)

1. In a 10-inch skillet, dissolve bouillon cubes over moderately high heat; add vermouth or wine and mushrooms and sauté for about 5 minutes, stirring occasionally.
2. Add shallots, green onions, celery, green pepper, and parsley. Sauté 3 minutes more.
3. Add yogurt, vegetable seasoning, and pepper.
4. Remove from heat and add pureed cottage cheese.
5. Toast bread (crusts removed) and rub in whole cloves of garlic when hot. Place 3 toast squares in bottom of a 2½-quart baking dish.
6. Layer mushroom mixture over toast.
7. Cube remaining 3 slices of toast and sprinkle over mushrooms.
*8. Beat egg whites with milk and pour over bread and mushroom mixture. Refrigerate overnight.
9. Remove from refrigerator 1 hour before baking and cover with mushroom soup.
10. Top with seasoned bread crumbs and bake uncovered in a preheated 325° oven for 45 minutes.

* Must be prepared the day before through step 8 for optimum flavor.

Serving Suggestions: This is wonderful served with steamed broccoli and carrots and a crisp green salad. It also is a delicious accompaniment to chicken or turkey. If you are fortunate enough to have leftovers, it's even good reheated.

Variation: If your diet allows, 2 tablespoons Parmesan cheese may be added with the bread crumbs.

Helpful Hint: Save bread crusts to make our Seasoned Bread Crumbs (see page 29).

Per serving: 104 calories; 6.8 gm protein; 2.2 gm fat; 14 gm carbohydrate; 1.7 gm fiber; 1 mg cholesterol; 1.1 mg iron; 115 mg sodium; 73 mg calcium; 99 mg phosphorus; 198 IU Vitamin A; 0.11 mg thiamine; 0.38 mg riboflavin; 10 mg Vitamin C; 317 mg potassium; 0.14 mg zinc; 2.6 mg niacin; 88 mcg Vitamin B_6; 0.13 mcg Vitamin B_{12}; 13 mcg folic acid

Noodle Lasagna

Serves: 12 (1 cup = 1 serving)

16 ounces whole wheat noodles
2 large onions, grated
2 cloves garlic, minced
3 tablespoons dry white wine, or 3 our Bouillon Cubes (see page 25)
1½ pounds ground flank steak or extra-lean ground beef
1 28-ounce can Italian plum tomatoes with basil, crushed
1 12-ounce can salt-free tomato paste
2 teaspoons Italian herb seasoning, crushed
1 bay leaf
2 16-ounce cartons Weight Watchers cottage cheese
2 egg whites
2 10-ounce packages frozen chopped spinach, cooked and well drained
3 tablespoons grated Sap Sago cheese, toasted (see page 15)

1. Cook noodles in boiling water until tender (about 10 minutes). Drain well.
2. Sauté onions and garlic in wine in nonstick skillet until transparent. Add ground meat and cook just until it turns pink.
3. Add crushed tomatoes, tomato paste, Italian seasoning, and bay leaf. Simmer 15 minutes. Remove bay leaf.
4. Combine cottage cheese and egg whites in blender or food processor and mix well. Add chopped, drained spinach and blend.
5. Spray a 3-quart casserole (13 x 9 x 2-inches) with nonstick spray.

*6. Place a layer of sauce, then noodles, then cheese, then sauce. Repeat layering and end with sauce.

7. Sprinkle with toasted Sap Sago cheese and bake in a preheated 350° oven for 45 minutes.

To Serve: To complete the meal, serve an Italian salad (mixed greens with garbanzo beans), crisp Italian bread, and Raspberry Mousse (page 288) for dessert.

Variations: If your diet allows, 3 tablespoons Parmesan cheese may be used instead of Sap Sago and, if you like, ½ pound coarsely shredded mozzarella cheese may be added between layers.

Per serving: 375 calories; 38.7 gm protein; 9.1 gm fat; 36 gm carbohydrate; 1.3 gm fiber; 54 mg cholesterol; 4.7 mg iron; 328 mg sodium; 164 mg calcium; 190 mg phosphorus; 4440 IU Vitamin A; 0.33 mg thiamine; 0.52 mg riboflavin; 26 mg Vitamin C; 760 mg potassium; 0.23 mg zinc; 5.5 mg niacin; 94 mcg Vitamin B_6; 0.01 mcg Vitamin B_{12}; 10 mcg folic acid

* May be prepared the day before through step 6, or frozen at this point for future use. If frozen, defrost 8 to 10 hours or the night before in the refrigerator before heating.

Sally's Vegetarian Lasagna

Serves: 12 (1 cup = 1 serving)

1 large onion, chopped
3 cloves garlic, minced
1 pound unpeeled eggplant, diced
2 zucchini, diced
¼ pound fresh mushrooms, sliced
¼ cup salt-free tomato juice
1 28-ounce can plum tomatoes in puree
½ cup dry red wine
2 carrots, shredded
¼ cup minced fresh parsley
2 teaspoons dried oregano, crushed, or 4 teaspoons fresh oregano
1 teaspoon dried basil, crushed, or 2 teaspoons fresh basil
Freshly ground pepper
9 whole wheat lasagna noodles
1 pound hoop cheese or skim-milk ricotta
2 egg whites
¼ cup chopped fresh parsley
3 tablespoons grated Sap Sago cheese, toasted (see page 15)

1. Cook onion, garlic, eggplant, zucchini, and mushrooms for 15 minutes in tomato juice.
2. Add tomatoes, wine, carrots, parsley, oregano, basil, and ground pepper. Bring to a boil and simmer for 30 minutes, stirring occasionally.
3. Cook, rinse, and drain lasagna noodles according to manufacturer's directions.*
4. Process hoop cheese in blender or food processor until creamy. Add egg whites and chopped parsley and process briefly.
5. Spray a 9 x 13-inch baking dish with nonstick spray. Spread a layer of vegetable sauce in dish, lay 3 strips of lasagna noodles lengthwise over sauce, and place 4 dollops of hoop cheese on each noodle.

**6. Proceed with a second layer of sauce, noodles, and hoop cheese, and a third layer of the same, ending with sauce.

7. Sprinkle with Sap Sago cheese.
8. Place dish on a baking sheet to catch those bothersome drips, and bake in a preheated 350° oven for 45 minutes.
9. Let stand 10 minutes before serving so that lasagna holds its shape.

To Serve: Vegetarian Lasagna may be served with Marinated Bean Salad (page 85) on shredded lettuce and crisp whole wheat garlic toast (page 14). A wedge of seasonal melon with lime would be an excellent dessert.

Variations: If your diet allows, grated Parmesan cheese may be used instead of Sap Sago, and shredded skim-milk mozzarella may be sprinkled on the dollops of hoop cheese in each layer (use 8 ounces mozzarella in all).

***Helpful Hint:** Add lasagna noodles one at a time to boiling water, so that you do not disturb boil and noodles do not stick together.

Per serving: 250 calories; 19.1 gm protein; 2.6 gm fat; 38.2 gm carbohydrate; 2.9 gm fiber; 7 mg cholesterol; 2.2 mg iron; 200 mg sodium; 62 mg calcium; 66 mg phosphorus; 2417 IU Vitamin A; 0.26 mg thiamine; 0.27 mg riboflavin; 26 mg Vitamin C; 438 mg potassium; 0.23 mg zinc; 2.6 mg niacin; 117 mcg Vitamin B_6; 0.01 mcg Vitamin B_{12}; 11 mcg folic acid

** May be prepared a day ahead through step 6, or frozen at this point for future use. If frozen, thaw 4 to 6 hours at room temperature and bake 1½ hours at 350°.

Creole Tuna Pie

Serves: 4 (⅔ cup = 1 serving)

3 our Bouillon Cubes (see page 25), or 3 tablespoons our Chicken Stock (see page 26)
1 small onion, sliced
½ green pepper, sliced
½ 28-ounce can plum tomatoes, crushed, with juice
1 bay leaf
½ teaspoon basil, crushed
1 7-ounce can salt-free tuna in water, drained and flaked in large pieces
1 7-ounce can artichoke hearts, rinsed, drained, and quartered
½ cup unsweetened whole-grain flake cereal, crushed, or 1 cup whole wheat garlic croutons (page 14)

1. Melt bouillon cubes in a nonstick skillet until boiling. Add onion and pepper and sauté until soft (about 10 minutes).
2. Add crushed tomatoes and juice, bay leaf, and basil, and cook 10 minutes, stirring constantly. Remove bay leaf.
3. Spray a shallow casserole or 9-inch glass pie plate with nonstick spray. Arrange tuna chunks and artichoke hearts in dish. Cover with tomato-onion mixture and sprinkle with crumbs.
4. Bake in a preheated 350° oven for 20 minutes, or until lightly browned.

To Serve: Serve with Steamed Brown Rice (page 254) and steamed vegetables for an easy Sunday night supper.

Per serving: 127 calories; 17.2 gm protein; 1 gm fat; 14.1 gm carbohydrate; 2 gm fiber; 31 mg cholesterol; 2 mg iron; 201 mg sodium; 40 mg calcium; 162 mg phosphorus; 1272 IU Vitamin A; 0.15 mg thiamine; 0.22 mg riboflavin; 41 mg Vitamin C; 559 mg potassium; 0.75 mg zinc; 8.3 mg niacin; 215 mcg Vitamin B_6; 0 mcg Vitamin B_{12}; 21 mcg folic acid

Christmas Eve Turkey Casserole

Serves: 8 (1½ cups = 1 serving)

This casserole is perfect for easy holiday entertaining. It can be made ahead of time and reheated so that you can enjoy the festivities.

¼ cup flour
1¼ cups nonfat milk
1 cup nonfat evaporated milk
1 slice onion
½ teaspoon thyme
1 bay leaf
½ teaspoon freshly ground white pepper
1 teaspoon low-sodium vegetable seasoning (see page 28)
2 tablespoons dry sherry or sauterne
3 our Bouillon Cubes, melted (see page 25), or 3 tablespoons our Chicken Stock (see page 26)
1 cup sliced fresh mushrooms
3 green onions, chopped
1 5-ounce can water chestnuts, drained and sliced
1 cup green pepper, chopped
1 2-ounce jar pimiento, drained and chopped
1 tablespoon mild soy sauce
1 6-ounce package soba noodles* or linguini, cooked *al dente*
1 bunch fresh broccoli, steamed and coarsely chopped
4 cups cooked turkey, cubed
4 tablespoons our Seasoned Bread Crumbs (see page 29)
2 tablespoons grated Sap Sago cheese, toasted (see page 15)

1. *To make sauce:* Mix flour with cold milk. Blend with a wooden spoon or whisk, place over heat, and stir constantly until mixture coats spoon. Add onion, thyme, bay leaf, freshly ground pepper, vegetable seasoning, and dry sherry and simmer 5 minutes more to evaporate alcohol. Remove from heat and cover until ready to use.

2. Place bouillon cubes in a 10-inch nonstick skillet. Add mushrooms and green onions and sauté 5 minutes.

3. Add water chestnuts, green pepper, pimiento, and soy sauce. Mix and simmer. Cover and simmer for 2 minutes more.

4. Place cooked, drained noodles on bottom of a 13 x 9 x 2-inch glass or earthenware casserole that has been sprayed lightly with nonstick spray.

5. Cover noodles with mushroom mixture. Spread chopped broccoli on top of mushroom mixture, reserving some florets for garnish.

**6. Add a layer of diced turkey and top with sauce (onion and bay leaf removed).

7. Sprinkle with seasoned bread crumbs and toasted Sap Sago cheese.

8. Bake in a preheated 350° oven for 30 to 35 minutes.

* Soba noodles, sometimes called Japanese noodles, may be purchased in your local market or health food store. The content is half buckwheat and half whole wheat flour.
** May be prepared the day before through step 6 or frozen at this point for future use.

To Serve: Garnish with reserved broccoli florets and serve. Complete the menu with a crispy green salad, hot sourdough rolls, and a chilled white wine. Our Festive Fruit Cake (page 269) provides a special ending for a holiday buffet.

Variation: If your diet allows, use Parmesan cheese instead of Sap Sago.

Per serving: 316 calories; 31.8 gm protein; 5.2 gm fat; 32.7 gm carbohydrate; 2.4 gm fiber; 64 mg cholesterol; 3 mg iron; 234 mg sodium; 190 mg calcium; 330 mg phosphorus; 1570 IU Vitamin A; 0.25 mg thiamine; 0.49 mg riboflavin; 61 mg Vitamin C; 725 mg potassium; 1.90 mg zinc; 7.1 mg niacin; 82 mcg Vitamin B_6; 0.23 mcg Vitamin B_{12}; 34 mcg folic acid

Red and Green Peppers Stuffed with Vegetables

Serves: 8 (½ stuffed green pepper and ½ stuffed red pepper = 1 serving)

4 red peppers, halved, seeds removed
4 green peppers, halved, seeds removed
1 pound russet potatoes, cooked and mashed with ½ cup skim milk
8 ounces skim-milk ricotta cheese
1 cup chopped onion
2 cloves garlic, minced
2 shallots, minced
½ pound zucchini, cooked and chopped
2 large carrots, shredded coarsely
1 10-ounce package frozen chopped broccoli, cooked, or 1 pound fresh broccoli, steamed and chopped
1 10-ounce package frozen petits pois
1 teaspoon low-sodium vegetable seasoning (see page 28)
1 teaspoon freshly ground pepper
1 quart salt-free marinara sauce, or 2 28-ounce cans crushed Italian plum tomatoes

1. Parboil the peppers for 5 minutes. Drain and cool.
2. Mix mashed potatoes, cheese, onion, garlic, shallots, zucchini, carrots, broccoli, and peas.
3. Season to taste with vegetable seasoning and freshly ground pepper.
4. Use mixture to fill pepper halves. Place filled peppers in a baking dish, alternating red and green peppers.
5. Bake in a preheated 375° oven for 30 to 35 minutes. While baking, heat tomato sauce.
6. Spoon sauce over stuffed peppers and bake another 10 minutes. May be prepared several hours ahead of time and preheated for serving.

To Serve: These delicious peppers are lovely served with Orange and Onion Salad (page 103) as an accompaniment.

Per serving: 200 calories; 12 gm protein; 3.1 gm fat; 34.9 gm carbohydrate; 7.5 gm fiber; 16 mg cholesterol; 3.3 mg iron; 134 mg sodium; 192 mg calcium; 232 mg phosphorus; 7999 IU Vitamin A; 0.38 mg thiamine; 0.3 mg riboflavin; 240 mg Vitamin C; 1047 mg potassium; 1 mg zinc; 3.4 mg niacin; 475 mcg Vitamin B_6; 0.14 mcg Vitamin B_{12}; 37 mcg folic acid

Baked Potatoes Provençale

Serves: 6 (1 cup = 1 serving)

2 large onions, sliced thin
1 clove garlic, minced
½ green pepper, seeded and chopped
3 tablespoons our Chicken Stock (see page 26)
2 tomatoes, peeled, seeded, and chopped, or 4 Italian plum tomatoes, drained and chopped
2 pounds russet potatoes, peeled and sliced ½-inch thick
2 teaspoons thyme, crushed
1 teaspoon low-sodium vegetable seasoning (see page 28)
Freshly ground pepper
2 cups our Chicken Stock
1 tablespoon mild soy sauce
2 tablespoons grated Sap Sago cheese, toasted (see page 15; optional)

Chopped fresh parsley, basil, or chives for garnish

1. Sauté onions, garlic, and pepper in the 3 tablespoons chicken stock until wilted. Add chopped tomato.
2. Place half the onion mixture in a 9-inch square or round glass baking dish sprayed with nonstick spray. Next spread on half of the potatoes. Sprinkle potatoes with crushed thyme, vegetable seasoning, and freshly ground pepper.
3. Repeat layers.
4. Pour the 2 cups stock and the soy sauce into the dish (just enough to cover potatoes). Cover dish with foil and bake 45 minutes in a preheated 375° oven.
5. Remove foil and bake 15 minutes more, or until potatoes are tender.
6. Sprinkle with grated Sap Sago cheese and brown potatoes under broiler.

To Serve: Garnish with chopped parsley, fresh basil, or chives. These potatoes may be served with a variety of entrées such as Barbecue-Style Broiled Chicken (page 151), Old-Fashioned Baked Meat Loaf (page 178), or Marinated Flank Steak (page 176).

Variation: If your diet permits, Parmesan cheese may be substituted for Sap Sago.

Per serving: 167 calories; 5.9 gm protein; 0.4 gm fat; 36.5 gm carbohydrate; 6.5 gm fiber; 0 mg cholesterol; 2.6 mg iron; 96 mg sodium; 53 mg calcium; 121 mg phosphorus; 530 IU Vitamin A; 0.23 mg thiamine; 0.11 mg riboflavin; 58 mg Vitamin C; 859 mg potassium; 0.27 mg zinc; 2.9 mg niacin; 131 mcg Vitamin B_6; 0 mcg Vitamin B_{12}; 19 mcg folic acid

Spanish Rice
(Add Leftover Chicken, and Would You Believe Paella?)

Serves: 6 (1 cup = 1 serving)

3 our Bouillon Cubes (see page 26)
2 cups brown rice
6 green onions, finely chopped
3 cloves garlic, minced
1 8-ounce can salt-free tomato sauce
5 cups our Chicken Stock (see page 26)
1 tablespoon mild soy sauce
1 stalk celery with leaves, chopped
2 carrots, chopped
½ teaspoon crushed red pepper
1 teaspoon low-sodium vegetable seasoning (see page 28)
1 bay leaf
1 green pepper, diced

1. Melt bouillon cubes in a heavy saucepan. Add rice, onions, and garlic. Stir over medium heat until rice browns slightly.
2. Add tomato sauce, chicken stock, soy sauce, celery, carrots, crushed red pepper, vegetable seasoning, and bay leaf. Stir, bring to a boil, lower heat to simmer, and cover. Cook 30 minutes.
3. Add diced green pepper, cover, and continue to cook 15 to 20 minutes, or until rice is tender and not too moist. (If rice is tender and still too moist, remove cover and let steam until dry.)

Variation: *To make a quick paella:* Add 2½ cups leftover diced roast or broiled chicken, 1 cup quartered artichoke hearts, 1 cup frozen peas, 1 8-ounce lobster tail (cut into 16 pieces), and ½ teaspoon powdered saffron with the pepper in step 3. Pour into a paella pan or a shallow casserole and cover. Place in a preheated 350° oven and finish cooking about 20 minutes. Garnish with tomato wedges and pea pods.

To Serve: Paella is a traditional dish in most parts of Spain. To start our meal in the Spanish tradition, we might serve a cup of chilled Gazpacho (page 75) and continue with our paella, a crisp green salad, and hot crusty sourdough rolls. A fruit bowl filled with tangerines (which resemble Seville oranges) would be an appropriate dessert.

Per serving: 272 calories; 7.6 gm protein; 1.1 gm fat; 50.9 gm carbohydrate; 5.1 gm fiber; 0 mg cholesterol; 1.7 mg iron; 110 mg sodium; 46 mg calcium; 140 mg phosphorus; 3648 IU Vitamin A; 0.24 mg thiamine; 0.07 mg riboflavin; 30 mg Vitamin C; 284 mg potassium; 0.13 mg zinc; 2.9 mg niacin; 83 mcg Vitamin B_6; 0 mcg Vitamin B_{12}; 5 mcg folic acid

Scalloped Sweet Potatoes and Apples

Serves: 8 (1 cup = 1 serving)

6 sweet potatoes,* peeled and sliced
6 apples (McIntosh, Spartan, or Golden Delicious), peeled and sliced
1 cup fresh orange juice
Grated zest of 1 orange
1 teaspoon cinnamon
1 cup crushed unsweetened corn flakes or fresh whole wheat crumbs made from Pritikin bread

1. Spray a 13 x 9 x 2-inch baking dish with nonstick spray.
2. Place alternate layers of sweet potatoes and apples in baking dish, ending with apples.
3. Pour orange juice mixed with zest over potatoes and apples and sprinkle with cinnamon.
4. Bake, covered with foil, in a preheated 375° oven for 40 minutes.
5. Remove foil and top with crushed cereal or bread crumbs. Bake 15 to 20 minutes more, until crumbs are lightly browned.

To Serve: This casserole is wonderful served with Addie's Broiled Chicken (page 155).

Variation: Substitute either pears or orange slices for the apples.

Per serving: 215 calories; 2.7 gm protein; 1 gm fat; 51.2 gm carbohydrate; 5.7 gm fiber; 0 mg cholesterol; 1.4 mg iron; 36 mg sodium; 52 mg calcium; 78 mg phosphorus; 10,921 IU Vitamin A; 0.2 mg thiamine; 0.14 mg riboflavin; 38 mg Vitamin C; 437 mg potassium; 0.47 mg zinc; 1.3 mg niacin; 68 mcg Vitamin B_6; 0 mcg Vitamin B_{12}; 10 mcg folic acid

* Leftover cooked sweet potatoes may be used instead of raw—a shorter total cooking time (35 to 40 minutes) will then be required.

Vegetables

ROOT, LEAF, OR SEED, THEY'RE WHAT YOU NEED

Basic Stir-Fried Vegetables
Nanette's Microwaved Oriental Vegetables
Bean and Vegetable Loaf
Bake Your Beets
Broccoli Puree
Chopped Broccoli Chinese Style
Hilda's Braised Red Cabbage
Carrot and Prune Tzimmes
Corn Cooked in Milk
Corn, Tomato, Onion, and Zucchini Casserole
Eggplant No-Crust Pizza
Sarah's Sweet and Sour Lima Beans
Larry's Crispy Potatoes
Potato Kugelettes
Spinach, Cheese, and Mushroom Squares
Spinach Ring
Steamed Summer Squash with Carrots
Just Plain Baked Sweet Potatoes
Vegetable Pie with a Cabbage Crust
Tomato Pie
Layered Vegetable Mold
Sesame, Zucchini, and Tomatoes
Zucchini Tian
Stuffed Zucchini

Vegetables are generally low in calories because of their high water content and low sugar content. They are a good source of carbohydrates, provide a generous supply of a wide variety of nutrients, and are a valuable source of fiber in our diets. Dried peas, beans, and lentils are important sources of protein.

When you buy vegetables, your first choice should always be fresh vegetables. Steam or cook them in as little water as possible, and for as short a time as possible. If you happen to have any vegetable liquid left after cooking the vegetables, save it for use in sauces or stocks at a future time. It would be foolish to waste the food value and flavor left in these liquids.

People frequently question the difference in the vitamin and mineral content of canned and frozen vegetables. There is little. However, canned vegetables do contain more sodium because of added salt, and sometimes because of preservatives. Canned vegetables also often contain added sugar. And the high temperatures used in the canning process change their texture, flavor, and nutrient content. So if you cannot buy fresh vegetables, I recommend you use frozen.

One of the main challenges in vegetable cookery is avoiding the boredom that comes from buying the same vegetables and cooking them in the same ways day in and day out. I've discovered incredible variety among vegetables. Cabbages alone include broccoli, cauliflower, red cabbage, green cabbage, brussels sprouts, kohlrabi, Chinese or Napa cabbage, and savoy cabbage, to name a few. The following lists will give you an idea of the wonderful range of vegetables you can learn to prepare (in addition to cabbages), and the recipes in this chapter will get you started.

Leaves—limestone lettuce, butter lettuce, iceberg lettuce, romaine, green leaf lettuce, red leaf lettuce, escarole, chicory, Belgian endive, sorrel, collard greens, turnip greens, kale, arugala, radicchio, spinach.

Roots—Salsify, radishes (red, black-white), daikons (Japanese radish), jicama, turnips, rutabagas, beets, carrots, celeriac, parsnips, potatoes, yams, sweet potatoes, Jerusalem artichokes (sunchoke), horseradish.

Pods and Seeds—corn, lima beans, wax beans, string beans, snow peas, bean sprouts, yard-long beans, peas, fava beans, sugar peas.

Vegetable-Fruits—eggplant, tomatoes, cherry tomatoes, Italian plum tomatoes, okra, cucumbers, red peppers, green peppers, European cucumbers, Japanese eggplant, white eggplant.

Stalks—green or white asparagus, celery, Swiss chard, bok choy, fennel.

Squash—zucchini, hubbard, buttercup, banana, butternut, acorn, summer, spaghetti, crookneck, chayote, pattypan, pumpkin.

Onions—red, white, yellow, boiling, Maui, Walla Walla, Vidalia; scallions, leeks, shallots, garlic.

Artichokes—globe, baby or French.

Mushrooms—white, brown, shiitake, chanterelles, morels, cepes, enoki. (Use fresh when possible; however, dried mushrooms after 30 to 60 minutes' soaking are delicious.)

Basic Stir-Fried Vegetables

The Glory That Was Not "Grease"

Serves: 4 (1 cup = 1 serving)

Chinese-style cooking lends itself to our methods of food preparation quite easily and happily, for several reasons. First of all, vegetables predominate; meat, fish, and poultry are used in small quantities as seasonings. Dairy products like butter, cheese, and milk are practically unknown to Chinese cooking. The soybean, whose protein resembles that of meat, has been converted to a frequently used cheese called tofu. Desserts rarely accompany family meals, and if served, they are frequently fresh fruit. The use of sweets is negligible, so that our fruit juice concentrate works quite well. The omnipresent rice gives us the whole grain we prefer—of course, we use brown rice instead of white.

Our method of Chinese cookery depends upon certain basic ingredients such as fresh vegetables, chicken, fish, flank steak, mild soy sauce, ginger root, garlic, scallions, crushed red pepper, and a good defatted, salt-free chicken stock (we use our own; see page 26). There are also some acceptable Chinese spices and seasonings—containing no fat, salt, MSG, or sugar—available through Chinese food stores (remember, read the labels carefully).

How does one teach an experienced chef how to cook without oil and MSG, and with only a minimal amount of mild soy sauce? Where do I begin? This was the dilemma I was confronted with when I was asked to teach a chef in Palm Springs, California. I was greeted with cordiality but skepticism—and so we began. The techniques of steaming and stir-frying are both great in our way of preparing food, so the transition was really not very difficult. I taught him how to use our Bouillon Cubes (page 25) instead of oil in stir-frying and to depend upon subtle spices instead of strong (sodium-laden) soy sauce, and he taught me some of the nuances I have incorporated into many of my recipes to share with you. The following recipe is a basic technique for stir-fried vegetables we perfected together.

Stir-fried vegetables are characterized by crispness, bright color, and natural flavor. The secret, of course, is minimal cooking time. The choice of stir-frying or steaming or a combination of both techniques is determined by the way the vegetable is cut. The diagonal or julienne cut is the traditional one for Chinese-style stir-frying, but this can certainly be varied with thin slices. What is important is uniformity of cut within each recipe so that the vegetables can cook evenly and be esthetically pleasing.

1 pound mixed fresh vegetables (1/4 pound carrots, 1/4 pound broccoli, 1/4 pound fresh mushrooms, 1/4 pound peas, fresh or frozen)
1/4–1/3 cup our Chicken Stock (see page 26) or Vegetable Stock (see page 60)
1 tablespoon mild soy sauce
1 tablespoon frozen unsweetened pineapple juice concentrate (optional, to vary taste)
2 our Bouillon Cubes (see page 25)
3 thin slices ginger root, minced or crushed, and 1 clove garlic, minced

1. Cut vegetables as desired, slicing by hand or using a 1/4-inch slicing blade in food processor.
2. Combine stock, soy sauce, and pineapple juice concentrate (if desired).
3. Heat bouillon cubes in a wok or a nonstick sauté pan.
4. Add garlic and ginger root and stir-fry 1/2 minute.
5. Add vegetables—if using a mixture, add slow-cooking ones first. Adjust heat. Stir-fry 3 minutes and steam covered 1 minute, then add remaining vegetables. Stir-fry to heat through.

6. Add stock mixture, stir gently, cover, and simmer over medium heat until vegetables are done *but crisp.*

To Serve: Vegetables may be placed in a bowl or on a platter and served as an accompaniment, or they may be served over steamed brown rice and used as a delicious entrée, in which case the recipe would serve only 2 people.

Variation: Add 1 teaspoon cornstarch and 2 tablespoons dry sherry in step 2. Use 1 minced clove garlic and 1 scallion cut into ½-inch pieces instead of the ginger root.

Suggested Vegetables for Stir-Frying: Choose one or more of the following; *add toughest first.*

asparagus
bamboo shoots (canned, rinsed, and drained)
bean sprouts
bok choy
broccoli
Chinese cabbage (Napa)
cabbage (raw green)
carrots
cauliflower
celery
cucumbers (peeled and seeded)
eggplant
winter melon
mushrooms (fresh or dried)
onions (red or white)
peas (fresh or frozen)
pepper (red or green)
potatoes (white or sweet)
snow peas
spinach
string beans
Swiss chard
turnips
water chestnuts (canned, rinsed, and drained)
zucchini

A Few Combinations:

1. 12 dried black mushrooms (soaked—see page 208); 1 cup sliced water chestnuts; ½ red pepper, sliced; 3 stalks Swiss chard, sliced.
2. ½ pound asparagus, cut in 1-inch pieces; 1 stalk celery, cut in 1-inch pieces; ½ pound bean sprouts.
3. ½ cup snow peas, whole; ½ pound carrots, thinly sliced; ¼ pound broccoli, thinly sliced or julienne; and ¼ pound Chinese cabbage, shredded.

Per serving: 59 calories; 4.4 gm protein; 0.3 gm fat; 13.8 gm carbohydrate; 3.3 gm fiber; 0 mg cholesterol; 1.3 mg iron; 144 mg sodium; 49 mg calcium; 98 mg phosphorus; 4009 IU Vitamin A; 0.17 mg thiamine; 0.25 mg riboflavin; 43 mg Vitamin C; 414 mg potassium; 0.19 mg zinc; 2.4 mg niacin; 126 mcg Vitamin B_6; 0 mcg Vitamin B_{12}; 24 mcg folic acid

Nanette's Microwaved Oriental Vegetables

Serves: 6 (½ cup = 1 serving)

The basics of stir-frying are replaced by the magic of microwave cooking.

12 ounces fresh Chinese pea pods (washed and strings and ends removed), plus 2 tablespoons water
1 cup sliced fresh mushrooms
4 ounces water chestnuts, rinsed, drained, and sliced
2 ounces chopped pimiento, drained
½ teaspoon garlic powder
½ cup sliced green onions
1½ cups fresh bean sprouts
¼ cup water or our Chicken Stock (see page 26)
4 teaspoons mild soy sauce

1. Place pea pods and the 2 tablespoons water in a 3-quart covered casserole.
2. Microwave on high for 2 minutes. Stir and microwave 2 additional minutes.
3. Add remaining ingredients to pea pods, mix gently, cover, and microwave on high 1 to 2 minutes, or *until crisp.*

To Serve: Serve immediately with an entrée of your choice.

Per serving: 86 calories; 5.8 gm protein; 0.4 gm fat; 16.1 gm carbohydrate; 7.7 gm fiber; 0 mg cholesterol; 1.9 mg iron; 119 mg sodium; 26 mg calcium; 115 mg phosphorus; 754 IU Vitamin A; 0.28 mg thiamine; 0.22 mg riboflavin; 33 mg Vitamin C; 426 mg potassium; 0.02 mg zinc; 2.6 mg niacin; 15 mcg Vitamin B_6; 0 mcg Vitamin B_{12}; 4 mcg folic acid

Bean and Vegetable Loaf

Serves: 10 (1 slice = 1 serving)

8 ounces dried white northern beans
4 cups water with 1 tablespoon mild soy sauce
1 bouquet garni (4 sprigs parsley, 1 teaspoon thyme, 1 bay leaf, ½ teaspoon crushed red pepper)
½ cup egg whites (4 to 5 large eggs), slightly beaten
3 cloves garlic, minced
1 teaspoon low-sodium vegetable seasoning (see page 28)
5 large Swiss chard leaves, stems removed
¼ pound fresh whole string beans or asparagus spears
¼ pound fresh whole okra
¼ pound fresh whole small carrots
5 artichoke bottoms or hearts

1. Cook beans in water and soy sauce with bouquet garni for 1½ hours. Drain and puree beans in blender or food processor.
2. Mix pureed beans with slightly beaten egg whites, garlic, and vegetable seasoning.
3. Blanch Swiss chard leaves, string beans, and okra for 3 minutes in boiling water and refresh with cold water.
4. Blanch carrots in boiling water 5 minutes and refresh with cold water.
5. Line a nonstick 6-cup loaf pan with overlapping Swiss chard leaves.
6. Spread a ¼-inch layer of bean puree, then a layer of vegetables. Continue alternating bean paste and vegetables. The first layer of vegetables should be okra, then the next layer artichokes, the next carrots, the next string beans. End with the bean puree.
7. Cover with waxed paper and place in a baking pan with 1 inch hot water. Bake in a preheated 350° oven for 30 to 45 minutes, or until mixture is firm.

To Serve: Serve hot with a tomato sauce or cold the next day with our Vinaigrette Dressing (see page 12). This makes a lovely luncheon entrée served with crisp Italian bread or whole wheat muffins and Apple Crisp (page 264) for dessert.

Per serving: 63 calories; 4.1 gm protein; 0.3 gm fat; 10.9 gm carbohydrate; 5.4 gm fiber; 0 mg cholesterol; 1.4 mg iron; 90 mg sodium; 48 mg calcium; 73 mg phosphorus; 2060 IU Vitamin A; 0.09 mg thiamine; 0.11 mg riboflavin; 11 mg Vitamin C; 334 mg potassium; 0.27 mg zinc; 0.6 mg niacin; 17 mcg Vitamin B_6; 0.01 mcg Vitamin B_{12}; 1 mcg folic acid

Bake Your Beets

Serves: 6 (2 beets = 1 serving)

Most cooks never think of baking beets. It is an incredibly more delicious and easy method of beet preparation than boiling. Once you try it, you will never go back to boiling them.

2 pounds fresh beets (about 2 bunches *small* beets)
12 butter lettuce leaves for serving
1½ cups nonfat yogurt for serving
3 carrots, shredded, for garnish
3 green onions, finely chopped, for garnish
Fresh dill, finely chopped, for garnish

1. Scrub beets with a vegetable brush. Cut off all but ½ inch of the tops and leave the tails.
2. Place in a covered casserole and bake in a preheated 450° oven for about 45 to 60 minutes, or until tender (test with the point of a paring knife).*
3. Cut off stems and slip off skins, leaving on the tails.**
4. Chill several hours in a covered container in refrigerator.

To Serve: Line a serving dish with butter lettuce. Place a bed of yogurt on the lettuce leaves, arrange two small beets on each leaf (tails up), garnish with shredded carrot and chopped green onion, and sprinkle with finely chopped dill. Lovely to serve with poached salmon (see page 126).

Per serving: 73 calories; 5.6 gm protein; 0.12 gm fat; 19.1 gm carbohydrate; 4.6 gm fiber; 0 mg cholesterol; 1.5 mg iron; 112 mg sodium; 144 mg calcium; 49 mg phosphorus; 3377 IU Vitamin A; 0.13 mg thiamine; 0.34 mg riboflavin; 15 mg Vitamin C; 488 mg potassium, 0.12 mg zinc; 1.4 mg niacin; 42 mcg Vitamin B_6; 0 mcg Vitamin B_{12}; 2.7 mcg folic acid

* Beets may also be wrapped individually in foil and baked at 325° for about 2½ hours. They tend to be juicier baked in foil at a lower temperature. For microwave cooking, place in a covered container with 1½ cups water and cook on high for about 20 minutes, or until tender.

** At this point, beets may be left whole, or sliced, diced, or shredded, depending upon the specific recipe.

Broccoli Puree

Serves: 6 (½ cup = 1 serving)

1 bunch broccoli, washed, cut into small pieces, and steamed until tender
1 to 2 tablespoons nonfat yogurt
1 teaspoon low-sodium vegetable seasoning (see page 28)
Crushed red pepper

1. Puree broccoli in blender or food processor. (Save 3 or 4 broccoli florets for garnish.) If mixture is too thick, add yogurt; *do not make soupy.*

2. Transfer puree to a saucepan and season with vegetable seasoning and pepper.

3. Heat through and serve hot. (If soupy, dry out over medium heat.)

To Serve: Serve from a casserole dish, or serve individually, pushed through a pastry tube as you so frequently see it served in French restaurants.

Variation: This method may be applied to carrots, green beans, peas, turnips, rutabaga, cauliflower, etc. Flavoring herbs may be added if you like.

Per serving: 37 calories; 4.5 gm protein; 0.33 gm fat; 7.5 gm carbohydrate; 3.07 gm fiber; 0 mg cholesterol; 1.3 mg iron; 22 mg sodium; 140 mg calcium; 63 mg phosphorus; 2080 IU Vitamin A; 0.17 mg thiamine; 0.37 mg riboflavin; 86 mg Vitamin C; 303 mg potassium; 0 mg zinc; 1.15 mg niacin; 0 mcg Vitamin B_6; 0 mcg Vitamin B_{12}; 0 mcg folic acid

Chopped Broccoli Chinese Style

Serves: 4 (½ cup = 1 serving)

3 our Bouillon Cubes, melted (see page 25), or 3 tablespoons our Chicken Stock (see page 26)
1 bunch green onions, sliced in ½-inch pieces
1 20-ounce package frozen broccoli cuts, thawed just enough to separate
1 cup our Chicken Stock
2 tablespoons mild soy sauce
1 tablespoon cornstarch

1. Heat bouillon cubes or stock in a wok or skillet; add onions and cook 1 minute.

2. Add broccoli cuts. Cover with lid and cook 1 minute; shake pan vigorously while cooking *with cover on.*

3. In a swirl cup or small jar, mix the 1 cup stock, the soy sauce, and the cornstarch vigorously to combine.

4. Add cornstarch mixture to broccoli and simmer, stirring gently until mixture thickens—it takes about 3 minutes.

To Serve: Serve family-style in a serving bowl. Delicious with Turkey Piccata (page 168).

Variation: Cook 1 10-ounce package frozen kernel corn with the broccoli, and add 1 2-ounce jar of chopped pimiento, drained, at the end of the cooking—just before serving.

Per serving: 65 calories; 6.1 gm protein; 0.5 gm fat; 12.9 gm carbohydrate; 2.1 gm fiber; 0 mg cholesterol; 1.2 mg iron; 150 mg sodium; 91 mg calcium; 91 mg phosphorus; 4042 IU Vitamin A; 0.11 mg thiamine; 0.19 mg riboflavin; 105 mg Vitamin C; 383 mg potassium; 0.05 mg zinc; 0.9 mg niacin; 0 mcg Vitamin B_6; 0 mcg Vitamin B_{12}; 2 mcg folic acid

Hilda's Braised Red Cabbage

Serves: 10 (⅔ cup = 1 serving)

⅓ cup our Chicken Stock (see page 26), or 3 our Bouillon Cubes, melted (see page 25)
½ cup finely chopped onions
1 medium red cabbage (about 1 pound), shredded
4–6 Pippin, Gravenstein, or other sweet apples, peeled, cored, and sliced
½ cup apple cider vinegar or raspberry wine vinegar
½ cup our Chicken Stock
½ cup red wine
⅓ cup frozen unsweetened apple juice concentrate
½ teaspoon freshly ground nutmeg
¼ teaspoon ground allspice

1. Heat the ⅓ cup chicken stock in a Dutch oven or casserole dish. Add onions, and cook over moderate heat 5 minutes. Add cabbage, apples, vinegar, and the ½ cup stock. Stir.

2. Simmer 2 hours on top of stove, or in a preheated 325° oven.

3. Add ½ cup red wine, apple juice concentrate, nutmeg, and allspice. Cook 30 minutes more and taste to adjust seasonings.

To Serve: Serve cabbage from casserole or in a warmed serving dish.

Variation: Add 1 pound chestnuts. Cut an X on the rounded side of each chestnut and parboil for 10 minutes. Remove outer and inner skins and chop coarsely. Add with the wine in step 3.

Per serving: 91 calories; 1.3 gm protein; 0.4 gm fat; 20.1 gm carbohydrate; 3.9 gm fiber; 0 mg cholesterol; 0.6 mg iron; 15 mg sodium; 36 mg calcium; 30 mg phosphorus; 106 IU Vitamin A; 0.05 mg thiamine; 0.05 mg riboflavin; 28 mg Vitamin C; 254 mg potassium; 0.24 mg zinc; 0.3 mg niacin; 102 mcg Vitamin B_6; 0 mcg Vitamin B_{12}; 19 mcg folic acid

Carrot and Prune Tzimmes

Serves: 6–8 (½ cup = 1 serving)

1¼ pounds carrots, sliced or diced
Our Chicken Stock (see page 26) or water, to cover
2 tablespoons flour
¼ cup unsweetened apple juice concentrate
4 ounces pitted prunes
1 beef bone, or 3 skinned chicken drummettes

1. Place carrots in a saucepan. Add chicken stock or water to cover and simmer 15 minutes.
2. Brown flour in a dry heavy skillet over medium heat. Shake pan or stir constantly with a wooden spoon to prevent scorching and add ½ cup of the carrot cooking liquid. Stir until smooth. Add apple juice concentrate and simmer 5 minutes.
3. Add browned liquid to carrots. Mix.
4. Place carrot mixture in a 3-quart casserole. Add prunes and bone.
5. Cover and bake in a preheated 350° oven for 35 to 40 minutes.

To Serve: Serve hot in a serving bowl. This is a delicious accompaniment to poultry or flank steak, or it may be served as a dessert.

Per serving: 135 calories; 2.4 gm protein; 0.3 gm fat; 33.1 gm carbohydrate; 3.5 gm fiber; 0 mg cholesterol; 1.6 mg iron; 49 mg sodium; 52 mg calcium; 56 mg phosphorus; 10,826 IU Vitamin A; 0.09 mg thiamine; 0.1 mg riboflavin; 8 mg Vitamin C; 504 mg potassium; 0.39 mg zinc; 1 mg niacin; 143 mcg Vitamin B_6; 0 mcg Vitamin B_{12}; 8 mcg folic acid

Corn Cooked in Milk

Serves: 6 (½ cup = 1 serving)

Corn is a good source of complex carbohydrates, and the technique of cooking it in milk seems to enhance its delicious flavor.

½ cup nonfat milk
1 tablespoon nonfat powdered milk
3 cups fresh corn kernels,* cut from the cob with a sharp knife and chilled until ready to use
½ cup chopped pimiento or chopped red pepper
½ teaspoon freshly ground white pepper
½ teaspoon low-sodium vegetable seasoning (see page 28)

* 3 cups frozen kernel corn may be substituted for fresh corn.

1. Heat milk in a saucepan until simmering.
2. Add corn, stir, and heat to a simmer. Lower heat, cover, and simmer 3 minutes.
3. Drain corn with a slotted spoon. Place in a heated serving dish and stir in pimiento, ground pepper, and vegetable seasoning.

Helpful Hint: Save remaining cooking liquid for a cream soup.

Per serving: 101 calories; 3.5 gm protein; 1.4 gm fat; 18.1 gm carbohydrate; 3.7 gm fiber; 0 mg cholesterol; 0.7 mg iron; 4 mg sodium; 10 mg calcium; 100 mg phosphorus; 897 IU Vitamin A; 0.14 mg thiamine; 0.12 mg riboflavin; 35 mg Vitamin C; 266 mg potassium; 0.02 mg zinc; 1.5 mg niacin; 2 mcg Vitamin B_6; 0.02 mcg Vitamin B_{12}; 0 mcg folic acid

Corn, Tomato, Onion, and Zucchini Casserole

Serves: 6 (1 cup = 1 serving)

2 10-ounce packages frozen kernel corn, defrosted
6 small zucchini, cut in ½-inch slices
4 ripe tomatoes, cut in ¼-inch slices
2 mild onions, thinly sliced
2 cloves garlic, minced
1 teaspoon low-sodium vegetable seasoning (see page 28)
Few grains crushed red pepper
Juice of ½ lemon
4 our Bouillon Cubes, melted (see page 25)

1. Place corn, zucchini, tomatoes, onions, garlic, vegetable seasoning, and crushed red pepper in a covered casserole. Sprinkle with lemon juice and mix together gently.
2. Pour melted bouillon cubes over vegetables.
3. Cover and bake in a preheated 325° oven for 45 minutes.

To Serve: Especially nice served with our Barbecue-Style Broiled Chicken (page 151) or turkey.

Per serving: 142 calories; 6.4 gm protein; 0.9 gm fat; 32.5 gm carbohydrate; 6.4 gm fiber; 0 mg cholesterol; 2.2 mg iron; 11 mg sodium; 67 mg calcium; 156 mg phosphorus; 1665 IU Vitamin A; 0.26 mg thiamine; 0.23 mg riboflavin; 58 mg Vitamin C; 751 mg potassium; 0.34 mg zinc; 3.5 mg niacin; 149 mcg Vitamin B_6; 0 mcg Vitamin B_{12}; 19 mcg folic acid

Eggplant No-Crust Pizza

Serves: 6 (1 slice = 1 serving)

6 slices unpeeled eggplant, ½ inch thick
¾ cup salt-free tomato sauce
1 teaspoon low-sodium vegetable seasoning (see page 28)
1 teaspoon oregano, crushed
Freshly ground pepper
6 slices ripe tomato, ½ inch thick
2 tablespoons grated Sap Sago cheese, toasted (see page 15)
6 thin slices our Yogurt Cheese (see page 305) or skim milk mozzarella cheese, shredded
12 thin slices green pepper
1 tablespoon chopped fresh basil

1. Squeeze eggplant slices with paper towels to remove bitter juices.
2. Dip eggplant slices in tomato sauce seasoned with vegetable seasoning, oregano, and ground pepper.
3. Heat an iron skillet sprayed lightly with nonstick spray and sear eggplant slices until browned on each side.
4. Arrange eggplant slices in 1 layer on a nonstick baking sheet. Sprinkle with freshly ground pepper.
5. Cover each slice with a tomato slice and sprinkle with toasted Sap Sago cheese.
6. Cover each pizza with a slice of Yogurt Cheese and bake in a preheated 325° oven for 10 minutes, or until Yogurt Cheese has melted.
7. Garnish with two crossed green pepper strips and sprinkle with freshly chopped basil.

To Serve: Serve hot as either part of an entrée on a vegetable plate or an accompaniment to roast chicken.

Variations: If your diet permits, grated Parmesan cheese may be substituted for the Sap Sago.

To make pizza appetizers, substitute small Japanese eggplant slices and Italian plum tomatoes, or use toasted Pritikin English muffins as a base instead of the eggplant and cut into quarters.

Per serving: 109 calories; 3.5 gm protein; 5.9 gm fat; 12.1 gm carbohydrate; 2.3 gm fiber; 1 mg cholesterol; 1.8 mg iron; 22 mg sodium; 80 mg calcium; 59 mg phosphorus; 1281 IU Vitamin A; 0.1 mg thiamine; 0.1 mg riboflavin; 27 mg Vitamin C; 261 mg potassium; 0.06 mg zinc; 1.3 mg niacin; 56 mcg Vitamin B_6; 0 mcg Vitamin B_{12}; 3 mcg folic acid

Sarah's Sweet and Sour Lima Beans

Serves: 4–6 (½ cup = 1 serving)

When I was a child, my mother frequently prepared vegetables with a simple sweet and sour sauce and served them as a separate course before or after the entrée.

3 cups boiling water, our Chicken Stock (see page 26), or our Vegetable Stock (see page 60)
1 cup dried lima beans, rinsed and drained
1 teaspoon mild soy sauce
1 sliced carrot
¼ cup unbleached flour
¼ small onion, grated
¼ cup frozen unsweetened apple juice concentrate
3 tablespoons apple cider vinegar

1. Add lima beans, soy sauce, and carrot to boiling liquid, cover, and simmer 1 to 1½ hours, or until beans are tender.
2. Brown flour in a heavy skillet (cast iron does well), stirring constantly with a wooden spoon until golden brown. *Be careful not to burn.*
3. Remove from heat, add grated onion, and blend.
4. Add browned flour mixture to cooked beans and blend.
5. Add apple juice concentrate and vinegar, and stir over low heat until a smooth sauce results. Simmer 20 minutes. Taste, and adjust seasonings. May be prepared the day before and reheated for serving.

To Serve: Serve in individual sauce dishes as an accompaniment to simply prepared entrées like roast chicken or turkey.

Variation: Any one of the following vegetables may be substituted for the lima beans: 16 ounces rutabaga, peeled and cubed; 16 ounces fresh green beans, sliced; 16 ounces potatoes, diced.

Helpful Hint: Leftover sauce can be frozen for future use.

Per serving: 85 calories; 3.8 gm protein; 0.25 gm fat; 17.6 gm carbohydrate; 9.3 gm fiber; 0 mg cholesterol; 1.6 mg iron; 53 mg sodium; 33 mg calcium; 65 mg phosphorus; 2178 IU Vitamin A; 0.15 mg thiamine; 0.07 mg riboflavin; 13 mg Vitamin C; 338 mg potassium; 0.1 mg zinc; 0.8 mg niacin; 36 mcg Vitamin B_6; 0 mcg Vitamin B_{12}; 3 mcg folic acid

Larry's Crispy Potatoes

Serves: 6 (1 cup = 1 serving)

When my son smells these potatoes baking in the oven, he's sure to stay home for dinner!

2 pounds russet potatoes, boiled in skins until tender
1 bunch green onions, chopped
2 teaspoons Italian herb seasoning or basil, crushed
Freshly ground pepper
½ cup our Chicken Stock (see page 26)
Hungarian paprika

3 tablespoons chopped fresh Italian parsley or fresh basil for garnish

1. Peel cooked potatoes and dice in 1-inch cubes.

*2. Place in an 8 x 11 x 2-inch baking dish that has been sprayed with nonstick spray. Sprinkle with chopped green onions, Italian seasoning, and freshly ground pepper. Mix gently with a fork to distribute the ingredients.

3. Pour chicken stock over the potatoes and spinkle generously with Hungarian paprika.

4. Bake in a preheated 400° oven on upper shelf. Stir every 15 minutes until nicely browned and crisp, about 45 minutes. Place under broiler to complete browning before serving.

To Serve: Garnish with freshly chopped Italian parsley or fresh basil. Because it is so easy to prepare, this dish lends itself nicely to outdoor entertaining for large parties. It's wonderful to serve with broiled flank steak or chicken.

Variation: In step 4, after stirring, spray with a mixture of 3 tablespoons mild soy sauce and ¼ cup water placed in a plastic spray bottle. Stir again. Spray and stir every 15 minutes. This will, of course, increase the sodium content of the recipe.

Per serving: 125 calories; 3.8 gm protein; 0.2 gm fat; 28.1 gm carbohydrate; 3.6 gm fiber; 0 mg cholesterol; 1.5 mg iron; 7 mg sodium; 35 mg calcium; 90 mg phosphorus; 553 IU Vitamin A; 0.15 mg thiamine; 0.08 mg riboflavin; 32 mg Vitamin C; 685 mg potassium; 0.49 mg zinc; 2.4 mg niacin; 266 mcg Vitamin B_6; 0 mcg Vitamin B_{12}; 13 mcg folic acid

* May be prepared through step 2 several hours ahead and refrigerated.

Potato Kugelettes

Serves: 8 (1 kugelette = 1 serving)

3 russet potatoes, peeled and diced
⅓ small onion
3 egg whites
Freshly ground white pepper
½ teaspoon low-sodium baking powder
Hungarian paprika

1. Place potatoes and onion in blender or food processor (using steel knife). Process until mixture is coarsely pureed. (Remember to scrape down sides of container with a spatula.)

2. Add egg whites, freshly ground pepper, and baking powder to potato mixture. Blend.

3. Using a nonstick muffin pan, preferably heavy ironware, add ⅓ cup of potato mixture to each muffin cup. Sprinkle top of each potato mixture with Hungarian paprika.

4. Place in a preheated 400° oven and bake 20 minutes. Lower heat to 350° and continue baking until lightly browned—around 20 minutes more.

To Serve: Invert baked kugelettes on a platter to show crisp bottoms and serve hot with bowls of either cold applesauce or cold Rosy Rhubarb Sauce (page 280) placed in center of platter.

To Freeze for Future Use: Place baked kugelettes on a baking sheet and flash-freeze, uncovered, until solid; then freeze in a tightly closed plastic bag with the air removed. *To defrost:* Place on a baking sheet with bottoms up in a preheated 500° oven and bake until thawed and crisp—about 7 to 10 minutes.

Per serving: 41 calories; 2.3 gm protein; 0.1 gm fat; 7.9 gm carbohydrate; 1.3 gm fiber; 0 mg cholesterol; 0.3 mg iron; 20 mg sodium; 12 mg calcium; 36 mg phosphorus; 78 IU Vitamin A; 0.04 mg thiamine; 0.05 mg riboflavin; 9 mg Vitamin C; 213 mg potassium; 0.02 mg zinc; 0.7 mg niacin; 5 mcg Vitamin B_6; 0.01 mcg Vitamin B_{12}; 1 mcg folic acid

Spinach, Cheese, and Mushroom Squares

Serves: 8 (1 4 x 3-inch square = 1 serving)

3 tablespoons dry white wine
¾ pound fresh mushrooms, cleaned and sliced
4 green onions, thinly sliced
1 teaspoon low-sodium vegetable seasoning (see page 28)
1 tablespoon Worcestershire sauce
3 10-ounce packages frozen chopped spinach, defrosted and well drained
1½ cups soft whole wheat crumbs made from Pritikin bread
1 pint Weight Watchers cottage cheese, rinsed and drained
6 egg whites

1. Bring wine to a boil in a nonstick skillet. Add mushrooms and green onions and sauté until just tender.
2. Add vegetable seasoning, Worcestershire sauce, and drained spinach. Blend well and transfer to a mixing bowl.
3. Add bread crumbs and drained cottage cheese. Blend.
4. Beat egg whites until stiff and fold into spinach mixture.

*5. Spray a 13 x 9 x 2-inch glass baking dish with nonstick spray and place spinach mixture in dish.

6. Bake, uncovered, in a preheated 350° oven for 30 minutes, or until firm.
7. Let stand 10 minutes before cutting into 8 portions for serving.

Variations: May be cut into smaller squares and served as an appetizer. Frozen chopped broccoli may be substituted for the spinach.

Per serving: 153 calories; 16.2 gm protein; 1.5 gm fat; 18.6 gm carbohydrate; 2.3 gm fiber; 0 mg cholesterol; 3.5 mg iron; 312 mg sodium; 189 mg calcium; 106 mg phosphorus; 8561 IU Vitamin A; 0.2 mg thiamine; 0.6 mg riboflavin; 34 mg Vitamin C; 657 mg potassium; 0.02 mg zinc; 3 mg niacin; 56 mcg Vitamin B_6; 0.02 mcg Vitamin B_{12}; 11 mcg folic acid

* If you wish to freeze this dish for future use, prepare through step 5, cool, wrap baking dish in an airtight plastic bag or foil, and freeze. To reheat, place at room temperature for several hours and bake at 350° for 30 minutes.

Spinach Ring

Serves: 4

Spinach and other leafy vegetables such as beet greens and Swiss chard are high in iron, Vitamin A, and calcium. However, they also contain oxalic acid, which inhibits the absorption of calcium in the body, so they should be eaten in limited amounts.

2 pounds fresh spinach, or 2 10-ounce packages frozen chopped spinach
¼ cup Weight Watchers cottage cheese, rinsed and drained
2 green onions
Dash freshly grated nutmeg

2 hard-cooked egg whites, chopped, for garnish
1 tablespoon chopped fresh parsley for garnish

1. Wash spinach carefully, discarding wilted leaves.* Cook in water that clings to leaves. Cover; start at moderate heat; cook 5 minutes, or until wilted, stirring once or twice.

2. Remove cover and stir until completely wilted. If there is any remaining liquid, drain it. (If using frozen spinach, cook according to package directions, drain, and squeeze dry.)

3. Puree cottage cheese in blender or food processor.

4. Add spinach and green onions to cheese and chop. Season with nutmeg.

5. Pack into a ring mold sprayed lightly with nonstick spray. Keep mold in a pan of hot water until ready to serve.

To Serve: Unmold onto a hot plate and sprinkle with chopped egg whites and parsley. For a more attractive presentation, fill the center of the ring with steamed carrots. Spinach cooked this way will retain its green color and fresh flavor.

Variation: Frozen chopped broccoli may be substituted for the spinach.

***Helpful Hint:** When washing fresh spinach, place in generous amounts of fresh water and rinse. Then *remove spinach from water*, rinse grit from container, refill container, and repeat until remaining water is clear. If you just remove the water and not spinach from bowl, grit remains in bowl with spinach.

Per serving: 82 calories; 11 gm protein; 1 gm fat; 11 gm carbohydrate; 8.1 gm fiber; 0 mg cholesterol; 7.2 mg iron; 218 mg sodium; 230 mg calcium; 121 mg phosphorus; 18,557 IU Vitamin A; 0.23 mg thiamine; 0.54 mg riboflavin; 119 mg Vitamin C; 1119 mg potassium; 1.82 mg zinc; 1.5 mg niacin; 637 mcg Vitamin B_6; 0.02 mcg Vitamin B_{12}; 176 mcg folic acid

Steamed Summer Squash with Carrots

Serves: 8 (1 squash = 1 serving)

This squash has different names depending upon where you live. It may be called scallop squash, pattypan, or summer squash. For a choice vegetable, look for a pale green (not yellow) squash that is firm and about 2 to 3 inches in diameter. Because it is harvested before it is mature, its skin and seeds are tender and delicious.

8 summer squash (2 to 3 inches in diameter)
1–1½ teaspoons low-sodium vegetable seasoning (see page 28)
4 small carrots, peeled and coarsely shredded
1 teaspoon dried chervil, crushed, or 2 teaspoons chopped fresh chervil

1. Wash squash thoroughly in cold water. Place squash with flat side down, stem up. With a grapefruit knife or small, sharp paring knife, scoop out enough flesh to make a small cavity.

2. Sprinkle each cavity with vegetable seasoning and top with about 1–1½ tablespoons shredded carrot. Sprinkle carrots with chervil.

3. Place a steamer basket in a saucepan; add 1 inch water. Arrange squash on steamer basket.

4. Cover pan and bring water to a boil over medium heat. Steam vegetables until tender when pierced with a sharp knife, about 10 minutes depending upon size of squash.

To Serve: This may be served as a separate vegetable or as part of a buffet platter including Wild Rice, Brown Rice, and Mushrooms (page 257) and broiled tomato halves. It also makes a colorful garnish served with roast turkey or broiled chicken.

Per serving: 39 calories; 1.8 gm protein; 0.2 gm fat; 8.7 gm carbohydrate; 4.7 gm fiber; 0 mg cholesterol; 0.9 mg iron; 19 mg sodium; 53 mg calcium; 50 mg phosphorus; 4613 IU Vitamin A; 0.1 mg thiamine; 0.12 mg riboflavin; 28 mg Vitamin C; 372 mg potassium; 0.15 mg zinc; 1.4 mg niacin; 56 mcg Vitamin B_6; 0 mcg Vitamin B_{12}; 3 mcg folic acid

Just Plain Baked Sweet Potatoes

Serves: 6 (1 potato = 1 serving)

6 medium-sized sweet potatoes or yams

Hungarian paprika or freshly ground nutmeg for garnish (optional)

1. Scrub sweet potatoes thoroughly, removing imperfections.

2. Place in a baking pan* and bake in a preheated 350° oven 40 to 60 minutes, or until soft.

3. Remove from oven. Cut lengthwise and crosswise to remove steam. Pinch potatoes, pressing up top of flesh so that it will show.

To Serve: Serve plain or with a sprinkling of paprika or nutmeg on each potato.

Variations: *To make stuffed sweet potatoes:* Cut baked sweet potato in half lengthwise. Carefully scoop out the inside, leaving a little as lining for the shell. Mash insides thoroughly and add ½ cup nonfat milk and ½ teaspoon cinnamon. Stuff back into shells and sprinkle with freshly grated nutmeg, grated orange zest, or cinnamon. May be prepared several hours ahead up to this point. Reheat in a 425° oven for 15 to 20 minutes.

***Helpful Hint:** Do not puncture sweet potatoes with a fork before baking; they will drip. They do not need puncturing as white potatoes do, since they contain less moisture.

Per serving: 187 calories; 2.8 gm protein; 0.8 gm fat; 42.9 gm carbohydrate; 4.1 gm fiber; 0 mg cholesterol; 1.2 mg iron; 16 mg sodium; 53 mg calcium; 77 mg phosphorus; 14,357 IU Vitamin A; 0.16 mg thiamine; 0.1 mg riboflavin; 34 mg Vitamin C; 399 mg potassium; 0 mg zinc; 1 mg niacin; 0 mcg Vitamin B_6; 0 mcg Vitamin B_{12}; 0 mcg folic acid

Vegetable Pie with a Cabbage Crust

Serves: 8–10 (1/10 of pie = 1 serving)

1 small green cabbage
3 green onions, cut in ½-inch slices
½ pound fresh mushrooms, sliced thin
2 our Bouillon Cubes, melted (see page 25), or 2 tablespoons our Chicken Stock (see page 26)
1 teaspoon Worcestershire sauce
½ teaspoon thyme
Freshly ground pepper
2 tablespoons our Chicken Stock
1 small onion, minced
1 small carrot, minced
¼ cup chopped fresh parsley
½ teaspoon garlic powder
1 teaspoon herbes de Provence
2 10-ounce packages frozen chopped spinach, thawed and well drained
8 ounces skim-milk ricotta or hoop cheese
Freshly ground nutmeg
2 egg whites, lightly beaten
½ cup salt-free tomato sauce, with ½ teaspoon oregano
2 tablespoons grated Sap Sago cheese, toasted (see page 15)

1. Remove hard center core of cabbage and parboil cabbage for 20 minutes.
2. Drain and separate cabbage leaves; try not to tear. Drain well on paper towels.
3. Sauté green onions and mushrooms in bouillon cubes and Worcestershire sauce for about 5 to 10 minutes. Add thyme and freshly ground pepper.
4. Place chicken stock in a nonstick skillet. Add onion, carrot, and parsley. Sauté until transparent. Add garlic powder, herbs, and drained, chopped spinach. Blend well.
5. Remove from heat, cool slightly, and add ricotta cheese, freshly ground nutmeg, and egg whites. Blend well.
6. Lightly spray a 10-inch glass pie plate with nonstick spray. Arrange cooked cabbage leaves around bottom and sides of pie plate. Overlap leaves to thickness of about 5 leaves. (Leaves should extend 1 inch over the edge of the plate.)
7. Spoon the drained mushroom mixture over the cabbage, spreading over bottom of plate. Then place the cheese mixture over the mushroom mixture.
8. Curl cabbage leaves over filling, leaving center of pie uncovered.
9. Spoon tomato sauce over top of pie and sprinkle with toasted Sap Sago.

10. Bake in a preheated 300° oven for 20 to 30 minutes, or until filling is set. Remove pie from oven and drain any excess liquid. Let pie set for 2 minutes and cut into 8 to 10 wedges for serving.

To Serve: Serve with roast chicken.

Variation: If your diet permits, substitute grated Parmesan cheese for the Sap Sago.

Per serving: 115 calories; 11.5 gm protein; 3.1 gm fat; 12.7 gm carbohydrate; 4.3 gm fiber; 7 mg cholesterol; 2.6 mg iron; 176 mg sodium; 179 mg calcium; 128 mg phosphorus; 6921 IU Vitamin A; 0.15 mg thiamine; 0.38 mg riboflavin; 62 mg Vitamin C; 617 mg potassium; 0.35 mg zinc; 2 mg niacin; 176 mcg Vitamin B_6; 0.01 mcg Vitamin B_{12}; 34 mcg folic acid

Tomato Pie

Serves: 6 (1/6 of pie = 1 serving)

4 slices fresh whole wheat Pritikin bread or sourdough bread
1 28-ounce can plum tomatoes, drained and mashed (juice reserved)
½ cup chopped onion
2 green onions, chopped
2 tablespoons chopped fresh basil, or 2 teaspoons dried basil
Few grains crushed red pepper
2 egg whites
2 teaspoons oregano, toasted*

1. Tear bread into small pieces. Pour juice from tomatoes over bread and mix.
2. Combine mashed tomatoes, onion, basil, and crushed red pepper in a bowl.
3. Beat egg whites until fluffy.
4. Combine tomato and onion mixture with bread mixture.
5. Fold egg whites into tomato and bread mixture. Spoon into a 9-inch pie pan that has been lightly sprayed with nonstick spray and bake in a preheated 375° oven for 45 minutes, or until lightly browned.

To Serve: Sprinkle with toasted oregano before serving.

Per serving: 82 calories; 4.4 gm protein; 0.8 gm fat; 15.6 gm carbohydrate; 1.4 gm fiber; 0 mg cholesterol; 1.7 mg iron; 235 mg sodium; 42 mg calcium; 38 mg phosphorus; 1443 IU Vitamin A; 0.1 mg thiamine; 0.1 mg riboflavin; 26 mg Vitamin C; 370 mg potassium; 0.32 mg zinc; 1.3 mg niacin; 135 mcg Vitamin B_6; 0.01 mcg Vitamin B_{12}; 9 mcg folic acid

* Toast dried oregano lightly in a dry skillet and enjoy the change of flavor.

Layered Vegetable Mold

Serves: 10–12 (⅔ cup = 1 serving)

Although this dish takes a bit of extra preparation, its different and elegant presentation is worth the extra effort.

3 our Bouillon Cubes (see page 25)
1 pound fresh mushrooms, finely chopped
4 green onions, finely chopped
3 tablespoons nonfat yogurt
1 egg white, slightly beaten
1 10-ounce package frozen chopped spinach, defrosted and well drained
¼ teaspoon freshly ground nutmeg
1 egg white, slightly beaten
Freshly ground pepper
10 carrots, steamed
1 teaspoon chervil, crushed
1 egg white, slightly beaten
1 head cauliflower, steamed
Freshly ground pepper
1 egg white, slightly beaten
1 tablespoon nonfat yogurt
½ cup frozen peas
2 our Bouillon Cubes
1 leek (white part only), cut in 1-inch julienne strips
1 carrot, cut in 1-inch julienne strips
3 soaked dried or 4 fresh mushroom caps, cut in 1-inch julienne strips
2 tablespoons chopped fresh parsley
½ teaspoon low-sodium vegetable seasoning (see page 28)
Freshly ground pepper
⅓ cup nonfat yogurt or nonfat evaporated milk

1. Melt the first bouillon cubes in a skillet; add mushrooms and onions and sauté until dry. Add the 3 tablespoons yogurt and the first egg white, and blend.

2. Puree spinach in blender or food processor. Add the second egg white, then nutmeg, and the freshly ground pepper, and blend.

3. Puree steamed carrots. Add chervil and the third egg white, and blend.

4. Puree cauliflower. Add freshly ground pepper, the fourth egg white, and the 1 tablespoon yogurt, and blend. Add frozen peas gently.

5. Dry each vegetable puree separately over low heat until thick, stirring constantly.

*6. Lightly spray a 2-quart soufflé dish with nonstick spray. Make equal layers of vegetables in this order: cauliflower, spinach, and carrots, and top with mushroom mixture.

* May be prepared a day ahead through step 6.

7. Set mold in an ovenproof dish with boiling water and bake in a preheated 375° oven 20 minutes, or until knife comes out clean.

8. While vegetables are baking, make sauce. Melt the remaining bouillon cubes in a heavy skillet and add julienne vegetables. Cook, covered, over medium heat for 10 minutes.

9. Season with parsley, vegetable seasoning, and freshly ground pepper.

10. Add the ⅓ cup yogurt just before serving. Heat, *do not boil.*

To Unmold and Serve: Loosen mold with a spatula, invert onto a platter, shake gently, and unmold. Spoon sauce over and around mold and serve immediately. Makes a wonderful accompaniment for Orange-Glazed Cornish Hens (page 139).

Variation: Add or substitute celery root, broccoli, rutabaga, or turnips.

Per serving: 120 calories; 7.9 gm protein; 0.3 gm fat; 15.1 gm carbohydrate; 4.7 gm fiber; 0 mg cholesterol; 2.6 mg iron; 87 mg sodium; 97 mg calcium; 132 mg phosphorus; 8600 IU Vitamin A; 0.16 mg thiamine; 0.4 mg riboflavin; 58 mg Vitamin C; 665 mg potassium; 0.32 mg zinc; 3 mg niacin; 84 mcg Vitamin B_6; 0.01 mcg Vitamin B_{12}; 15 mcg folic acid

Sesame, Zucchini, and Tomatoes

Serves: 2 (1 cup = 1 serving)

1 tablespoon sesame seeds
2 tablespoons our Chicken Stock (see page 26)
1 small clove garlic, minced
3 zucchini, sliced thin
3 green onions, chopped
6 cherry tomatoes, halved
2 tablespoons chopped fresh parsley

1. Toast sesame seeds in a dry skillet over low heat and set aside.
2. Heat chicken stock and garlic in a wok or sauté pan.
3. When hot, add sliced zucchini and green onions. Stir until crisp, cover, and steam 2 minutes.
4. Stir in cherry tomatoes and chopped parsley and heat through.

To Serve: Remove to a heated platter and sprinkle with toasted sesame seeds. Serve with Broiled Swordfish Steaks (page 133).

Variation: If your diet permits, use 1 teaspoon oil instead of chicken stock.

Per serving; 35 calories; 1.9 gm protein; 1.2 gm fat; 5.3 gm carbohydrate; 3.1 gm fiber; 0 mg cholesterol; 0.7 mg iron; 4 mg sodium; 36 mg calcium; 46 mg phosphorus; 708 IU Vitamin A; 0.06 mg thiamine; 0.09 mg riboflavin; 25 mg Vitamin C; 258 mg potassium; 0.05 mg zinc; 1.1 mg niacin; 18 mcg Vitamin B_6; 0 mcg Vitamin B_{12}; 3 mcg folic acid

Zucchini Tian

Serves: 8 (1 cup = 1 serving)

A tian is a vegetable casserole from the region of Provence in France. It is usually a mixture of vegetables or a combination of vegetables and rice that is baked in a gratin dish.

¼ cup our Vegetable Stock (see page 60), our Chicken Stock (see page 26), or dry vermouth
1 small onion, minced
1 clove garlic, minced
1 bunch green onions, finely chopped
2 pounds zucchini, sliced thin
1 teaspoon chopped herbes de Provence
1 cup Weight Watchers cottage cheese, rinsed and drained
½ cup chopped fresh parsley
3 egg whites, slightly beaten
⅔ cup brown rice, parboiled 30 minutes and drained
3 tablespoons our Seasoned Bread Crumbs (see page 29)
2 tablespoons grated Sap Sago cheese, toasted (see page 15)

1. Heat stock in a large skillet and add onion and garlic. Sauté until soft.
2. Add green onions, zucchini, and herbs. Cook, covered, 10 minutes over low heat, stirring occasionally. Remove from heat.
3. Combine cheese, parsley, egg whites, and cooked brown rice.
4. Add zucchini mixture to rice mixture and mix well.
5. Spray a gratin dish or a 10-inch glass pie plate with nonstick spray. Place vegetables in baking dish and sprinkle with a mixture of bread crumbs and cheese.
6. Bake uncovered in a preheated 350° oven for 35 minutes.

To Serve: Lovely with parslied potatoes and Filets de Poisson aux Tomatoes (page 120).

Variation: If your diet allows, use grated Parmesan cheese instead of Sap Sago.

Per serving: 91 calories; 8 gm protein; 1 gm fat; 13.2 gm carbohydrate; 4.6 gm fiber; 1 mg cholesterol; 1.5 mg iron; 102 mg sodium; 108 mg calcium; 71 mg phosphorus; 1055 IU Vitamin A; 0.1 mg thiamine; 0.24 mg riboflavin; 35 mg Vitamin C; 380 mg potassium; 0.07 mg zinc; 1.7 mg niacin; 25 mcg Vitamin B_6; 0.01 mcg Vitamin B_{12}; 7 mcg folic acid

Stuffed Zucchini

Serves: 6 as entrée (1 whole zucchini per person) or 12 as garnish (½ zucchini per person)

Many vegetables are appropriate in size and shape for stuffing, if they hold their shape after cooking. One of the most popular of these is zucchini. The following recipe adapts nicely to summer (pattypan) squash also.

6 medium zucchini (3 pounds squash)
1½ teaspoons low-sodium vegetable seasoning (see page 28)
1 medium onion, chopped fine
3 large cloves garlic, minced
1 shallot, minced
2 our Bouillon Cubes (see page 25)
1 cup fresh tomatoes, seeded and chopped, or 1 can plum tomatoes, drained and chopped (juice reserved)
1 canned green chili, chopped fine
1 carrot, shredded
½ cup brown rice, cooked in 1½ cups our Chicken Stock (see page 26) or Vegetable Stock (see page 60)
1 egg white, slightly beaten
¼ cup chopped fresh parsley
1 tablespoon mild soy sauce
1 cup leftover cooked chicken or beef, finely chopped
½ cup salt-free tomato sauce (if tomatoes are used)
1 cup fine whole wheat bread crumbs, made from Pritikin bread
3 tablespoons grated Sap Sago cheese, toasted (see page 15)

1. Wash zucchini thoroughly under cold running water. Cut in half lengthwise, scoop out pulp leaving a ¼-inch shell (a grapefruit spoon works well for this), and season with vegetable seasoning.

2. Chop pulp coarsely and set aside.

3. Sauté onion, garlic, and shallot in bouillon cubes for 2 to 3 minutes.

4. Add zucchini pulp, tomatoes, chili pepper, and carrot. Cook slowly for 7 to 10 minutes, until most of the liquid is removed. Stir occasionally.

5. Combine with brown rice and cool.

6. Add egg white, parsley, soy sauce, and chicken. Combine with a fork and taste for additional seasoning.

*7. Stuff zucchini shells and place in a glass baking dish that has been lined with ½ cup tomato sauce (reserved from the canned tomatoes, if used).

* May be prepared ahead through step 7.

8. Mix bread crumbs with toasted Sap Sago cheese and top zucchini heavily with mixture.

9. Bake in a preheated 400° oven for about 45 minutes to 1 hour, or until golden brown.

To Serve: You may serve this as a vegetable garnish with broiled chicken or as one of the entrées on a vegetable plate accompanied by a baked potato and parsleyed carrots.

Per serving: 187 calories; 14.1 gm protein; 1.8 gm fat; 30.7 gm carbohydrate; 9.6 gm fiber; 21 mg cholesterol; 2.7 mg iron; 166 mg sodium; 108 mg calcium; 177 mg phosphorus; 2875 IU Vitamin A; 0.26 mg thiamine; 0.33 mg riboflavin; 74 mg Vitamin C; 876 mg potassium; 0.19 mg zinc; 5.7 mg niacin; 84 mcg Vitamin B_6; 0.01 mcg Vitamin B_{12}; 11 mcg folic acid

Pastas and Grains

COMPLEX CARBOHYDRATES,
SIMPLE RECIPES

Pastas

Basic Marinara Sauce
Ragù alla Bolognese
Fresh Tomato Sauce with Fresh Basil
Bucatini Primavera
Japanese Soba Salad
Tuna-Pasta Salad
Marilyn's Linguini Salad
Pasta Salad Jardinière
Stuffed Large Pasta Shells
Quickie Luscious Lasagna
Zucchini with Linguini or Conchiglie
Harriet's Pasta Florentine
Noodle Pudding Duo
  Noodle Pudding I
  Noodle Pudding II—with Blueberry Topping

Grains

Barley Casserole
Steamed Brown Rice
East African Pavlava Sauce with Brown Rice
Cracked Wheat Pilaf
Wild Rice, Brown Rice, and Mushrooms
Basic Granola

There are two kinds of carbohydrates—sugars and complex carbohydrates (such as cellulose and starches). We need complex carbohydrates in our diets because they are a very efficient source of fuel. Sugar enters the bloodstream quickly; starches, however, must be broken down gradually and stored in the body to be released as needed. Good sources of complex carbohydrates are whole grains (in cereals and brown rice, flours, bread products, and whole grain pasta), legumes, and starchy vegetables such as corn, potatoes, and peas. Today, only approximately 25 percent of the calories Americans consume are derived from complex carbohydrates whereas people in Third World nations have approximately 75 percent of their calories derived from complex carbohydrates. We should avoid all refined cereals, flours, and cereal products—especially those with sugar or preservatives added. Processed and refined cereal products have had the bran (the outer covering of grains which is rich in cellulose or fiber, and vitamins and minerals) and sometimes the germ (which is rich in protein, fat, vitamins B and E) removed. Instead of having to add bran or wheat germ to our foods, why not eat the whole grain as nature has provided it—in proper proportions?

I remember when pasta used to mean just plain spaghetti and meat balls. Today, there is a whole new world of pasta out there, with many varieties of shape, size, and texture. Not just unbleached white flour is used; there is pasta made from whole wheat flour, corn flour, artichoke flour, buckwheat flour, soy flour, and combinations thereof. Because we now realize the importance of complex carbohydrates in our diets, people are eating more pasta and more often without fearing the calories. Pasta is like the much-maligned potato; its final caloric content is controlled by what you put on it. Hence, if we top our pastas with light sauces, less meat, and more vegetables or even fish, we have a calorie-controlled delight.

I suggest using mostly whole-grain pastas, or if not, at least those made without added fat or eggs. Remember to read your package labels. You will find more variety in your local Italian delicatessen than in most neighborhood supermarkets. Most pastas are variations of four general shapes: strands, twists, shells, and tiny pasta bits.

One of the most popular ways of serving pasta today is the cold pasta salad, which presents endless possibilities for creativity and variety. In this chapter I have given you a few hot and cold pasta suggestions I know you will enjoy. After trying some of the recipes here you can vary them by changing the pasta, dressing, or vegetables and adding meat, fish, or poultry. Be adventurous.

Pasta

Basic Marinara Sauce

Yield: 6 cups (1 cup = 1 serving)

The beauty of this classic Italian sauce is that by preparing it quickly, the fresh flavors are retained. It is not necessary to cook it all day.

1 small onion, chopped fine
1 small carrot, chopped fine
1 shallot, chopped fine
2 cloves garlic, chopped fine
3 tablespoons our Chicken Stock (see page 26), or 3 our Bouillon Cubes (see page 25)
3 pounds ripe, fresh tomatoes, peeled, seeded, and coarsely chopped, or 1 28-ounce can Italian plum tomatoes in sauce, chopped
3 tablespoons salt-free tomato paste, to be used with fresh tomatoes only
4 tablespoons chopped fresh basil, or 2 tablespoons dried basil
2 tablespoons chopped fresh Italian parsley
2 tablespoons grated Sap Sago cheese, toasted (see page 15; optional)

1. Sauté onion, carrot, shallot, and garlic in stock for 5 minutes.
2. Add tomatoes, tomato paste, basil, and parsley. Add Sap Sago cheese if desired.

To Serve: Serve over cooked spaghetti or soba noodles,* topped with additional chopped fresh basil or parsley if desired. Complete the meal with a crisp green salad and sourdough rolls.

Variations: Add 1 tablespoon dry red wine for last 5 minutes.

For a delicious and distinctive variation, "*Spaghetti Tonnato,*" add 2 7½-ounce cans of salt-reduced tuna in water (drained) to sauce in step 2 and simmer 30 minutes. Serve over spaghetti or soba noodles.

Per serving: 73 calories; 4.3 gm protein; 0.6 gm fat; 16.2 gm carbohydrate; 4.5 gm fiber; 0 mg cholesterol; 2.3 mg iron; 16 mg sodium; 75 mg calcium; 87 mg phosphorus; 3458 IU Vitamin A; 0.17 mg thiamine; 0.13 mg riboflavin; 62 mg Vitamin C; 745 mg potassium; 0.55 mg zinc; 2 mg niacin; 263 mcg Vitamin B_6; 0 mcg Vitamin B_{12}; 24 mcg folic acid

* Soba noodles may be purchased in your local market or health food store. The content is half buckwheat and half whole wheat flour. Because of the addition of the buckwheat, this pasta may be cooked *al dente,* which cannot be done with 100 percent whole wheat pastas. Linguini or spaghettini (without eggs) may be substituted.

Ragù alla Bolognese
(Meat Sauce Bolognese Style)

Yield: 8 quarts (1 cup = 1 serving)

Because this classic Italian meat sauce takes a lot of time to prepare, I have given you a large-quantity recipe so you can make enough for several meals. I always have some in my freezer to use in lasagna, with various pastas, and as a sauce on eggplant or chicken. Its delicate flavor is indescribably delicious.

½ cup our Chicken Stock (see page 26)
3 large onions, minced
4 shallots, minced
6 cloves garlic, minced
3 celery stalks, minced
4 carrots, minced
1 cup minced fresh parsley
4 pounds ground flank steak or lean ground beef
3 teaspoons Italian herb seasoning, crushed
2 teaspoons basil, crushed
2 teaspoons rosemary, crushed
4 bay leaves
10 fennel seeds, crushed
1 cup dry white wine or vermouth
1 13-ounce can nonfat evaporated milk
3 28-ounce cans Italian tomatoes in juice with basil, coarsely chopped
1 28-ounce can salt-free tomato sauce
1 28-ounce can salt-free tomato puree
1 12-ounce can salt-free tomato paste

1. Place chicken stock in a large stainless steel kettle (at least 10 quarts). Add onions, shallots, and garlic and sauté until translucent. Add celery and carrots and sauté gently 5 minutes.
2. Add parsley and ground beef, crumble, and cook meat until it has lost its red color *only* (do not overcook).
3. Add Italian seasoning, basil, rosemary, bay leaves, and crushed fennel. Stir.
4. Add wine and cook 10 minutes, stirring occasionally.
5. Add nonfat evaporated milk and cook 10 minutes more, stirring frequently.
6. Add canned tomatoes and juice, sauce, puree, and paste, and stir thoroughly. When sauce starts to bubble, reduce heat to a gentle simmer.
7. Cook uncovered about 3½ hours. Stir from time to time to be sure it does not catch! (If you are interrupted, you can finish cooking it the

next day.) The sauce may be stored in the refrigerator up to 5 days. If you do so, simmer for 30 minutes before using.

To Freeze for Future Use: Cool sauce and divide into batches in jars or freezer containers. Remember to leave 1-inch head space for expansion.

Per serving: 188 calories; 14.9 gm protein; 5.3 gm fat; 14.8 gm carbohydrate; 1.5 gm fiber; 40 mg cholesterol; 3.8 gm iron; 242 mg sodium; 74 mg calcium; 168 mg phosphorus; 3175 IU Vitamin A; 0.15 mg thiamine; 0.2 mg riboflavin; 36 mg Vitamin C; 757 mg potassium; 0.3 mg zinc; 4.2 mg niacin; 114 mcg Vitamin B_6; 0.02 mcg Vitamin B_{12}; 10 mcg folic acid

Fresh Tomato Sauce with Fresh Basil

Yield: 2½ cups (¼ cup = 1 serving)

This is *not* a sauce for all seasons! Prepare it *only* at the height of the tomato crop for best results.

1 small onion, minced
1 large garlic clove, minced
2 tablespoons dry white wine
8 large ripe tomatoes, peeled, seeded, and chopped
3 tablespoons chopped fresh basil
1 tablespoon chopped fresh Italian parsley
Freshly ground pepper
Low-sodium vegetable seasoning (see page 28) optional

1. Sauté minced onion and garlic in white wine until softened.
2. Add tomatoes; bring to a boil and simmer 10 to 15 minutes, or until most of the liquid has evaporated. (*Do not overcook.*)
3. Add basil, parsley, and freshly ground pepper.
4. Taste, and adjust seasonings with pepper and a little vegetable seasoning if desired.

To Serve: May be served with pasta or with broiled fish or chicken.

Variation: Just before serving, combine all ingredients and chop coarsely in food processor. Place in saucepan and heat. Pour over freshly cooked and drained pasta. In this method of preparation, the sauce retains even more of its fresh flavor.

Per serving: 41 calories; 1.9 gm protein; 0.3 gm fat; 8.5 gm carbohydrate; 2.6 gm fiber; 0 mg cholesterol; 1.4 mg iron; 6 mg sodium; 52 mg calcium; 49 mg phosphorus; 1385 IU Vitamin A; 0.09 mg thiamine; 0.06 mg riboflavin; 34 mg Vitamin C; 406 mg potassium; 0.31 mg zinc; 1.1 mg niacin; 150 mcg Vitamin B_6; 0 mcg Vitamin B_{12}; 14 mcg folic acid

Bucatini Primavera

Serves: 4 (2 ounces pasta and 1 cup sauce = 1 serving)

8 ounces bucatini*
4 quarts boiling water
½ pound asparagus, cut Chinese style
10 cauliflowerets
1 bunch broccoli, florets only
4 cups Basic Marinara Sauce (see page 239)
6 dried mushrooms, soaked in hot water for 30 minutes, rinsed well, squeezed dry, and slivered
1 teaspoon freshly ground nutmeg

3 tablespoons chopped fresh Italian parsley for garnish
1 tablespoon chopped fresh basil, or 1 teaspoon dried basil, for garnish

1. Cook bucatini in 4 quarts briskly boiling water until tender.
2. Steam vegetables until crisp while cooking pasta.
3. Drain bucatini thoroughly; combine with 2 cups of the marinara sauce and mushrooms and nutmeg. Heat gently for a few minutes.

To Serve: Place pasta on a heated platter or pasta dish. Arrange vegetables over pasta, reserving some of each vegetable. Pour the remaining marinara sauce over the vegetables. Garnish with the remaining vegetables and sprinkle with fresh basil or parsley. Serve hot pasta with crisp sourdough rolls. May also be chilled and served as cold pasta salad.

Variation: *A low-calorie pasta pretender is spaghetti squash.* Use 1 large whole or 2 small spaghetti squash and serve ¼ to ½ squash shell, respectively, per person.

1. Cut squash in half lengthwise, pierce skin with a fork, and remove seeds.
2. To bake, place cut-side-down in a baking dish and bake in a preheated 375° oven for 30 minutes, or until skin is soft to the touch. (May also be covered with plastic wrap and microwaved for 7 to 10 minutes.)
3. When tender, fluff up the inside of the squash with 2 forks until you have spaghetti-like strands.
4. Serve in shell. Cover with sauce, and if you like, the steamed vegetables.

Per serving: 371 calories; 17.7 gm protein; 2.1 gm fat; 75.6 gm carbohydrate; 12.3 gm fiber; 0 mg cholesterol; 6.8 mg iron; 51 mg sodium; 215 mg calcium; 330 mg phosphorus; 6361 IU Vitamin A; 0.93 mg thiamine; 0.46 mg riboflavin; 161 mg Vitamin C; 1661 mg potassium; 0.91 mg zinc; 8.5 mg niacin; 509 mcg Vitamin B_6; 0 mcg Vitamin B_{12}; 121 mcg folic acid

* Other pastas such as penne, spaghettini, or linguini may be substituted for bucatini.

Tuna-Pasta Salad

Serves: 4 as an entrée (1 ounce pasta = 1 serving), 8 as an appetizer

1 cup nonfat yogurt
2 tablespoons brown rice vinegar
1 teaspoon low-sodium vegetable seasoning (see page 28)
1 clove garlic, minced
½ cup chopped fresh Italian parsley
4 ounces fusilli (twisted macaroni), cooked *al dente*, rinsed, and drained
1 7½-ounce can salt-free tuna in water, rinsed, drained, and flaked
1 cup frozen peas or steamed fresh peas
1 cup sliced celery
½ cup chopped red onion
¼ cup chopped fresh dill, or 1 tablespoon dried dill weed

1 tomato, peeled, seeded, and diced, for garnish
Fresh parsley sprigs for garnish

1. In a large salad bowl, stir together yogurt, brown rice vinegar, vegetable seasoning, garlic, and parsley until smooth.
2. Add remaining ingredients (except garnish) and toss with 2 forks to coat well.
3. Cover and chill several hours.

To Serve: Garnish with diced tomato and sprigs of fresh parsley. Use as an entrée with our Banana Bread (page 294) for dessert.

Variation: Substitute 1 cup our Italian Dressing (see page 12) for the yogurt and vinegar dressing.

Per serving: 255 calories; 23.7 gm protein; 1.1 gm fat; 37.7 gm carbohydrate; 3.3 gm fiber; 31 mg cholesterol; 4.1 mg iron; 148 mg sodium; 170 mg calcium; 218 mg phosphorus; 1717 IU Vitamin A; 0.51 mg thiamine; 0.39 mg riboflavin; 38 mg Vitamin C; 596 mg potassium; 0.58 mg zinc; 10.3 mg niacin; 158 mcg Vitamin B_6; 0 mcg Vitamin B_{12}; 23 mcg folic acid

Japanese Soba Salad

Serves: 6 as an entrée (2 ounces pasta = 1 serving), 8 as an accompaniment

½ cup our Chicken Stock (see page 26)
1 tablespoon white wine
3 tablespoons brown rice vinegar or raspberry wine vinegar
¼ teaspoon powdered onion
¼ teaspoon garlic powder
½ teaspoon crushed red pepper
1 package (1½ ounces) dried Japanese shiitake mushrooms
2 tablespoons mild soy sauce
4 quarts boiling water
8 ounces soba noodles (see note page 239)
1 tablespoon mild soy sauce
1 tablespoon brown rice vinegar
1 clove garlic, finely chopped
½ red onion, chopped
1 teaspoon thyme
2 cups mixed steamed vegetables (peas, julienne carrots, peapods, julienne zucchini, cut green beans, chopped broccoli, sliced asparagus)

Lettuce leaves (not iceberg) for serving
2 tomatoes, peeled, seeded, and cut in ½-inch cubes, for garnish
2 tablespoons chopped fresh basil for garnish
2 tablespoons chopped fresh Italian parsley for garnish

1. *To make vinaigrette dressing:* Whisk first 6 ingredients in a bowl or shake in a jar. Chill.

2. Place dried mushrooms in a bowl, cover with boiling water and 1 tablespoon of the 2 tablespoons soy sauce, soak 30 minutes, rinse several times, squeeze dry, and remove stems. Cut mushrooms into slices.

3. Bring 4 quarts water to a boil, add the remaining 1 tablespoon soy sauce. Add noodles to boiling water slowly so as not to interrupt boil. Boil 4 to 6 minutes, or until cooked *al dente*.

4. Drain pasta thoroughly and place in a bowl with the 1 tablespoon soy sauce, the 1 tablespoon brown rice vinegar, and the garlic, red onion, thyme, and steamed vegetables. Toss and chill.

To Serve: Line a bowl or platter with lettuce leaves. Shortly before serving, toss noodle mixture with vinaigrette dressing, place over lettuce, and garnish with chopped tomatoes and fresh basil and parsley. Serve as an entrée with warm sourdough bread and the light and luscious Mrs. Latterman's Strawberry Chiffon Pie (page 281) as a dessert. A 1-ounce serving is quite adequate for an appetizer, which may be followed by

Chicken Breasts Supreme (page 145) and steamed broccoli spears. Top off the meal with a Perfect Pear (page 274).

Helpful Hint: Save strained mushroom liquid for soup or sauce at some other time.

Per serving: 184 calories; 7.8 gm protein; 1.1 gm fat; 35.4 gm carbohydrate; 2.9 gm fiber; 0 mg cholesterol; 2.6 mg iron; 171 mg sodium; 71 mg calcium; 65 mg phosphorus; 2590 IU Vitamin A; 0.23 mg thiamine; 0.2 mg riboflavin; 32 mg Vitamin C; 369 mg potassium; 0.13 mg zinc; 2.4 mg niacin; 79 mcg Vitamin B_6; 0 mcg Vitamin B_{12}; 31 mcg folic acid

Marilyn's Linguini Salad

Serves: 6

1 ounce shiitake mushrooms, soaked in hot water 30 minutes, then rinsed several times, squeezed dry, stemmed, and slivered
1 tablespoon mild soy sauce
8 ounces linguini or shells, cooked *al dente*, rinsed, and drained
1 teaspoon Chinese sesame oil
2 whole chicken breasts (16 ounces chicken) roasted and cut in chunks, or 2 cups leftover chicken or turkey
1 teaspoon low-sodium vegetable seasoning (see page 28)
1 cup defrosted frozen peas
1 7½-ounce can artichoke quarters, rinsed and well drained
3 green onions, sliced
1 red pepper, seeded and cut in slivers
1 cup our Vinaigrette Dressing (see page 12)

1 large ripe tomato, peeled, seeded, and diced, for garnish
2 tablespoons chopped fresh basil or Italian parsley for garnish

1. Marinate mushrooms in soy sauce for 30 minutes while preparing rest of salad.
2. In a large salad bowl, combine pasta, sesame oil, chicken, vegetable seasoning, peas, artichokes, green onions, and red pepper.
3. Add dressing and toss with 2 forks to coat well.
4. Cover and chill 1 hour. Before serving, add marinated mushrooms and toss.

To Serve: Garnish with diced tomato and fresh basil or Italian parsley, and serve. Serve with crisp Italian bread and Apple Crisp (page 264).

Per serving: 255 calories; 20.7 gm protein; 1.9 gm fat; 41.1 gm carbohydrate; 3.3 gm fiber; 38 mg cholesterol; 3.2 mg iron; 99 mg sodium; 55 mg calcium; 267 mg phosphorus; 1356 IU Vitamin A; 0.54 mg thiamine; 0.41 mg riboflavin; 53 mg Vitamin C; 625 mg potassium; 0.06 mg zinc; 8.1 mg niacin; 86 mcg Vitamin B_6; 0 mcg Vitamin B_{12}; 8 mcg folic acid

Pasta Salad Jardinière

Serves: 4 as an entrée, 6 as an appetizer

1 cup nonfat yogurt
2 tablespoons chopped green onion
1 tablespoon lemon juice
1 teaspoon dried basil, or 1 tablespoon chopped fresh basil
Freshly ground pepper
4 ounces soba noodles (see note page 239) or thin spaghettini, cooked *al dente*, rinsed, and drained
1½ cups chopped English cucumber, or 1 regular cucumber, peeled, seeded, and chopped
¼ pound green beans, cut in 1-inch pieces and steamed
1 cup thinly sliced carrots, steamed
1 cup thinly sliced zucchini, cut in half and steamed
½ cup thinly sliced radishes
½ cup chopped green pepper

½ cup chopped fresh Italian parsley for garnish

1. *To make salad dressing,* combine the first 5 ingredients in a large salad bowl.

2. Add pasta, cucumber, beans, carrots, zucchini, radishes, and green pepper. Toss with 2 forks to coat well.

3. Cover and chill.

To Serve: Garnish with parsley and serve. As an entrée, serve with sliced tomato salad, sourdough melba toast, and Helen's San Francisco Peach Surprises (page 286) for dessert.

Variation: Add 1 cup diced cooked chicken or turkey.

Per serving: 186 calories; 7.9 gm protein; 0.9 gm fat; 35.8 gm carbohydrate; 3.2 gm fiber; 0 mg cholesterol; 2 mg iron; 39 mg sodium; 111 mg calcium; 41 mg phosphorus; 3663 IU Vitamin A; 0.23 mg thiamine; 0.21 mg riboflavin; 42 mg Vitamin C; 304 mg potassium; 0.14 mg zinc; 1.9 mg niacin; 91 mcg Vitamin B_6; 0 mcg Vitamin B_{12}; 14 mcg folic acid

Stuffed Large Pasta Shells

Serves: 12 (2 stuffed shells = 1 serving)

1¼ pounds hoop cheese or skim-milk ricotta
3 10-ounce packages frozen chopped broccoli, defrosted and drained
½ cup chopped green onions
2 egg whites
1 teaspoon Italian herb seasoning
1 cup defrosted frozen peas
½ teaspoon freshly ground pepper or crushed red pepper
24 whole wheat pasta shells, cooked, rinsed, and drained
4 cups Basic Marinara Sauce (page 239) or salt-free canned marinara sauce
4 tablespoons grated Sap Sago cheese, toasted (see page 15)

1. Process cheese in blender or food processor until creamy; add defrosted and drained broccoli and green onions. Process briefly.
2. Add egg whites, Italian seasoning, peas, and pepper, and blend.
3. Use mixture to stuff drained shells.
*4. Place shells side by side, stuffed-side-up, in a single layer in a 13 x 9 x 2-inch baking pan sprayed with nonstick spray.
5. Spoon sauce over shells and bake in a preheated 350° oven for 30 minutes, or until sauce bubbles.
6. Sprinkle with toasted Sap Sago cheese before serving.

Variation: If your diet permits, Parmesan cheese may be substituted for the Sap Sago.

Per serving: 519 calories; 27.1 gm protein; 3 gm fat; 92 gm carbohydrate; 3 gm fiber; 0 mg cholesterol; 3.8 mg iron; 141 mg sodium; 106 mg calcium; 97 mg phosphorus; 3833 IU Vitamin A; 0.54 mg thiamine; 0.25 mg riboflavin; 94 mg Vitamin C; 508 mg potassium; 0.16 mg zinc; 4 mg niacin; 88 mcg Vitamin B_6; 0.01 mcg Vitamin B_{12}; 10 mcg folic acid

* May be frozen after step 4 has been completed.

Quickie Luscious Lasagna

Serves: 8 (1 cup = 1 serving)

6 strips whole wheat and spinach lasagna noodles
1 16-ounce package skim-milk ricotta cheese
2 egg whites
1 10-ounce package frozen chopped spinach, defrosted and squeezed dry
2 tablespoons chopped fresh parsley
1 clove garlic, minced
1 16-ounce jar salt-free meatless spaghetti sauce
2 small zucchini, sliced ⅛ inch thick
4 ounces skim-milk mozzarella cheese, shredded

1. Add lasagna noodles to boiling water one at a time so you do not stop the water from boiling. Boil 15 minutes, or until tender. Drain, rinse with cold water, and drain thoroughly again.
2. Blend ricotta cheese, egg whites, spinach, and parsley.
3. Add minced garlic to spaghetti sauce.
4. Spray an 11 x 7-inch rectangular baking pan with nonstick spray. Spoon a layer of sauce on the bottom of the casserole. Spread 2 strips of lasagna noodles and top with sauce again.
5. Dab ricotta mixture by tablespoonfuls on top of lasagna noodles, placing 4 dabs on each strip of lasagna.
6. Alternate rows of zucchini between rows of ricotta along edges of lasagna noodles.
7. Sprinkle mozzarella on top of ricotta.
8. Next, place a layer of lasagna noodles and repeat with sauce, ricotta, zucchini, and mozzarella.

*9. Top with a layer of lasagna noodles and end with sauce and mozzarella cheese.

10. Bake in a preheated 400° oven for 20 minutes.

To Serve: Accompany with a crisp green Italian salad with garbanzo beans, hot crusty Italian bread, and either a sorbet you may already have in your freezer or fresh fruit.

Variation: You may substitute Italian plum tomatoes with basil for the spaghetti sauce; however they will be higher in sodium because they are not salt-free.

Per serving: 303 calories; 19.6 gm protein; 8.7 gm fat; 36.9 gm carbohydrate; 2.4 gm fiber; 46 mg cholesterol; 2.3 mg iron; 175 mg sodium; 297 mg calcium; 242 mg phosphorus; 3316 IU Vitamin A; 0.36 mg thiamine; 0.38 mg riboflavin; 25 mg Vitamin C; 409 mg potassium; 1.34 mg zinc; 2.7 mg niacin; 107 mcg Vitamin B_6; 0.29 mcg Vitamin B_{12}; 17 mcg folic acid

* May be prepared the day before through step 9 and baked 30 minutes before serving.

Zucchini with Linguini or Conchiglie

Serves: 8 (2 ounces pasta = 1 serving)

½ cup our Chicken Stock (see page 26) or Vegetable Stock (see page 60)
½ large onion, finely minced
2 shallots, finely minced
1 clove garlic, finely minced
2 pounds small, firm zucchini, thinly sliced
2 teaspoons chopped fresh rosemary, or 1 teaspoon dried rosemary, crushed
Freshly ground pepper
1 pound linguini or conchiglie (pasta shells), cooked *al dente*, rinsed, and drained
⅔ cup Weight Watchers cottage cheese, rinsed and drained

3 tablespoons chopped fresh Italian parsley for garnish

1. Place stock in a large nonstick skillet. Bring to a boil. Add onion, shallots, and garlic and cook until transparent, stirring constantly.

*2. Add sliced zucchini, rosemary, and pepper. Stir and cook 2 to 3 minutes.

3. Add drained pasta and cottage cheese to skillet and stir until pasta is well coated and heated through (2 to 3 minutes).

To Serve: Turn onto a heated platter, sprinkle with chopped Italian parsley, and *serve immediately*.

Per serving: 253 calories; 11.2 gm protein; 1 gm fat; 49.4 gm carbohydrate; 5.8 gm fiber; 0 mg cholesterol; 2.4 mg iron; 48 mg sodium; 74 mg calcium; 131 mg phosphorus; 501 IU Vitamin A; 0.57 mg thiamine; 0.37 mg riboflavin; 25 mg Vitamin C; 393 mg potassium; 0.03 mg zinc; 4.7 mg niacin; 50 mcg Vitamin B_6; 0 mcg Vitamin B_{12}; 3 mcg folic acid

* The vegetable mixture may be prepared through step 2 to be combined with freshly cooked pasta at serving time.

Harriet's Pasta Florentine

Serves: 8 as an entrée, 12–14 as pasta course

A pasta casserole is always an enormous success for buffet service. It can be made the day before or frozen ahead. This Pasta Florentine is delicious and much lower in calories than the traditional recipe.

6 ounces soba noodles (see note page 239)
6 ounces linguini
2 packages frozen chopped spinach, defrosted and squeezed dry
1 pint Weight Watchers cottage cheese, rinsed and drained
1 bunch green onions, sliced
½ teaspoon freshly grated nutmeg
1 teaspoon low-sodium vegetable seasoning (see page 28)
7 cups Ragù alla Bolognese (see page 240)
1 cup skimmed evaporated milk
3 tablespoons grated Sap Sago cheese, toasted (see page 15)

1. Cook soba and linguini pastas separately, until *al dente*. Drain thoroughly.
2. Blend defrosted spinach with cottage cheese, green onions, nutmeg, and vegetable seasoning.
3. Spray a 3-quart shallow casserole with nonstick spray and place a layer of Ragù alla Bolognese in casserole, then follow with a layer of linguini.
4. Spread spinach mixture over linguini, follow with a layer of soba pasta, then top with the remaining Ragù alla Bolognese.
*5. Pour skimmed evaporated milk over entire casserole.
6. Sprinkle with Sap Sago cheese and bake in a preheated 350° oven for 35 to 45 minutes.

Variation: If your diet permits, substitute Parmesan cheese for the Sap Sago.

Per serving: 266 calories; 15.1 gm protein; 5.4 gm fat; 25 gm carbohydrate; 0.61 gm fiber; 0 mg cholesterol; 1.8 mg iron; 106 mg sodium; 147 mg calcium; 85 mg phosphorus; 3696 IU Vitamin A; 0.31 mg thiamine; 29 mg riboflavin; 14.8 mg Vitamin C; 216 mg potassium; 0.02 mg zinc; 2.8 mg niacin; 21.38 mcg Vitamin B_6; 0.05 mcg Vitamin B_{12}; 0.85 mcg folic acid

* May be prepared several days ahead of time through step 5, or frozen for future use at that point.

Noodle Pudding Duo

Noodle Pudding I

Serves: 18 (⅔ cup = 1 serving)

Here are two of my sister Ruth's favorite noodle puddings. Both make delicious desserts or wonderful accompaniments to poultry or fish.

16 ounces whole wheat noodles
16 ounces Weight Watchers cottage cheese, rinsed and drained
16 ounces nonfat yogurt
4 ounces frozen unsweetened apple juice concentrate
2½ teaspoons vanilla extract
1 20-ounce can crushed unsweetened pineapple, with juice
4 egg whites, beaten stiff
Cinnamon and nutmeg

1. Cook whole wheat noodles in boiling water until tender, about 10 minutes. Drain well.
2. Combine cottage cheese, yogurt, apple juice concentrate, vanilla extract, and crushed pineapple (juice and all). Blend well.
3. Add noodles to cheese mixture and blend.
*4. Beat egg whites until stiff and fold into noodle mixture.
5. Spray a 13 x 9 x 2-inch baking dish with nonstick spray. Pour noodle mixture into pan. Sprinkle with cinnamon and freshly ground nutmeg and bake in a preheated 375° oven for about 1 hour, or until lightly browned.

Per serving: 150 calories; 8.1 gm protein; 0.7 gm fat; 26.0 gm carbohydrate; 0.1 gm fiber; 0 mg cholesterol; 0.6 mg iron; 83 mg sodium; 61 mg calcium; 3 mg phosphorus; 83 IU Vitamin A; 0.13 mg thiamine; 0.16 mg riboflavin; 2 mg Vitamin C; 62 mg potassium; 0 mg zinc; 0.9 mg niacin; 23 mcg Vitamin B_6; 0.01 mcg Vitamin B_{12}; 0 mcg folic acid

* May be frozen for future use after step 4 has been completed.

Noodle Pudding II—with Blueberry Topping

Serves: 18 (⅔ cup = 1 serving)

16 ounces whole wheat noodles
16 ounces Weight Watchers cottage cheese, rinsed and drained
16 ounces nonfat yogurt
1 cup fresh orange juice
½ cup frozen unsweetened apple juice concentrate
2 teaspoons vanilla extract
6 egg whites, beaten stiff
2 tablespoons cornstarch
½ cup orange juice
½ cup water
1 tablespoon frozen unsweetened apple juice concentrate
2 tablespoons berry juice concentrate
12 ounces frozen blueberries

1. Proceed as for Noodle Pudding I, using the first 7 ingredients. While the pudding is baking, make blueberry topping.
2. Blend the cornstarch with a few tablespoons of orange juice. Add to remaining orange juice, water, apple juice concentrate, and berry concentrate.
3. Cook until slightly thickened, about 10 minutes, stirring constantly. Add frozen blueberries.
4. After the pudding has been in the oven for 1 hour, remove from oven, spread with blueberry topping, and return to the oven for 15 additional minutes.

Variation: Frozen cherries can be used instead of blueberries.

Per serving: 168 calories; 8.8 gm protein; 0.8 gm fat; 29.6 gm carbohydrate; 0.3 gm fiber; 0 mg cholesterol; 0.8 mg iron; 88 mg sodium; 62 mg calcium; 8 mg phosphorus; 122 IU Vitamin A; 0.13 mg thiamine; 0.18 mg riboflavin; 12 mg Vitamin C; 90 mg potassium; 0.01 mg zinc; 1 mg niacin; 9 mcg Vitamin B_6; 0.01 mcg Vitamin B_{12}; 1 mcg folic acid

Grains

Barley Casserole

Serves: 8 (⅓ cup = 1 serving)

Barley is a frequently neglected whole grain cereal that makes a satisfying and delicious casserole. This easy recipe is tasty with Hearty Steak with Peppers (page 181).

1 cup barley
4 cups our Chicken Stock (see page 26) or our Vegetable Stock (see page 60)
1 carrot, sliced
1 small leek (white part only), sliced
1 small onion, chopped
Few grains crushed red pepper
½ teaspoon thyme, crushed
½ teaspoon low-sodium vegetable seasoning (see page 28)

Chopped fresh Italian parsley for garnish

1. In a 2-quart casserole, combine all ingredients except parsley.
2. Cover and bake in a preheated 350° oven for about 2 hours. Stir barley with a fork from time to time while baking.
3. Remove lid and garnish with parsley before serving.

Variation: Add a 2-ounce jar of pimiento, chopped and drained, with the parsley before serving.

Per serving: 117 calories; 3.8 gm protein; 0.3 gm fat; 25.3 gm carbohydrate; 2.4 gm fiber; 0 mg cholesterol; 0.9 mg iron; 9 mg sodium; 19 mg calcium; 60 mg phosphorus; 1106 IU Vitamin A; 0.05 mg thiamine; 0.03 mg riboflavin; 3 mg Vitamin C; 113 mg potassium; 0.08 mg zinc; 0.9 mg niacin; 86 mcg Vitamin B_6; 0 mcg Vitamin B_{12}; 4 mcg folic acid

Steamed Brown Rice

Serves: 4–6 (½ cup = 1 serving)

Another outstanding and many times overlooked whole grain cereal is brown rice. It has far more food value than white rice and a better flavor (a nutlike quality), though because of its bran, it must be cooked longer.

1 cup brown rice, washed

2¼ cups water, our Chicken Stock (see page 26), or our Vegetable Stock (see page 60)

1. Place cold water or broth in saucepan and bring to a boil.*
2. Add washed rice to boiling liquid slowly and return to boil. Reduce to simmer.
3. Cover and cook 40 to 45 minutes, until all liquid has been absorbed. Fluff rice with a fork before serving.

To Serve: Brown rice may be served with Stir-fried Vegetables (see page 208) as an entrée, or steamed and combined with cooked zucchini, peas, mushrooms, or asparagus as an accompaniment.

Variations: Add 1 tablespoon soy sauce, 1 teaspoon basil, 2 tablespoons chopped fresh parsley, and 4 finely chopped green onions with the rice.

You may also add crushed red pepper, 1 teaspoon toasted, dehydrated onion, and 1 teaspoon soy sauce to cooking liquid.

The Armenians moisten their cooked rice with yogurt before serving. It's low-calorie and delicious!

Per serving: 116 calories; 2.7 gm protein; 0.7 gm fat; 28.1 gm carbohydrate; 2.6 gm fiber; 0 mg cholesterol; 0.6 mg iron; 3 mg sodium; 12 mg calcium; 80 mg phosphorus; 0 IU Vitamin A; 0.12 mg thiamine; 0.02 mg riboflavin; 0 mg Vitamin C; 78 mg potassium; 0 mg zinc; 1.7 mg niacin; 0 mcg Vitamin B_6; 0 mcg Vitamin B_{12}; 0 mcg folic acid

* Rice may be added to boiling liquid in an ovenproof casserole, covered, and baked at 350° for 45 minutes to 1 hour instead of being boiled on top of the stove.

East African Pavlava Sauce with Brown Rice

Serves: 8 (1½ cups = 1 serving)

My thanks to the students of the College of the Redwoods, Eureka, California, their teacher, Rose Stebbins, and Geoffrey Bain, who discovered this recipe during his stay in the Peace Corps in an African village. The recipe is adapted to ingredients available in the United States.

3 bunches (3–4 pounds) collard greens,* washed and drained thoroughly
1½ pounds boned, skinned, and defatted chicken breasts, diced
2 teaspoons low-sodium vegetable seasoning (see page 28)
4 cups our Chicken Stock (see page 26)
4 medium onions, finely chopped
4 hot African dried peppers (they look like dried red chili peppers), chopped, or 1 3-inch jalapeno pepper, chopped
1 5-ounce can unsalted tomato paste
4 cups Steamed Brown Rice (see page 254)

1. Cut washed greens into very small pieces.
2. Season diced chicken with vegetable seasoning.
3. Add ½ cup of the chicken stock to a large Dutch oven or sauté pan and bring to a boil. Add seasoned chicken pieces and sauté.
4. Remove sautéed chicken from pan and add chopped greens, onions, the remaining chicken stock, the peppers, and the tomato paste. Blend well.
5. Bring mixture to a boil, reduce to a simmer, cover, and cook for 15 to 20 minutes.
6. Add sautéed chicken pieces and simmer 10 to 15 minutes more.

To Serve: Serve sauce over the steamed brown rice.

Per serving: 347 calories; 32.4 gm protein; 3.5 gm fat; 50.8 gm carbohydrate; 5.6 gm fiber; 49 mg cholesterol; 4.1 mg iron; 164 mg sodium; 457 mg calcium; 383 mg phosphorus; 13,672 IU Vitamin A; 0.64 mg thiamine; 0.78 mg riboflavin; 199 mg Vitamin C; 1198 mg potassium; 1.05 mg zinc; 14.7 niacin; 532 mcg Vitamin B_6; 0.32 mcg Vitamin B_{12}; 21 mcg folic acid

* You may substitute turnip or mustard greens for collards; however, if using mustard greens, use only half the amount as they have a significantly stronger flavor.

Cracked Wheat Pilaf

Serves: 8 (½ cup = 1 serving)

A delicious alternative to brown rice is cracked wheat, or bulgur. Cracked wheat is rich in potassium, phosphorus, and niacin. It has a nutlike flavor and somewhat chewy texture.

3 our Bouillon Cubes (see page 25), or ¼ cup our Chicken Stock (see page 26)
⅓ cup chopped celery with leaves
2 shallots, chopped
1 medium onion, chopped
1 cup sliced fresh mushrooms
½ green pepper, seeded and chopped
1 teaspoon low-sodium vegetable seasoning (see page 28)
2 cups cracked wheat
Few grains crushed red pepper
4 cups our Chicken Stock
1 2-ounce jar chopped pimiento, drained

3 tablespoons chopped fresh Italian parsley for garnish

1. Melt bouillon cubes in a saucepan; when boiling, add celery, shallots, and onion. Sauté until transparent, stirring constantly.
2. Add mushrooms, green pepper, and vegetable seasoning. Sauté 2 minutes.
3. Place cracked wheat in a shallow pan under broiler and toast until golden. *Watch carefully and stir.*
4. Add browned cracked wheat to sautéed vegetables and stir over low heat a few minutes.
5. Add crushed red pepper and the 4 cups chicken stock. Bring to a boil and lower heat to simmer.
6. Cover and simmer cracked wheat mixture 15 minutes. Stir in pimiento.

To Serve: Place in a serving dish and sprinkle with chopped parsley. This may be served instead of the more commonly used brown rice or potatoes with Stir-Fried Vegetables (page 208) or with Orange-Glazed Cornish Hens (page 139).

Per serving: 81 calories; 3.7 gm protein; 0.4 gm fat; 16.8 gm carbohydrate; 1.3 gm fiber; 0 mg cholesterol; 1.1 mg iron; 16 mg sodium; 23 mg calcium; 83 mg phosphorus; 399 IU Vitamin A; 0.1 mg thiamine; 0.08 mg riboflavin; 20 mg Vitamin C; 189 mg potassium; 0.06 mg zinc; 1.1 mg niacin; 52 mcg Vitamin B_6; 0 mcg Vitamin B_{12}; 8 mcg folic acid

Wild Rice, Brown Rice, and Mushrooms

Serves: 12 (½ cup = 1 serving)

Wild rice is not a grain, but the elegant seed of a grass. Like pasta, it tastes best when cooked *al dente*—around 45 minutes. Wild rice is expensive, so frequently we combine it with brown rice (which also cooks for 45 minutes) to cut down on the cost as well as provide an interesting combination of flavors.

4 cups our Chicken Stock (see page 26) or our Vegetable Stock (see page 60)
1 teaspoon dried shallots
Few grains crushed red pepper
½ teaspoon thyme, crushed
1 bay leaf
1 cup brown rice
1 cup wild rice
2 our Bouillon Cubes (see page 25)
1 tablespoon dry white wine
1 small onion, finely chopped
½ pound fresh mushrooms, wiped clean and sliced
2 green onions, chopped
1 tablespoon lemon juice
1 tablespoon mild soy sauce
1 tablespoon salt-free Dijon mustard
1 4-ounce jar chopped pimiento, drained

1. Place stock, shallots, pepper, thyme, and bay leaf in a 3-quart saucepan. Bring stock to a boil; add brown rice and wild rice. Bring to a second boil, reduce heat, cover, and simmer 45 minutes.

*2. Remove any excess liquid.

3. While rice is cooking, melt bouillon cubes with wine in a nonstick skillet. When simmering, add onion and sauté 5 minutes, or until transparent.

4. Add mushrooms, green onions, and lemon juice. Sauté a few minutes. Add soy sauce and mustard; blend with mushrooms using a fork.

5. Blend mushroom mixture with precooked rice and pimientos.

6. Place in an ovenproof casserole sprayed with nonstick spray, cover with foil, and heat in a preheated 325° oven for 20 to 30 minutes, or until quite hot and ready to serve.

To Serve: This casserole combines nicely with roast turkey or Marinated Flank Steak (page 176).

Variation: When cold, this cooked rice mixture combines nicely with vegetables and leftover diced chicken for an unusual luncheon main dish.

* Can be prepared ahead or the day before through step 2 and chilled until needed. Bring precooked rice to room temperature before using.

Helpful Hint: If rice seems dry, add a little stock to moisten after 20 minutes.

Per serving: 115 calories; 4.4 gm protein; 0.5 gm fat; 23.2 gm carbohydrate; 1.8 gm fiber; 0 mg cholesterol; 1.2 mg iron; 50 mg sodium; 14 mg calcium; 96 mg phosphorus; 298 IU Vitamin A; 0.12 mg thiamine; 0.18 mg riboflavin; 12 mg Vitamin C; 178 mg potassium; 0.03 mg zinc; 2.2 mg niacin; 35 mcg Vitamin B_6; 0 mcg Vitamin B_{12}; 7 mcg folic acid

Basic Granola

Yield: 6 cups (½ cup = 1 serving)

1 cup rolled oats
1 cup four-grain cereal
½ cup wheat or rye flakes
½ cup steel-cut oats
1 cup unsweetened whole wheat flake cereal
½ cup triticale* or whole wheat flour
½ cup nonfat powdered milk
¼ cup millet
8 tablespoons frozen unsweetened apple juice concentrate with 2 teaspoons vanilla extract
3 tablespoons cinnamon
1 teaspoon nutmeg, freshly ground
½ cup raisins, plumped in hot orange juice to cover for 15 minutes, then drained
½ cup chopped dates
1 vanilla bean, split

1. Place oats, four-grain cereal, and wheat or rye flakes in a colander. Pour cold water over them to *just dampen*, then drain.
2. Add whole wheat flake cereal, triticale, powdered milk, and millet. Mix gently with a fork and place on 2 nonstick baking sheets.
3. Sprinkle with a quarter of the apple juice concentrate and vanilla mixture, and a quarter of the cinnamon and nutmeg.
4. Toast in a preheated 375° oven for 15 minutes; mix lightly. Add another quarter of the apple juice concentrate and vanilla, and a quarter of the cinnamon and nutmeg, and toast for another 15 minutes. Repeat every 15 minutes until granola is golden brown, about 45 minutes. After granola has toasted 30 minutes, add plumped raisins and dates and continue baking for 15 minutes more.
5. Cool and store in a tightly sealed jar to which you have added a split vanilla bean for flavor.

To Use: The finished cereal may be used for snacking, as a cereal topped with bananas, strawberries, blueberries, or peaches and cold

* Triticale is a hybrid high-protein grain of wheat and rye, originating in Africa and available in health food stores and many markets.

milk, or as a base for pie. It is also delicious as a topping for a fruit crisp or our Pumpkin Bread (see page 298).

Variation: *Make Granola Bars.* Prepare Basic Granola through step 3. Beat 2 egg whites until stiff. Add 1 small ripe banana mashed with 3 tablespoons frozen unsweetened orange juice concentrate, 1 cup grated carrot, and 2 teaspoons vanilla extract. Beat thoroughly. Add ⅔ cup plumped raisins and ⅓ cup chopped dates. Combine egg white mixture with half of the baked granola mixture. Let stand 3 minutes. Spread in a nonstick (or nonstick sprayed) 11 x 6 x 2-inch pan. Sprinkle with 1 tablespoon toasted sesame seeds and bake in a preheated 350° oven for about 20 to 25 minutes, or until lightly browned. Immediately cut into 24 bars and cool on plate.

Per serving: 93 calories; 3.2 gm protein; 0.7 gm fat; 19.7 gm carbohydrate; 1.2 gm fiber; 0 mg cholesterol; 1.3 mg iron; 16 mg sodium; 50 mg calcium; 87 mg phosphorus; 88 IU Vitamin A; 0.12 mg thiamine; 0.08 mg riboflavin; 1 mg Vitamin C; 152 mg potassium; 0.52 mg zinc; 0.7 mg niacin; 68 mcg Vitamin B_6; 0.07 Vitamin B_{12}; 8 mcg folic acid

Sweets and Treats

CALORIES *DO* COUNT!

Desserts

Apple Crisp
Apple Torte
Last-Minute Fruit Mélange
Baked Fruit Compote
Pantry Fruit Compote
Festive Fruit Cake
Heavenly Fresh Fruit Pie
Judith's Fruited Cheese Pudding—Munich Style
Floating Islands with Strawberry or Raspberry Sauce
Funny Fudge Balls
Grapefruit Baked Alaska
Your Perfect Pear
Persimmon Pudding
Luscious Lemony Cheese Pie with Strawberry Sauce
Sweet Potato Mélange
Sweet Potato Meringues
Yogurt-Pumpkin Pie
Rosy Rhubarb Sauce
Mrs. Latterman's Strawberry Chiffon Pie
Strawberries with Strawberry Sauce
Yogurt Dessert Mold
Molded Apricot Mousse
Poached Peaches Supreme
Helen's San Francisco Peach Surprises
Harold's Old-Fashioned Rice Pudding
Raspberry Mousse
Banana and Pineapple Sorbet
Boysenberry-Yogurt Sorbet
Cranberry, Pineapple, and Yogurt Freeze
Lila's Frozen Dessert
Citron Soufflé

Quick Breads

Banana Bread
Carrot Cake Muffins
Corn Bread, Corn Sticks, or Corn Muffins
Geneva's Extra-Special Muffins
Harriet's Pumpkin Bread
Old-Fashioned Whole Wheat Fruit Bars

Can you believe that the average person in the United States today consumes about 125 pounds of sugar per year? Remember that statistic when you reach for sugar to prepare foods or to sprinkle on top of various already prepared dishes.

Sugar-rich foods are generally highly concentrated foods—high in calories that are empty. They are also usually readily available for rapid consumption (candy, cookies, cakes, and the like).

In an interview with *Total Health* magazine, I was asked where people seem to "cheat" in their diets the most. Desserts and sweets are the foods where self-discipline is most lacking. Rich desserts are excessive in calories from sugars and fat—both of which should be avoided.

Desserts are meant to be a special finish to a meal. Rich desserts, however, raise our blood sugar level quickly and then let us down quickly—frequently accounting for that logy or de-energized feeling at the end of an otherwise lovely meal. Why not choose whole fresh fruits for dessert—and for snacks? They contain some sugar, but their relatively high roughage content slows down the absorption of sugar in the body. They are also high in vitamins and minerals. Wonderful, ripe fruits in season, attractively served, have a luscious but light flavor all their own, and a splash of kirsch or brandy adds that something extra for a very special dessert.

However, occasionally we still have a yen for a piece of cake or a mousse. I have found that the use of unsweetened fruit juice concentrates is helpful in developing a "sweet" taste in various desserts while not adding sugar. Our Festive Fruit Cake, Raspberry Mousse, sorbets, and dried fruit compotes present the diner with something special that he can enjoy "without guilt."

Apple Crisp

Serves: 6 (⅔ cup = 1 serving)

4 cups sliced, peeled, and cored apples (McIntosh, Spartan, or Rome Beauty)
¼ cup fresh orange juice
1 teaspoon cinnamon
Freshly ground nutmeg
1½ cups our Basic Granola (see page 258)

1. Spray a 9-inch-square shallow baking dish with nonstick spray.
2. Arrange apple slices in baking dish. Sprinkle with orange juice, nutmeg, and cinnamon.
*3. Sprinkle granola mixture on top of apples.
4. Bake in a preheated 375° oven for 25 to 30 minutes, or until apples are tender. (May also be baked in microwave on high for 15 minutes.)

To Serve: Serve immediately in fruit dishes or compotes, and top with ½ cup whipped nonfat milk (see page 17), thoroughly chilled.

Variations: Peeled, sliced peaches or pears or blueberries may be substituted for apples. When using fresh (or frozen) peaches, sprinkle fruit with 2 teaspoons almond extract and 1 tablespoon Amaretto before adding granola.

Per serving: 145 calories; 6.4 gm protein; 1.6 gm fat; 50 gm carbohydrate; 4.2 gm fiber; 1 mg cholesterol; 2.6 mg iron; 28 mg sodium; 96 mg calcium; 178 mg phosphorus; 188 IU Vitamin A; 0.26 mg thiamine; 0.02 mg riboflavin; 3 mg Vitamin C; 376 mg potassium; 1.03 mg zinc; 1.4 mg niacin; 135 mcg Vitamin B_6; 0.13 mcg Vitamin B_{12}; 16 mcg folic acid

* May be prepared several hours ahead of time through step 3 and baked before serving.

Apple Torte

Serves: 24 (1 slice = 1 serving)

My guests always ask, "Are you *sure* there is no sugar or fat in this delicious dessert?"

5 to 6 apples, peeled, cored, chopped, and marinated in 3 ounces unsweetened frozen orange juice and 1 tablespoon dry sherry for 4 hours or overnight
1 6-ounce can frozen unsweetened apple juice concentrate
⅔ cup ripe bananas, mashed
½ cup muscat raisins, plumped 15 minutes in hot water to cover
1¼ cups whole wheat pastry flour
1¼ cups unbleached white flour
¼ cup soya flour
2 teaspoons low-sodium baking powder
2 teaspoons baking soda
2 teaspoons cinnamon
⅛ teaspoon freshly ground nutmeg
⅛ teaspoon allspice
4 egg whites, stiffly beaten
1½ teaspoons pure vanilla extract
1 cup Grape-nuts

1. Combine apples, apple juice concentrate, raisins and bananas, in a bowl.
2. Sift dry ingredients into apple mixture.
3. Stir until flour disappears and fold in stiffly beaten egg whites and vanilla.
4. Pour into a nonstick bundt pan that has been sprinkled with Grape-nuts and bake in a preheated 325° oven for 1½ hours.
5. Cool and cover with plastic wrap; let stand several hours or overnight before serving.

To Serve: Place slices of torte on individual plates and serve each with a dollop of whipped nonfat milk (page 17).

Per serving: 124 calories; 3.3 gm protein; 0.4 gm fat; 29.2 gm carbohydrate; 1.4 gm fiber; 0 mg cholesterol; 1.8 mg iron; 75 mg sodium; 47 mg calcium; 69 mg phosphorus; 382 IU Vitamin A; 0.17 mg thiamine; 0.17 mg riboflavin; 7.6 mg Vitamin C; 276 mg potassium; 0.22 mg zinc; 1.7 mg niacin; 197 mcg Vitamin B_6; 0.38 mcg Vitamin B_{12}; 29 mcg folic acid

Last-Minute Fruit Mélange

Serves: 15 (⅔ cup = 1 serving)

I find it an enormous convenience to have packages of frozen unsweetened fruit on hand in my freezer—fresh fruits can be used in this mélange when in season.

1 pint fresh strawberries, washed, then hulled
1 tablespoon frozen unsweetened apple juice concentrate
¼ cup nonfat yogurt
1 teaspoon pure vanilla extract
1 20-ounce package frozen unsweetened peach slices*
1 20-ounce package frozen unsweetened blueberries*
1 20-ounce package frozen unsweetened bing cherries*
2 bananas, peeled and sliced (optional)

Fresh mint sprigs for garnish

1. *To make strawberry-yogurt dressing:* Place strawberries, apple juice, yogurt, and vanilla in blender or food processor. Process until pureed. Place in covered container in refrigerator until serving time.

2. About 30 minutes before serving, place frozen peaches, blueberries, and cherries in an attractive glass serving bowl.

3. When ready to serve, add dressing to fruit and mix gently. Sliced bananas may be added at this time if you desire.

To Serve: Garnish with sprigs of fresh mint and serve in glass coupes or small Chinese white lotus bowls.

Per serving: 86 calories; 1.1 gm protein; 0.5 gm fat; 21.1 gm carbohydrate; 1.3 gm fiber; 0 mg cholesterol; 1 mg iron; 4 mg sodium; 20 mg calcium; 22 mg phosphorus; 672 IU Vitamin A; 0.04 mg thiamine; 0.09 mg riboflavin; 31 mg Vitamin C; 181 mg potassium; 0 mg zinc; 0.7 mg niacin; 18 mcg Vitamin B_6; 0 mcg Vitamin B_{12}; 3 mcg folic acid

* 3 cups fresh sliced peaches, 3 cups pitted fresh bing cherries, and 3 cups fresh blueberries may be substituted for the frozen fruit.

Baked Fruit Compote

Serves: 12 (⅔ cup = 1 serving)

Most times, we think of fruit served cold. However, this hot fruit compote is a welcome change, particularly in the months when many fresh fruits are not in season.

1 16-ounce can unsweetened fruit salad, drained (save juice)
1 16-ounce package mixed dried fruit, no sulphur dioxide added
1 16-ounce package pitted prunes
½ lemon
3 bananas, sliced
2 tablespoons brandy
2 tablespoons dry sherry

1. Pour drained fruit salad juice over dried fruit and prunes, adding enough water to cover fruit, and soak overnight.

2. Add juice of lemon and lemon itself and cook 30 minutes. Remove lemon.

*3. Add canned fruit salad, sliced bananas, brandy, and sherry to cooked fruit and place in a 2½-quart covered casserole.

4. Bake in a preheated 350° oven for 30 minutes.

To Serve: Serve hot in individual fruit compotes.

Per serving: 208 calories; 1.9 gm protein; 0.5 gm fat; 52.9 gm carbohydrate; 3.6 gm fiber; 0 mg cholesterol; 2.5 mg iron; 7 mg sodium; 35 mg calcium; 58 mg phosphorus; 2019 IU Vitamin A; 0.05 mg thiamine; 0.11 mg riboflavin; 9 mg Vitamin C; 573 mg potassium; 0.06 mg zinc; 1.6 mg niacin; 201 mcg Vitamin B_6; 0 mcg Vitamin B_{12}; 4 mcg folic acid

* May be prepared a day ahead through step 3.

Pantry Fruit Compote

Serves: 16 (½ cup = 1 serving)

All those canned fruits on hand in your pantry can be prepared into a pleasant last-minute dessert.

1 16-ounce can pitted red sour cherries
1 20-ounce can unsweetened pineapple chunks
1 16-ounce can sliced peaches in juice
2 tablespoons frozen unsweetened apple juice concentrate
1 16-ounce can unsweetened apple-sauce
Cinnamon
Freshly ground nutmeg

1. Drain cherries, pineapple, and peaches.
2. When well drained, place a layer of each fruit in a 1-quart casserole.
3. Add apple juice concentrate to applesauce and pour a thin layer over the top. Sprinkle with cinnamon and freshly ground nutmeg.
4. Bake in a preheated 350° oven around 20 to 30 minutes, or until hot.

To Serve: Serve in sherbet glasses while still warm.

Per serving: 55 calories; 0.7 gm protein; 0.2 gm fat; 14.1 gm carbohydrate; 0.9 gm fiber; 0 mg cholesterol; 0.5 mg iron; 2 mg sodium; 13 mg calcium; 14 mg phosphorus; 500 IU Vitamin A; 0.05 mg thiamine; 0.04 mg riboflavin; 6 mg Vitamin C; 163 mg potassium; 0.03 mg zinc; 0.4 mg niacin; 26 mcg Vitamin B_6; 0 mcg Vitamin B_{12}; 1 mcg folic acid

Festive Fruit Cake

Serves: 24 (1 slice = 1 serving)

This luscious holiday fruit cake makes an impressive presentation. For once you can have your cake and eat it.

2 cups dried fruit, coarsely chopped
¼ cup apricot brandy
1 teaspoon grated lemon zest
5 egg whites
1 cup mashed ripe banana
½ cup dry sherry
1 cup frozen unsweetened apple juice or pear and grape juice
12 ounces mixed frozen unsweetened apple juice, orange juice, and pineapple juice
1 tablespoon vanilla
1½ cups whole wheat pastry flour
1½ cups unbleached all-purpose flour
¼ cup soya flour
2 teaspoons baking soda
½ teaspoon low-sodium baking powder
1 tablespoon cinnamon
1 teaspoon mixed nutmeg, cloves, and allspice
2 cups shredded zucchini
2 cups raisins

1. Simmer the dried fruit with the apricot brandy until liquid is absorbed. Stir in lemon zest and cool. Let marinate overnight.
2. Beat egg whites until fluffy; add mashed banana, sherry, all juice concentrates, and vanilla. Beat until stiff.
3. Sift dry ingredients and stir into egg white mixture.
4. Stir in zucchini, raisins, and marinated fruit mixture until just blended.
5. Spoon into 2 nonstick 9 x 5 x 4-inch loaf pans sprayed with nonstick spray or 1 nonstick bundt pan.
6. Bake in a preheated 325° oven until a toothpick comes out clean (1 hour 10 minutes if using loaf pans, 1 hour 45 minutes if using bundt pan).
7. Cool on a rack for approximately 1 hour. Wrap in plastic wrap and then foil. Store overnight before serving. This may be stored 2 weeks in refrigerator before using or 3 months in freezer.

Variation: For an added dimension of flavor, sprinkle 2 tablespoons of apricot brandy over the cake!

Per serving: 190 calories; 3.8 gm protein; 0.5 gm fat; 43.2 gm carbohydrate; 2.7 gm fiber; 0 mg cholesterol; 1.8 mg iron; 33 mg sodium; 58 mg calcium; 78 mg phosphorus; 856 IU Vitamin A; 0.09 mg thiamine; 0.1 mg riboflavin; 8 mg Vitamin C; 402 mg potassium; 0.09 mg zinc; 1.1 mg niacin; 112 mcg Vitamin B_6; 0.01 mcg Vitamin B_{12}; 4 mcg folic acid

Heavenly Fresh Fruit Pie

Serves: 8–10 (1 slice = 1 serving)

This gorgeous dessert is so easy to prepare that you'll spend more time reassuring guests of its low calorie content than you did in its preparation.

4 extra-large egg whites (¾ cup), at room temperature
¼ teaspoon cream of tartar
1½ teaspoons pure vanilla extract
¾ cup pureed ripe banana (skin practically black—it will be easier to mash and taste sweeter)
2 pints ripe strawberries, washed, then sliced
2 tablespoons kirsch or framboise liqueur
1 cup nonfat milk, whipped (see page 17)

1. Using an electric mixer (or a whisk and copper bowl), beat the egg whites until foamy, then add cream of tartar.
2. Beat at high speed. When soft peaks form, add vanilla and pureed banana gradually. Continue beating until whites are shiny and form stiff peaks that do not slide in bowl.
3. Spray a 10-inch glass pie plate with nonstick spray. Place spoonfuls of stiffly beaten egg white mixture in pie plate and form shell with back of spoon.
4. Bake in a *very slow oven* preheated to 225° for 1½ hours. Turn off heat, leave oven door partially ajar, and let shell dry in oven several hours. (This meringue will not be as crisp as one made with sugar, so don't compare tastes or texture.)
5. *While shell is baking, make fruit filling.* Sprinkle sliced berries with liqueur of your choice and let marinate several hours to develop flavor.
6. *To assemble pie,* fill shell with fruit just before serving, and top with whipped nonfat milk.

Variation: Peaches may be substituted for strawberries, in which case, use 4 cups sliced peaches, 1 teaspoon almond extract, and 2 tablespoons apricot liqueur.

Per serving: 57 calories; 3.1 gm protein; 0.4 gm fat; 10.4 gm carbohydrate; 1.8 gm fiber; 0 mg cholesterol; 0.7 mg iron; 36 mg sodium; 45 mg calcium; 42 mg phosphorus; 68 IU Vitamin A; 0.04 mg thiamine; 0.14 mg riboflavin; 37 mg Vitamin C; 219 mg potassium; 0.13 mg zinc; 0.5 mg niacin; 130 mcg Vitamin B_6; 0.11 mcg Vitamin B_{12}; 7 mcg folic acid

Judith's Fruited Cheese Pudding—Munich Style

Serves: 6 as dessert (½ cup = 1 serving) or 3 as entrée (1 cup = 1 serving)

My friend Judith lives in Munich. She serves this easy fruited pudding either hot as a main dish for lunch or cold as a dessert.

2 tablespoons frozen unsweetened apple juice concentrate
2 apples (McIntosh, Jonathan, or Spartan), cored and sliced
8 ounces hoop cheese or skim-milk ricotta
1 egg white
1 tablespoon Wheatena cereal
1 teaspoon grated lemon zest
2 tablespoons frozen unsweetened apple juice concentrate
1 teaspoon cinnamon (optional)

1. Heat the first apple juice concentrate in a heavy skillet. When juice is hot, add apple slices and braise gently.
2. Add cheese, egg white, Wheatena, lemon zest, and the remaining apple juice concentrate to blender or food processor. Blend until mixture is a creamy consistency.
3. Spread cheese batter over braised apples in skillet. Sprinkle with cinnamon if desired. Cover with tight-fitting lid and cook 10 minutes over medium heat.
4. Turn heat down to low and continue cooking. Total cooking time after cheese mixture is added should be 20 to 25 minutes.

To Serve: Serve hot as an entrée (preceded by Split Pea Soup, page 66, with melba toast) or chill and serve in fruit dishes as a dessert. You may want to serve a pitcher of cold skim milk with it.

Variation: You may substitute 2 cups of one of the following fruits for the apples: sliced bananas, apricots, pitted bing cherries, or leftover mixed stewed fruit.

Per serving: 70 calories; 6.8 gm protein; 0.5 gm fat; 10.4 gm carbohydrate; 1.1 gm fiber; 0 mg cholesterol; 0.2 mg iron; 81 mg sodium; 11 mg calcium; 7 mg phosphorus; 18 IU Vitamin A; 0.02 mg thiamine; 0.07 mg riboflavin; 1 mg Vitamin C; 58 mg potassium; 0.01 mg zinc; 0.1 mg niacin; 1 mcg Vitamin B_6; 0.01 mcg Vitamin B_{12}; 0 mcg folic acid

Floating Islands with Strawberry or Raspberry Sauce

(That Ol' White Magic)

Serves: 8 *(1 meringue = 1 serving)*

4 cups nonfat milk
½ vanilla bean, split
3 egg whites, at room temperature
Few grains cream of tartar
1 teaspoon pure vanilla extract
1 pint fresh strawberries or raspberries,* washed, then hulled
Juice of ½ lemon, or to taste
1 tablespoon kirsch or framboise liqueur
Frozen unsweetened apple juice concentrate to taste, depending upon sweetness of fruit

Fresh mint leaves for garnish

1. In a 10-inch skillet, bring milk to a boil with split vanilla bean. Lower heat to maintain a *gentle simmer.* Remove skin from milk.
2. Combine egg whites and cream of tartar in a metal or glass bowl and beat until stiff. Add vanilla.
3. With 2 oval soup spoons, form meringues into 8 ovals. Drop one by one into simmering milk.
4. Poach meringues 4 minutes on each side. Turn once with a slotted spoon.
5. Drain on paper towel; chill, covered with plastic wrap. (Will keep in refrigerator several days.)
6. *To make strawberry or raspberry sauce:* Puree berries in blender or food processor, reserving several whole berries for garnish. (You may strain sauce if desired.) Add lemon juice and kirsch or framboise. Taste, and adjust seasonings. If necessary, add apple juice concentrate to sweeten.
7. Chill sauce in a covered container in refrigerator until time to serve. Sauce may be refrigerated up to 1 week or frozen for future use.

To Serve: Choose lovely glass dessert dishes. Place ¼ cup sauce on each plate and gently float an island of meringue on sauce. Garnish with fresh strawberries or raspberries and mint leaves. If desired, grated orange zest may be sprinkled over meringue before serving.

Helpful Hint: Leftover cooked milk may be used in baking or in preparing hot cereals.

Per serving: 70 calories; 6 gm protein; 0.3 gm fat; 10.6 gm carbohydrate; 0.8 gm fiber; 0 mg cholesterol; 0.4 mg iron; 82 mg sodium; 158 mg calcium; 126 mg phosphorus; 23 IU Vitamin A; 0.06 mg thiamine; 0.28 mg riboflavin; 25 mg Vitamin C; 261 mg potassium; 0.49 mg zinc; 0.4 mg niacin; 74 mcg Vitamin B_6; 0.5 mcg Vitamin B_{12}; 5 mcg folic acid

* You may use frozen strawberries or raspberries instead of fresh.

Funny Fudge Balls

Serves: 22–24 (1 ball = 1 serving)

⅓ cup plus 3 tablespoons boiling water
⅔ cup seeded muscat raisins
2 cups nonfat *noninstant* dry milk
4 tablespoons unsweetened carob powder
4 tablespoons frozen unsweetened apple juice concentrate
2 teaspoons pure vanilla extract or almond extract
Grape-nuts

1. Pour boiling water over raisins and let plump for 10 to 15 minutes. Drain, reserving water.
2. Place dry milk and carob powder in a mixing bowl; blend well.
3. Combine apple juice concentrate, vanilla, and water drained off raisins. Add liquid to dry ingredients and knead together until smooth. Add raisins.
4. Shape and roll into 22 to 24 1-inch balls. Dip each ball into Grape-nuts and place in a fluted paper cup.
5. Refrigerate for several hours before serving. Store excess in refrigerator up to 1 week for future use.

Variation: 1 tablespoon Grand Marnier or brandy may be added with liquid.

Per serving: 45 calories; 2.7 gm protein; 0.1 gm fat; 9.3 gm carbohydrate; 0.5 gm fiber; 1 mg cholesterol; 0.2 mg iron; 36 mg sodium; 94 mg calcium; 74 mg phosphorus; 50 IU Vitamin A; 0.04 mg thiamine; 0.14 mg riboflavin; 1 mg Vitamin C; 146 mg potassium; 0.3 mg zinc; 0.2 mg niacin; 35 mcg Vitamin B_6; 0.21 mcg Vitamin B_{12}; 0 mcg folic acid

Grapefruit Baked Alaska

Serves: 6 (½ grapefruit = 1 serving)

Beneath a snowy topping, hot from the oven, lies a grapefruit, and as a surprise in the center, a spoonful of raspberry sorbet!

3 grapefruits (preferably seedless)
4 tablespoons frozen unsweetened apple juice concentrate
3 egg whites, at room temperature
Few grains cream of tartar
¼ cup frozen unsweetened apple juice concentrate
1 teaspoon pure vanilla extract
¾ cup our Boysenberry-Yogurt Sorbet (see page 290)

1. Cut each grapefruit in half and remove core. (Cut out more than usual.)

2. Section grapefruit and sprinkle each half with 2 teaspoons apple juice concentrate; chill thoroughly.

3. Beat egg whites until frothy; add cream of tartar, beat until soft peaks form; gradually add the ¼ cup apple juice concentrate and vanilla, beating until stiff and shiny.

4. When ready to serve, put 1 heaping tablespoon sorbet in center cavity of each grapefruit half.

5. Cover grapefruit completely with meringue.

6. Place on a baking sheet and brown meringue in a preheated 550° oven. Watch closely so that meringue does not burn.

7. Serve at once.

Per serving: 100 calories; 3.3 gm protein; 0.2 gm fat; 22.3 gm carbohydrate; 0.7 gm fiber; 0 mg cholesterol; 0.7 mg iron; 36 mg sodium; 44 mg calcium; 33 mg phosphorus; 144 IU Vitamin A; 0.06 mg thiamine; 0.06 mg riboflavin; 43 mg Vitamin C; 215 mg potassium; 0.04 mg zinc; 0.5 mg niacin; 37 mcg Vitamin B_6; 0.05 mcg Vitamin B_{12}; 3 mcg folic acid

Your Perfect Pear

Serves: 4 (1 pear = 1 serving)

4 ripe Bosc or Bartlett pears
4 tablespoons fresh orange juice or apple juice
½ teaspoon cinnamon
½ teaspoon freshly ground nutmeg

1. Core each pear starting at the bottom, and leave stem intact.

2. Peel 4 ½-inch strips down the sides of each pear.

3. Place pears in a glass baking dish and sprinkle with orange juice or apple juice, cinnamon, and nutmeg.

4. Cover baking dish and bake on high in microwave oven* for 13 minutes, or until barely fork-tender. *Do not overcook.*

To Serve: Serve warm in glass fruit coupes or white lotus cups. Pour some warm juice over each pear. For a special touch, add a green camellia or lemon leaf as a garnish.

Variations: Stuff 1 teaspoon seeded muscat raisins, prunes, apricots, or dates into the space of the removed core of each pear before baking. If you choose, you may mix the dried fruit with 1 teaspoon dry sherry or muscatel before stuffing the pear.

Per serving: 70 calories; 0.8 gm protein; 0.5 gm fat; 17.3 gm carbohydrate; 2.5 gm fiber; 0 mg cholesterol; 0.4 mg iron; 2 mg sodium; 13 mg calcium; 14 mg phosphorus; 52 IU Vitamin A; 0.04 mg thiamine; 0.04 mg riboflavin; 11 mg Vitamin C; 161 mg potassium; 0.01 mg zinc; 0.2 mg niacin; 21 mcg Vitamin B_6; 0 mcg Vitamin B_{12}; 2 mcg folic acid

* You may use a standard oven, baking for 30 to 40 minutes at 350°, but the results will not be nearly as delicious!

Persimmon Pudding

Serves: 8–10 (½ cup = 1 serving)

In the fall, a good cook's thoughts always turn to using persimmons. This yummy dessert also makes a wonderful accompaniment to turkey for a holiday dinner.

¾ cup whole wheat flour
½ cup unbleached white flour
1½ teaspoons low-sodium baking powder
2 teaspoons cinnamon
1 teaspoon baking soda
1 teaspoon ginger
½ teaspoon freshly ground nutmeg
2 cups ripe persimmon pulp, pureed (excess may be frozen)
1 teaspoon vanilla
4 tablespoons frozen unsweetened apple juice concentrate
1 cup skimmed evaporated milk
4 egg whites
Few grains cream of tartar
½ cup raisins, plumped for 15 minutes in ¼ cup hot, fresh orange juice
½ cup chopped dates
1 cup nonfat milk, chilled and whipped (see page 17)

1. Sift flours, baking powder, cinnamon, baking soda, ginger, and nutmeg together.
2. In a separate bowl, stir together persimmon puree, vanilla, frozen apple juice concentrate, and milk.
3. Add sifted dry ingredients to persimmon mixture. Blend well.
4. Beat egg whites with cream of tartar until stiff. Fold into flour and persimmon mixture.
5. Gently fold in raisins with juice and dates.
6. Lightly spray a 1½-quart ovenproof casserole with nonstick spray. Add persimmon mixture to casserole and bake in a preheated 350° oven for 1 hour, or until browned.
7. This may be prepared several days ahead of time. To reheat, place in a pan of hot water, tent with foil, and steam for about 20 to 25 minutes at 350°.

To Serve: Serve in individual coupes topped with whipped nonfat milk.

Per serving: 172 calories; 5.8 gm protein; 0.6 gm fat; 38.2 gm carbohydrate; 2.3 gm fiber; 0 mg cholesterol; 1.4 mg iron; 74 mg sodium; 119 mg calcium; 150 mg phosphorus; 1346 IU Vitamin A; 0.12 mg thiamine; 0.16 mg riboflavin; 8 mg Vitamin C; 420 mg potassium; 0.44 mg zinc; 1 mg niacin; 81 mcg Vitamin B_6; 0.07 mcg Vitamin B_{12}; 9 mcg folic acid

Luscious Lemony Cheese Pie with Strawberry Sauce

Serves: 10

1 16-ounce carton Weight Watchers low-fat cottage cheese*
5 egg whites
¾ cup evaporated skim milk
1 tablespoon instant nonfat milk
⅔ cup frozen unsweetened apple juice concentrate
3 tablespoons cornstarch
¼ cup fresh lemon juice
2 teaspoons grated lemon zest
1 teaspoon pure vanilla extract
¼ teaspoon cream of tartar
1½ cups unsweetened wheat flakes with raisins
½ cup sliced almonds
1 cup Strawberry Sauce (see page 272)

1. Process cheese, 2 of the egg whites, and ¼ cup of the skim milk in food processor or blender until creamy and smooth.
2. Add remaining milk, instant milk, and apple juice concentrate and blend thoroughly.
3. Add cornstarch, lemon juice, zest, and vanilla extract and blend.
4. Beat remaining 3 egg whites with cream of tartar until *stiff,* not *dry* (do not slide around bowl).
5. Pour cheese mixture over stiffly beaten egg whites and fold carefully.
6. Spray an 8-inch pie plate or spring-form pan with nonstick spray and sprinkle wheat flakes and raisins over bottom of pan.
7. Pour cheese mixture into pan and top with almonds.
8. Place in a preheated 325° oven and bake 50 to 60 minutes, until firm and lightly browned.
9. Turn off oven and let pie sit in oven 30 minutes.
10. Finish cooling on a rack at room temperature. Chill before serving.

To Serve: Cut pie in 10 wedges and serve with 1½ tablespoons strawberry sauce over each serving.

Variation: Almonds may be omitted from recipe and pie may be served topped with 1 cup sliced fresh strawberries and 1 cup strawberry sauce.

Per serving: 96 calories; 8.5 gm protein; 0.6 gm fat; 14 gm carbohydrate; 0 gm fiber; 3 mg cholesterol; 0.3 mg iron; 150 mg sodium; 89 mg calcium; 105 mg phosphorus; 93 IU Vitamin A; 0.02 mg thiamine; 0.18 mg riboflavin; 4 mg Vitamin C; 216 mg potassium; 0.37 mg zinc; 0.1 mg niacin; 66 mcg Vitamin B_6; 0.34 mcg Vitamin B_{12}; 10 mcg folic acid

* If you substitute 16 ounces partially skim-milk ricotta cheese for 16 ounces of the low-fat cottage cheese, you will raise each serving 30 calories.

Sweet Potato Mélange

Serves: 12–14 (3/4 cup = 1 serving)

This wonderfully tasty recipe makes a beautiful company presentation and satisfies your sweet tooth as a dessert as well. For a special treat, serve it as a deluxe accompaniment for chicken or turkey for a holiday dinner.

4 pounds Mackintosh apples, cored, peeled, and sliced 1/4-inch thick
1/2 can frozen unsweetened pineapple juice concentrate
3 1/2 pounds sweet potatoes, scrubbed and cooked in skins until tender
1 *very ripe* banana
1 16-ounce can unsweetened crushed pineapple, drained, juice reserved for glaze
Zest of 2 oranges and 1 lemon
1 teaspoon cinnamon
1 teaspoon freshly ground nutmeg
3 bananas, sliced
2 pears, peeled and cut in large dice
1 bunch grapes, in season
1/4 cup sherry
2 tablespoons frozen unsweetened orange juice concentrate

1. Layer apples in rows in a 3-quart rectangular casserole sprayed with nonstick spray.
2. Brush with frozen pineapple juice and bake in a preheated 350° oven for 30 minutes (or in microwave oven on high for 5 minutes).
3. Puree cooked, peeled sweet potatoes in blender or food processor; when pureed, add the very ripe banana, crushed pineapple, orange and lemon zest, cinnamon, and nutmeg. Blend well.
4. Place half of the sweet potato mixture over cooked apples and smooth.
5. Arrange half the sliced bananas, diced pears, and grapes in rows over the sweet potato mixture.
*6. Cover with remaining half of sweet potato mixture and arrange remaining fruit in rows on top.
7. Boil drained canned pineapple juice, sherry, and orange juice concentrate for 5 minutes.
8. Glaze the fruit mixture, using all of the glaze.
9. Bake in a preheated 375° oven for 30 minutes.

Per serving: 279 calories; 3 gm protein; 1.1 gm fat; 67.3 gm carbohydrate; 7.8 gm fiber; 0 mg cholesterol; 1.7 mg iron; 14 mg sodium; 60 mg calcium; 83 mg phosphorus; 9133 IU Vitamin A; 0.21 mg thiamine; 0.14 mg riboflavin; 36 mg Vitamin C; 659 mg potassium; 0.07 mg zinc; 1.3 mg niacin; 200 mcg Vitamin B_6; 0 mcg Vitamin B_{12}; 4 mcg folic acid

* This may be prepared the day before through step 6; cover with plastic and refrigerate until glazed and baked the next day. Bake for 45 minutes.

Sweet Potato Meringues

Serves: 8 (1 potato mound = 1 serving)

Satisfying enough to be a dessert, this may also be served as an accompaniment to chicken.

½ cup seeded muscat raisins
½ cup fresh orange juice
1 tablespoon dry sherry
6 medium sweet potatoes or yams, scrubbed and cooked in skin until tender
Grated zest of 1 orange and 1 lemon
¼ teaspoon allspice
¼ teaspoon freshly grated nutmeg
3 egg whites, at room temperature
Few grains cream of tartar
¼ cup *very ripe* banana, mashed until syrupy

1. Plump raisins in orange juice and sherry for 10 to 15 minutes. Reserve liquid.
2. Peel cooked sweet potatoes, cut each potato into 6 pieces, and puree in blender or food processor.
3. Add orange juice and sherry from plumped raisins to potato mixture and blend until smooth.
4. Add grated orange and lemon zest, allspice, and nutmeg, and blend.
5. Mix in plumped raisins.

*6. Shape seasoned sweet potato mixture into 8 mounds on a baking sheet. (I like to use an ice cream scoop; however, a ⅓-cup measure may also be used.)

7. Place egg whites in a metal or glass bowl. Add cream of tartar and beat until soft peaks form. Add mashed banana and continue beating until stiff. (Test to see if whites slide around bowl; if you want to be brave, turn bowl upside down—they'll stay in the bowl.)
8. Cover each potato mound with beaten egg whites, sealing potato to pan.
9. Bake at 450° in upper portion of oven until lightly browned, about 5 minutes. Remember to watch carefully—they burn quickly.

To Serve: Serve hot.

Per serving: 162 calories; 3.5 gm protein; 0.5 gm fat; 36.5 gm carbohydrate; 3.3 gm fiber; 0 mg cholesterol; 1.1 mg iron; 31 mg sodium; 44 mg calcium; 62 mg phosphorus; 8609 IU Vitamin A; 0.13 mg thiamine; 0.11 mg riboflavin; 31 mg Vitamin C; 385 mg potassium; 0.02 mg zinc; 0.8 mg niacin; 64 mcg Vitamin B_6; 0.01 mcg Vitamin B_{12}; 2 mcg folic acid

* May be prepared through step 6 several hours in advance and refrigerated. Remove from refrigerator 1 hour before adding meringue.

Yogurt-Pumpkin Pie

Serves: 8 (1 slice = 1 serving)

½ loaf raisin Essene bread*
(available in frozen food section of most health food stores)
1 cup canned pumpkin
⅓ cup frozen unsweetened apple juice concentrate
1 teaspoon cinnamon
¼ teaspoon ginger
½ teaspoon freshly ground nutmeg
1 4-ounce can nonfat evaporated milk, well chilled
8 ounces nonfat yogurt
1 teaspoon pure vanilla extract

1. Crumble raisin bread in blender or food processor (using steel knife).
2. Lightly spray a 9-inch glass pie plate with nonstick spray. Spread crumbs evenly over surface; press lightly with hand.
3. Bake in a preheated 375° oven for 8 minutes.
4. Blend pumpkin with apple juice concentrate, cinnamon, ginger, and nutmeg in a saucepan.
5. Cook for 6 minutes on medium heat. Cool.
6. Beat evaporated milk on high until stiff (see page 17).
7. Add stiffly beaten milk, yogurt, and vanilla to *cooled* pumpkin mixture and blend well.
8. Spoon into baked crust and chill 4 hours or overnight. Can be frozen for future use. If frozen, remove from freezer 30 minutes before serving.

Per serving: 148 calories; 5.1 gm protein; 1.2 gm fat; 30.7 gm carbohydrate; 1.6 gm fiber; 1 mg cholesterol; 0.9 mg iron; 51 mg sodium; 129 mg calcium; 81 mg phosphorus; 6482 IU Vitamin A; 0.06 mg thiamine; 0.18 mg riboflavin; 5 mg Vitamin C; 363 mg potassium; 0.12 mg zinc; 1.1 mg niacin; 65 mcg Vitamin B_6; 0.03 mcg Vitamin B_{12}; 9 mcg folic acid

* If unavailable, use 1½ cups unsweetened wheat flakes with raisins and make crust as described on page 276, Luscious Lemony Cheese Pie.

Rosy Rhubarb Sauce

Serves: 8 (½ cup = 1 serving)

Rhubarb is tart, but here we have managed to overcome this tart flavor *without added sugar.*

1 20-ounce package frozen unsweetened cut rhubarb
⅓ cup fresh orange juice
⅓ cup unsweetened cranberry and grape juice nectar
3 tablespoons frozen unsweetened apple juice concentrate*
1 cup fresh strawberries, washed, then hulled, sliced, and marinated in 1 tablespoon kirsch (optional)

1. Place frozen rhubarb in a saucepan.
2. Add orange juice and cranberry and grape nectar to rhubarb, cover, and simmer 30 minutes or until cooked, stirring occasionally.**
3. Add apple juice concentrate, stir, and add sliced strawberries if desired.
4. Chill several hours or overnight before serving.

To Serve: Serve as an accompaniment to poultry or Potato Kugelettes (page 221), or as a simple dessert.

Per serving: 31 calories; 0.6 gm protein; 0.1 gm fat; 7.4 gm carbohydrate; 1.9 gm fiber; 0 mg cholesterol; 0.6 mg iron; 2 mg sodium; 70 mg calcium; 15 mg phosphorus; 92 IU Vitamin A; 0.03 mg thiamine; 0.05 mg riboflavin; 12 mg Vitamin C; 200 mg potassium; 0 mg zinc; 0.3 mg niacin; 4 mcg Vitamin B_6; 0 mcg Vitamin B_{12}; 0 mcg folic acid

* 3 tablespoons unsweetened frozen pear and grape juice concentrate may be substituted for the apple juice concentrate.
** May also be cooked on high in a microwave oven for 15 minutes or until cooked.

Mrs. Latterman's Strawberry Chiffon Pie

Serves: 10–12 (1 slice = 1 serving)

As a young girl, I would go to a friend's summer cottage in Conneaut Lake, Pennsylvania. The recollection of those days at the lake and the tempting aromas wafting from Mrs. Latterman's kitchen still brings me a warm feeling.

½ loaf Essene raisin bread* (available in frozen food section of most health food stores)
1 envelope plain, unflavored gelatin
¼ cup cold fresh orange juice
Juice of 2 lemons, plus water to equal 1 cup
3 tablespoons unsweetened strawberry concentrate (available in most health food stores)
2 pints fresh strawberries, washed, then hulled and sliced
1 teaspoon grated lemon zest
1 tablespoon unsweetened strawberry concentrate
1 tablespoon framboise liqueur
1 13-ounce can nonfat evaporated milk, chilled overnight or in freezer several hours

Long-stemmed strawberries for garnish

1. Crumble raisin bread in food processor, using steel knife.
2. Lightly spray a 10-inch glass pie plate with nonstick spray. Spread crumbs evenly over surface and press lightly with hand.
3. Bake in a preheated 375° oven for 8 minutes.
4. Dissolve gelatin in cold orange juice.
5. Bring lemon juice, water, and the 3 tablespoons fruit concentrate to a boil. Add boiling liquid to dissolved gelatin and stir until liquefied. Chill in refrigerator until the consistency of unbeaten egg whites.
6. Chill mixer bowl and beaters in freezer.
7. Marinate sliced strawberries with grated lemon zest, the 1 tablespoon fruit concentrate, and the framboise while gelatin is thickening in refrigerator.
8. Beat chilled evaporated milk in *chilled* bowl until tripled in volume and stiff (see page 17).
9. Fold sliced strawberries into gelatin mixture, then fold fruited gelatin mixture into stiffly beaten evaporated milk.

* If unavailable, use 1½ cups unsweetened wheat flakes with raisins and make crust as described on page 276, Luscious Lemony Cheese Pie.

10. Spoon fruited milk mixture gently into baked pie shell. Chill 4 to 6 hours or overnight before serving.

To Serve: Garnish with long-stemmed strawberries, or if not available, with washed, unstemmed, whole berries.

Per serving: 99 calories; 4.3 gm protein; 0.8 gm fat; 18.8 gm carbohydrate; 1 gm fiber; 1 mg cholesterol; 0.7 mg iron; 46 mg sodium; 111 mg calcium; 86 mg phosphorus; 154 IU Vitamin A; 0.04 mg thiamine; 0.14 mg riboflavin; 28 mg Vitamin C; 235 mg potassium; 0.24 mg zinc; 0.5 mg niacin; 44 mcg Vitamin B_6; 0.07 mcg Vitamin B_{12}; 6 mcg folic acid

Strawberries with Strawberry Sauce

Serves: 6 (¾ cup = 1 serving)

An easy dessert that tastes wonderful and looks lovely.

3 pints strawberries, washed, then hulled
Strawberry Sauce (see page 272)
Fresh mint sprigs or stemmed strawberries for garnish

Place whole berries in a glass serving bowl, pour strawberry sauce over berries, and refrigerate several hours to develop flavor.

To Serve: Serve in glass brandy snifters or champagne glasses garnished with sprigs of fresh mint or stemmed strawberries.

Variation: Instead of strawberries as the basic fruit, use cubed cantaloupe, casaba melon, or pineapple and prepare in the same manner.

Per serving: 71 calories; 1.1 gm protein; 0.7 gm fat; 16.6 gm carbohydrate; 3.3 gm fiber; 0 mg cholesterol; 1.5 mg iron; 3 mg sodium; 31 mg calcium; 31 mg phosphorus; 89 IU Vitamin A; 0.04 mg thiamine; 0.1 mg riboflavin; 88 mg Vitamin C; 246 mg potassium; 0 mg zinc; 0.9 mg niacin; 82 mcg Vitamin B_6; 0 mcg Vitamin B_{12}; 13 mcg folic acid

Yogurt Dessert Mold

Serves: 6 (1 slice = 1 serving)

1 package plain, unflavored gelatin
1 cup fresh grapefruit juice, heated to boiling
1 cup nonfat yogurt
3 cups grapefruit segments, cut in 1-inch pieces (about 3 whole grapefruit, peeled and sectioned)
1 cup orange segments (about 2 navel oranges), cut in 1-inch pieces
¾ cup seeded red grapes, halved

Curly endive or red or green leaf lettuce for serving
2 kiwi fruit, peeled and sliced, for garnish
4 small sprays whole red grapes, for garnish

1. Dissolve gelatin in heated grapefruit juice.
2. Add yogurt to gelatin mixture. Stir with a whisk until smooth.
3. Chill until thick as unbeaten egg whites.
4. Reserve 6 grapefruit segments and 4 orange segments for garnish. Fold drained, cut grapefruit, orange, and grapes into chilled yogurt mixture.
5. Rinse a 1-quart mold with cold water and add fruit gelatin mixture.
6. Cover with plastic wrap and chill until firm or overnight.

To Unmold and Serve: Unmold onto a platter lined with one of the suggested greens. Run a metal spatula around the edge of the mold to loosen, then invert mold over platter and shake gently. Garnish with orange and grapefruit segments, sliced kiwi, and grape sprays. This would also be delicious served as a fruit salad.

Per serving: 114 calories; 6.7 gm protein; 0.3 gm fat; 23.3 carbohydrate; 0.8 gm fiber; 0 mg cholesterol; 0.7 mg iron; 27 mg sodium; 87 mg calcium; 31 mg phosphorus; 274 IU Vitamin A; 0.11 mg thiamine; 0.13 mg riboflavin; 68 mg Vitamin C; 387 mg potassium; 0.05 mg zinc; 0.8 mg niacin; 51 mcg Vitamin B_6; 0 mcg Vitamin B_{12}; 4 mcg folic acid

Molded Apricot Mousse

Serves: 24 (½ cup = 1 serving)

2 envelopes plain, unflavored gelatin
½ cup fresh orange juice, cold
½ cup fresh lemon juice, cold
6 ounces frozen unsweetened apple juice concentrate
6 ounces frozen unsweetened orange-pineapple juice concentrate
1 20-ounce can unsweetened crushed pineapple, drained, juice reserved
Grated zest of 2 lemons
1 egg white, unbeaten
3 tablespoons apricot brandy, Triple Sec, or Grand Marnier
1 20-ounce can whole unsweetened apricots, drained
1 cup nonfat evaporated milk, well chilled
1 20-ounce can unsweetened apricot halves, drained

Green or red leaf lettuce for serving
Fresh strawberries and pineapple wedges for garnish

1. Dissolve gelatin in cold orange juice and lemon juice. Liquefy over heat or hot water.
2. Add apple juice concentrate, frozen orange-pineapple juice concentrate, drained canned pineapple juice, grated lemon zest, egg white, and brandy to liquefied gelatin. Mix well.
3. Place in refrigerator and chill until thickened.
4. Whip thickened, chilled mixture until doubled in bulk.
5. Puree drained, whole apricots in blender or food processor.
6. Add pureed apricots and drained, crushed pineapple to beaten mixture.
7. Beat chilled nonfat milk until stiff (see page 17). Fold into fruit mixture.
8. Rinse a 3-quart mold with cold water or spray *lightly* with nonstick spray. Line bottom of mold with apricot halves.
9. Carefully spoon mousse mixture into mold. Cover with plastic wrap and chill overnight or freeze for future use.

To Unmold and Serve: Unmold onto a large platter lined with green or red leaf lettuce. Run a metal spatula around the edge of the mold to loosen, then invert mold over platter and shake gently. Fill center of mousse with fresh strawberries and surround with pineapple wedges for a spectacular presentation. This can also be served as a fruit salad.

Per serving: 68 calories; 2 gm protein; 0.1 gm fat; 15.1 gm carbohydrate; 0.9 gm fiber; 0 mg cholesterol; 0.3 mg iron; 16 mg sodium; 42 mg calcium; 33 mg phosphorus; 957 IU Vitamin A; 0.06 mg thiamine; 0.05 mg riboflavin; 16 mg Vitamin C; 238 mg potassium; 0.08 mg zinc; 0.4 mg niacin; 54 mcg Vitamin B_6; 0.03 mcg Vitamin B_{12}; 2 mcg folic acid

Poached Peaches Supreme

Serves: 8 (½ large peach, 1 tablespoon yogurt sauce, 2 tablespoons strawberry sauce = 1 serving)

2 cups water
1 cup chablis
1 6-ounce can frozen unsweetened apple juice concentrate
Zest of 2 lemons
1 vanilla bean, split lengthwise
4 ripe but firm large peaches or nectarines
1 cup nonfat yogurt (optional)
Strawberry Sauce (see page 272)

1. In a saucepan, combine water, wine, apple juice concentrate, lemon zest, and vanilla bean. Bring to a boil and simmer 20 minutes.
2. Drop peaches into simmering liquid and poach gently about 10 minutes, or until barely tender.
3. Let peaches cool in poaching liquid.
4. When cool, remove peaches and slip off skins. Halve peaches, remove pit, and slice.
5. At serving time, blend 1 cup yogurt with ½ cup of the strawberry sauce if desired.

To Serve: Divide sliced peaches into chilled coupes, brandy snifters, or large wine glasses. Place 1 tablespoon yogurt mixture over peaches and top with 1 tablespoon strawberry sauce. If you like, a stemmed strawberry or mint leaves may be used as a garnish.

Variation: *To make poached pears,* use the same poaching liquid and add 4 ripe pears, peeled, halved, and cored. Poach 7 to 8 minutes and cool in liquid. Serve pears from a large glass bowl in cooled poaching liquid. A sauce is not necessary.

Helpful Hint: Poaching liquid may be placed in an airtight container and refrigerated for several weeks for future use.

Per serving: 112 calories; 1.9 gm protein; 0.2 gm fat; 20.8 gm carbohydrate; 2 gm fiber; 0 mg cholesterol; 0.8 mg iron; 21 mg sodium; 58 mg calcium; 21 mg phosphorus; 756 IU Vitamin A; 0.04 mg thiamine; 0.12 mg riboflavin; 29 mg Vitamin C; 198 mg potassium; 0.1 mg zinc; 1 mg niacin; 46 mcg Vitamin B_6; 0 mcg Vitamin B_{12}; 5 mcg folic acid

Helen's San Francisco Peach Surprises

Serves: 6 (½ peach = 1 serving)

1 16-ounce can peach halves in fruit juice or water
2 tablespoons frozen unsweetened orange juice concentrate
½ teaspoon almond extract
½ teaspoon grated lemon zest
Freshly ground nutmeg
2 egg whites, at room temperature
Few grains cream of tartar
2 tablespoons frozen unsweetened apple juice concentrate
1 teaspoon pure vanilla extract
1 pint raspberries or strawberries, washed, then hulled
1 tablespoon frozen unsweetened apple juice concentrate
¼ cup nonfat yogurt
1 teaspoon pure vanilla extract

1. Drain peaches and place cup-side-up in a shallow glass or enamel baking pan.
2. Stir together orange juice concentrate, almond extract, and grated lemon zest. Spoon into peach halves and top with freshly ground nutmeg.
3. Add cream of tartar to egg whites. Beat until soft peaks form. Add the 2 tablespoons apple juice concentrate while continually beating until stiff peaks form and egg whites are stiff but not dry. Add the first teaspoon vanilla and mix.
4. Swirl meringues over each peach half and bake in a preheated 400° oven for 8 to 10 minutes, or until meringues are lightly browned.
5. Prepare fruit sauce while peaches are baking. Place raspberries, the 1 tablespoon apple juice concentrate, the yogurt, and the second teaspoon vanilla in blender or food processor and puree.

To Serve: Serve peaches immediately in individual dessert dishes, passing fruit sauce in a separate bowl so that guests can serve themselves.

Per serving: 72 calories; 2.4 gm protein; 0.4 gm fat; 16 gm carbohydrate; 1.4 gm fiber; 0 mg cholesterol; 0.8 mg iron; 24 mg sodium; 30 mg calcium; 25 mg phosphorus; 428 IU Vitamin A; 0.04 mg thiamine; 0.11 mg riboflavin; 40 mg Vitamin C; 234 mg potassium; 0.08 mg zinc; 0.9 mg niacin; 42 mcg Vitamin B_6; 0.01 mcg Vitamin B_{12}; 6 mcg folic acid

Harold's Old-Fashioned Rice Pudding

Serves: 8 (⅔ cup = 1 serving)

⅓ cup raw short-grain brown rice, cooked 25 minutes in 1 cup boiling water
3¼ cups nonfat milk
¼ cup dry skim milk
½ cup frozen unsweetened apple juice concentrate
2 teaspoons pure vanilla extract
4 egg whites, beaten just until foamy
1 ripe banana, pureed
⅔ cup muscat raisins, plumped 15 minutes in hot water to cover
1 teaspoon cinnamon
Freshly ground nutmeg
1 cup Grape-nuts

1. Scald nonfat milk and dry skim milk. Add apple juice concentrate, vanilla, egg whites, and pureed banana. Blend well.

2. Place rice in a 1-quart ovenproof casserole or individual ramekins. Add raisins and cover with milk mixture. Sprinkle with Grape-nuts, cinnamon, and freshly ground nutmeg.

3. Place casserole or ramekins in a baking dish with 1 inch of hot water and bake in a preheated 350° oven for 45 to 50 minutes. (When a sharp knife is inserted into custard, it should come out clean when pudding is done.)

Per serving: 174 calories; 6.3 gm protein; 0.3 gm fat; 37.3 gm carbohydrate; 3.7 gm fiber; 1 mg cholesterol; 1.2 mg iron; 56 mg sodium; 80 mg calcium; 115 mg phosphorus; 701 IU Vitamin A; 0.23 mg thiamine; 0.36 mg riboflavin; 7 mg Vitamin C; 267 mg potassium; 0.24 mg zinc; 2.2 mg niacin; 125 mcg Vitamin B_6; 0.19 mcg Vitamin B_{12}; 3 mcg folic acid

Raspberry Mousse

Serves: 8 (1 cup = 1 serving)

For extraordinary eye appeal, as well as delectable taste, try this raspberry mousse.

1 4-ounce can chilled nonfat evaporated milk, or 1½ cups nonfat yogurt
6 egg whites, at room temperature
1 tablespoon lemon juice
Few grains cream of tartar
2 envelopes plain, unflavored gelatin
½ cup fresh orange juice
1 teaspoon raspberry or pure vanilla extract
1 tablespoon kirsch
16 ounces freeze-dried unsweetened raspberries, thawed and pureed with 3 strips orange zest
1 cup sugar-free raspberry preserves* or pureed ripe banana

1. Whip chilled evaporated milk or stir yogurt in a chilled bowl (see page 17) and refrigerate.
2. Whip egg whites until soft peaks form. Add lemon juice and cream of tartar; whip until stiff.**
3. Dissolve gelatin in orange juice and liquefy over heat. Add to beaten egg whites.
4. Fold in extract and kirsch. Blend well. Gently stir in berries and preserves.
5. Add whipped milk or stirred yogurt. Blend gently.
6. Pour mousse into a 1-quart soufflé dish and chill thoroughly for 4 hours in refrigerator. Serve the day it is prepared for best flavor.

To Serve: Serve directly from soufflé dish. You may top with fresh fruit or a fresh fruit sauce (made by pureeing fruit in blender or food processor with lemon zest and apple juice concentrate if necessary). Budget allowing, long-stemmed strawberries add a special touch.

Per serving: 104 calories; 7.2 gm protein; 0.4 gm fat; 19 gm carbohydrate; 5 gm fiber; 0 mg cholesterol; 0.8 mg iron; 63 mg sodium; 80 mg calcium; 27 mg phosphorus; 260 IU Vitamin A; 0.07 mg thiamine; 0.24 mg riboflavin; 26 mg Vitamin C; 268 mg potassium; 0.06 mg zinc; 1.2 mg niacin; 185 mcg Vitamin B_6; 0.02 mcg Vitamin B_{12}; 6 mcg folic acid

* Fruit Preserves à la Suisse (page 303) may be used.
** If using pureed banana instead of raspberry preserves, beat into egg whites at this point.

Banana and Pineapple Sorbet

Serves: 16 (⅓ cup = 1 serving)

Sorbet is the French word for sherbet. It takes time as well as special equipment to prepare sorbet in the traditional manner. This fast recipe allows for either last-minute or do-ahead preparation with readily available ingredients.

3 cups ripe pineapple (1 ripe pineapple), cut into 1-inch chunks
2 ripe bananas, cut into 1-inch chunks
Juice of ½ lemon
1 cup nonfat evaporated milk, chilled in freezer
1–2 teaspoons pure vanilla extract

1. Flash-freeze pineapple and banana chunks on a baking sheet. When frozen solid, place fruit in separate bags. Store in freezer until ready to use.
2. Place half of the frozen banana and pineapple in chilled food processor or blender container. Add lemon juice. Process until mixture is pureed.
3. Add remaining fruit and puree.
4. Add half of milk, process until crème is formed, continue adding milk and vanilla.
5. Freeze in freezer container, or parfait glasses (or in lemons and oranges that have been hollowed out) for at least an hour. If you like, garnish with a lemon or camellia leaf before freezing, or with mint leaves at time of service. May be kept in the freezer for a month.

To Serve: Take from freezer 15 minutes before serving. (Or, if you forget, as I so frequently do, defrost in microwave oven on low for 10 seconds.)

Variations: Combined with your two ripe bananas, you may use 3 cups frozen ripe apricots, peaches, mangoes, strawberries, raspberries, boysenberries, or kiwi instead of the 3 cups of ripe pineapple.

You may also serve the sorbet with a *raspberry sauce* made by pureeing 1 pint fresh raspberries, straining, and adding 1 tablespoon kirsch. The sauce may be prepared ahead of time, stored in an airtight container, and refrigerated until used. This sauce also freezes well.

Per serving: 40 calories; 1.4 gm protein; 0.1 gm fat; 9.1 gm carbohydrate; 0.7 gm fiber; 0 mg cholesterol; 0.3 mg iron; 17 mg sodium; 50 mg calcium; 36 mg phosphorus; 109 IU Vitamin A; 0.04 mg thiamine; 0.06 mg riboflavin; 7 mg Vitamin C; 155 mg potassium; 0.15 mg zinc; 0.2 mg niacin; 111 mcg Vitamin B_6; 0.04 mcg Vitamin B_{12}; 5 mcg folic acid

Boysenberry-Yogurt Sorbet

Serves: 8 (1/4 cup = 1 serving)

Serve this to cleanse your palate between courses, or as a refreshing dessert.

1 16-ounce package frozen unsweetened boysenberries or strawberries

3 tablespoons frozen unsweetened apple juice concentrate

2/3 cup nonfat yogurt

1/4 cup instant nonfat dry milk

1. Place half the frozen berries in blender or food processor and puree.
2. Add remaining fruit and frozen apple juice concentrate. Puree.
3. Add yogurt and dry milk. Process until sorbet is formed.
4. Pour into an 11 x 7-inch metal or glass baking pan. Freeze until nearly frozen solid.
5. Return mixture to blender or food processor. Process until broken into small pieces; then process until creamy.
6. Place mixture into individual pot au crème dishes or hollowed lemon or orange shells, or in one large container, cover with plastic wrap, and return to freezer.

To Serve: Remove from freezer about 15 minutes before serving.

Variation: This sorbet works well in Grapefruit Baked Alaska (page 273).

Per serving: 53 calories; 2.5 gm protein; 0.2 gm fat; 11.2 gm carbohydrate; 1.5 gm fiber; 1 mg cholesterol; 0.9 mg iron; 24 mg sodium; 75 mg calcium; 42 mg phosphorus; 182 IU Vitamin A; 0.05 mg thiamine; 0.17 mg riboflavin; 17 mg Vitamin C; 167 mg potassium; 0.11 mg zinc; 0.8 mg niacin; 9 mcg Vitamin B_6; 0.08 mcg Vitamin B_{12}; 0 mcg folic acid

Cranberry, Pineapple, and Yogurt Freeze

Serves: 12 (½ cup = 1 serving)

2 cups raw cranberries
¼ cup unsweetened cherry fruit juice concentrate
1 20-ounce can crushed, unsweetened pineapple, drained
1 pint nonfat yogurt
½ 6-ounce can frozen unsweetened orange juice concentrate
½ cup Grape-nuts

1. Chop cranberries in blender or food processor with steel knife.
2. Add cherry concentrate and marinate 30 minutes.
3. Blend crushed pineapple, yogurt, orange juice concentrate, and marinated cranberries.
4. Line muffin tins with foil cupcake liners (or use hollowed lemon or orange cups) and fill with yogurt mixture. Sprinkle tops with Grape-nuts.
5. Freeze several hours, until firm. When firmly frozen, remove cups from muffin pan and store in freezer in airtight container for future use.

To Serve: Remove from freezer 15 minutes before serving. Freezes are delicious served either as an accompaniment to roast turkey or as a dessert.

Per serving: 86 calories; 2.7 gm protein; 0.2 gm fat; 19.3 gm carbohydrate; 1.5 gm fiber; 0 mg cholesterol; 0.5 mg iron; 32 mg sodium; 69 mg calcium; 22 mg phosphorus; 475 IU Vitamin A; 0.16 mg thiamine; 0.18 mg riboflavin; 30 mg Vitamin C; 160 mg potassium; 0 mg zinc; 1.2 mg niacin; 37 mcg Vitamin B_6; 0 mcg Vitamin B_{12}; 1 mcg folic acid

Lila's Frozen Dessert

Serves: 8 (⅔ cup = 1 serving)

2 6-ounce cans frozen unsweetened orange-pineapple juice concentrate
1 3½-ounce package nonfat dry milk
3½ cups cold water
1 tablespoon pure vanilla extract
Orange slices or pineapple wedges for garnish

1. Place all ingredients (except garnish) in blender, food processor, or mixer bowl. Blend well.
2. Pour mixture into a flat plastic freezer container and freeze until *nearly* frozen solid.
3. Put mixture back in blender, food processor, or mixer and process or beat until broken in small pieces, then increase speed and beat until creamy. (It takes about 3 to 5 minutes.)

4. Put mixture in pot au crème dishes or sherbet dishes—or in one large container—and refreeze for future use.

To Serve: Remove from freezer about 5 to 10 minutes before serving and garnish with orange slices or pineapple wedges.

Per serving: 85 calories; 1.9 gm protein; 0.1 gm fat; 19.6 gm carbohydrate; 0.1 gm fiber; 1 mg cholesterol; 0.3 mg iron; 18 mg sodium; 56 mg calcium; 49 mg phosphorus; 166 IU Vitamin A; 0.13 mg thiamine; 0.06 mg riboflavin; 44 mg Vitamin C; 300 mg potassium; 0.14 mg zinc; 0.5 mg niacin; 12 mcg Vitamin B_6; 0.1 mcg Vitamin B_{12}; 1 mcg folic acid

Citron Soufflé

Serves: 8–10 (1 cup = 1 serving)

1 envelope plus 1 teaspoon plain, unflavored gelatin
2 tablespoons cold fresh orange juice
Grated zest of 4 lemons
½ cup lemon juice
6 ounces frozen unsweetened apple juice concentrate
8 egg whites, at room temperature
⅛ teaspoon cream of tartar
1 cup nonfat evaporated milk, chilled several hours in freezer

1. Dissolve gelatin in cold orange juice. Liquefy gelatin over heat; transfer to a mixing bowl.

2. Add lemon zest, lemon juice, and apple juice concentrate to the liquefied gelatin. Place bowl with gelatin mixture in refrigerator until mixture thickens.

3. Beat egg whites until foamy, add cream of tartar, and beat until stiff.

4. Whip chilled nonfat evaporated milk in a *chilled* bowl until peaks form (see page 17).

5. Add thickened gelatin mixture to whipped milk.

6. *Fold* stiffly beaten egg whites into milk and gelatin mixture and place in a 2-quart soufflé dish.

7. Chill 3 to 4 hours or overnight before serving, or freeze for future use.

To Serve: Garnish with thin lemon slices and fresh mint leaves.

Variations: *Make a lemon chiffon pie* by adding mixture to a baked 10-inch pie shell (see page 276) and topping with sprinkled Grape-nuts.

To make an orange soufflé, substitute grated zest of 4 oranges and ½ cup frozen unsweetened orange juice concentrate for the lemon zest and ½ cup lemon juice.

Soufflé may also be divided into lemon or orange shells and frozen for future use.

Per serving: 69 calories; 5.7 gm protein; 0.1 gm fat; 11.2 gm carbohydrate; 0 gm fiber; 0 mg cholesterol; 0.1 mg iron; 69 mg sodium; 77 mg calcium; 54 mg phosphorus; 106 IU Vitamin A; 0.02 mg thiamine; 0.15 mg riboflavin; 10 mg Vitamin C; 153 mg potassium; 0.2 mg zinc; 0.1 mg niacin; 22 mcg Vitamin B_6; 0.09 mcg Vitamin B_{12}; 3 mcg folic acid

Quick Breads

Why pay more money for using a prepared mix with less nutritious food value, when you can easily prepare your own quick bread that is neither complicated nor time-consuming? Quick breads use a quick-acting leavening—baking powder, or baking soda and sour milk—instead of slow-acting yeast. The nutritious approach to preparing quick breads is to minimize their fat, sugar, and sodium content, and still make them delicious. We have done this by eliminating added fat or oil; substituting fresh or dried fruits and unsweetened fruit juice concentrates for sugar; eliminating salt; substituting low-sodium baking powder for regular baking powder; and, of course, using no preservatives such as BHA or BHT. Whenever possible, we have also used whole wheat flour instead of white flour.

Quick breads are easy to prepare and freeze well. Here are a few helpful hints that will make expert bakers out of beginners:

1. Always preheat your oven 25° higher than the recipe calls for—then lower it to the suggested temperature when baked goods are placed in the oven. (For example, if the recipe calls for 350°, preheat oven to 375°, and lower to 350° when you put the pan in the oven.)
2. Read recipe thoroughly, assemble ingredients, and have pan ready before you begin preparation.
3. Measure dry ingredients into a bowl first; then measure liquid ingredients into a separate bowl.
4. Add dry ingredients to wet. Stir only until flour disappears—overmixing results in batter not rising as much as it should and tunnels in bread.
5. Put in preheated oven *as soon as batter is placed in pan.*

If you follow these suggestions, you will be delighted with your results!

Banana Bread

Yield: 22 slices (1 slice = 1 serving)

2¼ cups whole wheat pastry flour
¼ cup soya flour
1 tablespoon low-sodium baking powder
¼ teaspoon baking soda
¼ cup bran
3 very ripe bananas, mashed and well blended
¼ cup frozen unsweetened apple juice concentrate
⅔ cup buttermilk, strained to remove fat globules
2 teaspoons pure vanilla extract
½ cup seeded muscat raisins, plumped in ¼ cup hot fresh orange juice for 15 minutes
3 egg whites, beaten until stiff

1. Preheat oven to 375°.
2. Spray a nonstick 9 x 5 x 3-inch loaf pan lightly with nonstick spray.
3. Combine whole wheat flour, soya flour, baking powder, baking soda, and bran in a mixing bowl.
4. In a separate bowl, combine mashed bananas, apple juice concentrate, buttermilk, vanilla, and raisins with orange juice.
5. Add dry ingredients to wet ingredients and stir quickly until flour disappears. (*Do not overmix.*)
6. Mix in beaten egg whites. Immediately fill loaf pan, place in oven, lower temperature to 350°, and bake for 1 hour, or until golden brown. Test for doneness by inserting toothpick. When it comes out clean, bread is finished baking. (Bread will also shrink slightly from sides of pan when done.)
7. Place loaf pan on cake rack for about 5 minutes. Remove bread from pan and complete the cooling on a rack.

Variation: Add ¼ cup poppy seeds to dry ingredients for an interesting additional flavor.

Per serving: 81 calories; 2.6 gm protein; 0.3 gm fat; 18 gm carbohydrate; 0.8 gm fiber; 0 mg cholesterol; 0.6 mg iron; 21 mg sodium; 44 mg calcium; 85 mg phosphorus; 38 IU Vitamin A; 0.04 mg thiamine; 0.05 mg riboflavin; 3 mg Vitamin C; 213 mg potassium; 0.2 mg zinc; 0.5 mg niacin; 108 mcg Vitamin B_6; 0 mcg Vitamin B_{12}; 6 mcg folic acid

Carrot Cake Muffins

Yield: 24 muffins (1 muffin = 1 serving)

These muffins are delicious served with a salad and savory enough to be served by themselves as a sweet with afternoon tea.

3 cups whole wheat pastry flour
½ cup soya flour
1 teaspoon baking soda
2 teaspoons low-sodium baking powder
1 tablespoon cinnamon
1 tablespoon ground ginger
1 tablespoon freshly ground nutmeg
½ teaspoon allspice
1 cup seeded muscat raisins
¾ cup chopped almonds or filberts, lightly toasted
1 tablespoon vanilla
1 cup buttermilk, strained to remove fat globules
1 cup mashed banana (approximately 3 whole bananas)
2 egg whites
1 6-ounce can frozen unsweetened apple juice concentrate
1 7½-ounce can unsweetened crushed pineapple
5 cups grated carrots (approx. 12 to 14 carrots)

1. Preheat oven to 400°. Sift together flours, baking soda, baking powder, cinnamon, ginger, nutmeg, and allspice in a large bowl.
2. Add raisins and nuts to flour mixture and stir.
3. Add vanilla, buttermilk, banana, apple juice concentrate, pineapple, and carrots to flour mixture.
4. Mix well by hand until all ingredients are well blended and no flour shows.
5. Fill nonstick muffin tins two-thirds to three-quarters full with batter and bake at 375° for 25 minutes.
6. Allow to cool in pans about 10 minutes before removing. Place muffins on rack to finish cooling.

Per serving: 130 calories; 3.5 gm protein; 2.9 gm fat; 24 gm carbohydrate; 1.4 gm fiber; 0 mg cholesterol; 1 mg iron; 42 mg sodium; 66 mg calcium; 84 mg phosphorus 2551 IU Vitamin A; 0.08 mg thiamine; 0.06 mg riboflavin; 4 mg Vitamin C; 360 mg potassium; 0.22 mg zinc; 0.5 mg niacin; 100 mcg Vitamin B_6; 0.02 mcg Vitamin B_{12}; 4 mcg folic acid

Corn Bread, Corn Sticks, or Corn Muffins

Yield: 12 muffins, 12 sticks, or 1 8 × 8-inch pan cut into 12 squares
(1 muffin = 1 serving)

1½ cups yellow cornmeal*
½ cup unbleached flour
1 tablespoon low-sodium baking powder
½ teaspoon baking soda
1⅓ cups buttermilk, strained to remove fat globules
2 tablespoons frozen unsweetened apple juice concentrate
2 egg whites, stiffly beaten

1. Preheat oven to 425°. Spray an 8-inch square pan, 12 muffin cups, or a 12-stick mold with nonstick spray.
2. Measure cornmeal, flour, baking powder, and baking soda into a bowl and mix with a fork.
3. In a large bowl, mix buttermilk and apple juice concentrate together.
4. Beat egg whites until stiff.
5. Add cornmeal mixture to buttermilk and apple juice mixture. Blend quickly with a fork. Add beaten egg whites, blend quickly with a fork.
6. Immediately place mixture into baking pan. Bake in 400° oven for 20 to 25 minutes, or until firm and lightly browned. Cool slightly on rack.

To Serve: This quick bread should be served warm. It is a delicious accompaniment to Old-Fashioned Black Bean Soup (page 65).

Variations: If your diet permits, you may add 1 tablespoon safflower oil to the buttermilk.

To make confetti muffins, add ¼ cup chili peppers and a 2-ounce jar of drained, chopped pimientos to the buttermilk.

Per serving: 92 calories; 3.6 gm protein; 0.3 gm fat; 18.2 gm carbohydrate; 1.1 gm fiber; 1 mg cholesterol; 0.6 mg iron; 41 mg sodium; 84 mg calcium; 117 mg phosphorus; 51 IU Vitamin A; 0.11 mg thiamine; 0.12 mg riboflavin; 0 mg Vitamin C; 177 mg potassium; 0.16 mg zinc; 0.8 mg niacin; 6 mcg Vitamin B_6; 0.01 mcg Vitamin B_{12}; 2 mcg folic acid

* For optimum food value, use whole-grain yellow cornmeal, not bolted or degerminated meal and substitute whole wheat flour for unbleached.

Geneva's Extra-Special Muffins

Yield: 12 muffins (1 muffin = 1 serving)

1 cup whole wheat flour
½ cup unbleached flour
½ teaspoon baking soda
2 teaspoons low-sodium baking powder
½ cup unprocessed bran
1 cup unsweetened whole wheat flakes
1 cup buttermilk, strained to remove fat globules, or sour milk (1 tablespoon vinegar in 1 cup cold milk)
⅔ cup mashed ripe banana
1 teaspoon pure vanilla extract
2½ tablespoons frozen unsweetened orange juice or apple juice concentrate
3 egg whites, beaten stiff
1 cup muscat raisins,* plumped in 1 cup hot water for 15 minutes, then drained

1. Preheat oven to 425°. Sift whole wheat flour, unbleached flour, baking soda, and baking powder together.
2. Add bran and whole wheat flakes and stir with a fork.
3. Combine buttermilk, banana, vanilla, and orange juice concentrate.
4. Add liquid to dry ingredients, stir *until flour disappears.* (The batter will look lumpy.)
5. Fold stiffly beaten egg whites into batter.
6. Add raisins; stir gently.
7. Fill nonstick muffin tins half to two-thirds full.
8. Bake in a 400° oven 15 to 20 minutes, or until lightly browned. Cool slightly on rack before serving.

Helpful Hint: If muffins are done a little ahead of the rest of the meal, loosen them and tip in muffin tin to keep warm. Second-day muffins may taste better split and toasted before serving.

Per serving: 126 calories; 5.6 gm protein; 0.8 gm fat; 33.3 gm carbohydrate; 2.4 gm fiber; 0 mg cholesterol; 2.5 mg iron; 56 mg sodium; 75 mg calcium; 240 mg phosphorus; 129 IU Vitamin A; 0.15 mg thiamine; 0.16 mg riboflavin; 2 mg Vitamin C; 387 mg potassium; 1.54 mg zinc; 3 mg niacin; 249 mcg Vitamin B_6; 0.01 mcg Vitamin B_{12}; 37 mcg folic acid

* 1 cup frozen unsweetened blueberries may be substituted for the raisins or ⅔ cup chopped toasted hazelnuts may be added with the raisins.

Harriet's Pumpkin Bread

Yield: 24 slices (1 slice = 1 serving)

1⅔ cups canned pumpkin
½ cup frozen unsweetened orange juice, pineapple juice, or apple juice concentrate
⅓ cup water
1 large, very ripe banana, mashed until syrupy
1 teaspoon pure vanilla extract
2¼ cups whole wheat flour
¼ cup soya flour
½ teaspoon baking soda
1½ teaspoons low-sodium baking powder
1 teaspoon pumpkin pie spice
1 teaspoon cinnamon
1 teaspoon freshly grated nutmeg
3 egg whites
½ ripe banana, mashed until syrupy
½ cup seeded muscat raisins, plumped in ¼ cup dry sherry or warm fresh orange juice for 15–30 minutes
½ cup chopped dates
½ cup Grape-nuts or our Basic Granola (see page 258)

1. Preheat oven to 375°. Place pumpkin, frozen fruit juice concentrate, water, the whole mashed banana, and vanilla in a mixing bowl; blend well.
2. Sift together flours, baking soda, baking powder, pumpkin pie spice, cinnamon, and nutmeg.
3. Add sifted flour mixture to pumpkin mixture. Stir to combine.
4. Beat egg whites until soft peaks form. Add the half syrupy banana and continue to beat until stiff (not dry).
5. Add beaten egg whites to pumpkin mixture and blend gently.
6. Add raisins with sherry and dates; blend.
7. Place mixture into a nonstick 9 x 5 x 4-inch loaf pan. Top with Grape-nuts or Basic Granola, and bake in a 350° oven for about 90 minutes. Pumpkin bread is done when an inserted toothpick comes out clean. Cool on rack before slicing.

Variation: Serve with a dollop of our Low-Calorie Whipped Topping (page 318).

Per serving: 87 calories; 2.6 gm protein; 0.3 gm fat; 19.3 gm carbohydrate; 1.6 gm fiber; 0 mg cholesterol; 0.8 mg iron; 17 mg sodium; 28 mg calcium; 72 mg phosphorus; 1256 IU Vitamin A; 0.11 mg thiamine; 0.08 mg riboflavin; 10 mg Vitamin C; 224 mg potassium; 0.25 mg zinc; 1 mg niacin; 98 mcg Vitamin B_6; 0 mcg Vitamin B_{12}; 7 mcg folic acid

Old-Fashioned Whole Wheat Fruit Bars

Yield: 30 1½ × 2-inch bars (1 bar = 1 serving)

If you're looking for a healthy snack or dessert to put in a lunch box, you'll be pleased with this fruit bar. Dried fruits are high in natural sugar, however, so limit your consumption.

8 ounces chopped dates
8 ounces dried apricots
3 tablespoons frozen unsweetened apple juice concentrate
3 tablespoons frozen unsweetened pineapple-orange juice concentrate
2 cups water
1½ teaspoons almond extract
1½ cups whole wheat flour
1½ cups regular rolled oats or 7-grain cereal
1 teaspoon low-sodium baking powder
3 tablespoons toasted sesame seeds
1 6-ounce can frozen unsweetened orange juice concentrate
⅔ cup very ripe banana, mashed until syrupy

1. Preheat oven to 425°. Mix together in a saucepan the dates, apricots, frozen apple juice concentrate, pineapple-orange juice concentrate, and water. Cover and simmer about 20 minutes, or until tender, stirring occasionally so fruit does not stick.
2. Remove from heat, stir until thick, add almond extract, and blend.
3. In a bowl, mix together flour, rolled oats, baking powder, and sesame seeds.
4. Mix orange juice concentrate and syrupy banana together. Slowly add to flour mixture, mixing with a fork until well blended.
5. Lightly spray an oblong 13 x 9 x 2-inch pan with nonstick spray. Press half of oat mixture into pan. Flatten with hands to cover bottom of pan.
6. Spread with fruit filling and crumble remaining oat mixture over top, patting lightly.
7. Bake in a 400° oven for 30 minutes, or until lightly browned. Cut into 30 bars while still warm. Cool bars in pan on a wire rack.

Per serving: 99 calories; 2.3 gm protein; 0.9 gm fat; 22.1 gm carbohydrate; 1.2 gm fiber; 0 mg cholesterol; 1.1 mg iron; 3 mg sodium; 23 mg calcium; 68 mg phosphorus; 884 IU Vitamin A; 0.09 mg thiamine; 0.04 mg riboflavin; 12 mg Vitamin C; 240 mg potassium; 0.29 mg zinc; 0.9 mg niacin; 76 mcg Vitamin B_6; 0 mcg Vitamin B_{12}; 7 mcg folic acid

Potpourri

A MISCELLANEOUS MÉLANGE: SPREADS, LIGHT MEALS, SNACKS, CONDIMENTS, SAUCES

Fruit Preserves à la Suisse
Unsweetened Apple Butter Spread
Yogurt Cheese
Frittata
No-Yolks Huevos Rancheros
Our Tostadas
Tuna Benedictine
Pissaladière
Hummus
Tickled-Pink Pickled Beets
Pilaf Mix Supreme
Chestnuts Roasted on an Open Fire
Mango-Cranberry Chutney
Raita
Cultured Cucumber Sauce
Two Sauces from Cuisine Minceur
A Low-Calorie Whipped Topping
Festive Nonalcoholic Fruit Punch
Instant Banana Milkshake

Webster defines a potpourri as a miscellaneous collection, brought together without a bond or connection. Well, here they are—all my left-over recipes, whose only bond or connection is my desire for you to enjoy them!

Fruit Preserves à la Suisse

Yield: 2–2½ cups (1 tablespoon = 1 serving)

1 20-ounce package frozen berries, or 16 ounces fresh berries in season
2 tablespoons lemon juice
2 tablespoons fresh orange juice or water
½ 1-ounce package powdered pectin

1. Combine fruit, lemon juice, orange juice, and pectin.
2. Stir over high heat. Bring to a boil.
3. Boil 2 minutes, or until shiny.
4. Store in sterile jars in refrigerator or freeze in containers for future use.

Per serving: 5 calories; 0.1 gm protein; 0.1 gm fat; 1.2 gm carbohydrate; 0.3 gm fiber; 0 mg cholesterol; 0.1 mg iron; 0 mg sodium; 3 mg calcium; 3 mg phosphorus; 9 IU Vitamin A; 0 mg thiamine; 0.01 mg riboflavin; 8 mg Vitamin C; 24 mg potassium; 0 mg zinc; 0.1 mg niacin; 7 mcg Vitamin B_6; 0 mcg Vitamin B_{12}; 1 mcg folic acid

Unsweetened Apple Butter Spread

Yield: 3 pints (1 tablespoon = 1 serving)

Those of you who have a bearing apple tree in your yard, or better yet, are fortunate enough to live in apple country, may like to try your hand at preparing your own apple butter—without sugar. The success of this recipe depends largely on the flavor of the apples used.

5 pounds apples (McIntosh, Northern Spy, Cortland, Baldwin, Jonathan, or Pippin)
2 cups water
1 cup fresh orange juice
2 cups unsweetened apple cider
1½ teaspoons cinnamon, or 2 large sticks cinnamon
1 teaspoon ground cloves, or 6 whole cloves
1 teaspoon allspice
½ teaspoon freshly ground nutmeg

1. Peel, core, and thinly slice apples (slicing can be done in food processor, using 3–4 mm. slicer).
2. Put apples, water, fresh orange juice, and apple cider in a saucepan and cook to a sauce, about 20 to 25 minutes. (If using microwave oven, cut water to 1 cup and cook on high heat about 10 to 12 minutes.)
3. Puree in blender or food processor until fairly smooth.
4. Turn sauce into a large, flat pan (an enamel roaster will do).
5. Cook, uncovered, in a preheated 325° oven for about 1 hour, or until reduced by about half. Stir from time to time.
6. Add cinnamon, cloves, allspice, and nutmeg. (If using whole cloves and cinnamon sticks, tie in cheesecloth for easy removal.) Stir to blend in spices.
7. Turn oven to 250° and bake apple mixture about 3 hours, or until very dark and thick. *Stir* frequently to prevent sticking.
8. Taste to adjust spices, place in hot, sterilized mason jars, and store in refrigerator for future use.

Per serving: 17 calories; 0.1 gm protein; 0.1 gm fat; 4.3 gm carbohydrate; 0.6 gm fiber; 0 mg cholesterol; 0.1 mg iron; 0 mg sodium; 3 mg calcium; 3 mg phosphorus; 15 IU Vitamin A; 0.01 mg thiamine; 0.01 mg riboflavin; 2 mg Vitamin C; 37 mg potassium; 0 mg zinc; 0 mg niacin; 3 mcg Vitamin B_6; 0 mcg Vitamin B_{12}; 0 mcg folic acid

Yogurt Cheese

Yield: approx. 1⅓ cups (1 serving = 1⅓ tablespoons)

1 pint nonfat yogurt

1. Line a triple-mesh strainer with 3 thicknesses of cheesecloth. Pour yogurt into lined strainer.
2. Place strainer over a bowl and refrigerate overnight. The curd that remains in the strainer the next day will be the yogurt cheese.

To Use: May be used in place of cottage cheese in salads and as a sandwich spread or piped onto halved artichoke hearts, split pea pods, or other vegetables for hors d'oeuvres or buffet (use pastry tube for prettier effect). *Please note:* Yogurt Cheese cannot be frozen.

Variation: Yogurt Cheese may be seasoned with 3 tablespoons fresh dill, an assortment of fresh herbs, chives, pimiento, or chili peppers. Mix seasonings into the yogurt before placing it in strainer.

The cheese can also be molded by puncturing holes in an empty milk carton, then adding yogurt and letting it drain over a bowl overnight. When you remove the remaining curd by cutting away the carton, you will have a square of cheese that slices nicely for sandwiches.

Per serving; 16 calories; 1.6 gm protein; 0.05 gm fat; 2.2 gm carbohydrate; 0 gm fiber; 0.4 mg cholesterol; 0.02 mg iron; 22 mg sodium; 57 mg calcium; 45 mg phosphorus; 2 IU Vitamin A; 0.01 mg thiamine; 0.07 mg riboflavin; 0.24 mg Vitamin C; 74 mg potassium; 0.28 mg zinc; 0.04 mg niacin; 15 mcg Vitamin B_6; 0.18 mcg Vitamin B_{12}; 3.5 mcg folic acid

Frittata

Yield: 1 serving

A frittata is an Italian omelet. Ours uses egg whites only, thus lowering the cholesterol content. It will be well received at breakfast, brunch, or lunch.

1 tablespoon chopped onion
1 clove garlic, minced
2 tablespoons salt-free tomato juice
1 tablespoon chopped zucchini
2 fresh mushrooms, sliced
1 tablespoon chopped green pepper
1 tablespoon chopped pimiento
Freshly ground pepper
Dash Tabasco
½ teaspoon thyme, crushed
2 extra-large egg whites
1 teaspoon cornstarch

¼ fresh tomato,* chopped, for topping
1 green onion,* chopped, or 1 teaspoon chopped fresh basil, for topping

1. In a nonstick pan, sauté onion and garlic in tomato juice for 5 minutes, or until transparent.

2. Add zucchini, mushrooms, green pepper, pimiento, ground pepper, Tabasco, and thyme. Blend and cook, covered, for about 2 to 3 minutes.

3. Beat egg whites and cornstarch together just until fluffy. Add to sautéed vegetable mixture.

4. Cook, covered, over medium heat until bottom is lightly browned.

5. Lift edge to see if ready. Loosen frittata, invert, and brown lightly on other side.

To Serve: Place on a warm plate and top with chopped tomato and green onion or basil.

Variation: Any 4 of the following vegetables may be added, chopped: bean sprouts, summer squash, tomato, crookneck squash, asparagus, cooked potatoes, chili pepper, artichoke bottoms.

Per serving: 92 calories; 10.5 gm protein; 0.4 gm fat; 12.4 gm carbohydrate; 2.5 gm fiber; 0 mg cholesterol; 2.7 mg iron; 128 mg sodium; 51 mg calcium; 73 mg phosphorus; 1128 IU Vitamin A; 0.09 mg thiamine; 0.036 mg riboflavin; 44 mg Vitamin C; 479 mg potassium; 0.14 mg zinc; 1.7 mg niacin; 90 mcg Vitamin B_6; 0.08 mcg Vitamin B_{12}; 13 mcg folic acid

* 2 tablespoons green chili salsa may be substituted for tomato and green onion.

No-Yolks Huevos Rancheros

(Ranch Eggs)

Serves: 4 (2 tortillas and 2 egg whites = 1 serving)

Our Mexican neighbors have a strong influence on the cooking of those of us living in Southern California. Corn tortillas, chili and jalapeno peppers, pinto beans, and salsa all add variety. This simple, economical, Mexican-style dish makes an excellent Sunday breakfast.

1¼ cups chopped onion
1 large green pepper, seeded and chopped
2 cloves garlic, minced
2 28-ounce cans plum tomatoes, drained and chopped (reserve juice)
½ teaspoon low-sodium vegetable seasoning (see page 28)
1 7-ounce can green chilies, chopped
1½ tablespoons chopped fresh coriander (Chinese parsley)
Freshly ground pepper
8 egg whites
8 corn tortillas
1 teaspoon low-sodium vegetable seasoning

1. In a large nonstick skillet, sauté onion, green pepper, and garlic in ¼ cup juice drained from tomatoes. Cook, stirring occasionally, until onions are transparent (about 5 minutes).
2. Add tomatoes, the ½ teaspoon vegetable seasoning, and the chilies, coriander, and pepper. Simmer sauce 30 minutes.
3. Make 8 indentations in the sauce with a spoon and drop 1 egg white into each indentation. Cover and cook eggs 3 minutes, or until set, basting with sauce from time to time.
4. Season tortillas with the 1 teaspoon vegetable seasoning and bake in a preheated 400° oven for about 3 to 5 minutes while the eggs are cooking.

To Serve: Place 2 tortillas on each warm serving plate. Arrange 1 egg white on each tortilla, spoon sauce over and around, and serve immediately. For hearty eaters, you may want to add some Steamed Brown Rice (see page 254).

Variation: Add a layer of pureed chili beans (¼ cup for each egg white) before arranging egg white on tortilla.

Per serving: 254 calories; 18.7 gm protein; 3.4 gm fat; 71.8 gm carbohydrate; 3.4 gm fiber; 0 mg cholesterol; 5.5 mg iron; 440 mg sodium; 81 mg calcium; 230 mg phosphorus; 3813 IU Vitamin A; 1.92 mg thiamine; 0.41 mg riboflavin; 106 mg Vitamin C; 1161 mg potassium; 1.87 mg zinc; 3.5 mg niacin; 483 mcg Vitamin B_6; 0.07 mcg Vitamin B_{12}; 32 mcg folic acid

Our Tostadas

Serves: 6 (1 tortilla = 1 serving)

You prepare the various ingredients and let the family assemble their own lunch or supper.

1 pound fresh mushrooms, sliced
1 bunch green onions, sliced
4 our Bouillon Cubes, melted (see page 25), or 4 tablespoons our Chicken Stock (see page 26) or our Vegetable Stock (see page 60)
6 corn tortillas
Garlic powder
Onion powder
Low-sodium vegetable seasoning (see page 28)
1 15-ounce can chili beans, without meat, pureed in blender or food processor
1 pint-basket alfalfa sprouts, or 2 cups shredded romaine
3 tablespoons our Sour Cream (see page 27)
3 ripe Roma tomatoes, chopped
4 tablespoons green chili salsa

1. Sauté mushrooms and green onions in bouillon cubes or stock for 5 minutes, or until limp.

2. Place tortillas on a nonstick baking sheet and sprinkle with garlic powder, onion powder, and vegetable seasoning. Bake in a preheated 350° oven for 5 minutes, or until crisp.

To Assemble: Place baked tortillas on individual serving dishes and spread with a layer of pureed beans. Next, spread with a layer of mushroom mixture. Then add a few alfalfa sprouts. Top with a dollop of sour cream, sprinkle with chopped tomatoes, finish with a spoonful of salsa, and serve.

Variation: *To make chicken tostadas,* substitute 2 cups leftover diced or shredded roast chicken for mushroom mixture, or add chicken to the mushroom mixture.

Per serving: 100 calories; 7.2 gm protein; 1.6 gm fat; 30.8 gm carbohydrate; 3.2 gm fiber; 1 mg cholesterol; 2 mg iron; 50 mg sodium; 25 mg calcium; 163 mg phosphorus; 670 IU Vitamin A; 0.93 mg thiamine; 0.41 mg riboflavin; 20 mg Vitamin C; 505 mg potassium; 0.63 mg zinc; 3.8 mg niacin; 178 mcg Vitamin B_6; 0 mcg Vitamin B_{12}; 27 mcg folic acid

Tuna Benedictine

Serves: 8 (½ muffin and ½ cup topping = 1 serving)

4 tablespoons unbleached flour
3 cups nonfat milk
1 bay leaf
½ teaspoon low-sodium vegetable seasoning (see page 28)
1 tablespoon grated onion
1½ teaspoons dry mustard
Few drops Tabasco
1 7-ounce can salt-free tuna in water, well drained
4 hard-cooked egg whites, sliced
4 Pritikin whole wheat muffins, split and toasted

Chopped fresh parsley for garnish

1. Blend flour and milk in a swirl cup or glass jar.
2. Place in a saucepan with bay leaf, vegetable seasoning, grated onion, mustard, and Tabasco.
3. Stir constantly with a wooden spoon over moderate heat until sauce is thickened and smooth.
4. Add tuna and egg slices and heat thoroughly.

To Serve: Top each muffin half with tuna and egg mixture and sprinkle with chopped parsley. If you like, serve with broiled tomato halves and steamed broccoli spears.

Variation: Substitute 8 egg whites poached in nonfat milk for hard-cooked egg whites. Place 1 poached egg white on each muffin half and top with tuna mixture.

Per serving: 148 calories; 15.6 gm protein; 1.47 gm fat; 218 gm carbohydrate; 0.33 gm fiber; 16 mg cholesterol; 0.9 mg iron; 185 mg sodium; 124 mg calcium; 143 mg phosphorus; 220 IU Vitamin A; 0.08 mg thiamine; 0.22 mg riboflavin; 1 mg Vitamin C; 247 mg potassium; 0.40 mg zinc; 3.5 mg niacin; 41 mcg Vitamin B_6; 0.36 mcg Vitamin B_{12}; 8 mcg folic acid

Pissaladière

(Pizza Provençale)

Serves: 8 as entrée, 16 as hors d'oeuvre

8 large Spanish onions, chopped
2 cloves garlic, minced
1 teaspoon rosemary, crushed, or 1 tablespoon chopped fresh basil
½ cup our Chicken Stock (see page 26)
4 large, long sourdough rolls
2 cups Italian plum tomatoes, drained, seeded, and chopped
1 teaspoon thyme, crushed
2 tablespoons grated Sap Sago cheese, toasted (see page 15)
½ green pepper, cut in strips

1. Mix onions, garlic, rosemary, and stock in a heavy iron skillet. Steam, covered, for about 30 minutes over low heat.
2. Uncover and stir. Cook uncovered until a lightly browned puree is formed. Stir frequently.
3. Split rolls and tear out centers, leaving a ⅓-inch shell.
4. Broil rolls until lightly toasted.
5. Spoon equal amounts of onion mixture on each toasted roll.
6. Cover with chopped tomatoes, sprinkle with thyme and cheese, and top with green pepper strips.
7. Bake in a preheated 375° oven until golden, about 8 to 10 minutes.

To Serve: Serve hot as an hors d'oeuvre or a main dish for a light supper or lunch. If using for supper, start with corn chowder, serve a green salad with the pizza, and end with a basket of fresh fruit.

Variation: If your diet permits, you may substitute Parmesan cheese for the Sap Sago.

Per serving: 128 calories; 6.5 gm protein; 2.4 gm fat; 34.6 gm carbohydrate; 5 gm fiber; 3 mg cholesterol; 2.4 mg iron; 183 mg sodium; 105 mg calcium; 114 mg phosphorus; 714 IU Vitamin A; 0.17 mg thiamine; 0.16 mg riboflavin; 36 mg Vitamin C; 469 mg potassium; 0.83 mg zinc; 1.5 mg niacin; 269 mcg Vitamin B_6; 0 mcg Vitamin B_{12}; 45 mcg folic acid

Hummus

Yield: 2½ cups (1 tablespoon = 1 serving)

This is a veritable staple in Middle Eastern cooking. (Americans usually serve it as an appetizer.)

2 cloves garlic
2 tablespoons toasted sesame seeds
2½–3 tablespoons lemon juice
Few grains cayenne pepper
¼ cup our Chicken Stock (see page 26) or juice from garbanzo beans (below)
1 15-oz. can garbanzo beans, drained

1. Place garlic, sesame seeds, lemon juice, cayenne, and stock or juice in blender or food processor. Puree.
2. Add drained garbanzo beans and continue to puree until creamy and smooth.
3. Taste, and adjust seasonings.
4. Place in an airtight refrigerator container and chill until ready to serve.

To Serve: Bring to room temperature. To serve as an appetizer, place in a bowl and surround with plain or toasted pita bread, or serve with our Caponata (see page 40). Hummus can also be served as an addition to a pita bread sandwich for lunch.

Variation: If your diet allows, 1 teaspoon olive oil may be added after step 3; blend well.

Per serving: 25 calories; 1.5 gm protein; 0.6 gm fat; 3.9 gm carbohydrate; 0.9 gm fiber; 0 mg cholesterol; 0.5 mg iron; 2 mg sodium; 15 mg calcium; 23 mg phosphorus; 3 IU Vitamin A; 0.02 mg thiamine; 0.01 mg riboflavin; 1 mg Vitamin C; 53 mg potassium; 0 mg zinc; 0.1 mg niacin; 1 mcg Vitamin B_c; 0 mcg Vitamin B_{12}; 0 mcg folic acid

Tickled-Pink Pickled Beets

Yield: 2 cups (½ cup = 1 serving)

2 pounds fresh beets
1⅓ cups cider vinegar
½ cup frozen unsweetened apple juice concentrate
2 tablespoons pickling spice
1 bay leaf
1-inch piece fresh ginger root, peeled and cut in half
2 bay leaves
½ teaspoon thyme
1 large white or red onion, thinly sliced

1. Cook beets in boiling water to cover for 30 to 40 minutes, or until tender.
2. Drain cooking liquid and save; cool, peel, and slice beets.
3. Combine beet juice, vinegar, apple juice concentrate, pickling spice, bay leaf, and ginger root in a saucepan. Bring to a boil and simmer 10 minutes.
4. Strain hot mixture and pour over sliced beets. Add bay leaves, thyme, and onion.
5. Place in a tightly covered container and refrigerate for 24 hours before serving.

To Serve: Drained pickled beets may be served as an individual salad on a leaf of butter lettuce, garnished with grated, hard-cooked egg white. Pickled beets are also delicious served as a condiment with poached fish or broiled chicken.

Per serving: 39 calories; 1 gm protein; 0.1 gm fat; 9.7 gm carbohydrate; 1.8 gm fiber; 0 mg cholesterol; 0.7 mg iron; 32 mg sodium; 14 mg calcium; 22 mg phosphorus; 26 IU Vitamin A; 0.02 mg thiamine; 0.03 mg riboflavin; 6 mg Vitamin C; 204 mg potassium; 0.03 mg zinc; 0.2 mg niacin; 11 mcg Vitamin B_6; 0 mcg Vitamin B_{12}; 2 mcg folic acid

Pilaf Mix Supreme

Yield: 8 cups dry mix (1 cup dry mix serves 6; ½ cup cooked = 1 serving)

Give as a holiday or hostess gift, or keep on your shelf at home.

1½ cups raw wild rice
1½ cups raw brown rice
2 cups dry lentils
1½ cups chopped dried mushrooms
1 cup raw barley or rye
3 tablespoons Rokeach dried vegetable mix
3 tablespoons dried parsley flakes
1 tablespoon dried shallots
1 tablespoon dried onion flakes
1 tablespoon Italian herb seasoning, crushed
1 tablespoon granulated garlic
2 tablespoons low-sodium vegetable seasoning (see page 28)
½ teaspoon crushed red pepper

1. Place wild rice, brown rice, and lentils in a colander; rinse thoroughly in cold water and drain.
2. Spread in a thin layer on a baking sheet and dry 10 to 15 minutes in a preheated 300° oven, stirring frequently.
3. Remove from oven and cool.
4. Place remaining ingredients in a large bowl; mix well.
5. Add cooled rice and lentils to mixture and blend well.
6. May be stored in airtight containers, at room temperature, indefinitely.

To Cook Mix: Stir mix before measuring. Combine 1 cup mix with 3 cups water or our Chicken Stock (see page 26) in a saucepan. Bring to a boil, reduce to a simmer, cover, and cook 50 to 60 minutes, or until grains are tender.

To Package for Gift-giving: Measure mix into plastic bags in the size portion of your choice and seal. Place each airtight bag in a colorfully decorated jar along with a copy of the cooking directions and you will delight the recipients.

Per serving: 56 calories; 1.7 gm protein; 0.2 gm fat; 12.1 gm carbohydrate; 0.9 gm fiber; 0 mg cholesterol; 0.7 mg iron; 2 mg sodium; 10 mg calcium; 43 mg phosphorus; 46 IU Vitamin A; 0.06 mg thiamine; 0.05 mg riboflavin; 0 mg Vitamin C; 53 mg potassium; 0.02 mg zinc; 0.8 mg niacin; 13 mcg Vitamin B_6; 0 mcg Vitamin B_{12}; 1 mcg folic acid

Chestnuts Roasted on an Open Fire
(Or in Your Oven)

Yield: Approx. ½ pound roasted chestnuts from 1 pound raw (2 chestnuts = 1 serving)

Each chestnut contains about 16 calories—it's the only nut that you can crack without feeling some guilt.

Roasting: (for chestnuts to eat as a snack)

1. Pick over chestnuts and discard any that are soft or wormy.
2. Cut an X on rounded side of each chestnut. Place cut-side-up on a nonstick baking sheet.
3. Place in a preheated 425° oven and roast for 1 hour, or until done. Sprinkle with a few tablespoons of water every 15 or 20 minutes during cooking. The chestnuts will burst open when ready.

To Serve: Remove outer shells and inner skins before eating.

Parboiling: (for chestnuts to use in cooking)

1. Pick over chestnuts and discard any that are soft or wormy.
2. Cut an X on rounded side of each chestnut and add to boiling water.
3. Bring to a second boil and simmer about 10 minutes.

To Use: Remove outer shells and inner skins before using. May be frozen for future use.

Per serving: 32 calories; 0.5 gm protein; 0.2 gm fat; 6.9 gm carbohydrate; 1.1 gm fiber; 0 mg cholesterol; 0.3 mg iron; 1 mg sodium; 4 mg calcium; 15 mg phosphorus; 0 IU Vitamin A; 0.04 mg thiamine; 0.04 riboflavin; 0 mg Vitamin C; 75 mg potassium; 0 mg zinc; 0.1 mg niacin; 0 mcg Vitamin B_0; 0 mcg Vitamin B_{12}; 0 mcg folic acid

Mango-Cranberry Chutney

Yield: 4 cups (1 tablespoon = 1 serving)

½ cup frozen unsweetened pineapple or grape-pear concentrate
1⅔ cups water
½ teaspoon curry powder
½ teaspoon ground ginger
¼ teaspoon cinnamon
½ teaspoon ground cloves, or 4 whole cloves
1 lemon, thinly sliced, slices cut in half
1 orange, thinly sliced, slices cut in quarters
1 cup ripe mango, peeled and diced
1 ripe pear, peeled and diced
3 cups raw cranberries
½ cup raisins

1. Combine fruit concentrate, water, and spices. Bring to a boil.
2. When mixture boils, add lemon, orange, mango, and pear.
3. Cook 12 minutes, or until fruit is transparent.
4. Add cranberries and raisins and cook about 10 minutes, until cranberries burst.
5. Cool and chill. Taste, and correct seasonings.
6. This will keep several months in sterilized mason jars in refrigerator.

To Serve: Chutney should be served at room temperature so that you can enjoy the full flavor.

Per serving: 22 calories; 0 gm protein; 0 gm fat; 3.3 gm carbohydrate; 0.2 gm fiber; 0 mg cholesterol; 0.1 mg iron; 1 mg sodium; 3 mg calcium; 2 mg phosphorus; 132 IU Vitamin A; 0.01 mg thiamine; 0 mg riboflavin; 3 mg Vitamin C; 23 mg potassium; 0 mg zinc; 0 mg niacin; 4 mcg Vitamin B_6; 0 mcg Vitamin B_{12}; 0.2 mcg folic acid

Raita

A Condiment for Curries

Yield: 2 cups (1 tablespoon = 1 serving)

1 cup nonfat yogurt
2 ripe bananas, thinly sliced
1 ripe peach, peeled and diced
2 teaspoons lime juice
1 tablespoon fresh coriander, finely chopped
1 teaspoon peeled, fresh ginger root, grated
1–1½ teaspoons cumin powder, lightly toasted in oven or dry skillet
½ teaspoon low-sodium vegetable seasoning (see page 28) optional

1. Combine yogurt, bananas, peach, lime juice, coriander, ginger root, toasted cumin, and vegetable seasoning in a bowl.
2. Blend well and store in a covered container in refrigerator for several hours before serving.

To Serve: Use as one of the condiments with Turkey Curry (page 169) or any favorite curry, or with Tandoori Chicken (page 149).

Per serving: 22 calories; 0.9 gm protein; 0.1 gm fat; 5.1 gm carbohydrate; 0.6 gm fiber; 0 mg cholesterol; 0.3 mg iron; 9 mg sodium; 25 mg calcium; 6 mg phosphorus; 147 IU Vitamin A; 0.02 mg thiamine; 0.05 mg riboflavin; 2 mg Vitamin C; 77 mg potassium; 0.04 mg zinc; 0.3 mg niacin; 77 mcg Vitamin B_6; 0 mcg Vitamin B_{12}; 2 mcg folic acid

Cultured Cucumber Sauce

Yield: Approx. 2 cups (1 tablespoon = 1 serving)

1 pound European cucumbers, or 2 regular cucumbers, peeled and seeded
½ onion, chopped fine
1 large clove garlic, minced
1½ cups nonfat yogurt
1 teaspoon onion powder
Freshly ground pepper
Few drops Tabasco

1. Shred cucumber in food processor.
2. Add chopped onion and garlic to cucumber and chop fine.

3. Squeeze and drain well.

4. Combine yogurt, onion powder, ground pepper, and Tabasco. Blend well.

5. Fold in cucumber mixture.

6. Chill 4 to 6 hours in the refrigerator.

To Serve: Use as a sauce for fish or as a dip.

Per serving: 8 calories; 0.6 gm protein; 0 gm fat; 1.4 gm carbohydrate; 0.2 gm fiber; 0 mg cholesterol; 0 mg iron; 8 mg sodium; 18 mg calcium; 4 mg phosphorus; 26 IU Vitamin A; 0.02 mg thiamine; 0.04 mg riboflavin; 2 mg Vitamin C; 28 mg potassium; 0 mg zinc; 0.2 mg niacin; 2 mcg Vitamin B_6; 0 mcg Vitamin B_{12}; 0.5 mcg folic acid

Two Sauces from Cuisine Minceur

Yield: Approx. 1½ cups (¼ cup = 1 serving)

Two low-calorie sauces to be used with vegetables or broiled or poached fish or poultry.

Piquant Sauce from Cuisine Minceur

½ onion, sliced
2 stalks celery, sliced
3 carrots, sliced
⅓ cup water or our Chicken Stock (see page 26) or our Vegetable Stock (see page 60)
3 fresh tomatoes, chopped
½ cup fresh sorrel leaves
1 clove garlic, crushed
1 bay leaf
½ teaspoon dried thyme, or 1½ teaspoons chopped fresh thyme
Freshly ground nutmeg
Few grains crushed red pepper

1. Cook onion, celery, carrots, and water or stock in a small saucepan for 15 minutes.

2. Add tomatoes, sorrel, garlic, bay leaf, thyme, nutmeg, and crushed red pepper. Simmer 15 minutes, adding water if necessary.

3. Puree and strain.

Per serving: 40 calories; 1.5 gm protein; 0.4 gm fat; 8.8 gm carbohydrate; 2.8 gm fiber; 0 mg cholesterol; 1.2 mg iron; 32 mg sodium; 37 mg calcium; 41 mg phosphorus; 4877 IU Vitamin A; 0.07 mg thiamine; 0.06 mg riboflavin; 21 mg Vitamin C; 355 mg potassium; 0.32 mg zinc; 0.8 mg niacin; 143 mcg Vitamin B_6; 0 mcg Vitamin B_{12}; 12 mcg folic acid

Mushroom Sauce from Cuisine Minceur

½ onion, chopped
2 carrots, chopped
2 stalks celery, chopped
4 fresh mushrooms, chopped
¼ cup chopped fresh Italian parsley
1 bay leaf
½ teaspoon herbes de Provence
1 cup nonfat yogurt

1. Place first 7 ingredients in a saucepan. Add water just to cover.
2. Cook 20 to 30 minutes, stirring occasionally.
3. Puree and strain. Add yogurt and combine.

Per serving: 37 calories; 2.5 gm protein; 0.2 gm fat; 7.2 gm carbohydrate; 1.5 gm fiber; 0 mg cholesterol; 0.9 mg iron; 47 mg sodium; 89 mg calcium; 27 mg phosphorus; 3205 IU Vitamin A; 0.05 mg thiamine; 0.15 mg riboflavin; 10 mg Vitamin C; 195 mg potassium; 0.13 mg zinc; 0.9 mg niacin; 67 mcg Vitamin B_6; 0 mcg Vitamin B_{12}; 8 mcg folic acid

A Low-Calorie Whipped Topping

Yield: 1¾ cups (1 tablespoon = 1 serving)

¼ cup instant nonfat dry milk
¼ cup ice water or iced orange or pineapple juice
1 teaspoon lemon juice
2 tablespoons frozen unsweetened apple juice concentrate

1. Chill beaters and a narrow, deep bowl.
2. Beat instant milk with ice water on highest speed for 3 minutes, or until soft peaks form.
3. Add lemon juice and beat until stiff.
4. Add apple juice concentrate and blend.

To Serve: Serve at once.

Per serving: 6 calories; 4 gm protein; 0 gm fat; 1.1 gm carbohydrate; 0 gm fiber; 0 mg cholesterol; 0 mg iron; 6 mg sodium; 14 mg calcium; 11 mg phosphorus; 0 IU Vitamin A; 0 mg thiamine; 0.02 mg riboflavin; 0 mg Vitamin C; 25 mg potassium; 0.05 mg zinc; 0 mg niacin; 5 mcg Vitamin B_6; 0.04 mcg Vitamin B_{12}; 1 mcg folic acid

Festive Nonalcoholic Fruit Punch

Yield: 1½ gallons (½ cup = 1 serving)

2½ quarts water
1 12-ounce can frozen unsweetened apple juice concentrate
1 12-ounce can frozen unsweetened orange juice concentrate
1 6-ounce can frozen unsweetened grapefruit juice concentrate
2 6-ounce cans frozen unsweetened pineapple juice concentrate
5 *very ripe* bananas, mashed with potato masher or fork until syrupy
2–3 quarts sparkling mineral water
2 pints fresh strawberries, hulled and sliced

1. Mix water, fruit juice concentrates, and mashed bananas in a large bowl. Blend thoroughly with a whisk.
2. Pour into 8 or 9 1-pint plastic containers and freeze.
3. Remove from freezer about 1 hour before serving.

To Serve: Make half a batch at first, and then replenish as needed. Place 4 pints frozen fruit juice mixture in a punch bowl and pour about 1 quart sparkling mineral water over; stir to combine. Float half of the sliced strawberries over punch and serve.

Variations: The sliced strawberries can be marinated in ¼ cup Grand Marnier for several hours before serving.

Health food stores stock fruit syrups in such unusual flavors as cassis (black currant), raspberry, wild strawberry, apricot, and cherry. They are expensive, but a small amount added to the punch enhances the flavor considerably.

Per serving: 49 calories; 0.5 gm protein; 0.1 gm fat; 12.1 gm carbohydrate; 0.6 gm fiber; 0 mg cholesterol; 0.3 mg iron; 1 mg sodium; 9 mg calcium; 13 mg phosphorus; 84 IU Vitamin A; 0.04 mg thiamine; 0.02 mg riboflavin; 26 mg Vitamin C; 151 mg potassium; 0.02 mg zinc; 0.3 mg niacin; 70 mcg Vitamin B_6; 0 mcg Vitamin B_{12}; 3 mcg folic acid

Instant Banana Milkshake

Serves: 2

1 cup chilled nonfat milk
2 tablespoons nonfat powdered milk*
1 tablespoon frozen unsweetened apple juice concentrate*
½ ripe banana, sliced
½ teaspoon pure vanilla extract

1. Combine milk, powdered milk, and fruit concentrate in a chilled 2-cup glass measuring cup. Beat with Bamix (see page 17) until milk starts to form peaks.

2. Add banana slices and vanilla and continue beating until thick and creamy.

To Serve: This delicious, nourishing snack should be served immediately in chilled glasses. (Since there is no fat in the milk, if not served immediately it will fall back; the only thing holding it up is the air you have beaten into it.)

Variations: Either ⅔ cup sliced strawberries, ½ cup drained unsweetened crushed pineapple, or ⅔ cup sliced fresh or frozen peaches may be substituted for the banana. My favorite is peaches with ½ teaspoon almond extract.

Per serving: 110 calories; 7.3 gm protein; 0.4 gm fat; 20.1 gm carbohydrate; 0.8 gm fiber; 4 mg cholesterol; 0.4 mg iron; 106 mg sodium; 249 mg calcium; 206 mg phosphorus; 309 IU Vitamin A; 0.09 mg thiamine; 0.31 mg riboflavin; 5 mg Vitamin C; 487 mg potassium; 0.87 mg zinc; 0.4 mg niacin; 238 mcg Vitamin B_6; 0.77 mcg Vitamin B_{12}; 13 mcg folic acid

* If you eliminate these ingredients, the calories in each serving will be reduced by almost 50 percent.

Bibliography

Brody, Jane, JANE BRODY'S NUTRITION BOOK: A LIFETIME GUIDE FOR BETTER HEALTH AND WEIGHT CONTROL BY THE PERSONAL HEALTH COLUMNIST FOR *THE NEW YORK TIMES*, Norton, 1981.

Bronfen, Nan, NUTRITION FOR A BETTER LIFE: A SOURCE-BOOK FOR THE 80s, Capra Press, 1980.

Dufty, William, SUGAR BLUES, Warner Books, 1976.

Farquhar, John W., THE AMERICAN WAY OF LIFE NEED NOT BE HAZARDOUS TO YOUR HEALTH, Norton, 1979.

Hausman, Patricia, JACK SPRATT'S LEGACY: THE SCIENCE & POLITICS OF FAT & CHOLESTEROL, The Center for Science in the Public Interest, 1982.

Jacobson, Michael F., A BRAND NAME GUIDE TO SALT, Workman, 1983.

Jacobson, Michael F., EATER'S DIGEST: THE CONSUMER'S FACT-BOOK OF FOOD ADDITIVES, Doubleday, 1982.

Kraus, Barbara, THE DICTIONARY OF SODIUM, FAT AND CHO-LESTEROL, Grosset & Dunlap, 1976.

Lappe, Frances Moore, DIET FOR A SMALL PLANET (rev. ed.), Ballantine, 1975.

Mayer, Jean, A DIET FOR LIVING, McKay, 1975.

Pritikin, Nathan, PRITIKIN PERMANENT WEIGHT LOSS MANUAL, Bantam, 1981.

Pritikin, Nathan, with Patrick McCrady, Jr., THE PRITIKIN PRO-GRAM FOR DIET AND EXERCISE, Grosset & Dunlap, 1979.

Pritikin, Nathan, THE PRITIKIN PROMISE: 28 DAYS TO A LONGER, HEALTHIER LIFE, Simon and Schuster, 1983.

Sims, Dorothy, DIABETES: REACH FOR HEALTH AND FREE-DOM, Signet, 1981.

U.S. Department of Agriculture, COMPOSITION OF FOODS: RAW, PROCESSED AND PREPARED, Agricultural Handbook #8.

———, SODIUM, THINK ABOUT IT, U.S. Department of Agriculture, U.S. Department of Health and Human Services Home & Garden Bulletin #237.

Yudkin, John, SWEET AND DANGEROUS, Ballantine, 1972.

PERIODICALS

Healthline	For information write to: The Robert McNeil Foundation for Health Education, 2855 Campus Drive, San Mateo, California 94403
Lifelines	For information write to: *Lifelines,* P.O. Box 1501, Ann Arbor, Michigan 48106
Nutrition Action	For information write to: Center for Science in Public Interest, 1501 16th Street, N.W., Washington, D.C. 20036
N.W. Diet Guide	For information write to: Dieters Service, Inc., 2020 23rd Ave. E, Seattle, Washington 98112
Lo Sodium Pantry	For information write to: Lo Sodium Pantry, 4901 Auburn Avenue, Bethesda, Maryland 20814

Appendix

PREFERRED PRODUCTS

Note: This is a partial list. There are acceptable products being added at your local markets because of consumer awareness and demand. Remember to read the labels before buying.

SEASONINGS

Allspice, sweet basil, caraway seeds, celery seeds, chervil, chili powder, cinnamon (whole stick), cloves (whole), coriander, cumin, curry powder, dill weed, fennel seeds, garlic powder, ginger, Italian seasoning, dry mustard, nutmeg (whole), onion powder, oregano, poppy seeds, red pepper (crushed), rosemary, saffron, sesame seeds, shallots, tarragon, thyme. Recommended brands: Wagners, Spice Islands

Szeged Hungarian Paprika

Gaylor Hauser Vegit and Herbal Bouquet, Select No-Salt Bar BQ Spice, Capello's Vegetable Seasoning, Wachters Seasoning, Yerba Encanta Seasoning, Health Valley No-Salt Seasoning

Bak On Herbs and Spices Salad Style

Wasabi Ko Powdered Horseradish

Salt-free Dijon mustard. Recommended brands: Paul Corcillet, Maître Jacques, Featherweight, Reine, Lifetone, Silver Palate

Chinese five spices

Capers (rinsed and drained)

Mild soy sauce (1 tablespoon has 465 mg. sodium—*use prudently*). Recommended brands: Kikkoman, San J. Tamari, Yamasi

Vinegars—brown rice, rice wine, red wine, white wine, champagne, pear, raspberry tarragon, Italian Balsamic. Recommended brands: Paul Corcillet, Gourmet France, Monair Federzoni, Harry & David, Dessaux Fils, Spice Islands, Silver Palate, Sterling Apple Cider Vinegar, Mitsukan Rice Vinegar

Pure vanilla extract (without sugar). Recommended brand: Nielsen-Massey

Pure almond extract

Angostura Aromatic Bitters

McIlheny Tabasco

French's Worcestershire Sauce (1 tablespoon has 150 mg. sodium plus sugar—*use prudently*)

MILK AND MILK PRODUCTS (1 percent milkfat or less)

Nonfat dry milk. Recommended brands: Carnation, Sanalac, Alba

Evaporated nonfat or skimmed milk. Recommended brands: Carnation, Pet

Dry curd cottage cheese. Recommended brands: Axelrod, Borden, Breakstone, Knudsen

Weight Watchers cottage cheese (rinse and drain before using)

Hoop cheese. Recommended brands: Knudsen, Tuttle

Sap Sago cheese

Nonfat yogurt. Recommended brands: Continental, Weight Watchers

TOMATO PRODUCTS

Del Monte (no salt added), Gathering Winds Spaghetti Sauce, Hunt's No Salt Spaghetti Sauce, Enrico's Spaghetti Sauce (no salt or sugar added)

Italian plum tomatoes in puree or tomato sauce. Recommended brands: Progresso, Contadina, Springfield (salt-free), Hunt's (salt-free), S & W 50 percent less salt

Green chili salsa. Recommended brands: Pace, Ortega, Hot Cha-Cha Texas Salsa (no salt added)

Low-sodium tomato juice. Recommended brands: Diet Delite, Nutra Diet, Hunt's (no salt added)

Nutra Diet Vegetable Juice, S & W 50 percent less salt

CANNED VEGETABLES

Garbanzo beans. Recommended brand: Nutra Diet

Dennison's Chili Beans

Rosarita *Vegetarian* Refried Beans

Libby's Pumpkin

Water chestnuts, bamboo shoots, artichokes (hearts or bottoms), hearts of palm

Green chilis. Recommended brands: Ortega, Hot Cha-Cha

Salt-free canned vegetables. Recommended brand: Nutra Diet

FROZEN VEGETABLES

Salt-free frozen vegetables (most frozen vegetables are blanched in salted boiling water). Recommended brand: C&W

CANNED FRUITS

Motts Sugar-free Applesauce, S & W Appletime

Dole Unsweetened Pineapple (crushed, chunks, slices)

Knudsen's Unsweetened Cranberry Nectar

Fruit in water pack or unsweetened natural fruit juice

Flavorland Unsweetened Berries, Cherries, Peaches

Overlake Blueberries

HOT CEREALS AND GRAINS

Brown rice, bulgur wheat, buckwheat or kasha, barley, millet, cornmeal (whole ground), rolled oats (not quick-cooking), wheat flakes, rye flakes, steel-cut oats, triticale. Recommended brands: Wheatena, Zoom, Ralston, Elams' Scotch style oatmeal, Arrowhead Mills 4-grain Cereal and 7-grain Cereal, Con Arga's Cream of Rye, Mother's Whole Wheat Hot Cereal

COLD CEREALS

Puffed rice, wheat, millet or corn (little food value present because of processing)

Shredded wheat (biscuit or bite size). Recommended brands: Nabisco, Skinners

Health Valley salt-free and sugar-free cereals, Golden Harvest Grainfields

Kellogg's Nutri-Grain (with or without raisins)

Uncle Sam

Grape-nuts (with or without raisins)

FLOURS

Barley flour, buckwheat flour, whole wheat flour, triticale flour, rice flour, soy flour (limited amounts because of fat content), potato flour, rye flour, unbleached white flour (in limited amounts because bran and germ have been removed), stone-ground cornmeal (not degerminated), matzo meal (in limited amounts because not whole grain)

Arrowhead Mills Pancake Flour

PASTAS

Whole wheat ribbon noodles, whole wheat lasagna noodles, whole wheat macaroni shells, soba (Japanese pasta, buckwheat and whole wheat flours used)

de Boles Corn Pasta

No Yolks Noodles

De Ceccio Spaghetti, Lasagna, Penne, Linguini, Macaroni, Shells, Bucatini, Whole Wheat Spaghettini, Cappellini, Fuscilli, Conchiglie

BREADS AND CRACKERS

Pritikin Whole Wheat Bread, Rye Bread, English Muffins

Sourdough bread or rolls (without shortening), whole wheat pita bread, corn tortillas (without preservatives and preferably without salt), Italian bread (no sugar or shortening), whole wheat water bagels

Wayfarer's Bread (plain or with raisins)

Ry-crisp (unseasoned)

Manischewitz Whole Wheat Matzo or Crackers

Finn-Crisp

Kavli whole rye or whole wheat flatbread

Ry-Vita (unsalted)

Wasa Brod

Hard Tack

Iverson's Slim Rye, Pumpernickel

Bran-a-Crisp Wheat Bran Wafers

Rice cakes: Arden or Chico San

Baked corn chips: Garden of Eating

MISCELLANEOUS

Dried fruits (in limited quantities)

Dried mushrooms (shiitake are particularly delicious)

Dried soup greens. Recommended brand: Rokeach, Springfield

Dehydrated soups (no salt or MSG). Recommended brand: Hain's (tomato, cream of mushroom, cream of chicken, minestrone, hearty vegetable)

Canned soups (no salt or MSG). Recommended brand: Health Valley (minestrone, lentil, split pea, vegetable)

French's Mashed Potato Granules

Frozen fruit juice concentrates (unsweetened): apple, orange, grape, pear, and pineapple

Bottled fruit juice concentrate. Recommended brand: Jensen's, Nu-Life

Apple butter preserves, unsweetened, Westbrae

Fruit preserves: Poiret, Whole Earth

Low-sodium baking powder. Recommended brands: Cellu, Featherweight

Carob powder. Recommended brand: El Molino

Coffee substitute: Bambu

Italian salad dressing. Recommended brands: Tillie Lewis (diluted), Walden Farms (no salt added)

Chestnuts (Marrons). Recommended brands: Minerve (roasted whole), Clement (puree, unsweetened)

Pam Nonstick Spray

Soken Plum Candy

Tuna. Recommended brands: Chicken of the Sea (50 percent salt reduced), Starkist (60 percent salt reduced)

IDEAL WEIGHT CHART

According to the Metropolitan Life Insurance Co., the following height-weight ratios are desirable for a longer life. Heights include one-inch heels for both men and women. Weights include five pounds of clothing for men and three pounds for women.

MEN

Height	*Small Frame*	*Medium Frame*	*Large Frame*
5′2″	128–134	131–141	138–150
5′3″	130–136	133–143	140–153
5′4″	132–138	135–145	142–156
5′5″	134–140	137–148	144–160
5′6″	136–142	139–151	146–164
5′7″	138–145	142–154	149–168
5′8″	140–148	145–157	152–172
5′9″	142–151	148–160	155–176
5′10″	144–154	151–163	158–180
5′11″	146–157	154–166	161–184
6′	149–160	157–170	164–188
6′1″	152–164	160–174	168–192
6′2″	155–168	164–178	172–197
6′3″	158–172	167–182	176–202
6′4″	162–176	171–187	181–207

WOMEN

Height	*Small Frame*	*Medium Frame*	*Large Frame*
4′10″	102–111	109–121	118–131
4′11″	103–113	111–123	120–134
5′	104–115	113–126	122–137
5′1″	106–118	115–129	125–140
5′2″	108–121	118–132	128–143
5′3″	111–124	121–135	131–147
5′4″	114–127	124–138	134–151
5′5″	117–130	127–141	137–155
5′6″	120–133	130–144	140–159
5′7″	123–136	133–147	143–163
5′8″	126–139	136–150	146–167
5′9″	129–142	139–153	149–170
5′10″	132–145	142–156	152–173
5′11″	135–148	145–159	155–176
6′	138–151	148–162	158–179

Metropolitan Life Insurance Co.

RECOMMENDED DAILY DIETARY ALLOWANCES

The Food and Nutrition Board of the National Academy of Sciences has estimated that practically all healthy people in the United States can maintain good nutrition if their diets provide safe and adequate daily amounts of certain nutrients. The chart on page 329 covers many of those recommendations. In general, eating a wide variety of common foods will provide every other nutrient required.

	Age (years)	Weight (lbs)	Height (in)	Energy (kcal)	Protein (g)	Iron (mg)	Sodium (mg)	Calcium (mg)	Phosphorus (mg)	Vitamin A (IV)	Thiamine (mg)	Riboflavin (mg)	Vitamin C (mg)	Potassium (mg)	Zinc (mg)	Niacin (mg N E)[e]	Vitamin B_6 (mg)	Vitamin B_{12} (μg)	Folacin (mg)
Infants	0–5	13	24	kg × 115 (95–145)	kg × 2.2	10	115–350	360	240	420	0.3	0.4	35	350–925	3	6	0.3	0.5	30
	5–10	20	28	kg × 105 (80–135)	kg × 2.0	15	250–750	540	360	400	0.5	0.6	35	425–1275	5	8	0.6	1.5	45
Children	1–3	29	35	1300 (900–1800)	23	15	325–975	800	800	400	0.7	0.8	45	550–1650	10	9	0.9	2.0	100
	4–6	44	44	1700 (1300–2300)	30	10	450–1350	800	800	500	0.9	1.0	45	775–2325	10	11	1.3	2.5	200
	7–10	62	52	2400 (1650–3300)	34	10	600–1800	800	800	700	1.2	1.4	45	1000–3000	10	16	1.6	3.0	300
Males	11–14	99	62	2700 (2000–3700)	45	18	900–2700	1200	1200	1000	1.4	1.6	50	1525–4575	15	18	1.8	3.0	400
	15–18	145	69	2800 (2100–3900)	56	18	900–2700	1200	1200	1000	1.4	1.7	60	1525–4575	15	18	2.0	3.0	400
	19–22	154	70	2900 (2500–3300)	56	10	1100–3300	800	800	1000	1.5	1.7	60	1875–5625	15	19	2.2	3.0	400
	23–50	154	70	2700 (2300–3100)	56	10	1100–3300	800	800	1000	1.4	1.6	60	1875–5625	15	18	2.2	3.0	400
	51+	154	70	2400 (2000–2800)	56	10	1100–3300	800	800	1000	1.2	1.4	60	1875–5625	15	16	2.2	3.0	400
Females	11–14	101	62	2200 (1500–3000)	46	18	900–2700	1200	1200	800	1.1	1.3	50	1525–4575	15	15	1.8	3.0	400
	15–18	120	64	2100 (1200–3000)	46	18	900–2700	1200	1200	800	1.1	1.3	60	1525–4575	15	14	2.0	3.0	400
	19–22	120	64	2100 (1700–2500)	44	18	1100–3300	800	800	800	1.1	1.3	60	1875–5625	15	14	2.0	3.0	400
	23–50	120	64	2000 (1600–2400)	44	18	1100–3300	800	800	800	1.0	1.2	60	1875–5625	15	13	2.0	3.0	400
	51+	120	64	1800 (1400–2200)	44	10	1100–3300	800	800	800	1.0	1.2	60	1875–5625	15	13	2.0	3.0	400
Pregnant				+300	+30	h		+400	+400	+200	+0.4	+0.3	+20		+5	+2	+0.6	+1.0	+400
Lactating				+500	+20	h		+400	+400	+400	+0.5	+0.5	+40		+10	+5	+0.5	+1.0	+100

Index